CAMBRIDGE LIBRARY COLLECTION

Books of enduring scholarly value

Linguistics

From the earliest surviving glossaries and translations to nineteenth-century academic philology and the growth of linguistics during the twentieth century, language has been the subject both of scholarly investigation and of practical handbooks produced for the upwardly mobile, as well as for travellers, traders, soldiers, missionaries and explorers. This collection will reissue a wide range of texts pertaining to language, including the work of Latin grammarians, groundbreaking early publications in Indo-European studies, accounts of indigenous languages, many of them now extinct, and texts by pioneering figures such as Jacob Grimm, Wilhelm von Humboldt and Ferdinand de Saussure.

Ethnological Studies among the North-West-Central Queensland Aborigines

Walter E. Roth's 1897 study of the Aborigines of North-West-Central Queensland was among the first of its kind in Australia, and established his international reputation as a leading anthropologist and ethnologist. Roth, a physician who was later appointed 'protector of Aboriginals' by the government, gained the confidence and trust of the Aboriginal people among whom he lived, and tried to stop the exploitation and injustice they suffered, in the face of fierce political opposition. His book provides a fascinating and closely observed account of the Aborigines' traditional way of life, including their language, kinship and customs. It describes social organisation, food, tools and weapons, personal decoration, travel and trade, birth and death, and even cannibalism. Containing over 430 illustrations and a glossary summarising key vocabulary, this thoroughly-researched book is widely recognised as a valuable and enduring anthropological record.

Cambridge University Press has long been a pioneer in the reissuing of out-of-print titles from its own backlist, producing digital reprints of books that are still sought after by scholars and students but could not be reprinted economically using traditional technology. The Cambridge Library Collection extends this activity to a wider range of books which are still of importance to researchers and professionals, either for the source material they contain, or as landmarks in the history of their academic discipline.

Drawing from the world-renowned collections in the Cambridge University Library, and guided by the advice of experts in each subject area, Cambridge University Press is using state-of-the-art scanning machines in its own Printing House to capture the content of each book selected for inclusion. The files are processed to give a consistently clear, crisp image, and the books finished to the high quality standard for which the Press is recognised around the world. The latest print-on-demand technology ensures that the books will remain available indefinitely, and that orders for single or multiple copies can quickly be supplied.

The Cambridge Library Collection will bring back to life books of enduring scholarly value (including out-of-copyright works originally issued by other publishers) across a wide range of disciplines in the humanities and social sciences and in science and technology.

Ethnological Studies among the North-West-Central Queensland Aborigines

WALTER EDMUND ROTH

CAMBRIDGE
UNIVERSITY PRESS

CAMBRIDGE UNIVERSITY PRESS

Cambridge, New York, Melbourne, Madrid, Cape Town, Singapore,
São Paolo, Delhi, Dubai, Tokyo

Published in the United States of America by Cambridge University Press, New York

www.cambridge.org
Information on this title: www.cambridge.org/9781108006170

© in this compilation Cambridge University Press 2009

This edition first published 1897
This digitally printed version 2009

ISBN 978-1-108-00617-0 Paperback

ETHNOLOGICAL STUDIES

AMONG THE

NORTH-WEST-CENTRAL

QUEENSLAND ABORIGINES.

BY

WALTER E. ROTH,

B.A. Oxon., M.R.C.S. Eng., L.R.C.P. Lond., J.P. Qu.; late Nat. Science Demy of Magdalen College, Oxford.

WITH 438 ILLUSTRATIONS.

BRISBANE:
BY AUTHORITY: EDMUND GREGORY, GOVERNMENT PRINTER, WILLIAM STREET.

LONDON:
QUEENSLAND AGENT-GENERAL'S OFFICE, WESTMINSTER CHAMBERS, 1 VICTORIA STREET.

1897.

PREFACE.

SINCE 1894 my tenure of office as Surgeon to the Boulia, Cloncurry, and Normanton Hospitals, respectively, has afforded unrivalled opportunities for making inquiry into the language, customs, and habits of the North-West-Central Queensland aboriginals. The following pages embody the notes collected during that period.

At Boulia, where strictly professional work was conspicuous by its absence, almost my whole time was devoted to a careful study of the local (Pitta-Pitta) language: only when this was sufficiently mastered did I find it possible to understand the complex system of social and individual nomenclature in vogue, and ultimately to gain such amount of confidence and trust among the natives as enabled me to obtain information concerning various superstitions, beliefs, and ceremonial rites which otherwise would in all probability have been withheld. To any future observers of, and writers on, the Queensland aboriginal, I would most strongly recommend this method of making themselves familiar with the particular language of the district before proceeding to make any further inquiries.

I would also draw the attention of the reader to the chapter on the Sign Language, which I first accidentally hit upon at Roxburgh Downs, on the Upper Georgina. I was out on horseback one day with some blacks when one of the "boys" riding by my side suddenly asked me to halt, as a mate of his in front was after some emus, consisting of a hen-bird and her young progeny. As there had been, apparently to me, no communication whatsoever between the boy in front and the one close to me, separated as they were by a distance of quite 150 yards, I naturally concluded that my informant was uttering a falsehood, and told him so in pretty plain terms, with the result that, after certain mutual recriminations, he explained on his hands how he had received the information, the statement to be shortly afterwards confirmed by the arrival of the lad himself with the dead bird and some of her young in question. The reported use of "masonic" signs attributed to the blacks by Captain Sturt, who had been in close proximity to these districts some half a century ago, immediately flashed across my mind, and the possibility of such signs being ideagrams, the actual expressions of ideas, led me on step by step to making a study of what I subsequently discovered to be an actual well-defined sign-language, extending throughout the entire North-West-Central districts of Queensland. It may be interesting to note that I have during the past few months discovered traces of a gesture-language, with some of the ideagrams expressed by identical signs, in the coastal district around Rockhampton.

The pronunciation of all aboriginal words from Chapter IV. onwards will be found in the Index and Glossary.

With regard to the chapter on Ethno-pornography, I am well aware that it is far from suitable for the general lay reader; the subject matter, however, being essential to a scientific account of these aboriginals, I have decided upon its publication, at the same time placing it at the very last, in the hope that those who do not wish to peruse its pages need not unwittingly find themselves doing so.

I take this opportunity of thanking my old friend and teacher, Mr. F. M. Bailey, Queensland Government Botanist, for his kindness in determining the various plants, grasses, &c., submitted to him for examination. Mr. C. de Vis, Curator of the Brisbane Museum, did me a similar service with regard to the fauna. I also wish to express my obligations to the many station-managers —notably, Mr. Sam. Reid, of Clonagh; Mr. J. Craigie, late of Roxburgh Downs (now of Stockport); Mr. J. Coghlan, late of Glenormiston; Mr. Reardon, of Carlo; Mr. A. Cameron, of Marion Downs; and Mr. Dan. Wienholt, of Warenda —for all their trouble and help in furthering my investigations. Messrs. R. Etheridge, junr., and Chas. Hedley, of the Australian Museum, Sydney, have also given me continuous advice and encouragement in carrying out these Ethnological studies: the former gentleman has laid me under a deep debt of gratitude in drawing up the Bibliography. My greatest thanks of all, however, are due to Mr. Parry-Okeden, Commissioner of Police, Brisbane, who has given me every facility and assistance in preparing the work for publication. I look forward to the day when Mr. Parry-Okeden will have the satisfaction of seeing his words verified, that "Queensland will be proud of her aboriginals"—a consummation in which he has made up his mind to take an active part.

In the arrangement of the tabular matter, and in the setting of the different types necessary for the elucidation of the text, the reader cannot fail to appreciate the many difficulties that have been so successfully overcome by the various officials at the Government Printing Office—Mr. E. Gregory, Mr. G. A. Vaughan, and the staff generally.

W. E. R.

Brisbane, Queensland, Sept., 1897.

ERRATA.

Sect. 62, subsection *f.—Omit* "an absence which was also met with around Rockhampton and Gladstone (sect. 70*d*)."

Sect. 70, subsection (*d*).—*Omit* " the gamo-matronyms being alone deficient."

BIBLIOGRAPHY.

A List of the More Important Publications bearing on the District and Tribes Described in the Following Pages, or that should be Referred to in Conjunction with the Matter therein Contained.

BY

R. ETHERIDGE, Junr.,

Curator of the Australian Museum, Sydney, N.S.W.

N.B.—While away in the North working at his MSS., Dr. Roth was unaware of the existence of the following literature, and hence has described certain tribes under names spelt differently from those given in Mr. Etheridge's List. To prevent ambiguity the accompanying table is appended :—

Names in Mr. Etheridge's List.		*Names in Dr. Roth's Work.*
Karrandee	=	Karunti
Kulkadoon	=	Kalkadoon
Miappe	=	Miubbi
Moorloobulloo	=	Mooraboola
Mykoolon	=	Mikoolun
Oonoomurra	=	Woonamurra
Ringa-Ringaroo	=	Ringo Ringo
Runga-Rungawah	=	Rungo Rungo
Wollongurma	=	Wollangama
Yanda	=	Yunda
Yelina	=	Yellunga

Armit, W. E.—
Vocabulary and Account of the Tribe at the Mouth of the Leichhardt River. "Curr's Australian Race, 1886," ii., pp. 300–305.
Vocabulary and Account of the Karrandee Tribe at the Mouth of the River Norman. "Curr's Australian Race, 1886," ii., pp. 306–309.
Vocabulary and Account of the Wollongurma Tribe on the Middle Norman River. "Curr's Australian Race, 1886," ii., pp. 310–313.

Bancroft, J.—
The Pituri Poison. "Trans. Phil. Soc., Queensland, 1859-72," 42nd Article, p. 2.
Pituri and Tobacco. "Trans. Phil. Soc., Queensland, 1878-82," iii., 2nd Article, p. 16; 2 Plates.

Barlow, H.—
Vocabulary of Aboriginal Dialects of Queensland. "Journ. Anthrop. Inst., 1872," ii., pp. 166–175.

Beddoe, J.—
On the Aborigines of Central Queensland. "Journ. Anthrop. Inst., 1877," vii., pp. 145–148.

Bedford, C. T.—
Reminiscences of a Surveying Trip from Boulia to the South Australian Border. "Proc. R. Geogr. Soc., Austr. (Queensland Branch), 1886-87 [1887]," ii. pp. 99–113.

CHARNOCK, ——

On Queensland Dialects. "Journ. Anthrop. Inst., 1873," ii., p. 175.

CHRISTISON, R.—

Vocabulary of Language used on the Upper Thomson (Lat. 22°, Long. 144°, or thereabouts). "Curr's Australian Race, 1887," iii., p. 10.

COWARD, T.—

Language of the Aborigines about Burketown. "Curr's Australian Race, 1886," ii., p. 298.

Cox, J. C.—

Notes on Some of the Habits and Customs of Australian Natives in Queensland. "Proc. Linn. Soc., N. S. Wales, 1881," v., pp. 633–636.

CRAIGIE, J.—

Vocabulary of the Runga-Rungawah Tribe, Roxburgh Downs Station. "Curr's Australian Race, 1886," ii., p. 356.

CURL, S. M.—

On Pituri, a New Vegetable Product that deserves further Investigation. "Trans. N. Zealand Inst. for 1878 [1879]," xi., pp. 411–415.

CURR, E. M.—

The Australian Race: Its Origin, Languages, Customs, Place of Landing in Australia, and the Routes by which it spread itself over that Continent. 3 vols. and atlas. 8vo and folio. Melbourne, 1886.

CURR, E.—

Language Spoken on the West Bank of the Leichhardt River, near the Sea. "Curr's Australian Race, 1886," ii., p. 314.

Language Spoken on the Leichhardt River, twenty miles below Kamilaroi Station. "Curr's Australian Race, 1886," ii., p. 316.

Vocabulary of the Birria Language. "Curr's Australian Race, 1886," ii., pp. 384-85.

Vocabulary of Language used at the Head of the Gilbert River. "Curr's Australian Race, 1886," ii., p. 416.

Vocabulary of the Goa Tribe, Middleton Creek, Diamantina River. "Curr's Australian Race, 1887," iii., p. 14.

CURR, M.—

Vocabulary of the Tribe at Kamilaroi Station, Leichhardt River. "Curr's Australian Race, 1886," ii., pp. 318–321.

Vocabulary of Language used at the Head of the Diamantina River. "Curr's Australian Race, 1887," iii., p. 12.

CURR, M. AND E.—

The Pooroga Language: Dialects of the Upper Flinders, Hughenden, and Dutton Rivers. "Curr's Australian Race, 1886," ii. pp. 460–463.

EGLINGTON, E.—

Vocabulary and Manners of the Yelina Tribe, Burke River. "Curr's Australian Race, 1886," ii., pp. 346–349.

Vocabulary and Customs of the Yanda Tribe, Head of the Hamilton River. "Curr's Australian Race, 1886," ii., pp. 360–363.

Vocabulary of a Tribe on the Hamilton River, near Boulia. "Curr's Australian Race, 1886," ii., p. 364.

ETHERIDGE, R., Junr.—

The Knife used by the Mulligan River (North-Central Queensland) Aborigines in the Mika Operation. "Proc. Linn. Soc., N. S. Wales, 1890," v. (2), pp. 251-258, pls. 9 and 10.

Additional Remarks on Mika Knives. "Proc. Linn. Soc., N. S. Wales, 1890," v. (2), pp. 289–291, pls. 11 and 12.

Spear Heads from Settlement Creek and Nicholson River. "Proc. Linn. Soc., N. S. Wales, 1891," vi. (2), p. 37, pl. 4, f. 2 and 3.

Contributions to a Catalogue of Works, Reports, and Papers on the Anthropology, Ethnology, and Geological History of the Australian and Tasmanian Aborigines. Parts i.–iii. "Pal. Mem. Geol. Survey, N. S. Wales," No. 8. 4to. Sydney, 1890-95. By authority.

FISON, L.—

On Australian Marriage Laws. "Journ. Anthrop. Inst. for 1879 [1880]," 354–57.

FRASER, J.—
Some Remarks on the Australian Languages. "Journ. R. Soc. N. S. Wales for 1890 [1891]," xxiv., pp. 231–253.
HEAGNEY, J.—
Vocabulary and Account of the Birria, Koongerri, and Kungarditchi Tribes, at the Junction of the Thomson and Barcoo Rivers, also the Whitula Creek. "Curr's Australian Race, 1886," ii., pp. 374–383.
HOWITT, A. W.—
Notes on the Australian Class Systems. "Journ. Anthrop. Inst., 1883," xii., pp. 496–512, pl. 15.
Further Remarks on the Australian Class Systems. "Journ. Anthrop. Inst., 1889," xviii., pp. 31–70, pl. 5.
The Organisation of Australian Tribes. "Trans. R. Soc. Vict., 1889. i., pp. 96–137."
Note on the Use of Gesture-Language in Australian Tribes. "Proc. Austr. Assoc. Adv. Sci. for 1890 [1891]," ii., pp. 637–646.
HOWITT, A. W., AND FISON, L.—
On the Deme and the Horde. "Journ. Anthrop. Inst., 1884," xiv., pp. 142–169.
LAMOND, M. S.—
Vocabulary and Account of the Mykoolon Tribe, between the Gregory and Leich-hardt Rivers. "Curr's Australian Race, 1886," ii., pp. 322-325.
LIVERSIDGE, A.—
The Alkaloid from Pituri. "Journ. R. Soc., N. S. Wales, for 1880 [1881]," xiv., pp. 123-132.
LUMHOLTZ, C.—
Among Cannibals: An Account of Four Years' Travels in Australia, and of Camp Life with the Aborigines of Queensland, pp. xx., 395. Plates, maps. 8vo. London, 1890.
MACGILLIVRAY, A.—
Manners and Languages of the Oonoomurra Tribe, Flinders and Cloncurry Country. "Curr's Australian Race, 1886," ii., pp. 340-345.
MACHATTIE, J. O.—
Vocabulary and Customs of the Moorloobulloo Tribe, at the junction of King's Creek and the Georgina or Herbert River. "Curr's Australian Race, 1886," ii., pp. 366–369.
MATHEW, J.—
The Australian Aborigines. "Journ. R. Soc., N. S. Wales, for 1889 [1890]," xxiii., pp. 335–349. Plate and map.
MIKLOUHO-MACLAY, N. VON—
Über die Mika-operation in Central Australien. "Zeitsch. für Ethnol. (Verhandl.), 1880," xii., p. 85.
Stellung des Paares beim Coïtus und das Ausschlendern des Sperma's vom Weibe. "Zeitsch. für Ethnol (Verhandl.), 1880," xii., p. 87.
Langheinigkeit der Australischen Frauen. "Zeitsch. für Ethnol. (Verhandl.), 1880," xii., p. 89.
Geschlechtlicher Umgang mit Mädchen vor der Geschlechtsreife. "Zeitsch. für Ethnol. (Verhandl.), 1880," xii., p. 88.
Bericht über Operationen Australischer Eingeborner. "Zeitch. für Ethnol. (Verhandl.), 1882." xiv., pp. 26–29.
MCLEAN, A.—
Vocabulary of the Ringa-Ringaroo Tribe, between the Georgina and Burke Rivers, between Lat. 20° and L. 21° S. "Curr's Australian Race, 1886," ii., p. 358.
MOWBRAY, H. M.—
Vocabulary and Customs of a Tribe at the Granite Range, close to the head of the Mitchell River, and east of the Hodgkinson Gold Fields. "Curr's Australian Race, 1886," ii., pp. 402–407.
MUELLER, F. VON—
Origin of the Stimulant called Pitury. "Smyth's Aborigines of Victoria, 1878," i., p. 222, note.
MURRAY, J. P.—
Pituri. "Pharm. Journ., 1879," i. (3). p. 638.

PALMER, E.—

Notes on Some Australian Tribes. "Journ. Anthrop. Inst., 1884," xiii., pp. 276–347.

On Plants used by the Natives of North Queensland, Flinders and Mitchell Rivers, for Food, Medicine, &c. "Journ. R. Soc. N. S. Wales for 1883 [1884]," xvii., pp. 93–113.

Vocabulary and Account of the Miappe Tribe, Cloncurry River. "Curr's Australian Race, 1886," ii., pp. 330–333 and 338.

Vocabulary and Account of the Mirkin Tribe, Akoonkoon, Palmer River. "Curr's Australian Race, 1886," ii., pp. 396–399.

PETIT, A.—

The Alkaloid of Pituri. "Pharm. Journ., 1879," ix. (3), p. 819.

SMYTH, R. B.—

The Aborigines of Victoria, with Notes relating to the Habits of the Natives of other parts of Australia and Tasmania, &c. 2 vols. R. 8vo. Melbourne, 1878. By authority.

TAPLIN, G.—

Notes on a Comparative Table of Australian Languages. "Journ. Anthrop. Inst., 1872," i., pp. 84–88, *table*.

THOZET, A.—

List of some of the Roots and Fruits used as Vegetable Food by the Aborigines of Northern Queensland, Australia. "Off. Record, Intercol. Exhib. Australasia, Melbourne, 1866–67 [1867]," pp. 259–263.

THRELKELD, L. E.—

An Australian Language, as Spoken by the Awabakal, &c., &c., Re-arranged, Condensed, and Edited, with an Appendix by John Fraser, B.A., LL.D., &c., pp. lxiv., x., 227, and 148. Map, plates. 8vo. Sydney, 1892. By authority.

URQUHART, F.—

Language and Account of the Kulkadoon Tribe, Seymour, Templeton, and Cloncurry Rivers. "Curr's Australian Race, 1886," ii., pp. 326–329.

WELLS, F. H.—

The Habits, Customs, and Ceremonies of the Aboriginals on the Diamantina, Herbert, and Eleanor Rivers, in East-Central Australia. "Proc. Austr. Assoc. Adv. Sci. for 1893 [1894]," v., pp. 515–522.

CONTENTS.

———◆———

CHAPTER I.

Section 1. Where Spoken. 2. Geographical Limits of the Boulia District. 3. Pronunciation. 4. Gender, Number, and Person. 5. Personal Pronouns—Nominative. 6. Personal Pronouns Objective—Direct Object. 7. Personal Pronouns Objective—Indirect Object. 8. Auxiliary Verbs. 9. Indefinite Articles. 10. Personal Pronouns—Possessive. 11. Nouns—Nominative. 12. Nouns—Vocative. 13. Nouns—Possessive. 14. Nouns—Objective. 15. Nouns—Plural and Dual. 16. Nouns—Gender. 17. Verbs—Active, Indicative. 18. Verbal Pronouns. 19. Verbs, Active—Imperative. 20. Adjectives. 21. Adverbs. 22. Prepositions—Motion. 23. Prepositions—Rest. 24. Prepositions—Purpose, Reason, Means. 25. Prepositions—Time. 26. Conjunctions. 27. Comparison of Adjectives. 28. Comparison of Adverbs. 29. Verbs—Active, Infinitive. 30. Verbs—Special Forms of the Future. 31. Verbs—Special Forms of the Imperative. 32. Reflexive Verbs. 33. Special Forms of Transitive and Intransitive Verbs. 34. Relative Pronouns. 35. Interrogative Pronouns. 36. Numerals, &c. 37. Ideas of Quantity and Size. 38. Ideas of Time. 39. Ideas of Place, Direction, and Distance. 40. Interrogation, Doubt, and Uncertainty. 41. Notes of Exclamation, &c. 42. Participles and Perfects. 43. Introduction to the Pitta-Pitta Vocabulary. 44. Pitta-Pitta Vocabulary.

CHAPTER II.

Section 45. Boulia District and the Various Tribes Occupying it. 46. Leichhardt-Selwyn District. 47. Cloncurry District. 48. Flinders District. 49. Upper Georgina District. 50. North-West-Central Queensland. 51. Introduction to the Philological Tables. 52. Words Relating to Parts of the Body. 53. Fauna and Flora. 54. Other Objects of Nature. 55. Weapons, Utensils, &c. 56. Numerals. 57. Abstract Ideas. 58. Family Relationships.

CHAPTER III.

Section 59. Introductory. 60. Patronym. 61. Gamomatronym. 62. Paedomatronym. 63. Heteronym. 64. Geneanym. 65. Genealogical Tree in the Pitta-Pitta Language. 66. Aboriginal and European Relationship Equivalents. 67. Autonym. 68. Climanym. 69. Summary of Nomenclature. 70. Similar Systems in Other Portions of Queensland. 71. Probable Interpretation of the Class Systems.

CHAPTER IV.

Section 72. Introductory. 73-74. Mammals. 75-76. Birds. 77-78. Reptiles. 79-80. Fish. 81-82. Molluscs. 83-84. Arthropoda. 85-86. Plants. 87-88. Other Objects of Nature. 89-90. Individuals, Family Relatives. 91-92. Ornaments, Weapons, Implements, Utensils, Huts. 93-94. Number. 95-96. Locality, Direction. 97-98. Time. 99-100. Interrogation. 101-102. Simple Acts, States, and Conditions. 103-104. Complex Conditions, Abstract Ideas.

CHAPTER X.

CHAPTER XI.

CHAPTER XII.

CHAPTER XIII.

ILLUSTRATIONS

LIST OF ILLUSTRATIONS.

———————◆———————

ETHNOLOGICAL STUDIES

AMONG THE

NORTH-WEST-CENTRAL QUEENSLAND ABORIGINES.

◆

CHAPTER I.

THE SPOKEN LANGUAGE OF THE PITTA-PITTA ABORIGINALS: AN ELEMENTARY GRAMMAR.

1. **The Pitta-Pitta language** is spoken mainly at Boulia, the chief encampment of the Pitta-Pitta blacks, as well as throughout the surrounding neighbourhood wherever any of their members may be scattered. It bears intimate relationship, as will subsequently be shown, to several other languages in close proximity, and ought rather to be considered in the light of one particular dialect out of many which together constitute the language of the Boulia district. Though the exact ethnographical limits of such a district must necessarily prove a matter of some difficulty, there is nevertheless a certain portion of country known to the Pitta-Pitta aboriginals as the "ooroo-ena mie-ena"—*i.e.*, "one-and-the-same country"—throughout which the various dialects spoken by the different tribes are pretty similar, and more or less mutually intelligible.

2. For present purposes, therefore, the **Boulia District** will be understood as comprising the area bounded :—On the north by Buckingham Downs, Mount Merlin, and Chatsworth ; on the east by Tooleybuck country and Springvale ; on the south by Cluny, Bedouri, and Sandringham ; on the west by Carlo (*vel* Mungerebar) and Glenormiston (*vel* Idamea) country. In other words, it includes the district drained by the Hamilton, Burke, Wills, King's Creek, Upper Mulligan, Cottonbush Creek, and Middle Georgina Rivers, and measures approximately about 10,000 square miles.

3. The following **Spelling**, upon an English basis, has been adopted throughout the text. Unfortunately, it was not until after I had taken my departure from Boulia that I learnt of the "continental" system now being followed in the old country. The vowel-sounds used are represented by—

ă = more of the sound of a short *u*, as in wom*a*nly. (Except in two or three proper names, the Pitta-Pitta blacks have no open-sounded short *a* as in c*a*n.)

ā = f*a*te	â = t*ar*	ĕ = b*e*t	ē = f*ee*t
ĭ = b*i*t	ī = b*i*te	ŏ = g*o*t	ō = m*o*te
ŭ = m*u*d	ū = n*ew*	oo = b*oo*t	ou = c*ow*
			oy = b*oy*

The consonant-sounds used are expressed by *b, c, d, g, j, k, l, m, n, p, r, t*, and *w*. There is no aspirate.

c is only used in the softened form of ch*a*.

g is pronounced hard ; it is often indistinguishable from *k*.

b with *p*, and *d* with *t*, is often interchangeable.

Accentuation is expressed by a syllable being printed in italics.

There can be little doubt that the absence of certain consonants, and various peculiarities of pronunciation, are due to the mutilation of the vocal apparatus, separately or conjointly, in the avulsion of the two upper incisor teeth (sect. 177), and the perforation of the nasal septum (sect. 175), the constant use of the nose-pin producing increased dilation of the nostrils. The circumstance that an aboriginal in this district is unable to utter the sounds of *f*, *th*, or *v* is incontestably due to the former defect, which may also account for the total absence in the language of all true sibilants, such as *c* (soft), *s*, *z*, although the sounds of *ch* and *sh* can be well expressed. He can pronounce *shirt* quite correctly, but when he comes to *fish* he calls it *bish* or *pish*, and speaks of a woman's husband or *Fancyman* as her *Benjamin*: he can only feebly imitate the sounds of *size* and *the*. On the other hand, a native who has not been so mutilated can articulate all the above fairly well. It is further probable that the true pronunciation of the initial *ng* in the first and second personal pronouns, and a few other words, also depends upon physical peculiarities. The nearest, though far from absolute, approach to this sound is the *ng* of *sing*, without a trace of the guttural tacked on to the succeeding syllable, but, even after months' careful practice, I have personally failed in giving it its proper utterance; its orthographical significance, unless very marked as in the first and second personal pronouns, has been omitted in the text. Except in the case of pronouns and personal nouns, which are fully analysed as they occur, the component syllables, accentuation, &c., of all words noted as being used in the Boulia District are described in the Pitta-Pitta vocabulary, which should be freely consulted (sect. 44), otherwise all words will be found in the main index.

1. There are three Numbers—singular, dual, and plural. In connection with the dual it is interesting to note that the Pitta-Pitta aboriginals reckon by twos—that is, on a dual notation as compared with the European decimal one; instead of the ten fingers they have only reached the stage of grouping with the two hands.

The sign of the dual would appear to be -lĭ or -lă, which can be recognised throughout the series of pronouns (sect. 5, 6, 7, &c.) in the dual imperative of the verbs (sect. 19, 31) in the word "pakoo-la" (=two), &c.

Each number has three persons, the third having two forms of the gender— one for the masculine and neuter, the other for the feminine. Furthermore, both genders have additional inflexions in the form of suffixes according as the person or object referred to is either (*a*) close up in front, or at side of, (*b*) close up at the back of, or (*c*) anywhere yonder, at some distance away from—the person speaking. In the first case (*a*) an additional variation takes place according as present and past, or future, time is referred to. Hence, the third person has six inflexions at least in the singular, three in the dual, and three in the plural: they are made up as follows:—

Number.	Proximity to Speaker's Front or Side.	Proximity to Speaker's Back.	Remoteness anywhere from Speaker.
—	-ĭ-é or -yé in present or past time; -ŭ in future time.	-kă in all tenses.	-á-rĭ in all tenses.
sing. m. n. ...	he, it, this	he, it, this	he, it, that, yonder.
„ f ...	she, this	she, this	she, that, yonder.
dual ...	these two, both these ...	these two, both these ...	those two, both those, yonder.
plur. ...	these all	these all	all those, yonder.

The special indication for proximity close to one's back is paralleled by the London "coster" pointing his thumb over his shoulder.

5. Personal Pronouns—Nominative.

Like other personal pronouns, these are inflexed according as they refer to present and past, or to future, time. In the latter, the suffix -ng-o, peculiar to nouns governing verbs in the future, should be noted. Besides acting as pronouns proper, these personal pronouns nominative are used to express the different forms of the European auxiliary verb "to be" (sect. 8, 18.)

Number.	Person.	a. Present or Past.	b. Future.
Singular.	1st.	*nŭn*-jă = I, I am, *or* I was	*nŭn*-yō = I, I shall be
	2nd.	*ĭm*-pă = thou, thou art, *or* wast	*ĭng*-ō = thou, thou shalt be
	3rd.	*noo*-ĭ-ĕ = he, it, this, close up in front *or* at side, is *or* was	*noong*-ō-ŭ = he, it, this, close up in front *or* at side, shall be
	,,	*noo*-ă-kă = he, it, this, close up at back, is *or* was	*noong*-ō-kă = he, it, this, close up at back, shall be
	,,	*noo*-â-(rĭ) = he, it, that, yonder, is *or* was	*noong*-ō-(â-rĭ) = he, it, that, yonder, shall be
	,,	*nŭn*-ĭ-ĕ = she, this, close up in front *or* at side, is *or* was	*nŭng*-ō-ŭ = she, this, close up in front *or* at side, shall be
	,,	*nŭn*-ă-kă = she, this, close up at back, is *or* was	*nŭng*-ō-kă = she, this, close up at back, shall be
	,,	*nŭn*-pâ-(rĭ) = she, that, yonder, is *or* was	*nŭng*-ō-(â-rĭ) = she, that, yonder, shall be
Dual.	1st.	*nŭl*-lĭ = we both, are *or* were	*nŭl*-lĭng-ō = we both, shall be
	2nd.	*noó*-lă = you both, are *or* were	*noo*-lăng-ō = you both, shall be
	3rd.	*poo*-lĭ-ĕ = they both, close up in front *or* at side, are *or* were	*poo*-lăng-ō-ŭ = they both, close up in front *or* at side, shall be
	,,	*poo*-lă-kă = they both, close up at back, are *or* were	*poo*-lăng-ō-kă = they both, close up at back, shall be
	,,	*poo*-lâ-(rĭ) = they both, yonder, are *or* were	*poo*-lăng-ō-(â-rĭ) = they both, yonder, shall be
Plural.	1st.	*nŭn*-ă = we are *or* were	*nŭn*-ăng-ō = we, shall be
	2nd.	*noo*-ră = you, are *or* were	*noo*-răng-ō = you, shall be
	3rd.	*tŭn*-ĭ-ĕ = they close up in front *or* at side, are *or* were	*tŭn*-ăng-ō-ŭ = they, close up in front, *or* at side, shall be
	,,	*tŭn*-ă-kă = they close up at back, are *or* were	*tŭn*-ăng-ō-kă = they, close up at back, shall be
	,,	*tŭn*-â-(rĭ) = they yonder are *or* were	*tŭn*-ăng-ō-(â-rĭ) = they, yonder, shall be

The final syllables of certain of the third persons in preceding and succeeding pronomial tables are placed in parentheses to indicate that they may often b omitted in quick conversation.

6. Personal Pronouns Objective—Direct Object.

In this series can be recognised traces of the objective case which is -nă for the present or past, and -kō for future, tenses (sect. 14).

Number.	Person.	a. Present or Past.	b. Future.
Singular.	1st.	*nŭn*-yă = me	*nŭn*-jō-kō = me
	2nd.	*ĭn*-nă = thee	*ĭng*-kō = thee
	3rd.	*ĭn*-nĭ-ĕ = him, it, close up in front *or* at side	*nō*-kō-ŭ = him, it, close up in front *or* at side
	,,	*ĭn*-nă-kă, &c.	*nō*-kō-kă, &c.
	,,	*ĭn*-nâ-(rĭ)	*nō*-kō-â-(rĭ)
	,,	*nŭn*-nĭ-ĕ	*nŭn*-kō-ŭ
	,,	*nŭn*-nă-kă	*nŭn*-kō-kă
	,,	*nŭn*-nâ-(rĭ)	*nŭn*-kō-â-(rĭ)
Dual.	1st.	*nŭl*-lĭ-nă = us both	*nŭl*-lĭ-kō = us both
	2nd.	*noo*-lă-nă, &c.	*noo*-lă-kō, &c.
	3rd.	*poo*-lă-nĭ-ĕ	*poo*-lă-kō-ŭ
	,,	*poo*-lă-nă-kă	*poo*-lă-kō-kă
	,,	*poo*-lă-nâ-(rĭ)	*poo*-lă-kō-â-(rĭ)
Plural.	1st.	*nŭn*-ă-nă = us all	*nŭn*-ă-kō = us all
	2nd.	*noo*-ră-nă, &c.	*noo*-ră-kō, &c.
	3rd.	*tŭn*-ă-nĭ-ĕ	*tun*-ă-kō-ŭ
	,,	*tŭn*-ă-nă-kă	*tŭn*-ă-kō-kă
	,,	*tŭn*-ă-nâ-(rĭ)	*tŭn*-ă-kō-â-(rĭ)

7. Personal Pronouns Objective—Indirect Object.

As will be seen when dealing with prepositions (sects. 22, 23) the ideas of "motion towards" and "rest with, at" are indicated by the suffixes -ē-nō and -ē-nă respectively: traces of these prepositional inflexions can be recognised in the two following series of personal pronouns objective (a), (b) where the indirect object is either:—

Number.	Person.	a. Person—motion towards (in all tenses).	b. Person—rest with (in all tenses).
Singular.	1st.	nŭn-yō-ŭ-nō = towards me	nŭn-yō-ē-nă = with me, by my side
	2nd.	Ĭng-ō-ŭ-nō = towards thee	Ĭng-ō-ē-nă = with thee, by thy side
	3rd.	noong-ō-nō-ŭ = towards him, it, close up in front *or* side	nĭng-ē-nī-ĕ, &c.
	,,	noong-ō-nō-kă, &c.	nĭng-ē-nă-kă
	,,	noong-ō-nō-(m)ă-rĭ	nĭng-ē-nă-(m)ă-rĭ
	,,	nŭng-ō-nō-ŭ	nŭng-ē-nī-ĕ
	,,	nŭng-ō-nō-kă	nŭng-ē-nă-kă
	,,	nŭng-ō-nō-(m)ă-rĭ	nŭng-ē-nă-(m)ă-rĭ
Dual.	1st.	nŭl-lĭ-ē-nō = towards both of us	nŭl-lĭ-ē-nă = alongside, with, both of us
	2nd.	noo-lă-ē-nō, &c.	noo-lă-ē-nă, &c.
	3rd.	poo-lă-ē-nō-ŭ	poo-lă-ē-nī-ĕ
	,,	poo-lă-ē-nō-kă	poo-lă-ē-nă-kă
	,,	poo-lă-ē-nō-(m)ă-rĭ	poo-lă-ē-nă-(m)ă-rĭ
Plural.	1st.	nŭn-ă-ē-nō = towards us all	nŭn-ă-ē-nă = alongside, with, all of us
	2nd.	noo-ră-ē-nō, &c.	noo-ră-ē-nă, &c.
	3rd.	tŭn-ă-ē-nō-ŭ	tŭn-ă-ē-nī-ĕ
	,,	tŭn-ă-ē-nō-kă	tŭn-ă-ē-nă-kă
	,,	tŭn ă ē nō-(m)ă-rĭ	tŭn-ă-ē-nă-(m)ă-rĭ

The parenthesised "m" in the above third persons is euphonic.

There are no personal pronouns objective, indirect object, indicating motion *from* the actual person; this idea being expressed with the help of possessive pronouns indicating motion from the person's place-of-residence or location (sect. 10).

Again, the suffix -ēn-yă also bears prepositional traces (sect. 24b) and expresses the person or place whence something is obtained, brought, or received; tacked on to pronouns, as in the following series (c), it demonstrates the personal pronoun objective, indirect object, person whence something is obtained or received. The suffix undergoes further inflexion according as the act referred to takes place in present and past, or future time, by the additional -nă or -kō respectively of the objective case (sect. 14).

c. Person—from whom something is obtained or received.

Number.	Person.	I.—In Present or Past Time.	II.—In Future Time.
Singular.	1st.	nŭn-yĭ-ēn-yă-nă = obtained, received from me	nŭn-yĭ-ēn-yă-kō = obtained, received from me
	2nd.	Ĭng-ĭ-ēn-yă-nă = obtained, received from thee	Ĭng-ĭ-ēn-yă-kō = obtained, received from thee
	3rd.	nĭng-ĭ-ēn-yă-nī-ĕ, &c.	nĭng-ĭ-ēn-yă-kō-ŭ, &c.
	,,	nĭng-ĭ-ēn-yă-nă-kă	nĭng-ĭ-ēn-yă-kō-kă
	,,	nĭng-ĭ-ēn-yă-nă-rĭ	nĭng-ĭ-ēn-yă-kō-ă-rĭ
	,,	nŭng-ĭ-ēn-yă-nī-ĕ	nŭng-ĭ-ēn-yă-kō-ŭ
	,,	nŭng-ĭ-ēn-yă-nă-kă	nŭng-ĭ-ēn-yă-kō-kă
	,,	nŭng-ĭ-ēn-yă-nă-rĭ	nung-ĭ-ēn-yă-kō-ă-rĭ
Dual.	1st.	nŭl-lĭ-ēn-yă-nă = obtained, received from us both	nŭl lĭ-ēn-yă-kō = obtained, received from us both
	2nd.	noo-lă-ēn-yă-nă, &c.	noo-lă-ēn-yă-kō, &c.
	3rd.	poo-lă-ēn-yă-nī-ĕ	poo-lă-ēn-yă-kō-ŭ
	,,	poo-lă ēn-yă nă-kă	poo-lă-ēn-yă-kō-kă
	,,	poo-lă-ēn-yă-nă-rĭ	poo-lă-ēn-yă-kō-ă-rĭ
Plural.	1st.	nŭn-ă-ēn-yă-nă = obtained, received from us all	nŭn-ă-ēn-yă-kō = obtained, received from us all
	2nd.	noo-ră-ēn-yă-nă, &c.	noo-ră-ēn-yă-kō, &c.
	3rd.	tŭn-ă-ēn-yă-nī-ĕ	tŭn-ă-ēn-yă-kō-ŭ
	,,	tŭn-ă ēn-yă-nă-kă	tŭn-ă-ēn-yă-kō-kă
	,,	tŭn-ă-ēn-yă-nă-rĭ	tŭn-ă-ēn-yă-kō-ă-rĭ

The remaining series (*d*) of personal pronouns objective, indirect object, refer to the person's benefit, use, or advantage: their inflexions are similar to those characterising the possessive pronouns (sect. 10*b*), and take the additional -nă or -kō already referred to, according as the action takes place in present and past, or future time.

d. Person—for whose benefit, use, or advantage, something is done.

Number.	Person.	I.—In Present and Past Time.	II.—In Future Time.
Singular.	1st	*năn*-yâ-tĭ-nă = for me, for my benefit, for my advantage	*năn*-yâ-tĭ-kō = for me, for my benefit, for my advantage
	2nd	*ĭng*-kâ-tĭ-nă = for thee, for thy benefit, for thy advantage	*ĭng*-kâ-tĭ-kō = for thee, for thy benefit, for thy advantage
	3rd	nō-kâ-tĭ-*nĭ*-ĕ, &c.	nō-kâ-tĭ-*kō*-ū, &c.
	,,	nō-kâ-tĭ-nă-kă	nō-kâ-tĭ-kō-kă
	,,	nō-kâ-tĭ-*nă*-rĭ	nō-kâ-tĭ-kō-*á*-rĭ
	,,	nŭn-kâ-tĭ-*nĭ*-ĕ	nŭn-kâ-tĭ-*kō*-ū
	,,	*năn*-kâ-tĭ-nă-kă	*năn*-kâ-tĭ-kō-kă
	,,	nŭn-kâ-tĭ-*nă*-rĭ	nŭn-kâ-tĭ-kō-*á*-rĭ
Dual.	1st	*năl*-lĭng-ă-nă = for the benefit, use, advantage of us both	*năl*-lĭng-ă-kō = for the benefit, use, advantage of us both
	2nd	noo-lăng-â-nă, &c.	noo-lăng-ă-kō, &c.
	3rd	poo-lăng-â-nĭ-ĕ	poo-lăng-ă-kō-ū
	,,	poo-lăng-ă nă-kă	poo-lăng-ă-kō-kă
	,,	poo-lăng-ă-nâ-rĭ	poo-lăng-ă-kō-*á*-rĭ
Plural.	1st	*năn*-ăng-ă-nă = for the benefit, use, advantage of us all	*năn*-ăng-ă-kō = for the benefit, use, advantage of us all
	2nd	noo-răng-ă-nă, &c.	noo-răng-ă-kō, &c.
	3rd	tŭn-ăng-ă-nĭ-ĕ	tŭn-ăng-ă-kō-ū
	,,	tŭn-ăng-ă-nă-kă	tŭn-ăng-ă-kō-kă
	,,	tŭn-ăng-ă-*nă*-rĭ	tŭn-ăng-ă-kō-*á*-rĭ

8. The Auxiliary Verbs "to be" and "to have."

The verb "to be" is in reality not expressed; it is only understood by the various inflexional forms of the personal pronouns nominative which, as we have seen (sect. 5), undergo modification in present and past, or future time. There is, however, a verb "kunna-linga" == "to be," in the sense of "to become."

With regard to the verb "to have," *i.e.*, "to possess," the Pitta-Pitta aboriginals adopt the following method of translating, or rather transposing it: thus, instead of saying, like a European, "I have, had, *or* shall have, a boomerang," they would express themselves, literally, as "I am, was, *or* shall be, the boomerang-possessor." The possessor, the sign of possession, &c., is rendered by the suffix -*má*-rō (*cf.* mur-ra = hand) in present and past, or -*má*-rō-ngō in future time (sect. 22); hence the sentence would read either "bibapooro-maro nunja" or "bibapooro-marongo nunyo" as the tense requires.

[The Mitakoodi blacks of the Cloncurry district have a similar means of denoting possession by means of the suffix -*boo*-nă.]

Another form of the verb "to have," *i.e.*, in reply to a question involving a transitive verb, can be translated by the transitive verbal pronouns (sect. 18).

9. The Indefinite Articles "a" and "the" are not Translated.

Example 1.

1. Nunkartinari. 2. Ingoena. 3. Ningienyanaka [toka-ka nutto]. 4. Nungonou [pun-ni-a noo-a]. 5. Poolakoari [pite nunyo]. 6. Inna [pite-a nutto]. 7. Poolanganaka. 8. Nulliena. 9. Nooraenyana [toka-ka nutto]. 10. Poolaenoka [pun-ni-a noo-a].

Translation.

1. For the benefit of that woman yonder. 2. At thy side. 3. [I brought (it)] from the man close-up-at-the-back-of-me. 4. [He is running] towards the woman-in-front. 5. [I will strike] both of them. 6. [I am beating] you. 7.

For the advantage of these two-people at-the-back-of-me.   8. Close beside us two.
9. [I brought (it)] from all of you.   10. [He is running] towards the couple at
the back.

Example 2.

1. Nunkou [pite nunyo].   2. Noolana [pite-ka nutto].   3. Tunanari [pi-pi-a
nutto].   4. Ingkatina.   5. Nunyoena [nung-ki-a tun-a].   6. Ingienyana [toka-ka
nutto].   7. Tunaenomari [pun-na nunyo].   8. Nunnari [pipa-ka nutto].   9. Noolako
[pite nunyo].   10. Nokatinie.

Translation.

1. [I will strike] this-woman-here-in-front.   2. [I was beating] both of you.
3. [I see] those-people-yonder.   4. For thy benefit.   5. [They are sitting down]
alongside me.   6. [I brought (it)] from thee.   7. [I will run] to those-folks-
yonder.   8. [I saw] that-woman-over-there.   9. [I will strike] both of you.   10.
To the advantage of this fellow-close-in-front-of-me.

Example 3.

1. Noolaena.   2. Poolaenyanari [toka-ka nutto].   3. Nunyouno [pun-ni-a
noo-a].   4. Nokoka [pipa nunyo].   5. Nooie.   6. Poolie.   7. Tunanganaka.   8.
Tunaenamari.   9. Nungienyanaka [toka-ka nutto].   10. Noolangana.

Translation.

1. Alongside both of you.   2. [I brought (it)] from those-two-people-yonder.
3. [He is running] towards me.   4. [I shall see] him-close-up-at-the-back-of-me.
5. This fellow close-up-at-my-side.   6. This couple in-front-of-me.   7. For the
benefit of all-those-behind.   8. Alongside those-people-yonder.   9. [I brought
[(it)] from this-woman-here-at-the-back.   10. For the benefit of both of you.

10. Personal Pronouns—Possessive.

There are two forms of these pronouns, according as the article possessed is a
person or thing.   In the former case, it must be borne in mind, however, there is
no pronoun possessive expressed for the first person : this is somewhat after the
style of a European speaking of " Father" or " Mother," the " my" being understood.   In the latter case, where the article possessed is a thing, the pronoun of
the first person is used only for distinctiveness or emphasis ; otherwise it is always
understood.

In either case, for purposes of subsequent inflexion, the possessive pronoun
and the article possessed together form one word, the article possessed being
placed first.

Number.	Person.	a. Article Possessed—a Person.	b. Article Possessed—a Thing.
Singular.	1st	...	năn-yă-tĭ = my [dog, boomerang, &c.]
	2nd	măl-lă = thy [mother, son, &c.]	ĭng-kă-tĭ = thy „ „
	3rd	wă-rá, &c.	nŏ-kă-tĭ-yĕ, &c.
	„	wă-rá	nŏ-kă-tĭ-kă
	„	wă-rá	nŏ-kă-tĭ-á-rĭ
	„	wă-rá	năn-kă-tĭ-yĕ
	„	wă-rá	năn-kă-tĭ-kă
	„	wă-rá	năn-kă-tĭ-á-rĭ
Dual.	1st	năl-lĭng-ă = [the sister] of us two	năl-lĭng-ă = [the spear] belonging to us two
	2nd	noo-lăng-ă, &c.	noo-lăng-ă, &c
	3rd	wă-rá	poo-lăng-ă-yĕ
	„	wă-rá	poo-lăng-ă-ka
	„	wă-rá	poo-lăng-á-rĭ
Plural.	1st	năn-ăng-ă = [the father] of us all	năn-ăng-ă = [the trees] belonging to us all
	2nd	noo-rang-ă, &c.	noo-răng-ă, &c.
	3rd	wă-rá	tăn-ăng-ă-yĕ
	„	wă-rá	tăn-ăng-ă-kă
	„	wă-rá	tăn-ăng-á-rĭ

From the personal pronouns possessive, article possessed—a thing, certain groups of secondary possessives are formed : the thing possessed is now understood to be the particular individual's place of residence or location, while the prepositional suffixes -ĕ-nă, -ĕ-nō, ĕn-yă (sects. 22, 23) indicate respectively "rest in, motion towards, direction whence." Thus :

nunyati-ena = in, *or*, at my place, residence, hut, &c.
nunkatiko-eno = towards the hut, &c., belonging-to-the-woman-at-the-back-of-me.
nooranga-enya = from the direction of your camp, &c.

Example 4.
1. Bibapooro ingkati.　2. Berdaje nunkatiye.　3. Poolangaka-ena.　4. Nunkatika-ena.　5. Kokooro noolanga.　6. Tunangari-eno.　7. Makowata nokatiye.　8. Mali nunkatiari.　9. Nullinga-enya [pun-ni-a noo-a].　10. Piouli nokatika.

Translation.
1. Thy boomerang.　2. This woman's dilly-bag.　3. At their [dual] place. 4. At this woman's camp.　5. The yam-stick belonging to you two.　6. Towards the hut, &c., belonging-to-those-people.　7. The spear belonging-to-this-man-close-up-in-front.　8. Yonder-woman's net.　9. [He is running] from the direction-of-our-place.　10. The dog belonging-to-the-man-at-the-back-of-me.

Example 5.
1. Titi mulla.　2. Wungata nunyati-ena.　3. Koopa-koopa ingkati-ena.　4. Koonpara nokatiari.　5. Poolangaye-ena.　6. Bibapooro poolangari.　7. Koorooi noolanga.　8. Pooti nunyati.　9. Tarembola nunkatiye.　10. Pooti nunyati-ena.

Translation.
1. Thy brother.　2. A woman (is) at-my-place.　3. (There is) an old man at-your-camp.　4. The shield belonging-to-that-man-yonder.　5. At the camp of-those-two-men-in-front.　6. The boomerang belonging-to-that-couple-yonder.　7. A hut belonging-to-you-both.　8. My fire-wood.　9. The pituri belonging to-this-woman-here-beside-me.　10. (There is) firewood at-thy-place.

Example 6.
1. [Oota-na] ingkati-eno.　2. [Punna-na] nunkatika-enya.　3. Pokara nooranga-ena.　4. Untitiri nokatiye.　5. Berdaje nullinga.　6. Kootakapo nunyati-ena.　7. [Kunda-na] tunangari-eno.　8. Koonpara noolanga-ena.　9. Piouli poolangaka nullinga-eno [oo-ti-a].　10. Konupa nunkatika nokatika-ena.

Translation.
1. [Come back] to-thy-place.　2. [Run] from-this-woman's hut, &c.　3. Grass (grows) at-your-residence.　4. A sword belonging-to-this-man.　5. Our dilly-bag. 6. (There is a) white-flower at-my-place.　7. [Go] to yonder-people's camp, &c. 8. (My) shield (is) at-your-place.　9. The dog belonging-to-the-couple-at-the back-of-me [is returning] to-our-hut, &c.　10. Her necklace (is) at-his-place.

11. Nouns—Nominative.
The nominative denotes the subject, and is usually placed foremost in the sentence. If the subject governs a transitive verb in present or past time, it takes the suffix -lō (sect. 18): with an intransitive verb, under similar conditions, no addition is made (sect. 18). In future time, with both transitive and intransitive verbs, the subject take the suffix -ng-ō.

kana [nung-ki-a] = the man [sits-down].
machoomba-lo [tiche-a] = a kangaroo [eats].
kana [nungka-ka] = a man [sat-down].
machoomba-lo [tiche-ka] = the kangaroo [was eating].
kana-ngo [nungka] = the man [will sit-down].
machoomba-ngo [tiche] = a kangaroo [will eat].

12. Nouns—Vocative.

The vocative is used only in connection with persons, and has no special inflexion of its own. However, when any North-West-Central Queensland aboriginal wishes to greet, or attract another's attention, at a comparative distance away, he will shout " Hoo ! " sharply and abruptly, followed may be by " upperi," " titi," etc., *i.e.*, " father, brother," etc. When at closer quarters, a Boulia district native would begin with " *kou-ă* !" *i.e.*, " Hullo ! come here !" etc., according to the context of the conversation which is about to take place. Strictly speaking, this "kou-a" is a defective verb, used only in the imperative (sect. 31*c*), and undergoing the usual inflexions for the singular, dual, and plural : its remaining moods and tenses are supplied by " ka-ki-a nutto" = " I call, beckon to," etc. The resemblance of " Hoo" and " Kou-a" to the anglicised " Coo-ee ! " is very striking. [The Kalkadoon shout out "*nă*-wŏ !" when attracting someone's attention at a distance.]

13. Nouns—Possessive.

The inflexions of the possessive case vary according as the possessor, and that which is possessed, are persons or not :

a. When the possessor is a person, -ng-ă is suffixed—
koopa-koopa-nga bibapooro = an old-man's boomerang.

b. When that which is possessed is also a person, the latter takes the suffix -wă-ră
koopa-koopa-nga titi-wara = the old man's brother.
koopa-koopa-nga titi-wara-nga bibapooro = the old-man's brother's boomerang.

c. When both possessor and that which is possessed are things, the two nouns are put into close apposition without flexion—
machoomba wapa = a kangaroo's pup.

It must be borne in mind that in all these cases the terms signifying possessor and possessed constitute one word, so far as any subsequent inflexions are concerned. (*See* Examples 11, 12.)

14. Nouns—Objective.

a. Where the object is in the direct action of the verb, the noun objective takes the suffix -nă in present or past time, and -kō in future time (sect 6)—
wungata-lo uttapeukka-na [pite-a] = the woman [strikes] the child.
kana-lo upperi-na [pite-ka] = the man [struck] the father.
koopa-koopa-ngo nopo-ko [pite] = an old man [will strike] the wife.

b. In those cases where the object is in the indirect action of the verb, recourse is had to the various prepositional inflexions (sects. 22-25).

15. Nouns—Plural and Dual.

The plural is indicated by the suffix -*pĭt*-yĭ-rĭ, the compound so formed undergoing similar inflexions as the original word—
wungata [oo-ti-a] = a woman [returns].
wungata-pityiri [kun-di-a] = the women [depart].
uttapeukka-pityiri-lo [tiche-a] = children eat.
upperi-lo uttapeukka-pityiri-na [pite-a] = the father [strikes] the children.
umma-lo uttapeukka-pityiri-wara-na [pite-a] = a mother [is striking] her children.

The dual is expressed by *pa*-koo-lă = " two," which is used in exactly the same manner as *pityiri*.

16. Nouns—Gender.

Gender is expressed either by separate words, *e.g.*,
ka-na = man, wungata = woman,
kooliungo = he-dog, kenja = slut ;
or affixing the two latter terms, which are then treated as adjectives,
kenja tinnapulli = female opossum,
kooliungo kooridala = male eagle-hawk.

Example 7.

1. Upperi-nga mali. 2. Kooridala wapa. 3. Moyerjo-nga uttapeukka-wara. 4. Munguni-maro-nga nopo-wara. 5. Piouli wapa. 6. Koopa-koopa-nga kako-wara. 7. Moyerjo-nga titi-wara. 8. Upperi mulla. 9. Jummi-pityiri nullinga. 10. Uttapeukka-pityiri.

Translation.

1 (My) father's net. 2. The eagle-hawk's young-one. 3. An old woman's child. 4. The doctor's wife. 5. A dog's puppy. 6. The old-man's sister. 7. The old-woman's brother. 8. Your father. 9. Our aunts. 10. (My) children.

Example 8.

1. Ullo-wara. 2. Koopa-koopa-nga uttapeukka-pityiri-wara. 3. Moyerjo-nga uttapeukka-wara-ngo berdaje. 4. Ullo-mulla-nga bibapooro. 5. Titi-wara-nga uttapeukka-wara. 6. Kenja kooridala. 7. Upperi-mulla-nga makowata-pityiri. 8. Umma-wara-nga berdaje. 9. Kako-pityiri-wara. 10. Kako-nullinga-nga koorouі.

Translation.

1. Their uncle. 2. The old-man's children. 3. A dilly-bag belonging to the old-woman's child. 4. Thy uncle's boomerang. 5. Her brother's child. 6. A female eagle-hawk. 7. Thy father's spears. 8. His mother's dilly-bag. 9. Their sisters. 10. Our sister's hut.

Example 9.

1. Titi-wara-nga koonpara. 2. Konupa jummi-mulla-nga. 3. Kenja machoomba wapa. 4. Munguni-maro-nga kako-pityiri-wara. 5. Kako-wara-nga uttapeukka-pityiri-wara. 6. Nopo-mulla-nga titi-wara. 7. Umma-wara-nga uttapeukka-pityiri-wara. 8. Chata-mulla-nga untitiri. 9. Upperi-nga makowata. 10. Umma noolanga berdaje-pityiri.

Translation.

1. Her brother's shield. 2. Thy aunt's necklace. 3. A female kangaroo's young one. 4. The doctor's sisters. 5. Their sister's children. 6. Thy wife's brother. 7. Her mother's children. 8. Thy grandfather's sword. 9. (My) father's spear. 10. Your mother's dilly-bags.

17. Verbs—Active: The Indicative.

In the indicative mood the verb agrees with its subject in point of time only, as shown by means of special inflexions for present, past, and future: the particular number and person is indicated only by the subject noun or verbal pronoun (sect. 18).

The root-stem of all verbs ends either in a- or e-, whence the three tenses are formed as follows:—

Root-stem.	Present.	Past.	Future.
a-	the a- becomes -ĭ-ă	-kă is added to the root-stem	either— *ling*-ă is added to the root-stem;
e-	the e- becomes -ē-ă		or— the root-stem is unaltered, but the terminal vowel emphasised and lengthened.
oo-ta-	oo-*tĭ*-ă = come-back	*oo*-tă-ka = came back	oo-tă-*ling*-ă, oo-*tā* = will come-back
pun-na-	pŭn-*nĭ*-ă = run	*pŭn*-nă-ka = ran	pŭn-nă-*ling*-ă, pŭn-*nā*=will run
kun-da-	kŭn-*dĭ*-ă = go	*kŭn*-dă-ka = went	kŭn-dă-*ling*-ă, kŭn-*dā* = will go
ti-che-	tĭ-*chē*-ă = eat	*tĭ*-chē-ka = ate	tĭ-chē-*ling*-ă, tĭ-*chē* = will eat
pi-te-	pĭ-*tē*-ă = strike	*pĭ*-tē-kă = struck	pĭ-tē-*ling*-ă, pĭ-*tē* = will strike
woon-je-	woon-*jē*-ă = give	*woon*-jē-kă = gave	woon-jē-*ling*-ă, woon-*jē* = will give

For certain special forms of the future *see* sect. 30.

18. Verbal Pronouns.

The particular pronouns used with the verbs to distinguish the required number and person may be spoken of as verbal pronouns : there are three series of them—

(a) With intransitive verbs, in present and past time, they are identical with the personal pronouns nominative for the corresponding tenses (sect. 5) ;

(b) With transitive verbs, in present and past time, these verbal pronouns take on a special inflexion, identical with the -lō, already referred to in sect. 11 (which indicates a subject governing a transitive verb) ;

(c) With transitive and intransitive verbs, in the future, the pronouns are identical with the personal pronouns nominative used in the corresponding tense (sect. 5).

Number.	Person.	a. Present and Past. Intransitive.	b. Present and Past. Transitive.	c. Future. Intrans. and Trans.
Singular.	1st	nŭn-jă ootia, ootaka	nŭt-tō tichea, ticheka	nŭn-yō oota, tiche
	2nd	ĭn-pă ,, ,,	nĭn-dō ,, ,,	ĭng-ō ,, ,,
	3rd	noo-ī-ĕ ,, ,,	noo-loo-ū ,, ,,	noong-ō-ū ,,
	,,	noo-ă-kă ,, ,,	noo-loo-kă ,, ,,	noong-ō-kă ,,
	,,	noo-â ,, ,,	noo-loo-á-rĭ ,,	noong-ō-(á-rĭ) ,,
	,,	nŭn-ī-ĕ ,, ,,	nŭn-doo-ū ;,	nŭng-ō-ū ,,
	,,	nŭn-ă-kă ,,	nŭn-doo-ka ,,	nŭng-ō-kă ,,
	,,	nŭn-pâ ,, ,,	nŭn-doo-á-rĭ ,,	nŭng-ō-(á-rĭ) ,,
Dual.	1st	nŭl-lĭ ootia, ootaka	nŭl-lĭ-lō tichea, ticheka	nŭl-lĭng-ō oota, tiche
	2nd	noo-lă ,, ,,	noo-lă-lō ,, ,,	noo-lăng-ō ,,
	3rd	poo-lĭ-ĕ ,, ,,	poo-lă-lō-ū ,,	poo-lăng-ō-ū ,,
	,,	poo-lă-kă ,,	poo-lă-lō-kă ,,	poo-lăng-ō-kă ,,
	,,	poo-lă ,, ,,	poo-lă-lō-á-rĭ ,,	poo-lăng-ō-(á-rĭ) ,,
Plural.	1st	nŭn-ă ootia, ootaka	nŭn-ă-lō tichea, ticheka	nŭn-ăng-ō oota, tiche
	2nd	noo-ră ,, ,,	noo-ră-lō ,,	noo-răng-ō ,,
	3rd	tŭn-ī-ĕ ,, ,,	tŭn-ă-lō-ū ,,	tŭn-ăng-ō-ū ,,
	,,	tŭn-ă-kă ,,	tŭn-ă-lō-kă ,,	tŭn-ăng-ō-kă ,,
	,,	tŭn-â ,, ,,	tŭn-ă-lō-á-rĭ ,,	tŭn-ăng-ō-(á-rĭ) ,,

The forms " nutto," " nindo," &c., may sometimes do duty as translations for the expressions " I have or had," " You have or had," in reply to a query involving a transitive verb : thus, " Who has taken my spear ?" might quite grammatically be answered by " nutto !" = " I have !" the verb itself, the word " taken," being understood (sect. 8).

In ordinary conversation, verbal pronouns are placed immediately after the verbs they qualify, and generally at the very end of the sentence.

Example 10.

1. Moyerjo-nga uttapeukka-wara-lo koondara-na tiche-ka. 2. Munguni-maro-nga nopo-wara-ngo koopa-koopa-nga-ko kako-wara-ko pite. 3. Jummi-pityiri-noolanga-lo upperi-nga mali-na mare-ka. 4. Koopa-koopa-nga uttapeukka-pityiri-wara-lo berdaje-na umma-wara-nga mare-ka. 5. Ullo-wara-lo kenja-na kooridala-na tiche-ka. 6. Upperi-nullinga-lo bibapooro-na ullo-mulla-nga marea. 7. Titi-wara-nga uttapeukka-wara-ngo nungka. 8. Umma-wara-nga kako-pityiri-wara-lo tichea. 9. Upperi-nga titi-wara-lo umma-mulla-na tarea. 10. Kenja-lo machoomba-lo wapa-lo pokara-na tichea.

Translation.

1. The old woman's child was eating a snake. 2. The doctor's wife will beat the old man's sister. 3. Your aunts brought my father's net. 4. The old man's children fetched his mother's dilly-bag. 5. Their uncle was eating the female eagle-hawk. 6. Our father is bringing thy uncle's boomerang. 7. Her brother's child will sit down. 8. Her mother's sisters are eating. 9. (My) father's brother is kicking thy mother. 10. The female-kangaroo's pup is eating the grass.

Example 11.

1. Munguni-maro-nga kako-wara-lo munta-na mare-ka. 2. Upperi-wara-nga makowata-ngo machoomba-ko wapa-ko touela. 3. Umma-nullinga-lo wungata-na pite-ka. 4. Kako-wara-lo berdaje-pityiri-na tarea. 5. Kooridala wapa [pinji-ena] nungkia. 6. Koopa-koopa-nga titi-wara-lo upperi-nga koonpara-na mare-ka. 7. Ullo-ngo kuttamulla-ko tima. 8. Munguni-maro-nga kako-pityiri-wara-ngo pappa-ko wire. 9. Upperi-lo titi-mulla-na pitea. 10. Koopa-koopa-nga nopo-wara-ngo uttapeukka-pityiri-mulla-ko mullo pite.

Translation.

1. The doctor's sister was bringing the food. 2. His father's spear will hit the kangaroo's pup. 3. Our mother was beating the woman. 4. Her sister was weaving dilly-bags. 5. The eagle-hawk's young-one is sitting [in the nest]. 6. The old-man's brother brought my father's shield. 7. (My) uncle will drink the water. 8. The doctor's sisters will grind the pappa-seed. 9. (My) father is beating your brother. 10. The old-man's wife will not strike thy children.

Example 12.

1. Koolpari wapa-pityiri [punna-mia]. 2. Upperi-lo kako-pakoola-mulla-na kite-ka. 3. Kako-mulla-ngo titi-ko kite. 4. Moyerjo-nga uttapeukka-pityiri-wara nungkia. 5. Titi-wara-lo munta-ingkati-na tiche-ka. 6. Kako-ngo pooti-ingkati-ko mare. 7. Untitiri ingkati munna. 8. Berdaje-nunkatiye-ko mare nunyo. 9. Makowata-ingkati-lo machoomba-na-touela-ka. 10. Umma-lo munta-nokatiari-na tichea.

Translation.

1. The emu's young-ones [are running about]. 2. (My) father married thy two sisters. 3. Thy sister will marry (my) brother. 4. The old-woman's children are sitting down. 5. His brother was eating thy food. 6. (My) sister will bring thy fire-wood. 7. Thy sword (is) bad. 8. I will fetch the dilly-bag belonging-to-this-woman-here-in-front. 9. Thy spear hit the kangaroo. 10. (My) mother is eating yonder-man's food.

19. Verbs—Active: The Imperative.

The imperative is formed by the addition to the root-stem of—

-nă for the singular.

-nă-lă for the dual.

-nă-ră for the plural.

Thus—

tiche-na = eat thou!

kunda-nala = go, both of you!

oota-nara = come back, all of you!

For certain special forms of the imperative *see* sect. 31.

20. Adjectives.

a. Adjectives are generally placed before the nouns they qualify, and take the same inflexions—

tuari-lo machoomba-lo piouli-na tare-ka = a tall kangaroo was kicking the dog.

munna-ngo kana-ngo kunda = the bad man will go away.

b. But when an adjective qualifies a noun in the plural, the plural sign is attached to the noun only—

munna-lo kana-pityiri-lo uttapeukka-na pitea = the bad men are beating (my) child.

c. All adjectives can be, and very often are, used by themselves as nouns—

kooyungo = good, a good fellow, a good thing.

munna = bad, a bad fellow, a bad thing.

d. With one exception, all adjectives can be used with the suffix -ng-oo-rō to signify more distinctly a noun, person or thing, understood. This -ng-oo-ro = ng (interpolated for euphony) + oo-roo-roo (one, unity); hence—

kooyungo-ngooro = a good fellow, a good thing.

munna-ngooro = a bad fellow, a bad thing.

The exception mentioned above is nuno = tired, which interpolates the verb kunna = to become : thus, nuno-kunnia-ngooro = a tired fellow, a weary body.

e. Adjectives may also sometimes be used as adverbs—
kana malooaka punnia = the man is running quickly.

21. Adverbs.

Adverbs may be formed from adjectives by means of the suffix -*mŭn*-dă
    munna = bad   kooyungo = good.
    munna-munda = badly   kooyungo-munda = well.

It is interesting to note that this adverbial suffix is identical with the prepositional term denoting, from direction, neighbourhood, of-a-place (sect. 22*d*).

The use of adjectives as adverbs has already been referred to.

Example 13.

1. Koopa-koopa-nga titi-wara-ko marali pipa nunyo.   2. Mierli-ngo wungata-pakoola-ngo berdaje-pityiri-ko tare.   3. Kanari-pakoola-lo pappa-na wire-ka. 4. Upperi-lo uttapeukka-pityiri-na pitea.   5. Wungata-pakoola-na kite-ka nutto. 6. Machoomba-lo wapa-lo pooriti-na pokara-na tichea.   7. Perkilli-lo koolpari-lo kindooro-na kuttamulla-na timia.   8. Uttapeukka-pityiri-ngo nungka.   9. Munna-ko wungata-pityiri-ko pite nunyo.   10. Papatooro-ngooro-ngo tuari-ko untitiri-ko mare.

Translation.

1. I will see the old-man's brother to-morrow.   2. The two good women will be weaving dilly-bags.   3. Two girls were grinding pappa-seed,   4. The father is beating his children.   5. I married two women.   6. The kangaroo's pup is eating all the grass.   7. A big emu is drinking the clear water.   8. (My) children will sit down.   9. I will beat the bad women.   10. The short-fellow will fetch the long swords.

Example 14.

1. Papatooro bibapooro [tikkara-ena] malooaka-munda punnia.   2. Wungata-lo kooyungo-na berdaje-pityiri-na mare-ka.   3. Umma-lo mie-mie-na kutta-mulla-na timia.   4. Makowata-ngo kenja-ko machoomba-ko touela.   5. Koopa-koopa-nga kako-wara prinna-na [tunpa-mulle-ka].   6. Koondungari-pityiri-na tichea nunalo.   7. Mierli-ko munta-ko mare poolangoka.   8. Munna-lo kana-pityiri-lo kooyungo-na bibapooro-pityiri-na tare-ka.   9. Berdaje-pityiri-na tarea poolaka.   10. Mie-mie-na kuttamulla-na tima-ka nullilo.

Translation.

1. A short boomerang flies (*i.e.*, runs) swiftly [along the sky].   2. The women fetched the good dilly-bags.   3. Mother is drinking dirty water.   4. A spear will hit the female kangaroo.   5. The old-man's sister [cut] (her) leg. 6. We are eating diver-birds.   7. They will both bring good food.   8. The bad men were making good boomerangs.   9. Both are weaving dilly-bags.   10. We were both drinking the muddy water.

Example 15.

1. Tie-na takoko-na tarea nindo.   2. Wallara machoomba punnia.   3. Parawanga-lo munguni-maro-lo [punjea-ngooro-na] pokara-na woonjea.   4. Pulye-ngooro-lo pari-na munta-na tichea.   5. Yarimungkora-lo wungata-pityiri-lo tano-na kanari-pityiri-na pite-ka.   6. Wallara-ugo koolpari-ngo pari-ko kuttamulla-ko tima.   7. Chalo-chalo-ngo kana-ngo parawanga-ko wungata-ko tare. 8. Munna-ngo wungata-pityiri-ngo mullo nungka: kunda.   9. Kooyungo-lo umma-pityiri-lo munna-na uttapeukka-pityiri-na pitea.   10. Munna-ko pappa-ko mullo wire poolangou.

Translation.

1. Thou art kicking (my) little infant.   2. A young kangaroo is running. 3. The mad doctor gives grass [to the sick-fellow].   4. A fat-fellow eats a lot-of food.   5. Strong women were striking the weak girls.   6. A young emu will drink plenty of water.   7. The clever man will kick the mad woman.   8. The bad women will not sit down : they will go-away.   9. Good mothers thrash (their) bad children.   10. These two-people-here will not grind bad pappa-seed.

22. Prepositions—Motion.

Prepositions, or what would correspond to them in our own language, are signified in the Pitta-Pitta language by various suffixes added to both adjective and noun, or by separate words, and may be classified according as they refer to motion, rest, purpose, or time. Motion will be considered first—

a. To, in, into, at = -ē-nō (sect. 7*a*)—

koorooui-eno punnia nooaka = he is running to the hut.

munna-eno wungata-eno makowata-na touelia nutto = I am throwing a spear at the bad woman.

wungata-lo makowata-na nuna-eno touelia = the woman is throwing a spear at us.

b. From, person or place = -ēn-yă (sect. 7*c*)—

oora-enya kundia nuna = we are going from the camp.

kanari-enya oota-ka noora = you came-back from the girl.

c. From the direction, neighbourhood, of a person = -ēn-yăng-ŏ

munna-enyango wungata-pityiri-enyango kunda nunango = we will go-away from the neighbourhood of bad women.

d. From the direction, neighbourhood, of a place = -mŭn-dă (sect. 21)—

Boolyo-munda oota-ka poolie = both these people came from the direction of Boulia.

e. Across, over = -kō

perkilli-ko miriwinni-ko punna tunango = they will run across, over, the big mountain.

f. After, to be after, on the look out for, to hunt, &c. = -ng-ă

upperi-mulla koolpari-nga kundia = thy father is going after an emu.

pari-pari-nga tinungara-eno kunda nunango = we will go northwards after (our) belongings.

g. Around, round about = koo-dĭ-jă-kŏ-rē-ă (sect. 43*g*) with the suffix -na attached to the object referred to (sect. 23*b*)—

koodijakorea koorooui-na upperi punnia = father is running around the hut.

h. Among, up, through, alongside of = -ē-nă

tinnapulli moorra-ena katea = an opossum is climbing up among the branches.

koopa-koopa-nga bibapooro tikkara-ena punnia = the old-man's boomerang flies (*i.e.*, runs) through the sky.

k. In company with, things or persons = -mâ-rō in present or past time, -mâ-rŏ-ngō in future time (*cf.* the verb "to have" in sect. 8)—

kana nopo-maro kundia = the man is going away with (his) wife.

tunari-maro kundia nunja = I am going away with them.

bibapooro-maro-ngo kunda noongou = he will depart, taking his boomerang with him.

[NOTE.—" With, in company with," including two persons only—provided these two persons are not represented by pronouns—can also be expressed by the double use of the third personal pronoun dual (sect. 18*a*)—

kana poola wungata poola kundia = the man and the woman go away together, in company.]

Example 16.

1. Marali koorooui-eno kunda nunango. 2. Munna-ngo kana-pityiri-ngo tikkara-eno mullo kunda. 3. Munguni-maro-lo makowata-na koolpari-eno touelaka. 4. Bibapooro-na machoomba-eno touea nutto. 5. Poolaka punnia oora-enya. 6. Kanari-pityiri-ngo umma-pityiri-wara-enya oota. 7. Munna-enyango kana-pityiri-enyango kunda noolango. 8. Teriwa-munda punna-ka nooaka. 9. Perkilli-ko miriwinni-ko kunda noorango: nari, parapi-ko. 10. Machoomba-nga kurri kunda nunango.

Translation.

1. To-morrow we will all go to the hut. 2. Bad men will not go to heaven (*i.e.*, to the sky). 3. The doctor threw a spear at the emu. 4. I am throwing a boomerang at the kangaroo. 5. They are both running away from the camp. 6. The girls will return from their mothers. 7. You both will go away from the neighbourhood of bad men. 8. This man was running from the direction of the east. 9. You all will go over a big mountain; also, across a creek. 10. We will all go a-hunting (*i.e.*, after) kangaroos to-day.

Example 17.

1. Teriwa-eno pari-pari-nga kunda nunyo. 2. Moyerjo oota-ka perkilli-maro piouli-pityiri-maro. 3. Titi punna-ka koodijakorea kooroui-na. 4. Piouli-maro bibapooro-maro [nopo-ena] nooaka nungkia. 5. Yuppieri-pityiri-ngo pari-marongo munta-marongo marali oota. 6. Tunangari-eno tunari-marongo kunda nunyo. 7. Uttapeukka-marongo punna nullingo. 8. Koopa-koopa-ngo biba-pooro-pityiri-ko punnare. 9. Kanari-pityiri kooyungo-maro berdaje-pityiri-maro. 10. Takoko-pityiri-marongo noolango.

Translation.

1. I shall go eastward after (my) possessions. 2. The old woman returned with (her) big dogs. 3. (My) brother was running round the camp. 4. He is sitting down [alongside his wife] with his dog and boomerang. 5. The boys will come-back with plenty of food to-morrow. 6. I will go with them to-their-place. 7. We will both run (and take) the child with us. 8. The old man will steal the spears. 9. The girls have good dilly-bags. 10. Both of you will have babies.

23. Prepositions—Rest.

a. In, at, close to, among, alongside of, &c. = -ĕ-nă (*cf.* Personal Pronouns, indirect object, rest with whom, sect. 7*b*)—

kooroui-ena nungkia nunja = I am sitting down in the hut.

mulkari! tikkara-ena = Lord! (who dwellest) amongst the sky.

tarembola kana-ena nara-ena echea = the pituri rests on (behind) the man's ear.

b. Around, round about = koodija korea and -nă (used similarly as in sect. 22*g*)—

koodijakorea tillimurri-na koopa-koopa-pityiri nungkia = the old men are sitting around the gidyea-tree.

c. Between, persons = nă-kă, used as an adjective—

naka-ena wungata-pityiri-ena nungka ingo = thou shalt sit down between the women.

d. Between, things = koon-mī-ă, with -lō suffixed to that which limits; if there is no verb in the sentence, that which is limited, that which is between, takes -nă

miriwinni-pakoola-lo koonmia parapi echea = the stream lies between two mountains.

miriwinni-pakoola-lo koonmia parapi-na = between two mountains (is) a stream.

prinna-pakoola-lo koonmia merkoo-na = a lizard (is) between (my) legs.

prinna-pakoola-lo koonmia merkoo punnia = a lizard is running between (my) legs.

e. Above, on top of = kă-tĭ-ŭm-pă-kă-lă (*i.e.*, the "crown-of-the-head"), used as an adjective—

tinnapulli katiumpakala-ena kooroui-ena nungkia = the opossum is sitting on the top of the hut.

f. Under, below, beneath, things = kĕ-rĕ-prĕ-tĕ, with -lō suffixed to that which is above; if there is no verb in the sentence, that which is beneath takes -nă

koonpara-lo kereprete tarembola echea = the pituri lies beneath the koolamon.

koonpara-lo kereprete tarembola-na = under the koolamon (is) the pituri.

g. Under, below, beneath, persons = -*ē*-nă (sect. 23*a.*). With pronouns personal, the form of indirect object—person with whom, rest (sect. 7*b.*)—is used : a slight modification is found only with the first and second persons singular which become *nŭn*-yĭ-ē-nă, *ĭng*-ĭ-ē-nă respectively (*i.e.*, " underneath me, underneath thee").

h. On this side of, in front of = ĭk-kĭl-lĭm-mĕ-*wā*-rĭ, with- lō suffixed to that which is behind; if there is no verb in the sentence, that which is in front takes -nă

    ikkillimmewari parapi-lo nungkia tuna = they are sitting down on this side of the creek.

    ikkillimmewari moolka-lo machoomba tukkia = the kangaroo is standing in front of the tree trunk.

    ikkillimmewari miriwinni-lo parapi-na = on this side of the mountain (is) a stream.

k. On the other side of, behind =

  (i.) *oo*-rō-koo-nă-wă-ră (*cf.* ooro- = unity, and ko-ko = the back, dorsum) used as an adjective—

    oorokoonawara-eno kokotoongo-eno punna-na = run to the other side of the hill.

    oorokoonawara-ena kooroui-ena tinnapulli-lo merichi-pityiri-na tichea = the opossum is eating leaves behind the hut.

  (ii.) *kō*-kō (*i.e.*, the back, dorsum, of a person) used as a noun—

    nungka-na koko-ena = sit down (at-my-back, *i.e.*) behind me.

    nungka-na kana-ena koko-ena = sit down (at the man's back, *i.e.*) behind the man.

  (iii.) mă-*rē*-kă, with -lō suffixed to that which is in front; if there is no verb in the sentence, that which is behind takes -nă—

    kokotoongo-lo mareka = on the other side of the hill.

    kokotoongo-lo katiumpakala-lo mareka kana-pityiri moochea = behind the top of the hill the men are sleeping.

    kokotoongo-lo mareka parapi-na = on the other side of the hill (is) a creek.

24. Prepositions—Purpose, reason, means.

a. To, donation, &c. = -nă in present or past, and -kō in future, time (*cf.* the simple objective case, sect. 14*a*)—

    upperi-lo makowata-na munguni-maro-na woonjea = (my) father gives a spear to the doctor.

    umma-ngo berdaje-ko kanari-ko woonje = mother will give the girl a dilly-bag.

b. From—obtained or received—person or place = *ĕn*-yă (sect. 7*c*) with the additional -nă in present or past time, and -kō in future time (sect. 14*a*)—

    koopa-koopa-enya-na makowata-na mare-ka nutto = I brought the spear from the old man.

    tillimurri-enya-na bibapooro-na tinchia nindo = thou art cutting a boomerang from a gidyea tree.

    wungata-enya-ko berdaje-ko mare nunyo = I will fetch the dilly-bag from the woman.

c. For—advantage, benefit, use—person or thing = -ng-ă, with the additional -nă in present or past time, and -kō in future time (sec. 14*a*)—

    kana-lo wungata-nga-na munta-na indamullea = the man is begging food for the woman.

    piouli-nga-ko pokara-ko toka nunyo = I will bring grass for the dog (to lie upon, etc.)

    woonje-na nunya toota-na makowata-nga-na = give me grease for (*i.e.*, to smear on) a spear.

d. For—bargaining, swapping, exchanging something for something = -ng-ă for all tenses—

yuppieri-lo makowata-na bibapooro-nga pulkiwoonjea = the boy swaps a spear for a boomerang.

kana-lo wungata-na berdaje-na tarembola-nga pulkiwoonje-mullea = the man is exchanging a dilly-bag for pituri with-the-woman.

e. For—manufacturing, constructing, or building = -ng-ăng-ă—

kunda-na moorra-nga koorroui-nganga = go after (*i.e.,* to fetch, sect. 22*f*) wood for a hut (*i.e.,* to build it with).

mali-nganga pokara-na tinchia nunpa = she is cutting grass for a net (*i.e.,* to make it with).

f. With, by, through—the physical agency of = -lō in present or past time, -ng-ō in future time—

yuppieri-lo kope-na mali-lo kachea = the boy is catching a fish with the net.

kana-pityiri-lo machoomba-na bibapooro-lo toue-ka = the men struck the kangaroo with a boomerang.

wungata-ngo kanari-ko moorra-ngo pite = the woman will hit the girl with a stick.

g. With, by, through—the effects of = -lă

kanari bilba tarembola-la kundia = the girl's fore-head goes-away (*i.e.,* is dizzy) through the effects of pituri (*i.e.,* drunk with pituri).

munta-la poolki-kunnia nunja = I am become full-up from the effects of food (*i.e.,* I have had enough food).

Example 18.

1. Piouli wapa moolka-ena nungkia. 2. Merichi-pityiri moorra-pityiri-ena echea. 3. Merkoo prinna-pakoola-lo koonmia punnia. 4. Me-pakoola lo koonmia koongari-na. 5. Muona-ngo kana-ngo uaka-ena wungata-pityiri-ena nungka. 6. Tarembola ingiena. 7. Koko-ena wungata-pītyiri-ena nungka nunyo. 8. Tuari-ena moolka-ena yatea impa. 9. Machoomba-pakoola parapi-ena punna-ka. 10. Kooridala tikkara-ena punnia.

Translation.

1. The dingo's pup lives (*i.e.,* sits down) in the tree-trunk. 2. Leaves rest on branches. 3. A lizard is running between (my) two legs. 4. The nose (is) between the two eyes. 5. The bad man will sit down between the women. 6. The pituri (is) underneath you. 7. I will sit down behind the women. 8. You are climbing up along the tall tree-trunk. 9. Both kangaroos ran alongside the creek. 10. The eagle-hawk is flying (*i.e.,* running) through the sky.

Example 19.

1. Perkilli-na berdaje-na kako-lo titi-na woonjea. 2. Upperi-ngo uttapeukka-ko bibapooro-ko woonje. 3. Koonpara-lo kereprete tarembola-na. 4. Wungata-enyako munta-ko indamullo nunyo. 5. Pinkipoora-na munta-na: nunyatina: nunkatinie. 6. Kana-ngo pulye-ngo munta-la poolki-kunna. 7. Koopa-koopa-ngo koolpari-ko mali-nga kache. 8. Moyerjo-lo wakerdi-na miriwinni-lo touea. 9. Kooyungo-na bibapooro-pityiri-na kako-lo nunya woonje-ka. 10. Tie merichi-pityiri perkilli-ena moorra-pityiri-ena echea.

Translation.

1. The sister is giving a big dilly-bag to (her) brother. 2. The father will give a boomerang to (his) child. 3. The pituri (is) under the shield. 4. I will ask-for food from the woman. 5. Divide the food: for me: for her. 6. The fat man will be full-up with food. 7. The old man will catch an emu with the net. 8. An old woman is hitting the crow with a stone. 9. (My) sister gave me good boomerangs. 10. Small leaves rest on big branches.

25. Prepositions—Time.

There are no prepositions signifying specially time, duration, how long (sect. 38).

 a. Time when—relating to the future = -*ē*-nō

  wolka-wirea-eno pretipamulle nunango = we two will meet when the sun goes down (*i.e.*, at sunset).

  oorooroo-eno jungi-eno nungka-linga nunyo = I shall stay here (*i.e.*, sit down) for one month.

  jungi-pakoola-eno oota ingo = thou wilt return in two months' time.

 b. Time when—relating to the present or past = *ē*-nă (sect. 42*a*)—

  wolka-pakoola-ena innaka pretipaka nunja = I met him two days (*i.e.*, suns) ago.

  wolka-pakoola-ena prinnapoorte-ka nunja = I walked for two days.

 c. Time after or since, with a past verb = -*ēn*-yă (sect. 42*b*)—

  nunya tare-ka-enya machoomba-lo, nungka-ka nunja = after *or* since the kangaroo kicked me, I sat down.

Example 20.

1. Pakoolangooro-ena wolka-ena oota-ka nuna. 2. Pakoolangooro-eno wolka-eno oota nunyo. 3. [Wolka-wunjea-eno] pooriti-ngo katiwire nunango. 4. [Koopa-koopa-ena kunda-ka-ena] munguni-maro-lo nopo-na punnare-ka. 5. [Upperi-ngo tiche-le] kunda nunyo. 6. Ooro-wolka-ena koondara-na pite-ka nutto. 7. Pakoola-wolka-eno koopa-koopa-ko pite nunyo. 8. Munna-ngo munguni-maro-pityiri-ngo jungi-eno oota. 9. Pulye-ngo wungata-ngo munta-ko jungka-ko piouli-ko marali woonje. 10. Kindooro-ena kuttamulla-ena utia noolooka.

Translation.

1. We all returned three days ago. 2. I will come back in three days' time. 3. [At sunrise] we will all go for a dive. 4. [While the old man went away] the doctor stole the wife. 5. [When my father will be eating] I shall go away. 6. I hit a snake yesterday. 7. The day after to-morrow (*i.e.*, in two sun's time) I will strike the old man. 8. The wicked doctors will return in a month. 9. The fat woman will give (her) thin dog (some) food to-morrow. 10. He is swimming in the clear water.

26. Conjunctions.

 a. Also, and, = *nâ*-rĭ, but only expressed when particular emphasis is required—

  woonje-na nunya bibapooro-na nari makowata-na = give me a boomerang, and also a spear.

 b. Too, = *mŭt*-tō, taking past and present, or future, suffixes, but like the preceding only used to express particular emphasis—

  tinnapulli parapi-ena nungkia: machoomba-mutto = an opossum is sitting down alongside the creek : and there's a kangaroo too.

  kana -ngo bibapooro-ko mare: makowata-mutto-ko = the man will fetch a boomerang : and a spear too.

 c. Or, = *kâ*-tĭ—

  [wara pulye-yetcha?] kana kati wungata? = [who (is) the fatter?] the man or the woman?

Example 21.

1. Woonje-na wungata-na berdaje-na: tarembola-mutto-na. 2. Yarimung-kora wungata kokooro-maro punnia. 3. Kana ootia oora-eno: nopo-mutto. 4. Koopa-koopa-pityiri-ngo bibapooro-pityiri-ko mare: makowata-pityiri-mutto-ko. 5. Kako-lo koondara-na tichea: titi-mutto-lo. 6. Bibapooro-pakoolangooro-maro nooari. 7. Nokatiari-na makowata-pakoolangooro-na punnare-ka nindo. 8. Uttapeukka-pityiri-ngako untitiri-pityiri-maro-ngo noorango. 9. Koôdijakorea kooroui-na punna nunango. 10. Koopa-koopa-ngo nopo-ena nungka

B

Translation.

1. Give the woman a dilly-bag: and pituri too. 2. The strong woman is running with a yam-stick. 3. The man is returning to camp : and his wife too. 4. The old men will bring the boomerangs ; and the spears too. 5. (My) sister is eating a snake: and so is (my) brother. 6. That fellow yonder has three boomerangs. 7. You stole that individual's three spears. 8. You shall have the swords for the benefit of (your) children. 9. We will run around the hut. 10. The old man will sit down alongside (his) wife.

27. Comparison of Adjectives.

a. Equality = ĭl-lă-*pá*-koolâ (*cf.* pakoola)—

poolie illapakoola koopa-koopa = these-two (are) equally old — *i.e.*, one is as old as the other.

kana wungata, poolie illapakoola koopa-koopa = the man (and) the woman, these-two (are) equally old—*i.e.*, the man is as old as the woman.

Another method of giving expression to the same idea would lie in the omission of illapakoola, and the substitution of adjectives by nouns, *e.g.*—

nooie koopa-koopa : nunnie moyerjo = he is an old man : she is an old woman.

b. Similarity = *yŭn*-ŭn-ă

poolie yununa bibapooro-pakoola = these two boomerangs (are) similar, the same.

woonje-na nunya yununa-na makowata-pakoola-na = give me two similar spears.

c. Difference = *oo*-roo-yără

poolari oorooyara berdaje-pakoola = those two dilly-bags (are) different.

When the special sign of the plural or dual (pityiri, pakoola) is not employed, oorooyara becomes duplicated—

tunari untitiri oorooyara-oorooyara = all those swords (are) different.

oorooyara-na oorooyara-na bibapooro-na woonje-na innaka = give him different boomerangs.

d. Comparative. The comparative of adjectives may be said to be formed in four different ways, all of which are applicable to persons or things : the adjective denoting the opposite attribute is brought into requisition in three of the cases—

(i.) *-yĕt*-chă used with both things compared—

kooyungo-yetcha nunja : munna-yetcha impa = good-more I am : bad-more you are—*i.e.*, I am better than you.

wungata munna-yetcha : kana kooyungo-yetcha = the woman (is) bad-more : the man is good-more—*i.e.*, the woman is worse than the man.

bibapooro papatooro-yetcha : untitiri tuari-yetcha = the boomerang (is) short-er : the sword is long-er—*i.e.*, the boomerang is shorter than the sword.

(ii.) *-yĕt*-chă used only with the person or thing about whom or which the comparison is made. Thus the three preceding sentences can be as correctly stated—

kooyungo-yetcha nunja : munna impa.

munna-yetcha wungata : kooyungo kana.

bibapooro papatooro-yetcha : untitiri tuari.

(iii.) Similar use of *-yĕt*-chă as in (ii.) but the second adjective takes the suffixal form -ng-oo-rō (sect. 20*d*). Thus the preceding sentences may again be quite correctly spoken of as—

kooyungo-yetcha nunja : munna-ngooro impa.

munna-yetcha wungata : kooyungo-ngooro kana.

bibapooro papatooro-yetcha : untitiri tuari-ngooro.

Though every adjective may be used with -yetcha, it must be remembered that "nuno" (= tired) always, and "poolki" (= full up) sometimes, has the intervening "kunnia" (= to become)—

nuno-kunnia-yetcha = more tired.
poolki-kunnia-yetcha = more full-up.

(iv.) It sometimes happens that the exactly opposite attribute may be temporarily forgotten, or is non-existent: for instance, there are no adjectives indicative of the opposite to " glad, thirsty, tired," &c.   In such cases recourse is had to the use of the negation *mŭl-lō*, used either by itself in its primary form, or secondary adjectival form (mullo-ngooro, sect. 20*d*), or true comparative (mullo-yetcha) form.

poolela-yetcha nunja: wungata $\left\{\begin{array}{l} \text{mullo} \\ \text{mullo-ngooro} \\ \text{mullo-yetcha} \end{array}\right\} =$

Thirsty-more I-am: the woman $\left\{\begin{array}{l} \text{not} \\ \text{not fellow} \\ \text{not more} \end{array}\right.$

i.e., I am more thirsty than the woman.

yuppieri kitye-yetcha : kanari $\left\{\begin{array}{l} \text{mullo} \\ \text{mullo-ngooro} \\ \text{mullo-yetcha} \end{array}\right\} =$

The boy (is) glad-more: the girl (is) $\left\{\begin{array}{l} \text{not} \\ \text{not fellow} \\ \text{not more} \end{array}\right.$

i.e., The boy is more glad than the girl.

e. Superlative = *nà*-rĭ *yĕt*-cha (*i.e*, nari = and, also, still more, + -yetcha = sign of the comparative)—

koopa-koopa yarimungkora-nari-yetcha pari-ena = the old-man (is) the strongest among the lot.
kooridala perkilli-nari-yetcha pia-ena = the eagle-hawk (is) the biggest among birds.
innie moorra tuari-nari-yetcha = this tree (is) the longest, very long.

28. Comparison of Adverbs.

Adverbs can also undergo comparison just like adjectives.

malooaka-munda-yetcha punnia nunja, kunjo-munda-yetcha noòaka punnia = I run more swiftly than he does. (Literally, = I run more swiftly: he runs more slowly.)

Example 22.

1. Makowata-pakoola nullinga yunuua.   2. Bibapooro nunyati mie-mierli-yetcha ingkati mullo-ngooro.   3. Piouli machoomba: poola illapakoola malooaka punnia.   4. Kana tinnapulli: poola illapakoola kunjo-munda prinnapoortea. 5. Wungata kope: poola illapakoola pari-na timia.   6. Kokooro ingkati untitiri nunyati: poola illapakoola tuari.   7. Nooie pulye-yetcha: piouli jungka.   8. Nooari poolela-yetcha: wungata mullo-yetcha.   9. Nundata-yetcha tunie noongaye: pari-yetcha tuna noongari. 10. Koonpara taroua-yetcha: makowata choporo-ngooro.

Translation.

1. Our two spears are similar.   2. My boomerang is smoother than yours. 3. A dog runs as quickly as a kangaroo.   4. The man is walking as slowly as an opossum.   5. The woman drinks as much as a fish.   6. Your yam-stick is as long as my sword.   7. This man is fatter than a dog.   8. That fellow is more thirsty than the girl.   9. There are fewer people here, than there.   10. A shield is broader than a boomerang.

Example 23.

1. Kooliungo nuno-kunnia-yetcha kenja mullo-ngooro.   2. Wallara-yetcha nunja: mullo-ngooro impa,   3. [Wara pulye-yetcha?]   Kana kati wungata?

4. Wungata poolela-yetcha: impa mullo. 5. Kitye-yetcha impa: mullo-ngooro nooaka. 6. Kana-ngo poolki-kunna-yetcha-ngo nopo-ngo mullo. 7. Nooie miriwinni-pityiri peripa-nari-yetcha. 8. Nooari kokotoongo perkilli-nari-yetcha. 9. Malooaka-nari-yetcha punna-ka nunie. 10. Koopa-koopa tie-nari-yetcha pari-ena.

Translation.
1. The dog is more tired than the slut. 2. I am younger than you. 3. [Who is the fatter?] the man or the woman? 4. The woman is more thirsty than you. 5. You are happier than he is. 6. The man will be more full-up than his wife. 7. These mountains (are) the highest. 8. That hill (is) very big. 9. This woman-here was running very quickly. 10. The old-man (is) the smallest among the lot.

Example 24.
1. Pijerdo malooaka-nari-yetcha pia-ena. 2. Untitiri-ko tuari-nari-yetcha-ko mare nunyo. 3. Berdaje-maro tie-yetcha-maro oota-ka impa. 4. Titi-mulla-lo papatooro-yetcha-na bibapooro-na marca. 5. Umma uttapeukka: poola illapa-koola parawango. 6. Pulkiwoonje nunyo koonpara-ko papatooro-nari-yetcha ko makowata-nga tuari-nari-yetcha-nga. 7. Woonje-na tie-yetcha-na untitiri-na. 8. Tie-nari-yetcha-eno kooroui-eno punna noongoka. 9. Oorooyara-na oorooyara-na berdaje-na mare-ka nundooari. 10. Woonje na yununa-na makowata-na.

Translation.
1. The hawk (is) the swiftest among birds. 2. I will bring the longest sword. 3. You were coming back with a smaller dilly-bag. 4. Your brother is fetching a shorter boomerang. 5. The mother is as mad as her child. 6. I will exchange the shortest shield for the longest spear. 7. Give me a smaller sword. 8. He will be running to the smallest hut. 9. That woman yonder was bringing different dilly-bags. 10. Bring a similar spear.

29. Verbs: Active. The Infinitive.
The infinitive is formed by adding -*lĭng*-ă to the root-stem—
oota-linga = to come back;
tiche-linga = to eat;
and is often used to denote purpose or design.

Example 25.
1. Upperi-ngo uttapeukka-ko mierli-korelinga pite. 2. Oora-ena Pitta-Pitta-na parari-kunna-linga nungkia nunja. 3. Wungata-lo nopo-na yunka-ka nunjo-ko pitelinga. 4. Titi-na machoomba-nga kunda-linga yunkia nindo. 5. Koopa-koopa-nga-ko illa-ko tiche-linga woonje nullingo. 6 Titi-na tapo-kunna-linga yunka-ka nindo. 7. Nunkoka Boolyo-munda kunda-linga yunka nunyo. 8. Munta-na oora eno woonje-linga indamullea nooie. 9 Umma-lo takoko-na uta-linga woonje-woonjea. 10. Moyerjo-ngo kanari-ko woonje-woonje berdaje-ko tare-linga.

Translation.
1. A father will beat his son to keep-him-good. 2. I am sitting down in the camp to learn Pitta-Pitta. 3. The woman told her husband to hit me. 4. You are telling my brother to hunt kangaroo. 5. We will both give the old-man something to eat. 6. You told (my) brother to be silent. 7. I will tell her to go away from the direction of Boulia. 8. This man is asking for food to bring to the camp. 9. A mother teaches her infant to swim. 10. The old woman will teach the girl (how) to weave a dilly-bag.

30. Some Special Forms of the Future.
   a. About to, just, &c. By means of the lengthened future form of the verb, with the present or past transitive or intransitive verbal pronouns as the case may be—
oota-linga nunja = I am about to come back, I am just now going to return.
tiche-linga nutto = I am about to eat, I am just going to eat.

    b. May, perhaps, might, &c.—

        (i.) Similar to preceding, but an intervening *wĕ-rĭ*

          kunda-linga weri nunja = I may perhaps, might, go.

          tiche-linga weri nutto = I may perhaps, might, eat.

        (ii.) Translated by the ordinary future tense with the intervening *mŭn-nă*

          kunda munna nunyo = I may perhaps, might, go.

          tiche munna nunyo = I may perhaps, might, eat.

    c. Must. Translated by means of the lengthened future form of the verb, the present or past transitive or intransitive verbal pronoun, as the case may be, and the intervening *ná-rĭ*

        kunda-linga nari nunja = I must go.

        tiche-linga nari nutto = I must eat.

    d. Would, would like to, &c.: *-mŭl-lă* or *-mŭl-lă-tŭl-lă* is added to the stem-root, and the present or past transitive or intransitive verbal pronoun, as the case may be—

        kunda-mulla nunja, *vel* kunda-mulla-tulla nunja = I would go, I would like to go.

        tiche-mulla nutto, *vel* tiche-mulla-tulla nutto = I would like to eat, I would eat.

Example 26.

1. Kako-mulla-eno kooroui-eno kunda-mulla-tulla noongoka. 2. Koolpari-ko marali tiche-munna-nunango. 3. Wolka-pakoola-eno oota-linga weri nunja. 4. Munna-ko wungata-pityiri-ko pite-linga nari nutto. 5. Munna-enyango kana-pityiri-enyango punna-linga nulli. 6. Nungka-mulla nunja ingkati-ena. 7. Wolka-pakoolangooro-eno oota-linga nari impa. 8. Koolpari-nga kurri kunda-mulla-tulla tunangoka. 9. Mali-maro-ngo oota-linga weri nooaka. 10. Papatooro-ngo kana-ngo tuari-ngooro-ko munna pite.

Translation.

1. He would like to go to your sister's hut. 2. We might eat the emu to-morrow. 3. I may perhaps come back in two days. 4. I must beat the bad women. 5. We-two are about to run away from the direction of the bad men. 6. I would like to sit down (*i.e.*, live) at your place. 7. You must return in three days. 8. They would like to go emu-hunting soon. 9. He is thinking-about (*i.e.*, may be) coming with a net. 10. The short fellow might hit the tall one.

31. Some Special Forms of the Imperative.

The suffixes already given for the singular, dual, and plural in the imperative (sect. 19), indicate the required order or command without any limitation or reservation—

    a. Certain conditions can, however, be accentuated in the command—

        (i.) Proximity to person commanding = -tă, -tă-lă, -tă-ră

          oota-ta = come (thou!) here, close up!

          tiche-tala = eat (you two!) here, close up!

          tukka-tara = stand (all of you!) here, close up!

        (ii.) Remoteness from person commanding = -nă-pă, -nă-pă-lă, -nă-pă-ră

          kunda-napa = go (thou!) over there, far yonder.

          tiche-napala = eat (you two!) over there, far yonder.

          tukka-napara = stand (all of you!) over there, far yonder.

        (iii.) Reiteration of a command already given, &c. = -lĭ-kō, -lĭ-kă-lă, -lĭ-kă-ră

          kunda-liko = go (thou!) whither-you-are-told, &c.

          mare-likala = fetch (you two!) what-you-are-told, &c.

          tukka-likara = stand (all of you!) where-you-are-told, &c.

    b. The suffix -kō (*cf. kou-*ă, sect. 12 and sect. 31*c*) with an object by itself in the simple singular form expresses the idea of bringing or conveying that same object or objects to the person speaking, with an imperative force—

        bibapooro-ko! = fetch the boomerangs up here!

c. The use of *kou*-ă in the imperative mood has already been referred to, when dealing with the vocative case (sect. 12). It is defective, being used only in the singular, dual, and plural imperative—

kou-ă = come (you) here !
kou-ă-lă = come (both of you) here !
kou-ă-ră = come (all of you) here !

d. The second person singular, dual, and plural of the simple imperative can be supplemented as follows by the remaining persons :—

(i.) Let me, allow me to, &c. This can be translated in two ways :

Either: The past-tense form of the verb and suffix -*ē*-nō, with nunyo (the future verbal pronoun, sect. 18*c*) —

kunda-ka-eno nunyo = let me go,
tiche-ka-eno nunyo = allow me to eat ;

Or: By the use of the verb "nungkala-" (= to permit) in the imperative, the objective case, and the infinitive—

nungkala-na nunya punna-linga = permit me to run.

(ii.) Let him, her, it, &c. = *mŭl*-lă added to the root-stem, with the future verbal pronouns (sect. 18*c*)—

kunda- ⎱
tiche— ⎰ mulla noongou = let him, close up at front *or* side, go, eat.

„   noongoka = let him, close up at back,   „
„   noorgoari = let him, close up yonder,   „
„   nungou = let her, close up at front or side,   „
„   nungoka = let her, close up at back,   „
„   nungoari = let her, close up yonder,   „

Of course, as in the preceding case, the verb nungkala- may be again used: nungkala-na innie, &c., kunda-linga, tiche-linga, &c.

(iii.) Let us, &c. The past-tense form of the verb and suffix -*ē*-nō with the future pronouns (nullingo or nunango, &c., sect. 18*c*), according as the dual or plural is referred to—

kunda-ka-eno nullingo = let us both go.
tiche-ka-eno nunango = let us all eat.

Or again, the form—

nungkala-na nullina, nunana, &c., can be used.

(iv.) Let them, &c. Formed similarly to that of the 3rd person singular

kunda-mulla poolungoka = let these two-at-the-back-of-me go.
tiche-mulla tunangoari = let those-folks-yonder eat.

Or again, the same idea can be stated as—

nungkala-na poolanaka, tunanari, &c.

32. Verbs. Reflexive.

a. Self: translated by *moon*-dĭ, inflexed like a noun—

berdaje-na moondi-lo tare-ka nutto = I myself weaved the dilly-bag.

b. Reflexive verbs are formed by adding -mŭl-le- to the root-stem, and inflexing the compound so formed according to the ordinary rule (sect. 17), *e.g.*—

Present tense— mul-le-a
Past tense—mul-le-ka
Future tense—mul-le, mul-le-linga.

The transitive verb so transformed will of course be rendered intransitive.

bibapooro-na oondia nutto = I am greasing a spear.
oonda-mullen nunja = I am greasing myself.
moorra-na koorea nindo = thou art cutting wood.
koore-mullea impa = thou art cutting thyself.
kanari-na pite-ka nooloou = he struck the girl.
pite-mulle-ka nooie = he struck himself.
makowata-na poondia nutto = I am breaking a spear.
prinna-na poonda-mullea nunja = I break (myself, my) leg.

In addition to this meaning of "self," -mulle has an additional interpretation in the sense of " one another, one with the other, each other," &c.:—

> pite-mulle-ka nuna = we were all striking one another—*i.e.*, we were fighting.
>
> woonje-mulle poolungou = they-both will-be-giving one-with-the other —*i.e.*, they both will barter.
>
> koore-mullea tunaka = they are cutting one another.
>
> yunka-mullea nuna = we all are telling one with the other—*i.e.*, we are all chattering together.
>
> pretipa nunyo noko = I will meet him.
>
> pretipa-mulle nullingo = we two will meet one another.

33. Some Special Forms of Transitive and Intransitive Verbs.

a. A transitive verb can be made intransitive by the addition of -*le* to the root-stem, and conjugating accordingly.

> tichea nutto = I eat.
> tiche-le-a nunja = I am at-eating, at dinner, &c.
> tiche-ka nutto = I ate.
> tiche-le-ka nunja = I was at-eating, at dinner, &c.
> tiche nunyo = I will eat.
> tiche-le nunyo = I will be at-eating, at dinner, &c.

Similarly :—

> katipulka- = to hit someone on the heal.
> katipulka-le-a = a headache.
> timia nutto = I drink.
> tima-le-a nunja = I am at-drinking, at the bottle, &c.
> pipia nutto = I see.
> pipa-le-a nunja = I am at-seeing, on the look-out, &c.

b. A transitive verb can be made intransitive by means described in sect. 32*b*.

c. A certain indefiniteness of action is indicated by the addition of -*ma* to the root-stem of an intransitive verb, and conjugating accordingly—

> punnia nunja = I run.
> punna-mia nunja = I run about here and there.
> punna-ka nunja = I ran.
> punna-ma-ka nunja = I ran about here and there.
> punna nunyo = I will run.
> punna-ma nunyo = I will run about here and there.
> utia nunja = I swim.
> uta-mia nunja = I swim about here and there.

[South of Boulia, *e.g.*, Bedouri, the suffix -*cha* is used in place of -*ma*, and hence we find occasionally the forms punna-chia, punna-cha-ka, &c., used by the Pitta-Pitta aboriginals.]

d. Special definiteness or purpose, &c., is sometimes expressed by the addition of -*re* to the root-stem of an intransitive verb, which is thus rendered transitive—

> punnia nunja = I run.
> punna-re-a nutto = I run with-special-attention-to something, taking-something-with-me—*i.e.*, I steal.
> nungka-ka nunja = I sat down.
> nungka-re-ka nutto = I sat down with-special-attention to somebody, &c.—*i.e.*, I attended to, looked after, took care of, &c.

Example 27.

1. Kunda-napala! mullo oota-tala. 2. Perkilli-na koolpari-na tiche-likara.
3. Oota-ta! munguni-maro! tiche-ta! 4. Yunka-na pooriti-na tapo kunna-linga. 5. Woonje-woonje-ta Pitta-Pitta-na yunka-linga: parari kunna-linga

nunyo. 6. Woonje-na nuna-na munta-na kurri tiche-linga. 7. Nungkala-na nunya munna-enyango wungata-enyango kunda-linga. 8. Nungka-ka-eno nunyo umma-wara-ena kooroui-ena. 9. Perkilli-na moolka-na mullo yuppieri-ngo yate-mulla. 10. Mullo pite-mulle-mulla tunangoka: makowata-ko.

Translation.

1. Go away! you two fellows! far yonder!—don't come back to me here. 2. Here! all you people! eat the big emu as you are bidden. 3. Come-back here, doctor! and dine with me! 4. Tell the whole-lot-of-them to be quiet. 5. Teach me to speak Pitta-Pitta: I will learn. 6. Give us this day food to eat. 7. Let me avoid (*i.e.*, go-away from the direction of) a bad woman. 8. Let me rest in mother's hut. 9. Do not allow the boy to climb the big tree-trunk. 10. Do not let them fight: bring the spears up here!

Example 28.

1. Pooriti munguni-maro-pityiri pite-mulle-ka. 2. Kulli-na wolka-pa-koola-ena poonda-mulle-ka nunja. 3. Marali toota-ngo oonda-mulle noongoka 4. Makowata-na bibapooro-nga pulki-woonje-mullea nulli. 5. Wolka-wirea-eno pretipa-mulle poolangoka. 6. Miriwinni-lo pite-mulle-ka nooaka. 7. Noko kulla-pakoola-ena pretipa-mulle ingo. 8. Kooroui-ena nunkatiari-ena yunka-mulle-ka tunaka. 9. Moyerjo-ngo koopa-koopa-ngo bibapooro-pityiri-ngo pite-mulle. 10. Prinna-ko poonda-mulle-linga weri nunja.

Translation.

1. The whole lot of the doctors were fighting between themselves. 2. I broke my arm two days ago. 3. He will smear himself with fat to-morrow. 4. We are bartering together a spear for a boomerang. 5. They two will meet one another when-the-sun-goes-down. 6. He was hitting himself with a stone. 7. You will meet him at-the-two-rivers (*i.e.*, where the rivers meet). 8. They were all chattering together in that woman's hut. 9. The old man and the old woman will be hitting each other with boomerangs. 10. I might break my leg.

Example 29.

1. Moyerjo-nga uttapeukka-pityiri-wara kulla-ena uta-mia. 2. Machoomba wapa-pityiri pokara-ena punna-ma-ka. 3. Kana tiche-le-ka: wungata tima-le-ka. 4. Upperi kurri mullo kunda: bilba tarembola-la kunda-lea. 5. Kenja-ngo wapa-pityiri-ngo parapi-ena uta-ma. 6. Punjea-na wungata-na nungka-rea noolooka. 7. Tano-ko kanari-ko nungkare nullingo. 8. Bibapooro-na mullo punnare-mulla noongoka. 9. Koopa-koopa-ngo tiche-le. 10. Kooyungo-ngo kana-pityiri-ngo mullo eche-le.

Translation.

1. The old woman's children are swimming about in the river. 2. The kangaroo's pups were running about among the grass. 3. The man was at-dinner: the woman was having-a-drink. 4. Father will not go away to-day: he is drunk (*i.e.*, the forehead is "going" with pituri). 5. The slut's pups will be swimming about in the creek. 6. He is attending-to the sick woman. 7. We will both look-after the delicate girl. 8. Do not let him steal the spear. 9. The old man will be at-dinner. 10. Good men will not die.

34. Relative Pronouns.

  a. Nominative. Who, which, &c., are not translated, the relative sentence being put into close apposition with the subject: thus,—

  "The man, who takes care of his wife, is a good fellow" becomes "The man takes care of his wife; (he is) a good fellow"—*i.e.*, kana-lo nopo-na nungkarea; kooyungo-ngooro.

So again,

  wallara nunja koopa-koopa-na nungkarea = I, who am young, attend upon the old.

b. Objective. The relative " whom, which " is again omitted : the whole sentence, however, is put into the objective case, verb as well as noun bearing the suffixal inflexions -na or -ko, as the tense directs.

Thus, " I see the man whom you are beating," becomes " I see the you-are-beating man "—*i.e.*, pipia nutto innaka indo-pitea-na.

Similarly :—

innaka ingo-woonje-linga-na makowata-ko pipa-ka nutto = I saw the you-will-give-a-spear-to man—*i.e.*, I saw the man to whom you will give a spear.

[Note that in the future relative sentence the lengthened form only of the future is used.]

c. Possessive.

(i.) Relative to persons only, " whose" = -*wă*-ră-ngă inflexed of course as usual (*cf*. *wă*-ră in sects. 10, 35, and the possessive suffix -ng-ă in sect. 13*a*).

tare-ka nutto yuppieri-na waranga-na bibapooro-na mare-ka nindo = I kicked the boy whose boomerang you took.

pite-ka nindo kanari-na waranga-ko berdaje-ko mare nunyo = You struck the girl whose dilly-bag I propose taking (I will take).

(ii.) Relative to things—not translated.

35. Interrogative Pronouns.

a. Relating to persons : who ? which ? = *wă*-ră, inflexed like any other noun—

wara nungkia ? = who is sitting ?

wara-lo tichea ? = who is eating ?

wara wungata kundia ? = which woman goes-away ?

wara-lo wungata-lo timia ? = which woman is drinking ?

wara-nga bibapooro ? = whose boomerang ?

wara-enya-na ? -enya-ko ? = from whom ? (present *or* past, future).

b. Relating to things : which ? what ? = *mĭn*-nă, also inflexed like any other noun or adjective—

minna punnia ? = what is running ?

minna-nga kundia impa ? = what are you going after ?

minna-na marea nindo ? = what are you bringing ?

minna-la ? = (through-the-effects-of what ? *i.e.*) why ?

minna-mundi ? = (what much ? *i.e.*) how much ? how many ?

Example 30.

1. Nopo, koopa-koopa-nga kako, kundia. 2. Pipia nutto kooroui-na ingo mooche-linga-na. 3. Woonjeta bibapooro-na nindo toka-ka-na. 4. Tincha-ka nindo moolka-na yuppieri-lo yate-ka-na. 5. Pite nunyo piouli-ko ingo-woonje-linga-ko nopo-ko. 6. Pipa-ka nullilo wungata-na ingo woonje-linga-na berdaje-ko. 7. Kana-lo tichea pari-na munta-na poolki-kunnia. 8. Amachiella-ngooro-ngo pari-ko tiche. 9. Moyerjo-ngo puoti-ko tineha. 10. Munguni-maro, titi-mulla, nungkia nunkatiye-ena.

Translation.

1. My wife, who is the sister of the old-man, is going away. 2. I see the hut you will be sleeping in. 3. Give-me-here the boomerang which you fetched. 4. You were cutting the tree which the boy climbed. 5. I will strike the dog which you intend-giving-to your wife. 6. We both saw the woman whom you will give the dilly-bag to. 7. The man who eats too much food will be full-up. 8. A fellow who is hungry will eat plenty. 9. The old-woman will cut the fire-wood. 10. The doctor, your brother, is sitting-down at-her-place.

Example 31.

1. Mierli impa mullo eche-le. 2. Ooranga-ko bibapooro-pityiri-ko punnare nunyo. 3. Makowata-ko ingkati-ko poonda noongoka : ingko ooroo-ko woonje nunyo. 4. Pipa-ka nutto kanari-na waranga-na berdaje-na punnare-ka nindo.

5. Pipia nutto wungata-na waranga-ko uttapeukka-ko punnare ingo. 6. Toua noongoka machoomba-ko wapa-ko tiche-linga-ko nunyo. 7. Kache-linga nunyo kope-ko ingo tiche-linga-ko. 8. Koopa-koopa waranga-na makowata-pityiri-na toka-ka nindo nunyati-ena nungkia. 9. Pite noongoa kana-ko waranga utta-peukka twinjea. 10. Tiche nunyo tinnapulli-ko wapa-pityiri punna-mia-na.

Translation.

1. Thou, who art good, will not die. 2. I will steal another-man's boome-rangs. 3. He will break your spear: I will give you another. 4. I saw the girl whose dilly-bag you stole. 5. I see the woman whose child he is going to steal. 6. He will hit the kangaroo whose pups I intend eating. 7. I will catch the fish which you will eat. 8. The old man, whose spears you brought, is sitting-down at-my-place. 9. He yonder will strike the man whose child is crying. 10. I will eat the opossum whose young are running-about.

Example 32.

1. Wara-lo woonje-ka inna bibapooro-na? 2. Wara wungata takoko-maro? 3. Wara-eno kundia impa? 4. Wara-ngo uttapeukka? mulla. 5. Wara-ena nungkia nunpari? 6. Minna-eno mie-eno prinnapoortea nooa? 7. Minna-la punjea impa? 8. Minna-enyana moorra-enyana tinnapulli-na tincha-ka noolooka? 9. Yunka-na nunya, upperi, minna-na? 10. Minna-ko machoom-ba-nga-ko tiche nunango?

Translation.

1. Who gave you the boomerang? 2. Who is the woman that has a baby? 3. To whom are you going? 4. Whose child? thine. 5. Alongside whom is that woman-yonder sitting? 6. To which country is that fellow travelling? 7. Why (through the effects of what) are you sick? 8. From which branch did he fetch the opossum? 9. Tell me, father, what (do you want, &c.)? 10. Which kangaroo shall we eat?

36. Numerals, &c.

The Pitta-Pitta aboriginal has words for the two first numerals only.

one = *oo*-roo-roo, shortened into *oo*-roo or *oo*-rō, (*cf.* oora-nga = another's, another person's).

two = *pá*-koo-lä (sect. 43*h*).

Remaining numbers are compounded from these, thus:

three = pakoola-ng-ooro, the -*ng*- being inserted for euphony.
four = pakoola-pakoola.
five = pakoola-pakoolangooro.

Beyond four, the savage will generally speak of everything as *pá*-rĭ, *i.e.*, a lot, a large number. He certainly has visible conceptions of higher numbers, and I have often had a practical demonstration of this fact by asking him to count how many fingers and toes he has, and telling him to mark the number in the sand. Thus, he commences with the hand open, and turns the fingers down by twos, and for every two he will make a double stroke in the sand. [This method of closing the fingers into the palm after counting is like that of a Japanese boy: an English lad will generally close his fingers on to the palm previous to enumeration, and then extend them as he calls them.] The strokes he makes in the sand are parallel one beside the other, and when the numeration is complete, he calls "pakoola" for every two of them. This method of counting is common throughout the district, and often practised by the elders of the tribe to ascertain the number of individuals in camp. Pĕn-te- = to count: pĭu-kĭ-poo-ra- = to divide, to share equally.

Other ideas of number are the following:—

nŭn-dă-tä = few, scarce—used as adjective or noun.
pá-rĭ, *poo*-rĭ-tĭ, *poo*-nĭ = a large crowd, all, the whole lot, &c.: also used as adjective or noun (sect. 43 *h*).
pá-rĭ *pá*-rĭ = belongings, possessions, property, one's "all" (sect. 43*h*).
lı-ĕ = together, collectively, in a body.

37. Quantity and Size.

Ideas on these matters are very limited, and apparently interchangeable :—

tĭ-ē = small in quantity as well as small, diminutive, in size.

mŭn-dĭ = much, many.

mŭng-kŏr-ă = (the largest size of dilly-bag made, and hence =) large both in quantity, number, and size.

minna-mundi? = how much? how many?

minna-mungkora? = what size? what quantity?

pĕ-rĭ-pâ = big, large (*cf.* pari-pari).

pĕr-kĭl-lĭ = large, immense, big, in size and extent (sect. 43*h*).

tū-*â*-rĭ = big in length, long.

Example 33.

1. Tie-maro tarembola-maro nunaka. 2. Pari-maro-ngo munta-maro-ngo koopa-koopa-ngo. 3. Woonje-na nunnari pari-na. 4. Mungkora-maro tarembola-maro nunja. 5. Mungkora-ko kope-ko mali-ngo kache nunyo. 6. Pari-pari-maro-ngo oota tunangoka. 7. Pooriti-ngo kana-ngo kulla-pakoola-eno kunda. 8. Wungata-pityiri pooriti Boolyo-munda ootia. 9. Koopa-koopa oora-eno oota-ka : wungata mutto. 10. Yuppieri-lo tichea : wungata mutto-lo.

Translation.

1. She has a small quantity of pituri. 2. The old man will have a lot of food. 3. Give that woman yonder a large quantity. 4. I have a great deal of pituri. 5. I shall catch a large quantity of fish with my net. 6. They will come with all their possessions. 7. All the men will go to where-the-rivers-meet (to the two-rivers). 8. The whole lot of women are returning from the direction of Boulia. 9. The old-man returned to camp : and so did the woman. 10. The boy is eating—and the girl too.

Example 34.

1. Kana-ngo bibapooro-ko mare : makowata-mutto-ko. 2. Munguni-maro—pakoolangooro lie nungkia. 3. Minna-mundi makowata-pityiri ingkati? 4. Minna-mungkora uttapeukka? 5. Yunka-na licha minna-mundi-na tarembola-ingkati-na. 6. Minna-mungkora-na kope-pityiri-na mare-ka nindo? 7. Kache-ka noolooa nundata-na kope-pityiri-na : kache-ka nutto mungkora-na. 8. Koondungari-pityiri tie : nari nundata. 9. Wungata-pityiri tillimurri-ena lie nungkia. 10. Koolpari-pityiri perkilli : nari pari.

Translation.

1. The man will fetch the boomerang: and the spear too. 2. Three doctors are sitting together-apart. 3. How many spears are yours? 4. How big is the child? 5. State correctly how much pituri you have. 6. What quantity of fish have you brought? 7. He caught a few fish : I caught a lot. 8. Diver-birds are small : and they are also scarce. 9. The women are sitting apart-in-a-body near the gidyea tree. 10. The emus are large : they are also plentiful.

38. Ideas of Time.

As has already been mentioned under prepositions (sect. 25), Time-when is indicated by -ena or -eno according as it refers to the present and past, or to the future.

Time—duration, how long—is measured in days by the number of suns, and in months by so many moons :—

wolka-pakoolangooro-ena = during the past three days (*i.e.*, three suns in past-time).

jungi-pakoola-eno = during the next two month's (*i.e.*, two moons in future time).

The length of the day is measured by sun-rise, sun-risen (*i.e.*, mid-day), and sun-sinking—

wolka-wunjea = sun-rise (the sun rises).

wolka-wunje-ka = mid-day (the sun risen).

wolka-wirea = sunset (the sun sinks, dives).

wolka-wunjea-eno oota nunyo = I will return at sunrise.

wolka-wunje-ka-ena kunda-ka nunja = I went away at mid-day.

The following are some terms, other than those already given, relating to ideas of time :—

wĕn-kō ? = when.

kŭ-rĭ = now, immediately, soon, to-day.

wŏl-kă-nă, mâ-rä-lĭ = to-morrow.

ē-lă-lĭ-ĕ = to-morrow.

tŭn-ă-ē-lă-lĭ-ĕ = every-day, daily, always, ever and ever.

yâ-kä yâ-kă-ĕ = night-time.

too-rō, wăn-tä, kŭn-nă = by-and by, later on.

ŭng-kă-lă .... â-koo-nă = before .... after.

tiche-linga nunyo ungkala: tima-linga nunyo akoona = I will eat before I drink (lit. = I will eat betore : I will drink after).

Beyond a few months' duration, Time-when cannot be accurately expressed : reference is made to some event of more than passing importance—such as a big flood, or drought, or some special initiation ceremony, or a tribal fight, perhaps. Very long lapses of time are called to memory by expressions somewhat after this fashion : "When I was a child," "Before the white-fellow came," "Before the blackfellow jumped-up here," "When the animals and birds were all black-fellows," represent pretty accurately the comparative and progressively increasing past eras of the aboriginal calendar.

39. Ideas of Place, Direction, and Distance.

Attention will be directed elsewhere to local nomenclature (sect. 226) as well as to the limits of direction (sect. 227), the cardinal and intermediate points of the compass being known.

The following are some of the more ordinary terms used to define place and direction :—

ĭl-lā = hither (to front or side).

ĭl-lă-kă = hither (to close-up-at-the-back).

ĭl-lâ-rĭ = thither (yonder).

noong-ă-yĕ = here (at front or side).

noong-ă-kă = here (at close-up-at-the-back).

noong-â-rĭ = there (yonder).

ĭn-tă-lĭm-mĕ ? = whither ?

ĭn-tă ?, wĭn-tă ? = whereabouts ? what, which, place ?

wâ-ră-ră, tō = a long-way off, far away from.

moong-kă-tă = in the neighbourhood of, close to.

yĕ-nĭ-moong-kă-tă ? = how far ?

Distance is measured by the number of "suns" or "sleeps" taken in performing the journey—the day's travel of course varying in different directions according to the waterholes, &c., or else by enumerating the number of creeks, hills, &c., which require to be traversed.

40. Interrogation—Doubt or Uncertainty.

a. The direct question is indicated by—

(i.) Some form of the relative interrogative, already referred to in sect. 35—

wara ? = who ? which ? minna ? = what ? which ? mĭn-nă-lĭ = why ?

(ii.) The suffix -pä ? when the answer "yes" or "no" only is expected—

kooyungo-pa ? = was it (is it) a good man ?

munna-pa ? = was it (is it) a good one ?

(iii.) In all other cases nâ-rĭ is used, placed immediately after the verb—

mare-nari nunyo nokou makowata-ko ? = shall I bring this spear ?

kunda-linga-nari nunyo tinungara-eno pari-pari-nga ? = shall I go northwards after my belongings ?

b. Expressions of doubt or uncertainty.

(i.) May, perhaps, might, &c. = wĕ-rĭ (already referred to in sect. 3 b).

(ii.) "It is doubtful whether," "One hardly knows," "One would think so, but can't be sure," &c. = kŭl-lĭ kŭl-lĭ (sects. 99, 100), mä-rä.

41. Notes of Exclamation, &c.

The only examples (besides those mentioned in sect. 12) which I can gather in this connection are the following :—

  mâ = thanks ! thank you !

  kă-tē ! = right-you-are ! all-right !

  nă-rĭ = ready ! off ! &c.

  nŭng-kă-nă......*kŭn*-dă-nă-pă ! = ta-ta ! good-bye !

[It will be noticed that here we have " sit down"......" go away" in the imperative : the former expression is used by the individual departing, the latter by the one remaining.]

  kō ! *ē-ă* ! = yes !

  mŭl-lō ! = no !

Example 35.

1. Mierli mara nooaka. 2. Kulli-kulli mierli munna nunaka. 3 Kulli-kulli kunda-ka nooa. 4. Machoomba mara utia. 5. Piouli-ko munta-ko woonje nari nunyo ? 6. Tukka-nari kati nungka-nari nunango. 7. Minnali wungata-pityiri nungkia ? 8. Oora-eno ingkati-ngako punna-nari nunyo ? 9. Tunaelalie wolka wunjea. 10. Oota-nari ingo kunna ? ea !

Translation.

1. One hardly knows whether this fellow is a good one. 2. This woman may be good or bad—I don't know. 3. One hardly knows whether he went or not. 4. One would think that a kangaroo swims, but you can't be sure. 5. Shall I give the dog (some) food ? 6. Shall we stand or sit ? 7. Why are the women sitting-down ? 8 Shall I run up to the camp for you (*i.e.*, for your advantage, to save you trouble, &c.) ? 9. The sun rises daily. 10. Will you return later on ? Certainly !

Example 36.

1. Tima-linga ingo ungkala : tiche-linga ingo akoona. 2. Berdaje-na woonje-na nunya ungkala : kunda-na akoona. 3. Oora-enya kunda nunyo ungkala : kunda noongoka akoona. 4. Inta-enyana bibapooro-na toka-ka nindo. 5. Minna-ena nungkia kokola ? mie-ena. 6. Intalimme kundia impa ? 7. Wara-nga -ena nungkia nooaka ? 8. Yenimoongkata Boolyo ? warara. 9. Oota-linga nunango. wenko ? kurri. 10. Ma ! nungkana-kundanapa.

Translation.

1. You shall drink before you eat. 2. Give me a dilly-bag before you go. 3. He will be going away from the camp after I do. 4. From whereabouts did you fetch the boomerang ? 5. In what (place) does a bandicoot live ? In the ground. 6. Whither are you going ? 7. At whose (place) is he staying ? 8. How far is Boulia ? A long way off. 9. We shall come back. When ? Soon. 10. Thanks ! good-bye !

42. Participles and Perfects.

  a. Present. The present participle can be indicated by adding the suffix -*ē*-nă = time-when (sect 25*b*) to the present or past tense of the verb.

  kana punnia = the man runs.

  kana punnia-ena prinna-na tunpa-mullea = the man, while running, cuts (his) leg.

  makowata-na pukka-ka noolooka = he was making a spear.

  pukka-ka-ena noolooka makowata-na, mooche-ka nooaka = while making a spear, he fell asleep.

  b. Past and Perfect. These are translated by the suffixes -*ēn*-yă = time-after, since (sect. 25*c*) or -*mâ*-rō = sign of possession (*i.e.*, act possessed, and so, done-with), with the past tense of the verb.

  punna-ka nunja = I ran.

  punna-ka-enya, *vel* punna-ka-maro, nunja, &c. = (after I ran, I have run, I had run—the act done with, *i.e.*) having run, I &c.

c. Future. Expressed by -enya-ngo = time-after or since (in its future form), with the past tense (act completed) of the verb : this suffix is often contracted into -ngo.

tiche-ka nutta = I ate.

tiche-ka-enya-ngo, *vel* tiche-ka-ngo, nunyo, &c. = when I shall have eaten, having eaten, I will, &c.

[It will thus be seen in the following examples how various are the English methods by which these perfects and participles may be translated.]

Example 37.

1. Kulli-na poondomulle-ka-enya kanari oora-eno punna-ka.   2. Tiche-ka-enya nindo poolki-kunna-ka impa.   3. Inna pite-ka-enya nutto, nieri-nieri kunna-ka impa.   4. Twinje-ka nunja, nunya tare-ka-enya nindo.   5. Koopa-koopa prinna-na poondo-mulle-ka-enya nungka-ka.   6. Murra-na koore-ka-enya wungata nunyouno oota-ka.   7. Uta-ka-enya-ngo (nunyo) toota-ngo oonda-mulle nunyo.   8. Kunda-ka-ngo nunyo, takoko-na nungkare-na.   9. Moyerjo-lo uta-ka-ena tinna-na miriwinni-lo tunpa-mulle-ka.   10. Punna-ka-ena prinna-na poonda-mulle-ka nooa.

Translation.

1. Having broken (her) arm, the girl ran up to the camp.   2. After having had-your-food, you were full-up.   3. Being struck by me (after I had struck you) you got away.   4. I cried because you kicked me (after you kicked me).   5. Having broken his leg, the old man sat down.   6. The woman came back to my place : she had cut her hand.   7. When I (shall) have had a swim, I will grease myself with fat.   8. Look-after (my) child when I am (shall have) gone.   9. While swimming, the old woman cut (her) foot with a stone.   10. That fellow yonder broke his leg when running.

Example 38.

1. Tinnapulli-nga-ena kulli-na poondamulle-ka nunja.   2. Kunda-na upperi-lo yunkaka-enya.   3. Tarembola oota-ka-ko nunjo-ko oora-eno woonje-nari ingo ?   4. Umma-lo yunka-ka-enya nungka nullingo.   5. Yunka-ka-enya-ngo noongoka kunda ingo.   6. Mierli-lo umma-lo yunka-ka-ko tiche noongoka.   7. Ooro-wolka-ena munta-na yappieri-na oota-ka-na woonje-ka nutto.   8. Tiche-ka-enya punna-ka nooa.   9. Pite-ka-enya wungi-lo yuppieri twinjea.   10. Nung-ka-na ! kunda-napa ! nuno-kunnia nunja.

Translation.

1. While after opossums, I broke my arm.   2. Go where you father told you [time-when, since, your father told you to].   3. Will you give me pituri if (when) I come back to camp ? [Note the relative sentence : me-who-have-come in future time].   4. We shall stay (where) mother told us.   5. You will go when he shall have told you.   6. He will eat what his good mother told him [relative sentence : the-good-mother-told-him-what in future time].   7. I gave food yesterday to the boy who came up.   8. Having had his dinner, that fellow ran away.   9. The boy is crying because his brother hit him.   10. Good-bye ! I am tired.

43. Introduction to the Pitta-Pitta Vocabulary.

In the following vocabulary, formed of words noted as being used by the Pitta-Pitta aboriginals, it must be remembered that the spelling as originally transcribed into my note-books was purely phonetic, the subsequent etymological orthography, such as it is, being only gradually learnt and understood in proportion as my familiarity with the language increased.

Verbs are given in their crude or root form, in order that the subsequent inflections may be the more easily applied. Individual proper names are not included here. Personal pronouns also are omitted, these parts of speech having been already detailed both in spelling and pronunciation in their respective sections 5, 6, 7, 10 : the repetition of upwards of two hundred of these particular parts of speech was considered unnecessary and cumbersome. With these exceptions, all Pitta-Pitta words used throughout the entire text will be found included in the vocabulary.

Opportunity must be taken here of drawing attention to certain root-stems possibly indicating a correspondence of origin in the names applied to things with common attributes, properties, or peculiarities. The more important of these may be tabulated as follows :—

a. KOO :—Signifying that which is moist or wet, water.

*koo*ta = water. *ku*ttamulla = creek.

*koo*roui = a particular kind of hut specially designed for withstanding rain (sect. 159).

*koo*roomundo = the rain-stick (sect. 294).

*koo*ndea = wet, moist. *ku*nta-*ku*nta = rain. *ku*nga = water-spring.

*koo*ndungari = any species of diver-bird.

*ko*pe = fish. (= *koo*pa, among the neighbouring Ulaolinya blacks of the Upper Mulligan River ; sect. 53.)

*cf. koo*ria = rain, a Miorli word (sect. 54) ; also *ko* = rain, and *koa*= water, creek (both Kalkadoon words, sect. 54).

b. KA :—Expressing a tree, timber of any sort, bushes, &c.

*ka*lara = stick for digging up yams (sect. 158).

*ka*lori = letter- or message- stick (sect. 235).

*ka*lorungoro = tree-grub (sect. 119).

*ka*louari = ti-tree.

*ka*rapari = coolibar seed-food (sect. 108).

*ka*rabadi = coolibar-tree.

*ka*lo = native-flax plant (sect. 124).

*ka*roora = tree-root.

*ka*toora = sp. of barley-grass (sect. 107).

(koota)-*ka*po = sp. of white flower (growing along water's edge).

ya*ka*pari = grass allied to the katoora (sect. 107).

po*ka*ra = short meadow-grass (see root *po*).

po*ka*ngudye (sect. 287) = sp. of penny-royal (see root *po*).

poo*ka*tika (sect. 147) = sp. of wattle (see root *po*).

moor*ka* = tree-root.

mool*ka* = tree-butt, trunk.

yara*ka* = grass allied to the katoora (sect. 106).

c. PO :—Indicating grass, and so, hairs or feathers It may be noted here that grass and hair are terms often used synonymously by these aboriginals when speaking "pidgin" English; indeed, in the Pitta-Pitta language itself the word "wunje" means either hair or grass.

*po*kara = short meadow-grass (see root *ka*).

*po*kangudye (sect. 287) = sp. of penny-royal (see root *ka*).

*po*okatika (sect. 147) = sp. of wattle (see root *ka*).

*po*onjo = hair of the head, hair-string (sect. 52).

*po*orono = feather.

(koota)-ka*po* = sp. of white flower, &c. (see root *ka*).

d. KO :—Signification similar to root *PO*.

*ko*ne = hair.

*ko*nupa = grass necklace (sect. 179).

*koo*ni = pig-weed (sect. 109).

*ko*naro = feather.

*koo*ramara = spinifex grass.

e. PI :—That which travels or lives in the air.

*pi*a = any bird in general (sect. 53).

*pi*jerdo = small hawk (sect. 53).

*pi*ralko = " native companion " bird (sect. 53).

*pi*pinmia = lightning.

*bi*bapooro = any boomerang in general (sect. 55).

chin*bi* = star. *cf.* chi*ba* = moon (sect. 54).

f. MOO :—Expressing the idea of straightness, a straight stick.

moorra = branch, stick (*cf.* tilli*murri* = gidyea-tree).

moorka = tree-root.

moolka = tree-butt, trunk.

moorro = straight throwing-stick toy (sect. 214).

morro = "nulla-nulla" (sect. 214).

moorrindi = thumb, big toe.

murra = hand. This connection of the hand, thumb, big toe, with the idea of straightness, straight sticks, is not over-estimated when it is remembered that in the Boulia district itself among the Ulaolinya blacks (sect. 52) we find

mooroo = arm, fore-arm.

jaba*moko* = little toes (where "jaba" = small, diminutive).

uri*mooko* = elbow.

Furthermore as emphasising the above, there is the Pitta-Pitta word "mingko" = the "forks" of the fingers and toes, the fork of a tree, a forked stick, and so a netting-needle.

g. KOO :—Indicating that which is crooked, bent, curved, or rounded.

koondi-koondi = crooked.

kundi-kundi = bent throwing-stick toy (sect. 214).

koondara = snake in general (sect. 53).

koorimara = carpet-snake (sect. 53).

koompata = bent-handled native chisel (sect. 149).

koonpara = shield, koolamon (sect. 55).

koondachi (sect. 110) ▬ crayfish (*cf.* rounded claws, tail).

koodingberi = zig-zag wavy line (sect. 241).

koodija-koodija = a wavy zig-zag ornamentation (sect. 241).

koodijakorea = around (sect. 22*g*, 23*b*).

wer*koo* = two lines placed cross-wise (sect. 241).

koolyo = testicles (sect. 52).

wa*koola* = waist-belt (sect. 183).

uron*gooto* = circle (sect. 199*c*).

poorn*koo* = knee (sect. 52).

ko-ko = back, dorsum of the body (sect. 52).

h. PA :—Signifying quantity, number, or size.

pakoola = two, more than one (sect. 36).

pari = a lot (sect. 36).

pari-pari = property, belongings, possessions (sect. 36).

peripa = big, large.

perkilli = big, large (sect. 37).

pooriti = all, the whole lot (sect. 36).

k. UTTA :—Expresses blood-relationship.

*utta*peukka = child (sect. 58).

uttareka = nephew on sister's side (sect. 58).

uttana = maternal grandfather, paternal grandmother (sect. 58).

uttakalo = relationship between husband's and wife's mothers (sect. 64*b*).

put*ta* = a young boy.

yut*ta* — = to love, copulate.

unja*kootta* = a man's daughter-in-law, a woman's father-in-law (sect. 64*b*).

l. KA :—Indicates the female sex.

kalari = a woman's mother-in-law, a mother's daughter-in-law (sect. 58).

kabudyo = nipple, breast, milk.

kanari = young woman.

kanyini = a man's son's-daughter, a man's mother's-mother (sect. 58).

kariouo = widow.

kako = sister, whether by blood or not (sect. 58).

chata = female cousin (sect. 58).

utta*kalo* = relationship between husband's and wife's mothers (sect. 64*b*).

44. A Vocabulary of Pitta-Pitta words.

A.

â-*koo*-nă = afterwards, secondly (*cf.* pakoola).

â-mă-chĭ-*ĕl*-lă = hungry.

B.

bă-lă-bă-*lĭng*-ă = big spoonbill (water-bird).

lăm-bō = (what is inside, hence) egg, brain.

bĕr-dă-jĕ = dilly-bag in general.

bĭ-bă-poo-rō = boomerang in general.

bĭl-bă = forehead, penis (whether or not circumcised or introcised).

bĭl-bĭ = species of bandicoot (a doubt-fully local word).

boom-bō = short variety of throwing-stick-toy.

bŭl-kă-bŭr-ĭ = species of black bream.

bŭn-bŭr-ĭ = one of the four paedo-matro-nyms.

C.

chá-kĕr-tĭ *chá*-kĕr-tĭ = rough (to the touch).

chá-lō *chá*-lō = clever.

chá-tă = sister-in-law, female cousin.

chĕ-kŭl-*ă*-rĭ = pearl-shell phallocrypt.

chĕl-kĕ-rĭ = loud, noisy.

chĭ-bă = moon.

chĭn-bĭ = star.

chĭ-rĭ = handle of stone-tomahawk.

chĭ-roo-kō = instrument for producing venereal and other diseases.

choon-dă = dirty, muddy (*e.g.*, water).

chŏp-ō-rō = narrow.

chŭk-ŭl-bŭr-ră = hook-boomerang.

D.

dŭk-kă *dŭk*-kă = a bough-shed or green room for the corrobborees, formed by *standing* up saplings resting at the top against each other (*cf.* tukka).

E.

ē-ă = yes, certainly, etc.

ē-chă-lă-mŭl-le- = to dance (in a cor-robboree).

ē-che- = to lie down, to rest, to die.

ē-lă-*li*-ĕ = to-morrow.

ē-pă-lă = species of gum-tree.

ē-ră-kă-lă = flat.

ēr-rŭl-lĭ = bush-palisading, built at the first of the initiation rites.

c

I.

ĭk-kĭl-lĭm-mĕ-*wā*-rĭ = this side of, in front.

ĭk-oo-*ŭr*-ră = wild spotted cat.

ĭl-lă = something.

ĭl-*lā* = hither, close up at front or side.

ĭl-lă-kă = hither, at the back.

ĭl-lă-*pá*-koo-lă = both, equally (*cf.* pakoola).

ĭl-*lá*-rĭ = thither.

ĭn-dă-mŭl-le- = to ask for, to beg.

ĭng-gă-mŭl-le- = to kiss.

ĭn-tă = what, which, place? (*cf.* winta).

ĭn-tă-lĭm-mĕ = whither?

ĭn-*tī*-nō = whitherabouts? (=inta-eno).

J.

jă-ră *jă*-ră = the larger sandstone grinding slab.

jĭl-*lŏr*-ă = spin-ball toy.

jĭm-bă = black, blue.

jĭ-*ŭng*-kă = a man's son's-son, a man's father's-father.

joo-rō = road-track.

jŭng-ĭ = moon, month.

jŭng-kă = thin, lean.

jŭm-mĭ = father's sister.

K.

kă-bŭd-yō = milk, breast, nipple.

kâ-che- = to catch with a net (*e.g.*, fish, emus).

kâ-ka- = to call, beckon to (*cf.* koua).

ká-kō = elder sister.

kâ-*kō*-mă = rat.

kâ-*kŭm*-bō-lĕ = wooden netting-needle.

kă-lă-ră = yam, a special stick for digging it up.

kă-lă-rĭ = a woman's mother-in-law, a woman's daughter-in-law.

kă-lă-*wá*-rĭ = paddymelon.

ká-lō = native-flax plant.

kă-*lŏr*-ĭ = message-stick.

kă-lō-*rŭng*-ō-rō = a larger kind of edible grub found in trees.

kă-*lou*-â-rĭ = ti-tree.

ká-lō-wâ-rĭ = a baby just born.

ká-nă = adult man in general.

kă-*ná*-rĭ = young woman at full puberty.

kán-mă-rĕ = huge supernatural water-snake.

kĕn-yĭ-nĭ = a man's son's-daughter, a man's mother's-mother

kă-pă-ră = smaller kind of edible grub and caterpillar.

kă-*ră*-bă-dĭ = coolibar-tree.

kă-*ră*-mŭl-le- = to tie round (head, arm, stomach, etc.)

kă-ră-pă-rĭ = coolibar seed

44. A Vocabulary of Pitta-Pitta words—*continued*.

kâ-*rĭng*-ă-ră = small iguana.

kâ-rĭn-gâ-rĭ = cough, cold.

kă-*rĭng*-ō = young, youthful.

kă-rĭ-*ou*-ō = widow.

kă-*roo*-ră = tree-root, root.

kâ-rŭm-mĭn = wommera.

kâ-tă = head-louse (*cf.* kati).

kă-tă-pă *kă*-tă-pă = hornet.

kâ-tē = all right! right you are!

kă-te- = to climb.

kâ-tĭ = or.

kâ-tĭ = head, top, etc.

kâ-tĭ-â-*koo*-nă = (head secondly, *i.e.*) feet first.

kâ-tĭ *kâ*-tĭ *má*-rō = the head-covering possessor, an individual of 2nd degree (*cf.* kati, maro).

kă-tĭ-lō-ă = large species of frog.

kâ-tĭ-moong-ka- = to nod the head vertically.

kâ-tĭ-*nĭ*-â-pă = bald-headed.

kâ-tĭ-pĭ-te- = to hit a peg, etc., on its head (*cf.* pite-).

kâ-tĭ-pŭl-ka- = to hit someone on the head.

kâ-tĭ-pŭl-kă-*lē*-ă = head-ache (*cf.* kati-pulka-)

kâ-tĭ-*tō*-kă-ră = a short-haired individual (*cf.* tokara).

kâ-tĭ-*ŭm*-pă-kă-lă = crown of the head, crest of a hill, etc., top.

kâ-tĭ-*ŭng*-kă-lă = head-first (*cf.* ung-kala).

kâ-tĭ-wă-re- = to nod the head laterally.

kâ-tĭ-wĭ-re- = (head, to sink, *i.e.*) to dive (*cf.* wire-).

kă-*too*-ră = species of Ayrshire Downs Barley Grass.

kât-yō-pŭl-le- = to pierce with a spear.

kēl-pĭ = bush-palisading for the second and subsequent initiation ceremonies.

kē-*lŭn*-jĭ = galah-parrot.

kĕn-jă = she-dog, slut, sign of the female gender.

kĕ-rĕ-prĕ-tĕ = under, below, beneath.

kĭ-bŭl-yō = whistler-duck.

kĭ-kĭ = vagina.

kĭm-bă (often pronounced *gĭm*-bă) = blood.

kĭm-bă mâ-rō=(the blood-possessor, *i.e.*) a woman during her menstrual period.

kĭn-doo-rō = clear, pure, (e g., water).

kĭ-te- = to copulate, marry (*cf.* kiki).

kĭ-yĕ = happy, pleased.

kō = yes.

kō-kă = blood-wood -gum, -tree (*see* rechindi).

kō-kō = back, dorsum.

kō-kō-lă, or *kō*-kō = bandicoot.

kō-koo-rō = fighting pole.

kō-kō-tō-ka- = to carry on the back, (*cf.* koko, toka-).

kō-kō-*toon*-gō = hill (*cf.* koko = back).

kŏl-loo-ră = white-cockatoo, corella.

kō-mă = bandicoot's nest in ground (*cf.* kokola).

kō-nĕ = short-hair at back and nape of the neck.

kō-nū-pă = grass necklace.

koo-dĭ-jă *koo*-dĭ-jă = trilinear bodily ornamentation of red or yellow ochre.

koo-dĭ-jă-kŏ-*rē*-ă = around.

koo-*dĭng*-bĕ-rĭ = a zig-zag wavy line.

koo-ē-rĭ = a boy at earliest sign of puberty.

koo-koo-rĭ = yellow ochre.

koo-koo-rĭ má-rō = the yellow-ochre possessor: an individual of the third degree.

koo-lă-bĭ-lă = kangaroo.

koo-*lĭn*-jĕ-rĭ = white-shell ornament worn on chest.

koo-*lĭ*-ŭng-ō = he-dog, sign of male-sex (*cf.* koolyo).

kool-kă = tail (of kangaroo, etc.)

kool-pă-rĭ = emu (the bird with the nodding head).

kool-poo-roo = netted head-cap.

kool-yō = testicle.

koom-pă-ră = opossum-string tassel, covering the privates: phallocrypt.

koom-pâ-tă = stone-chisel (*cf.* pata-).

koo-nă = excrement, faeces.

koo-*nā*-pă = shadow, reflexion.

koon-dă-chĭ = cray-fish.

koon-dă-ră = snake (in general).

koondara-lō-pă-*chĭ*-ă = snake-bite.

koon-*dē*-ă = wet, moist.

koon-dĭ *koon*-dĭ = crooked.

koon-dō-mō = beef-wood tree.

koon-*dăng*-ă-rĭ = diver-bird, shag, etc.

koon-gă-rĭ = nose.

koo-nĭ = pig-weed.

koo-nĭn-je- = to take away, to remove.

koon-*mĭ*-ă = between.

koon-pă = sp. of frog.

koon-pă-ră = cork-tree shield, koolamon.

koon-tă = corpse, male or female.

koo-*năn*-jĕ-rĭ = common house-fly.

koo-pă *koo*-pă = old, old-man, "boss."

koo-poo-roo = one of the four paedo-matro-nyms.

koo-ră-mă-ră = spinifex-grass.

koo-*rá* = the pubes.

koor-dō = large koolamon.

koo-re- = to cut with a (stone) knife, to incise (*cf.* kooya).

44. Vocabulary of Pitta-Pitta words—*continued.*

koo-*rĕ*-ă̆ = a cut, incision (*cf.* koore-).

*k*oo-rĕ-kō = red-ochre (*cf.* koorikoori).

*k*oo-rĭ-dă̆-lă̆ = large eagle-hawk.

*k*oo-rĭ *k*oo-rĭ = red.

koo-*rĭm*-ă̆-rä = carpet-snake.

koor-kĭl-lä = one of the four paedo-matro-nyms.

koo-roo-mŭn-dō = "rain"-stick.

koo-*rou*-ĭ = hut specially designed for withstanding rain.

*k*oo-tä = water.

*k*oo-ta-kă̆-pō = small white flower grow-ing along the water edge.

*k*oo-yă̆ = stone, stone-knife, stone-chisel.

koo-*yŭng*-ō = good.

*k*ō-pĕ = fish.

*k*ō-pī = a sort of white plaster, gypsum; *not* a true N.W.C. Queensland word, though much used (*see* pata).

*k*ō-pō = spider.

*k*ŏr-dă̆ = navel, umbilicus.

kō-re- = to remain, keep, continue, in same condition.

*k*ō-tō = smoke.

kō-tō-ŭn-jĕ- = to make a smoke-signal, etc.

kou-ă̆ = hullo! come here! (Impera-tive singular, etc.)

kou-ă̆-rä = dog, dingo.

kou-ă̆-rō = feather.

*k*ŭl-kâ = west.

*k*ŭl-lä = river, creek, water (*cf.* kutta-mulla).

*k*ŭl-lĭ = arm, fore-arm.

*k*ŭl-lĭ *k*ŭl-lĭ = expression of doubt, etc.

*k*ŭl-yĭ-kă̆ = green.

*k*ŭm-bō = bone-apparatus used for pro-ducing sickness and death, death itself.

kŭn-da- = to go, depart.

*k*ŭn-dĭ *k*ŭn-dĭ = curved throwing-stick toy.

kŭn-*dŏr*-ă̆ = variety of reed-spear.

*k*ŭng-ă̆ = water-spring.

*k*ŭn-jō = slow (in movement).

*k*ŭn-jŭng-ō = steady.

*k*ŭn-kŭr-ĭ = stone-knife.

*k*ŭn-nä = bye and bye, later on.

kŭn-na- = to become, to remain.

*k*ŭn-tä *k*ŭn-tä = rain.

*k*ŭn-tĭ = a tenacious cementing-substance, made from porcupine grass, etc.

kunti-maro = (cementing-substance pos-sessor, *i.e.*) handle of a stone-knife.

*k*ŭr-râ = wind, storm.

*k*ŭr-rĭ = now, immediately, soon, to-day.

*k*ŭt-tă̆-mŭl-lä = water, creek, small stream.

L.

*l*ī-chä = correctly, "no gammon."

*l*ī-ĕ = together, collectively, in-a-body.

lŭng-ä̆ *lŭng*-ă̆ = variety of boomerang.

M.

mâ! = thanks! thank you!

mâ-*choom*-bä = kangaroo.

*m*ă̆-kă̆ = fire.

*m*ă̆-kă̆ *m*ă̆-kă̆ = hot, hot water, etc.

*m*á-kē = return-boomerang.

mâ-kŏ-*wá*-tä = spear in general.

mâ-*kŭn*-yĕ = one of the terminal posts supporting the emu net.

*m*ă̆-lă̆-kă̆ = dog, dingo.

*m*á-lĭ = fishing-net.

mă̆-*loo*-ă̆-kă̆ = swift, quick.

mám-bō = elbow.

*m*á-nō = large intestines.

mâ-pă̆-la- = to take one's departure.

*m*ă̆-rä = may be, perhaps, expressive of doubt.

*m*á-rä-lĭ = to-morrow.

*m*ă̆-rä *m*ă̆-rä = nude, *i.e.*, not painted.

mă̆-re- = to fetch, bring with the hand (*cf.* murra).

*m*á-rē-ă̆ = axe (tomahawk) head, or whole implement.

mă̆-*rē*-kă̆ = on the other side of.

*m*ā-rĭ-mō = a variety of hand spear.

*m*á-rō = sign of possession (*cf.* murra)

*m*á-tĭ = a knot (in net, piece of string, etc.).

*m*á-tĭ = fingers, toe.

mē = eye.

*m*ē-kō = the vulva.

meko-maro = the vulva-possessor, *i.e.*, the penis which has been introcised, a "whistle-cock."

mĕl-*il*-bō = eye-brow (*cf.* me).

*m*ēl-yă̆ = nose.

melya-*pĕr*-kĭl-lĭ = (nose-big) nose-pin ornament.

melya-*pŭl*-tă̆-*pŭl*-tă̆ = flat-nosed (*cf.* pulye).

melya-*wá*-kă̆-rä = big-nosed.

melya-wĭl-yĕ-rĭ-kŭn-na- = to make grimaces (*cf.* wallichimpa-).

mē-pŭk-koo-*rē*-ă̆ = the punishment of blinding another (*cf.* me, pukka-).

*m*ĕ-rĭ-chĭ = leaf.

*m*ĕr-koo = lizard.

mĕr-pŭl-lĭ-*mŭng*-ĭ = a "whirler," "roarer," etc. (rather a Roxburgh word).

*m*ī-ē = country, district.

*m*ī-ē *m*ī-ĕ = earthy, muddy, dirty.

mī-ē-mĭ-*ĕr*-lĭ = smooth.

*m*ī-ĕr-lĭ = good.

44. A Vocabulary of Pitta-Pitta words—*continued.*

mĭl-kă̆ = tooth, tooth-ornament.
mĭl-*yá̆*-dō = bandicoot (*cf.* melya).
mĭng-kă̆ = nostril.
mĭng-kă̆-ră̆ = toe- or finger-nail, a claw, a claw-ornament, a scratch or mark.
mĭng-kō = fork of the fingers, toes: fork of a tree, a forked stick, a netting needle.
mĭn-mă̆ = *mŭl*-tă̆-ră̆.
mĭn-nă̆ = which ? what ?
mĭn-nă̆-lĭ = why ?
mĭn-nă̆-*mŭn*-dĭ = how many ? how much ?
mĭn-tă̆-ră̆ = *mŭl*-tă̆-ră̆.
mĭ-rĭ = young girl (from four or five years of age up to first signs of puberty).
mĭ-rĭ *mĭ*-rĭ = netted fore-head band.
mĭ-rĭ-*wĭn*-nĭ = mountain, rock, small stone.
mō-*á*-rĭ = poisonous white powder for producing sickness or death. (Rather an Upper Georgina word.)
mō-kĭ = small fly in general.
mōk-*wá*-rĭ = specially-shaped pigeon-net.
mŏl-lō-rō = mountain-top.
mō-mă̆ = "ghost" or "spirit" of those departed.
mō-nă̆ = upper-part front-of-chest.
mŏng-kă̆ = thunder.
moo-che- = to sleep.
mool-kă̆ = tree-trunk, -butt.
moo-nă̆-mŭl-*yá*-rĭ = opossum - string apron belt.
moo-nă̆-tĭm-pĭ-*ĕl*-lă̆ = sp. of small red tit.
moon-dĭ = -self.
moon-dō = a circumcised penis.
moong-kă̆-lă̆ = opossum-string, and the various ornaments, etc., made from it.
moong-kă̆-tă̆ = close up, near, in the neighbourhood of.
moon-tă̆-bĭl-lă̆ = opossum-string sheath of a stone-knife.
moor-kă̆ = tree-root.
moor-ră̆ = branch, stick.
moorra-kumbo = (sticks-death, *i.e.*, referring to the piling over with branches), grave.
moor-*rĭn*-dĭ = thumb, big-toe.
moor-rō = large variety of throwing-stick toy.
moo-too-roo = vertical "flash" cuts on the shoulders.
mō-*rool*-kă̆ = mosquito (*cf.* moki).
mŏr-rō = nulla-nulla.
moy-ĕr-jō = old-woman.
mŭl-jĕ-rĭ = flank, side, of the body.

mŭl-kă̆ = north-west.
mŭl-kă̆ *mŭl*-kă̆ = painted, decorated.
mŭl-kă̆-rĭ = a benevolent, omnipresent, supernatural being. Anything incomprehensible.
mŭl-lă̆ = thigh.
mŭl-lĕ = cold.
mŭl-le- = reflexive suffix added to the root-stem of certain verbs.
mŭl-lĭ-mŭr-rō = pelican.
mŭl-lō = sign of negation, no, not.
mŭl-tă̆-ră̆ = roll of emu feathers worn over portion of body wherever pain is.
multara-maro = (emu-feather-roll possessor, *i.e.*) the emu.
mŭn-da- = to kill with the munguni.
mŭn-dă̆ = the adverbial suffix.
mŭn-dă̆-koo-*ĕ*-ă̆ = a flattened spindle-shaped chest-ornament.
mŭn-dē-*lĭ*-ă̆ = round, curved.
mŭn-dĭ = much, many (*cf.* mundia, mungkora)
mŭn *dĭ* ă̆ = heavy.
mŭng-ă̆-roo = seed of a sp. of edible nut-grass.
mŭng-kŏr-ă̆ = largest kind of dilly-bag, and so, very great in size or quantity.
mŭng-ŭn-ĭ = bone-apparatus used for producing sickness or death.
munguni-maro = bone-apparatus-possessor, *i.e.*, medicine-man, doctor.
mŭng-ŭn-ĭ-pa-rĭ = porcupine.
mŭn-jĭ = sp. of fibrous flax-plant.
mŭn-nă̆ = may, perhaps, might.
mŭn-nă̆ = bad, evil (*cf.* munda-, munguni).
munna-kō-re- = to make a mistake (= evil, bad, to keep).
munna-moorra = the brothers and sisters of a deceased adult male.
mŭn-tă̆ = food of any description.
mŭr-ră̆ = hand (*cf.* moorra).
mŭr-ră̆-*kŭn*-tă̆ = small square-shaped dilly-bag.
murra-*too*-nō = boulder pebble held in hand, used for crushing nardoo (*cf.* murra toua-).
mŭr-ŭk-*kŭn*-dĭ = individual initiated into the fourth degree.
mŭt-tō = too, also, in addition.

N.

ná-kă̆ = between.
ná-ră̆ = ear.
nâ-ră̆-*á*-pă̆-rĭ = porcupine (sect. **74**, fig. 10).
nâ-ră̆-poon-ga- = to forget (sect. **104**, fig. 205).

44. A Vocabulary of Pitta-Pitta words—*continued.*

ná-ră-rō = flood.

nâ-ră-we- = to hear (*cf.* nara).

ná-rĭ = and, also, still yet.

ná-rĭ! = now! ready! off!

ná-rĭ = sign of interrogation.

ná-rĭ-mŭn-tă = flood (*cf.* nararo).

ná-roo-ă = spear in general.

năr-pĭ = river-bank, the water's edge with its ripples (*cf.* nararo)

nĕ-má-kă = smallest species of edible frog.

nēng-ō = any small frog in general.

nĭ-ĕ-rĭ nĭ-ĕ-rĭ = angry.

nĭl-pa = native animal-hide water-bag.

nĭ-ŭ-mŏr-ă = soft to the touch.

noong-ă-kă = here, at the back.

noong-á-rĭ = there, yonder.

noong-ă-yĕ = here, in front or side.

nō-pō = wife, husband.

nŭl-lă = skin, flesh.

nulla-maro = (the skin-possessor, *i.e.*) a penis that has not yet been circumcised.

nŭl-loo-chă = sp. of pear-shape-fruited vine.

nŭl-yă = cheek (*cf.* nulla).

nŭn-dă-tă = few, scarce.

nŭng-ka- = to sit-down, stay, reside, live.

nŭng-kă-la- = to allow, permit.

nŭng-kă-lĕn-yă = old, aged.

nŭng-kă-re- = to attend to, to wait-on, to look-after.

nŭn-mō-ɪō = long-pointed (like a spear).

nŭ-nō = tired, exhausted, faint.

nŭn-tĕ-rĭ = slip-noose for catching ducks, etc.

O.

ŏl-lō = fore-head.

ool-lō = bee.

oon-da- = to grease.

oo-nō = sand-fly.

oo-ră = camp (*cf.* oorooroo).

oo-răng-o = another's („)

oo-rō-koo-nă-wă-ră = other side of („)

oo-roo-roo, oo-rō = one, unity.

oo-roo-yă-ră = different (*cf.* oorooroo).

oo-ta- = to come back, return.

oo-tă-roo = one of the two gamo-matro-nyms.

P.

pá-koo-lă = two, dual.

pâ-koo-lăng-oo-rō = three (*cf.* pakoola, oorooroo).

pá-koo-tă = one of the two gamo-matro-nyms.

păl-lă = rain.

pă-pă-*too*-rō = short.

pá-pŏl-lă = shoulder.

păp-pă = any kind of seed-food in general.

pâ-ră-pă-ră = large species of iguana.

pă-ră-rĭ-kŭn-na- = to learn.

pă-ră-pĭ = creek, stream.

pă-ră-wăng-ă = mad.

pá-rĭ = plenty, a lot of, big mob of.

pá-rĭ pá-rĭ = property, belongings, possessions.

pá-roo = yellow, pale.

pă-rou-lĭ = flock-pigeon.

pă-ta- = to hold in the hand.

pá-tă = "kopi," white-plaster, gypsum.

pa-ta-maro = white-plaster possessor, *i.e.*, the one who mourns, a mourner.

pĕn-te- = to count.

pĕr-chă = a wooden-peg, -hook.

percha-marro = the peg-possessor, *i.e.*, a variety of hooked spear.

pĕ-rĭ-pă = big, large.

pĕ-rĭ-rĭ = soft, low (sound).

pĕr-kĭl-lĭ = big, large.

pĕ-tă-bŭr-ĭ = edible water-lily root: the whole plant.

pī-ă = bird in general.

pĭ-jĕr-dō = small hawk.

pĭn-dĭ pĭn-dĭ = sp. of "Mitchell"-grass.

pĭng-kă-ră = eagle-hawk feather ornament.

pĭn-jă-nĕ = the breast.

pĭn-jĭ = bird's nest (*cf.* pia).

pĭn-kĭ-poo-ra- = to divide, share.

pĭn-nă = bone.

pĭn-tă = short-pointed.

pĭn-tă-*poon*-dă-kă = finished entirely, completed.

pī-*ou*-lĭ = dog, dingo.

pĭ-pa- = to see.

pĭ-pĭn-*mī*-ă = lightning.

pĭ-răl-kō = native-companion bird.

pĭ-te- = to hit, strike (with anything except a spear).

pitc-mŭl-lĕ- = to fight (*cf.* mulle).

pĭt-yĭ-rĭ = sign of the plural.

pō-kăn-*gŭd*-yĕ = sp. of penny-royal.

pō-kă-ră = short meadow-grass.

poo-chō-*poo*-cho-tou-ē-mŭl-le- = to play at stick and ball (*cf.* tou-a-).

poo-ká-tĭ-kă = sp. of wattle used in the preparation of pituri.

pool-kĭ = full-up.

pool-lĕ = dry.

pool-lĕ-lă = (dry with the effects of, *i.e.*), thirsty.

poolle-kō-re- = (dry, to keep, *i.e.*), to dry something.

44. A Vocabulary of Pitta-Pitta words—*continued*.

poon-da- = to break a bone, leg, etc. (in Miorli, poonda = bone).

poo-nĭ = all, the whole lot.

pŏon-jō = hair of the head, human-hair twine.

poon-ta- = to suck a wound.

poor-rǎ = urine.

poor-rǎ-*chī*-ǎ = bitter, salty, taste (*cf.* poorra).

poo-rĭ-tĭ = all, the whole lot.

poorn-koo = knee.

poo-rō-nō = feather.

poo-roo-rō = (poorono, oorooroo, *i.e.*) the feathered one, the emu.

poor-pâ-lĕ = rhythmic clapping with the hands on the groin at corrobborees.

poo-tĭ = fire-wood.

prĕ-tĭ-pa- = to meet.

prŭl-líng-ǎ = the whirring-stick toy.

prŭl-lĭ *prŭl*-lĭ = black, blue

prŭn-nǎ = leg, the side-scaffolding of a hut.

prinna-poor-te- = to walk (*cf.* prinna).

pŭk-ka- = to cut with the chisel, etc., to manufacture (a spear, boomerang, etc.) (*cf.* pukkangi).

pŭk-*kǎng*-ĭ = native chisel (a word used more in the extreme west of the Boulia district).

pŭl-kĭ-woon-je- = to take in exchange, to swap (*cf.* woonje-).

pŭl-lǎ = lip.

pŭl-yĕ = fat, stout.

pŭn-dĕ-*pŭn*-dĕ-yǎ = yellow.

pŭn-dĭ-rǎ = sweetheart, wife of one's choice.

pŭn-jǎ = knee.

pŭn-jǎ-*pŭn*-jĭ-ǎ = sweet (taste).

pŭn-jē-ǎ = sick, ill, diseased.

pŭn-na- = to run.

pŭn-nǎ-re- = to steal.

pŭt-tǎ = a boy from four or five years of age up to the first signs of puberty.

R.

rē-chĭn-dĭ = "bloodwood"-tree (a doubtful Pitta-Pitta word).

T.

tǎ-kǎ = small variety of koolamon (*cf.* toka-).

tá-kǎ-lĕ = the cross-stick head-ornament worn at certain corrobborees, rites, etc.

tá-kō-kō = a child, male or female, up to four or five years of age (*cf.* tano).

tá-lĕ = tongue.

tá-nō = weak, helpless, delicate, sickly.

tā-pō = mountain.

tâ-pō = quiet, silent, silence (*cf.* tale).

tǎ-*rǎl*-kō = biggest variety of bull-frog.

tǎ-re- = to kick.

tǎ-re- = to weave a dilly-bag, net, etc.

tǎ-*rĕm*-bō-lǎ = pituri (*cf.* tare—to kick, as expressive of its therapeutic effects).

tâ-rō-pŭl-le- = to speak, articulate (*cf.* tale, pulla).

tǎ-*rou*-ǎ = broad, wide.

tá-tǎ = ant.

tĕ-rǎ = door, entrance, of hut.

tĕ-*rǎng*-ǎ-rǎ = high river-bank.

tĕ-rǎ-tō-*kǎ*-rǎ = open country.

tĕ-rĭ = the "pointer"-portion of the "bone"-apparatus.

tĕ-rĭ-nŭng-ka- = to quarrel, have words with.

tī-che- = to eat.

tī-ē = small in size or quantity.

tĭk-kǎ-rǎ = clouds, sky.

tĭl-lĭ-mŭr-rĭ = gidyea tree (*cf.* moorra)

tĭl-*yǎ*-rĭ = bunch of emu-feathers for hanging over the buttocks.

tĭ-ma- = to drink.

tĭn-cha- = to cut down, gather, collect grass or wood.

tĭn-ĕr-tǎ = sp. of small brown tit.

tĭn-jǎ = the rough marks on handle of boomerang, nulla-nulla, etc, to prevent the weapon slipping out of thrower's hand.

tĭn-jǎ = one of the intermediate sticks supporting the emu-net.

tĭn-jĭn-nǎ = kind of miniature koompara, but fixed on the pubic hair.

tĭn-nǎ = foot, road-track.

tĭn-nǎ-pŭl-lĭ = opossum.

tĭ-*nŭng*-ǎ-rǎ = north.

tĭ-pâ-dō = transverse "flash" incisions on chest.

tĭ-tĭ = elder brother.

tō = a long way off.

tō-ka- = to bring, fetch, carry.

tō-kǎ-rǎ = short hair on temples, nape of neck, etc.

tŏl-koo-roo = a plain, a flat piece of country.

too-chĕ-rǎ = straight, straight-line.

too-chĕ-rǎ = south-east.

tool-chĭ = small-intestines, the "guts."

toolchi koondi-koondi = (guts crooked, *i.e.*) stomach-ache.

toor-*kǎ*-pǎ-lō = white.

toor-kĭn-jĕ = fire-stick.

too-rō = by-and-by (*cf.* to).

too-*rool*-kǎ = freshwater mussel.

too-tǎ = grease, fat.

44. A Vocabulary of Pitta-Pitta words—*continued.*

tō-pō = buttock.

tŏ-tō-kă-nă = child.

tou-a- = to hit (with anything except a spear).

tou-ē-la- = to hit (with a spear only).

tou-ĕr-lĭ = concavity, cup, hole, receptacle of the " bone "-apparatus.

tū-*ă*-rĭ = long, tall.

tŭk-ka- = to stand up.

tŭm-*bā*-ră = variety of spear.

tŭn-ă-ē-lă-*lĭ*-ĕ = always, ever, every day (*cf.* elalie).

tŭn-pa- = to cut with a stone-knife, stone, etc.

twĭn-je- = to cry.

U.

ŭl-lō = mother's brother.

ū-*lŏr*-ă = south-west.

ŭm-bă = abdomen, belly,

umba *pŭt*-yă-*pŭt*-yă-mŭl-*lē*-ă = belly-ache (*cf.* umba).

ŭm-ma, *ŭm*-mă-ră = mother, mother's sister.

ū-mō-lō = night, darkness.

ŭng-kă = beard, chin.

ŭng-kă-lă = before, first-time, previous to.

ŭn-jă-koot-tă = a man's daughter-in-law, a woman's father-in-law.

ŭn-nă-*kŭd*-yĕ = a hut specially constructed for withstanding cold.

ŭn-tĭ-*tĭ*-rĭ = two-handed sword.

ŭp-pĕ-rĭ = father, father's brother (*cf.* yuppieri).

ū-rō-*mō*-kō = north-east.

ū-rŏn-*goo*-tō = a circle.

ŭr-rŭng-gă-rĭ = sugar-bag, honey.

ū-ta- = to swim.

ŭt-tă-kă-lō = relationship between husband's and wife's mothers.

ŭt-tă-nă = paternal grandmother, maternal grandfather.

ŭt-tă-pē-*ŭk*-kă = child, boy or girl.

ŭt-tă-*rē*-kă = nephew on sister's side.

ū-*wŭn*-nă = top-cord supporting the length of the extended emu-net.

W.

wă-chă-mâ = handle of a stone tomahawk.

wă-kă-jĕ = emu.

wă-kă-lă = black crow.

wă-kĕr-dĭ = black crow.

wā-kō = the smaller of the two sandstone grindstones.

wă-koo-lă = human-hair waist-belt.

wăl-lă-ră = young, youthful.

wăl-lĭ-chĭn-pa- = to rest the side of the face on arm or hand, when lying on ground.

wân-doo = heel.

wăn-tă = by-and-by.

wâ-pă = pup, litter.

wă-ră = who, whose, etc.

wă-ră-pĕr-tă = tomahawk.

wâ-râ-ră = a long way off.

wĕn-kō = when ?

wĕ-pĕ *wĕ*-pĕ = quiet, silent.

wĕ-rĭ = perhaps, may be.

wĕ-rĭ *wĕ*-rĭ = sandy channel.

wĕr-koo = two lines placed cross-wise; a sign of mourning, etc.

wĕ-yĕ-rō = hard to the touch.

wĭl-lă-kŭn-na- = to shield the face with the arm or hand (*cf.* walli chinpa-).

wĭl-pă = a punctured wound (*e.g.* from a spear).

wĭn-jĭ *wĭn*-jĭ = any temporary grass-shed for protection from rain.

wĭn-ne- = to come up to, to arrive at.

wĭn-nĭ-*mŭn*-nă-rĭ = connecting-string of the bone apparatus (*cf.* muuguni).

wĭn-*nŭ* = witooka.

wĭn-tă = whereabouts (rest) ? (*cf.* inta).

wĭ-re- = to grind, seed, etc.

wĭ-re- = to sink.

wĭ-too-kă = a radish-like edible root.

wŏl-kă = sun, day.

wŏl-kă-nă = to-morrow (*cf.* wolka).

wŏm-mă = snake in general.

wŏn-yĕl-lă = black-headed snake (*cf.* womma).

woom-*bŭn*-yĕ = wild orange.

woong-kō = one of the four paedo-matro-nyms.

woon-je- = to give.

woon-jĕ-mŭl-le- = to swap, exchange (*cf.* woonje-).

woon-jĕ-woon-je- = to teach (*cf.* woonje-).

wŏr-ă-kă = emu-feather amulet worn over the chest (*cf.* warkaje)

wŏr-kă-ră = south.

wŏr-ră = shield.

wŭl-lō-ă = a break-wind on either side of a hut, built of twigs, grass, etc.

wŭl-*loo*-kă = a modification of the munguni.

wŭl-*lŭng*-ă-ră = stone tomahawk as a whole, its stonehead.

wŭl-pă-ră = sp. of stickleback, a very small kind of fish.

wŭn-dă-roo = the backbone, and so the curved framework of a hut.

wŭng-ă-tă = adult woman in general.

wŭng-ĭ = younger, brother or sister.

44. A Vocabulary of Pitta-Pitta words—*continued.*

wŭn-je- = to rise.

wŭn-jĕ = hair, grass.

wŭn-jĕ-la- = to make hair or grass, to grow (*cf.* wunje).

wŭn-ka- = to sing at a corrobboree (*cf.* wunni).

wŭn-nĭ = corrobboree as a whole.

Y.

yă-kă-pă-rĭ = a grass allied to the katoora.

yá-kă *yá*-kă-yĕ = night-time.

yá-kĭ = light in weight.

yăl-kà = drought.

yăl-kă-ră = dark, heavy, clouds.

yăl-lŏ-wŭn-je- = to send (*cf.* woonje).

yá-ră-kă = species of star-grass

yă-rĭ-*mŭng*-kŏr-ă = strong, powerful (*cf.* mungkora).

yă-te- = to build a hut, palisade, etc.

yĕl-kă = neck.

yĕl-kă *yĕl*-kă = bush alley-way into which the hunted emus are driven

yĕl-pĭ = emu-net.

yĕ-nĭ-*moong*-kă-tă = how far? how near? (*cf.* moongkata).

yŭm-bĭ = a man's mother-in-law, a woman's son-in-law.

yŭn-dĭ = brother-in-law, male cousin.

yŭng-kō = wulloa.

yŭn-ka- = to tell, to report, inform.

yŭn-ŭn-ă = similar.

yŭp-*pī*-ĕ-rĭ = young lad at full development of puberty (*cf.* upperi).

yŭt-ta- = to like, love, copulate.

CHAPTER II.

TABULAR COMPARISON BETWEEN VARIOUS SELECTED WORDS USED IN THE
DIFFERENT ETHNOGRAPHICAL DISTRICTS OF NORTH-WEST-CENTRAL
QUEENSLAND.

CONTENTS.—Section 45. Boulia District—the various tribes occupying it. 46. Leichhardt-Selwyn District. 47. Cloncurry District. 48. Flinders District. 49. Upper Georgina District. 50. North-West-Central Queensland. 51. Introduction to the Philological Tables. 52. Words relating to parts of the body. 53. Fauna and Flora. 54. Other Objects of Nature. 55. Weapons, Utensils, &c. 56. Numerals. 57. Abstract Ideas. 58. Family Relationships.

45. The Boulia District, the limits of which have already been defined in section 2, comprises in all a score or so of tribes, each having its head centre or chief encampment. Speaking generally, these same tribes are able to render themselves pretty mutually intelligible, and possess in common various trade-routes, markets, and hunting-grounds, customs, manners, and beliefs; in other words they might, as a whole, be well described as "messmates," though in the aboriginal language there appears to be no one word which would express them collectively. Still deeper bonds of comradeship connect them in that all these tribes, within certain individual limitations to be subsequently discussed, are inter-marriageable, and furthermore, in cases of warfare with outsiders, would join in making common cause against the enemy.

Owing to the opening up of the country with the advent of the Europeans, some of these tribal camps have been shifted of late years from their original quarters or else amalgamated with others, while in a few cases, what with priva-tion, disease, alcohol, and lead, the whole community has been annihilated. Even during my sojourn at Boulia, the head-centre of the Pitta-Pitta tribe, I have never seen more than about 50 of these individuals congregated there on any one occasion, though this number might occasionally have been augmented by visitors coming in from neighbouring districts for purposes of trade and barter. At the present day I do not suppose that the whole tribe numbers more than 200 souls, scattered here, there, and everywhere. So again, the Yellunga people of Noran-side are fast disappearing, while the Yunda folk, originally of Warenda, are now scarcely ever to be met with on that station, their quarters having been shifted northwards towards Tooleybuck. The tribes indigenous to the Boulia district can therefore only be located within certain limits, as follows:—The Boinji, Dun-gadungara, Yunnateunnea, Ringo-Ringo, &c., in the neighbourhood of Marion Downs, the Pitta-Pitta at Boulia, the Ooloopooloo at Bedouri, the Rukkia and Tinka-Tinki at Cooraboolka, the Rungo-Rungo in the country between Herbert and Roxburgh Downs, the Koonkoolenya at Mooraboola, the Kwokwa and Weelko at Pilliou Creek, the Yellunga along Noranside and the Burke River, the Yunda at Booloo-Booloo, Warenda, Muckunda Creek, and Tooleybuck, the Karanya at Cluny, the Yuntauntaya at Breadalbane, the Ulaolinya at Carlo (*vel* Mungerebar) and Upper Mulligan River, the Miorli at Springvale, the Lakes, Cork, and Middle Diamantina River, the Wonkajera in the neighbourhood of Glenormiston (*vel* Idamea) and Herbert Downs, &c. Why there should be such a multiplicity of communities in this particular district, as compared with the others, it is somewhat difficult to understand, except on the supposition that a composite society is actually undergoing a process of agglutination; on the other hand, some of the above tribes cannot boast of more than a score or two of individuals.

The Miorli have only of late years amalgamated with the Boulia District aboriginals so far as general friendly intercourse and trade relationship is concerned, a circumstance which will explain the fact that while many of their words possess roots in common with those given in the contiguous lists (section 52, &c.), there is a large proportion of others which are totally peculiar and independent. The Miorli language seems, indeed, to connect that of the Goa (Upper Diamantina), itself allied by common roots to the Woonamurra and Mitakoodi (Upper Flinders and Cloncurry) with the Pitta-Pitta and other Boulia District dialects. Again, in the lists of words of the Wonkajera and Ulaolinya, two neighbouring tribes of the Boulia District, are to be found a few roots in common with one another, yet distinct from those belonging to the district in general : a proportion of these common roots indicates a connection with the language of the Undekerebina aboriginals occupying the contiguous Toko country.

The Boulia District tribes, whence words have been chosen for comparison, are the Pitta-Pitta, Wonkajera, Ulaolinya, Karanya, and Miorli. Unfortunately, I never succeeded in obtaining a reliable Yunda or Yellunga vocabulary—*e.g.*, a dialect spoken in the northerly portions of the district.

46. The Leichhardt-Selwyn District includes the Selwyn Ranges and the highlands (Barkly Tableland, &c.) drained by the Leichhardt and various tributaries (*e.g.*, Buckley River, Moonah Creek) of the Upper Georgina : its southern limits extend to Chatsworth, Mount Merlin, and Buckingham Downs. In the main, this area may be described as wild mountainous country, watered by natural springs. It is occupied chiefly by the Kalkadoon tribes, though in what particular portion of it is their main camp, if any, it is difficult to learn. Messmates of theirs are the Workoboongo, Iujilinji, and Oboroondi. Their eastern and northern neighbours, the Mitakoodi of the Cloncurry District, sometimes speak of these Kalkadoon as consisting of two main divisions—the Muntaba (*i.e.*, southern) and the Roongkari (*i.e.*, western). It is the southern Kalkadoon who are referred to throughout the following text. Contrary to what might have been expected, there are very few words or roots common to the Leichhardt-Selwyn and Cloncurry Districts, which, being contiguous, have their lists (section 52, &c.) accordingly placed in apposition.

47. The Cloncurry District comprises all the country drained by the Cloncurry River and its branches as low down as its junction with Dismal Creek. It is occupied by the Mitakoodi, with their head encampment at Fort Constantine: around Canobie messmates of theirs are the Mikoolun and Miubbi. On the west and south this district is bounded by Kalkadoon, and on the east by Woonamurra, country.

48. The Woonamurra inhabit the watershed of the Saxby and Flinders, as far as Cambridge and Richmond Downs, an area which for present purposes may be referred to as the **Upper Flinders District.** Southwards it extends to the Ranges and to Kynuna, where it becomes contiguous with Goa country. The Nouun tribes at Mullangera are messmates both of the Woonamurra and Mitakoodi. Both the latter, as well as the Wommin, come to barter here at Mullangera.

49. In the **Upper Georgina District**, stretching along the river between Roxburgh and Carandotta and onwards, with head-quarters at the latter locality, are the Elookera or Walookera, a small tribe using words absolutely distinct, showing no traces of contact with neighbouring peoples. The Yunnalinka, who also had their head-quarters at Carandotta only a few years ago, are now probably extinct. Beyond the Walookera are the comparatively numerous Yaroinga, scattered from between Urandangie and Headingly ; these extend northwards along the Georgina as far as Lake Nash, and westwards along the course of Gordon's Creek. Here the Yaroinga come into contact with the Undekerebina of the Toko Ranges and surrounding country, with whom they are friends and messmates, and, as will be noticed in the lists referring to their respective dialects, the similarity of many of their words is very marked. The Yaroinga are also messmates with the powerful and warlike Workia people, who live north of them.

50. An examination of the map (Plate 1.) will show pretty clearly how the five foregoing ethnographical districts together constitute the major portion of the area henceforth to be referred to as **North-West-Central Queensland.** The distinctiveness with which these various districts are separated one from the other, even in language alone, is well illustrated in the succeeding comparative philological tables.

51. In drawing up the following lists, not a little care has been exercised in eliminating all words concerning the meaning of which, to the aboriginal mind, there could be the least suspicion of doubt. This possibility I was confirmed in when studying the personal and other pronouns, family and individual relationships, &c., among the Pitta-Pitta blacks, and even as it is, the various names for certain genera among the fauna may still be open to this objection. With this purpose in view, the particular words selected for philological comparison are confined to the various portions of the human body, to animals, plants, and other objects of nature, to weapons, implements, and numerals, a few abstract ideas, and certain family relationships (with limited significations). It will be noticed that the various tribes are tabulated in the lists not only collectively according to their ethnographical districts, but also individually in such manner that neighbouring communities are placed in close proximity. This has been done in order to show more forcibly how many a word will undergo gradual yet marked transformation within comparatively limited tracts of country. All words are analysed into their component syllables, and accentuated and pronounced according to the basis laid down in section 3. Opportunity may be taken here of drawing attention to the words "galah," "corella," "womuera," for comparison with their respective Australian aboriginal terms used in these districts.

52.—Parts of the Body.

Tribe.	adult man.	adult woman.	head.	hair of head.	fore-head.	eye.	eye-brow.	nose.	nostril.
Walookera(¹)	kĭ-rō	yă-ră-yă-na	koo-roo-kă-roo	bool-gă	mĭd-tĕr-ă	mŭng-ă	mĭl-ĭl-ă-rĭ	ŏr-tō	ŏr-tō
Yaroinga	ŭr-twĕĭ	ŭmb-bă	kă-pō-dă	ĕr-kĕ-ră	ool-lă	ŭng-ă	tĭn-năm-pŭl-yă	ŭl-lă	ŭng-gŏl-lă
Undekerebina	{tĭp-prĕĭ-lă / yĕl-kă	bŭl-gĭ-ă	ă-kă	ă-kŭl-dă	wŭl-lă	tĭlk-nă	tĭn-ŭng-bĭ-lă	ūl-tĭn-jĕ-ră	ōl-lă
Ulaolinya	wŏĭ-pĕl-lă	moo-roo-ă	kă-tĭ	koo-nă-rĭ	bĭn-jă-oo-nĭ	nă-kă	măl-pō-pō	kool-kă-rĭ	ă-rĭ-tĭm-ō-kō
Wonkajera	kĭ-nă	moo-roo-wŏ-chY	kă-tĭ	koo-nă-rĭ	bŭl-bă	mĕl-ă-dĭ	mĕl-ŭl-bō	goon-gă-rĭ	nă-rĕ-ă
Karanya	kĭ-nă	pă-rĕ-chă	kă-tĭ	poon-jō (³) (⁵)	pĭn-jĭ-rĭn-nĭ	mō	mĕl-pō-pō	mĕl-yă	mĭng-kă
Pitta-Pitta	kă-nă	wŭng-ă-tă	kă-tĭ	{kŏ-nĕ (²) / poon-jō (³)}	{bĭl-bă / ōl-lō}	mō	mĕl-ŭl-bō	{mĕl-yă / koon-gă-rĭ}	mĭng-kă
Miorli	kă-nă	pă-rĕ-chă	kăn-ă-rĕ	pŭn-jă (³)	ŭl-lō	ŭng-ă	mĕl-ŭl-bō	mĕl-yă	mĭng-ō
Goa	kŭn-dō	bŭn-yă-nă	kŭ-tă	yăk-kō	gō	tŭl-lY	ŏĕrĭ-gă	nĭng-ō	nĭng-ō
Woonamurra	ă-gŭr	bŭn-yă	kăn-dă	kŭn-dă	goo-mō	mēl	goo-mŏ-jĭ-rĭ-rĭ	ŏr-rō	ŏr-rŏ-kă-rŏ
Mitakoudi	{ĭ-gŭr / pŭn-yĭl	wŏm-mă-lŏng-oo-ltĭl / pŭn-yă	ŭng-gool	kăn-tă	yă-chēr	ū-kō (⁴)	mĕl-jĕ-rĭn	nĭng-kă	nĭng-kă
Kalkad-oon	ŭ-rō	mĭ-tă-bĭ	kŭn-tă	wŏr-ă-pō	moon-tă	mĭl-tĭ	mĭng-tŭng-gă-rĭ	ĕ-jĭn-jĭ	ĕ-jĭn-jĭ

(¹) Sect. 49.   (²) Particularly the short hair growing on nape of neck.   (³) Cf. Goa and Woonamurra terms for "meadow-grass."

(⁴) Cf. Mitakoudi term for "eye."   (⁵) Sect. 43 c.

52.—Parts of the Body—continued.

Tribe.	lip, mouth.	tongue.	tooth.	chin, beard.	cheek.	ear.	neck.	shoulder.	arm, fore-arm.
Walookera ...	lā-rǎ	ǔl-tǎ-lǎ	koo-tǔn-ǎ	tou-ǎ-oo-noo	tou-ǎ-lō	mǔn-kǎ-rō	bō-tōr-ǎ	yēl-bǐ	ǔm-pě
Yaroinga ...	mǎ-nǎ	ǔn-jě-rǎ	ǔr-dǎ-dǎ	chěl-kǎ, ǔr-rō-dǎ (²)	ǔr-rǎl-yǎ	ěl-pǎ	ǐn-dǎ-rōk-ōr-ǎ	ǔl-goo-dǎ, ǔl-goo-dǎ	ǎ-kwǒ
Undekerebina.	ǎ-rǒ-goo-tǎ	ǔn-jě-rǎ	ǔn-dǎ-kǎ	ǔr-rō-tǎ	ǔr-rǎl-ǎ	yǎl-bǎ	yěr-tǎ	ǔy-pǎ-rǎ	ǎ-kwǒ
Ulaolinya ...	pǔl-lǎ	yǔn-mō-rō	mǔl-kǎ	wǒng-kǎ	nǔl-yǎ	nǎ-rǎ-wǐ-dǔ-lǎ	yěl-kǎ	pǎ-pōl-lǎ	hǎ-doo-ǎ-lǐr (⁰), moo-roo (⁷)
Wonkajera ...	pǔl-lǎ	tǎ-lě	mǔl-kǎ	wǔn-kǎ	ǔl-yǎ	nǎ-rǎ-wǎ	ěl-kǎ / kǎ-kě-rǐ	pǎ-pōl-lǎ	kǔl-lǐr
Karanya ...	pǔl-lǎ	tǎ-lě	mǔl-kǎ	ǔng-kǎ	nǔl-yǎ	nǎ-rǎ	yǔl-kǎ	pǎ-pǔl-lǎ	kǔl-lǐr
Pitta-Pitta ...	pǔl lǎ	tǎ-lě	mǔl-kǎ	ǔng-kǎ	nǔl-yǎ	nǎ-rǎ	yěl-kǎ	pǎ-pōl-lǎ	kǔl-lǐr
Miorli ...	pǔl-kǎ	tǔm-bǎ-rǎ	mǔl-kǎ	pǔm-jō-lō (¹)(⁵) / ǔng-kǎ	ǔl-yǎ	nǎ-rǎ	ǔl-kǎ	pǎ-pōl-lǎ	kǔl-kǎ
Goa	bě-wō	tō-lǔn-yǎ	rǔr-rǎ	ǔl-tǔn-yǎ	ǔrǐ-gǎ	mǔng-ǎ	bǒm-bǎ (³) / tōr-ō-mō (⁴)	wǒng-kǎ	mǔl-lǎ (⁶), mǔng-gō (⁷)
Woonamurra ...	ǎ-gǎ	ǔl-lǔn-dǐ	yǎr-dǐ-dǎ	mǔng-goo-rǎ	tǔng-gǎ-ǔl-mǎ-rǎ	bǐ-nǎ	mǔng-goo-rǐ	kǎ-nǐ	pǐ-gǎ-rǎ
Mitakoodi ...	tǔng-goo-lǎ	nǔl-lǔn-dě / tǔm-měn-gool	yǎ-chě-rǐn	mǔng-goo-rǎ (³) / yǔn-bǎ	wǔl-lěn-dō	pǐ-nǎ	mǔng-goo-rǎ (⁴) / kě-ǎ-too-rǐ-too-rǐ (⁵)	kǎ-ně	wǔl-joor (⁶), bǔl-gǔl (⁷)
Kalkadoon...	ǔn-tǎ	mǎ-lě	ǎ-dǐn-tǎ	yǔn-pǔl	ō-kō	ǔn-tǎ	kǎ-lǎ-rǎ	nǎ-nǐ	yǔn-tō

(¹) (²) (³) Beard.   (³) Throat.   (⁵) Back of neck, nape.   (⁵) Arm.   (⁷) Fore-arm.

(⁵) Cf. Pitta-Pitta term for "hair-of-head"; also Goa and Woonamurra terms for "meadow-grass."

52.—Parts of the Body—*continued.*

Tribe.	elbow.	hand.	thumb.(15)	fingers.(16)	thigh.	knee.	leg (shin).	ankle.	foot.
Walookera ...	mǐ-*mǔl*-kǎ	mǐr-kǎ-nǎ	bǔr-*tǔl*-lǎ(5)	*tou*-t-ou-(4)	tǎ-*tǔm*-mǎ	mě-rǐ-*mǔl*-lǎ	ō-*tǔ*-rō	mǔn-dǐ-mǐl-lě	pǎ-*mǎ*-rǎ
Yaroinga ...	ǎ-*mǔg*-gǎ	ěl-jǎ	mǎ-kō *mǎ*-ko	yěr-tǎ-pǎ	ē-*lǔb*-ǎ-rǎ	ǔm-boo-tǎ	ěl-*lou*-ǎ	tǐn-*nǔlg*-pǎ tǐn-*nǔlg*-pǎ	ǔm-bǐ-lǎ(11)
Undekerebina	*mǔk*-kǎ	yěl-kǎ	yěl-kǎ	yěl-kǎ	ē-*lǐp*-ǎ-rǎ	ǔm-boo-tǎ	jǒr-ǎ	tǐlk-*nǔl*-pǎ tǐlk-*nǔl*-pǎ	yǔng-kǎ
Ulaolinya ...	ū-rǐ-*moo*-kō	*mǔr*-rǎ	moor-rǐn-dǐ	*mǔr*-rǎ	wǔn-dǐ wǔn-dǐ	poom-kō	prǐn-nǎ(12)	oon-dǎ-roo-koo	tǐn-nǎ
Wonkajera ...	ū-rō-*mō*-kō	*mǔr*-rǎ	boor-*dǔn*-yě	*mǔr*-rǎ	*mǔl*-lǎ	pǔnk-yǎ	pǐn-nǎ(12)	oon-dǎ-koo	tǐn-nǎ
Karanya ...	*mǎm*-bō	moor-roo	*boor-dǐn-yě*	mǎ-rǎ	*mǔl*-lǎ	poorn-kō	prǐn-nǎ	mǎ-tǐ	tǐn-nǎ
Pitta-Pitta	*mǎm*-bō	*mǔr*-rǎ	moor-rǐn-dǐ	mǎ-tǐ	*mǔl*-lǎ	{ poorn-koo(13) pǐn-jǎ }	prǐn-nǎ		tǐn-nǎ wǔn-doo(10)
Miorli ...	ū-rǐ-*mō*-kō	*mǔr*-rǎ	ōr-tō	*mǔr*-rǎ	*mǔl*-lǎ	yǔng-kō	prǐn-nǎ	mǎ-rǎ-wě	tǐn-nǎ
Goa	ū-rǐ chǐ-mō	*mǔr*-rǎ	yǔp-pō	nǔn-yō-lǎ-(3) *mǔr*-rǎ	tǎ-rǎ	moo-rǐn-dǐ	mō-kō(8) poom-mǎ-rǎ(9)	pǎ-rǎ-kō	tǐn-nǎ
Woonamurra		*mǔl*-lǎ	mǎ-rǎ-bǔng-gō	*mǔl*-lǎ	tǎ-rǎ	boong-gool	mō-kō		tǐn-nǎ
Mitakoodi ...	ǎ-rō-*mō*-kō	mǐm-bě-lǎ	*mǔm*-bě-lǎ *mǎ*-dō(1)	*mǔm*běla-wǔl-kǎ-jǎ-kǎ-jǎ-koo-rō(2)	tǎ-rō-rō koo-yě-mǎ-rǎ	poong-kool	ǐn-dǎ-rǎ	prě-nǎ(14)	chǎ-nǎ
Kalkadoon ...	*wǔn*-yǐ	*mǎ*-kǎ-tǐ	*mǎ*-kǎ-tǐ	*mǎ*-kǎ-tǐ	*nǒl*-tō(6) ně-*ǔn*-tǎ(7)	*ǐp*-pǒr-ō poo-roo poo-roo	*wǔng*-kǎ	nō-kō	tǎ-pǔn-tō

(1)(5) *Cf.* words for "big, large," in sect. 57.   (2)(3)(4) *Cf.* words for "small" in sect. 57.   (6) Thigh.   (7) Projection of hip-bone.   (8) Shin.
(9) Calf.   (10) Heel.   (11) *Cf.* Mitakoodi word for "hand,"   (12) *Cf.* Wonkajera, etc, terms for "bone, shin-bone."   (13) Sect. 43 *g.*
(14) *Cf.* Boulia district words for "leg."   (15)(16) *Cf.* terms for "big toe" and "little toe" respectively.

52.—Parts of the Body—continued.

Tribe.	big-toe (15).	little-toes (16).	breast.	abdomen.	umbilicus.	penis.	testicles.	vulva.	flank.
Walookera...	bŭr-tŭl-lă	tou-ɾ-ou (5)	tŭl-lŏr-grĕ	poong-kă	koo-nă-bă-dă	tō-bō	bŭl-lō	mă-kă-nă / mă-ră	bă-lɾ-wɾ-ă
Yaroinga ...	mā-kō mā-kō	ŭm-bɪ-lă	tɪn-grĕl-yă	tɪn-nŭl-jă	bŏ-mă-ră	poor-ră (14)	tɪn-nŭl-gwă	ĕ-rɪl-lă	wool-dă
Undekerebina	yŭng-kă	yŭng-kă	tɪn-grŭl-yă	ŭŕ-nɪ-tă	pŭ-mă-ră	pŏr-ră (14)	tɪl-lō-tă	yĕ-rɪl-lă	tɪn-gŏr-rĕl-yă (12)
Ulaolinya ...	moor-rĭn-dɪ	jă-bă-mō-kō (2)	kă-bood-yō	ŭm-pă	koor-tă	noor-ră	kool-yō	too-tɪ (10)	pă-roon-gŭl-ɾ
Wonkajera...	boor-dŭn-yĕ	wă-bă-bă	mō-nă	ŭm-pă	kŏr-tă	noor-ră	poor-tō	pɪng-ă / yĭăm-ră	pŏr-ŏn-gŭl-ɪ
Karanya ...	boor-dɪn-yĕ	mĕr-kɪ	kă-pood-yō	toorn-dō	koor-tă	pɪl-pă	kool-yō	yĭăm-nɪ / kɪ-kɪ	poor-oon-gŭl-ɪ
Pitta-Pitta...	moor-rĭn-dɪ	mă-tɪ	mō-nă / pŏn-jă-nĕ (6)	ŭm-bă	kŏr-dă	bŭl-bă (13)	kool-yō (15)	mĕ-kō / kɪ-kɪ (10) / koo-ră (11)	mŭl-jĕ-rɪ
Miorli ...	mŏr-rĭn-dɪ	tɪn-na	mō-nă	ŭm-bă	koor-tă	pɪl-pă	kool-yō	kɪ-kɪ (10)	mŏr-rō
Goa	yŭp-pō	tɪn-nă-nŭn-yō-lă (4)	pō-yō (8) / ŭm-mɪ-nă (9)	mɪ-chă	noorn-dɪn-yă	wŏn-dɪ	oor-dō	tɪm-lĕ / bĕr-gă	bɪ-băl-bɪ-băl-ă
Woonamurra	tɪn-nă-bŭng-gō	tɪn-nă	ŭm-mă-gō-ră	ŭb-bŏr-ă	jɪm-bō	wɪn-nɪ	kă-pă-gŏr-ă	yĕr-lă	pŏ-bă gĭ-bă
Mitakoodi ...	chă-nă mă-dō (1)	chă-nă-wŭl-kă-jă-kă-jă-koo-rō (3)	ŭm-mă-koo-ră / tăm-bō (7)	ŭp-pĕr-ă	rŏng-kō	mĕ-nō	kă-pō-koo-ră	mĕ-nē	kă-pă kă-pă
Kalkadoon...	tă-pun-tō	tă-pun-tō	wă-kĕ-tă	pō-tō	oo-nŏk-ŏ-rō	kăn-tō	nŏr-tō	tɪn-tɪ	tŭl-pō

(1) Cf. word for "big," in sect. 57.   (2) (3) (4) (5) Cf. words for "small," in sect. 57.   (6) Upper portion of the chest.   (7) Milk.   (8) Chest.   (9) Breast. (10) Vagina.   (11) Pubes.   (12) Cf. breast.   (13) Penis in general. Cf. moon-do, nul-la ma-ro, and me-ko ma-ro in Pitta-Pitta Vocabulary, sect. 44. (14) Cf. Ulaolinya, etc., terms for "urine."   (15) Sect. 43 g.   (16) (16) Cf. terms for "thumb" and "fingers," respectively.

52.—Parts of the Body—*continued.*

Tribe.	dorsum, back.	buttocks.	nails.	bone.	blood.	bowels.	excrement.	urine.
Walookera	too-roon-doo-roo	tō-nă	jĕ-nŭm-mĭ-ĕ-rĭ	wŭn-măr-I	oon-doo-roo	poong-kă	goo-nă	mă-choo-kă-mă-tĭ
Yaroinga	ŭr-dă-pă	ŭd-dĭ-lă	....	gwoon-nă	tĭr-roo-ă	tŭn-nŭl-jă (4)	ŭn-nă	tŭm-bă
Undekerebina	ār-tă-pă	mŭn-tă	ĕng-gă-tă-lĭk	gwoĭn-nă	trk-nă	tŭt-nŭl-yă	tĭt-nă	oom-bod
Ulaolinya	kŏ-kŏ	tŏ-bŏ	mĭng-gă-ră	toom-poo-nō	gĭm-pă	tool-chĭ	{ koo-nă / kŭn-tă	poor-ră (7)
Wonkajera	mŏl-lŏ-rŏ	ŭ-ră	mĭng-kă-ră	pĭn-nă (6)	gĭm-pă	oon-tĭ	goo-nă	pŏr-ră (7)
Karanya	mool-loo-rō (5)	tŏ-bŏ	nĕ-rĭ	{ prĭn-nă (6) / măng-ŭn-Y	gĭm-pă	tool-kĭ	koo-nĭ-ă	pŏr-ri-ă
Pitta-Pitta	kŏ-kŏ (8)	tŏ-pō	mĭng-kă-ră	pĭn-nă	{ gĭm-bă / kĭm-bă	{ tool-chĭ (2) / mă-nō (3)	koo-nă	poor-ră
Miorli	toor-gŭm-bō	tŏ-bŏ	mĭng-gă-ră	poon-dă (1)	ŏr-kĭ	tŏrt-yĭ	koo-nă	kĭp-pă-ră
Goa	tăl-kŏ-pă-ră / toom-goo	mĭ-rĭ	mĭn-jĭ-lĭ	tăl-lĭk	gwă-rō	mŭn-dă mŭn-dă	koo-nă	gĭ-bă-ră
Woonamurra	tăl-kŏ-pă-ră	bŏ-gō	mĕn-jĭl	tĭm-mŭl	gwă-rō	oon-dŏ-băng-gō	oon-dō	gĭ-bŏr-ă
Mitakoodi	roon-dō	bŏ-kō-tŭm-bō	mŭl-pĕ-jĕ	tĭm-mool mŏ-koon	kwă-rĭ	oon-dŏ-băng-gō	oon-dō	gĭ-bă-ră
Kalkadoon	mĕnt-yĕ	mĭ-tĭn-tĭ	pĕ-kō	koon-kă	ŏĭ-chĭ	ŏ-nō	wŏn-nō / oo-tŭm-bĕ-rĭ (5)	koor-ki-ĕ

(1) Cf. the Pitta-Pitta "poonda," to break a bone, etc.   (2) Small intestines.   (3) Large intestines.

(5) Only used in bad language, swearing, etc. (sect. 333).   (6) Cf. Ulaolinya, etc., terms for "shin."

(4) Also = abdomen.   (7) Cf. Yaroinga, etc., terms for "penis."

(8) Cf. Pitta-Pitta, etc., term for "hill."

53.—Fauna and Flora.

Tribe.	kangaroo.	opossum.	porcupine.	dog, dingo.	slut.	bird (in general).	emu.	ordinary small hawk.	big eagle-hawk.
Walookera ...	tǐn-kǔn-nǎ	wǐ-rǒ-ǎ	nǔl-lǐ-noo-kǎ	wǎ-rou-lǎ	yǒ-bǐ / yǎ-rǎ-yǔ-nǎ / wǎ-rou-lǎ [9]	oor-pǎ	poon-joo-rō-ǎ	ǒr-tǒm-oo-doong	wǐm-pě-tǎ
Yaroinga ... Undekerebina	ǔr-rǎ / ǔr-gǎ-rō	ǔn-dǐ-nǎ / ǔn-dǒ-nǎ	yě-nǎ-pǎ	ǔl-ǎ-grǎ / mǎ-tǎ	ěr-kwǔn-nǎ / mǎ-lǎ	too-rǎ	tǔng-gōr-ǎ / ǔn-kōr-ǎ	yǔng-gō-lǎ / yǔng-wǎng-ǎ	yě-rǐ-jǎ / yě-rěk-kǎ
Ulaolinya ...	wǒ-kě-rǎ	wǒm-pě-lǎ	tn-noo-ǎ-lǐng-ǎ	{ mǐ-ǎ mǐ-ǎ / kou-ǎ-rǎ { mǎ-kǎ-rǎ [6] / kou-rǎ	ǔn-dǎ-w-ǎ-rǎ	pǐ-ǎ	kool-pǎ-rǐ	koom-dǎ-lǎ	tǔl-lǎ-wǒ-rǎ
Wonkajera ...	wǒ-kǎ-rǎ	wǒm-pǎ-lǎ	tn-nōr-lǐng-ǎ	{ mǎ-kǎ-rǎ [6] / kou-rǎ	{ wǎ-bǎ-bǎ / tǐn-dou-rǎ [8]	bǔr-rǐ	kool-pǎ-rǐ	mǔr-rǎ mǔr-rǎ	koo-rǐ-dǎ-lǎ
Karanya ...	koo-lě-bǐ-lǎ	tǐn-nǎ-bǐtl-lǐr	ǔn-noor-lǐng-gǎ [21]	pǐ-ou-lǐ	mǐng-kǎ	pǐ-ǎ	kool-pǎ-rǐ	pǐ-jěr-dō	koo-rǐ-dǎ-lǎ
Pitta-Pitta {	{ koo-lǎ-bǐ-lǎ / mǎ-choom-bǎ	tǐn-nǎ-pǐtl-lǐr	nǎ-rǎ-ǎ-pǎ-rǐ	{ koo-lǐ-tǔng-ō [5] / pǐ-ou-lǐ / kou-ǎ-rǎ	kěn-jǎ	pǐ-ǎ [16]	{ wǒ-kǎ-jě / kool-pǎ-rǐ [13][20] / poor-oo-rō [14] / mǒl-tǎ-rǎ mǎ-rō [15]	pǐ-jěr-dō [19]	koo-rǐ-dǎ-lǎ
Miorli {	{ mǎ-choom-bǎ / kǎ-jǔm-bǐ	jou-rǎ	kō-kō-bǎ-rō	pǐ-ou-lǐ	ǔm-mǎ-rō	pǐ-ǎ	kool-pǎ-rǐ	mǔn-ǔn-dǎ-lō	{ ǔm-bǎ-pǎ-rǐ / koon-gǎ-pǎ-rǐ
Goa ...	mǐng-gō-rǒng-ō / nǎ-goon-ǎ	mǐng-ǎ-rǎ / wǒ-jǎ-lǎ [17]	pǎ-kǎ-ǔn-lǐr / koon-jō-pǎ-rǐ [18]	mǐk-kǎ-mō			kool-pǎ-rǐ	kǎ-chǎ-pǎ-rǐ	oo-lō-pǎ-rǐ
Woonamurra	ǒ-goon	kǎ-kō-ǐn / pě-kō-rǎ [17]	kǎ-roo-ka [18]	yǔm-bǐ	yǔǒ-bō-rō		jǔng-gō-pǎ-rǐ	wōr-ktǐn	koo-rǐ-dǎ-lǎ
Mitakoodi ...	{ nǔl-ǐn-gǎ-lǐ [1] / mǎ-choom-bǎ [2] / nǎ-koon [3]	kǎ-koon	wǒ-jě-nǔn	yǔm-bě [7] / moor-ktǔn [5]	yǔp-poo-rō		joong-gō-pǎ-rǐ	kǎ-chǎ-pǎ-rǐ	koo-rǐ-dǎ-lǎ
Kalkadoon ...	{ nǔl-ǐn-gǎ-lǐ [1] / mǎ-choom-bǎ [2] / nǎ-koon [3]	ǔ-kǎ-moon-tǎ / pě-kō-rǎ [17]	jō-rō-ytǐn [4]	tō-kō [7] / koo-lǐ-tǔng-ō [5]	gǐm-jǎ	nǐp-pǔng-ǔp-pǎ [10] / wǔng-gǎ-nǔl-tǎ [11] / nǐ-ǒl-lǐ [12]	wō-dǐng-ǎ	kǎ-chǎ-pǎ-rǐ	wǒl-lǎ-ytǐn / wǔl-kǎ-rǐ-pǎ-rǐ [16]

[1] Rock wallaby. [2] Scrub kangaroo. [3] Mountain kangaroo. [4] Also a rat. [5] He-dog. [6] An old aged dog; often applied to an old man. [7] Dog in general.
[8] Aged slut. [9] = Woman-dog. [10] = Scrub turkey. [11] Native companion. [12] Diver-bird, shag. [13] = Nodding-head. [14] Feather-one.
[15] Multara (sect. 286) in possession. [16] Pelican. [17] Bandicoot. [18] Rat. [19] Sect. 43e. [20] Sect. 43m. [21] See sect. 74.

D

53.—Fauna and Flora—continued.

Tribe.	black crow.	corella, white cockatoo.	galah parrot.	whistler duck.	flock pigeon.	snake (in general).	iguana.	lizard.	frog.
Walookera ...	koo-nă-mă-yă-dă	ŭn-gă-pă-tŭn-gō	gŭ-lă gŭ-lă		mĭt-ĭt-bĭ-nă	too-ŭn-nă	ŏn-nă-mĭ-tă (9) kĕr-rō (10)	tă-dă-lĭ	ŭl-lĭ-mŭr-rĭ
Yaroinga ...	ŭng-gō-lă	ō-lĕt-lă-kă	ō-lĕn-jă	tŭm-bĭ-lă-lĕn-dă (2)	ŭl-ŭl-goo-lă	ŭr-dŭr-ră	{ ĕr-kĕr-kă (11) wool-kă-dă (12) lō-ŭd-jĕ-ră (10) }	â-mool-yă	mă-mō-tă
Undekerebina	ŭn-gă-lă	{ ă-rō-ră ŭng-ō-lă }	yŭ-ŭn-chĭ-ă		ŭl-ŭl-gă-lă	{ ŭp-mă lă-ră-ning-ă }	{ wŏl-kă-dă (9) lō-ŭd-jōr-ă (10) }	â-mool-yă	ŏr-grŭl-gă
Ulaolinya ...	wă-kĕr-dĭ	wŏ-ră-wĭd-dă	ō-lĭn-jă	kĭ-bĭl-yō	wŭl-ŭl-goo-lă	ŭl-yŭ-tĕ-rō	wŏl-koo-jă	moor-koo	kă-tĭ-lō-ă
Wonkajera...	wă-kĕr-dĭ	wâ-rĭ-wĭd-dă	ō-lĭn-jă	kĭ-bĭl-yō	wŏl-ŭl-goo-lă	wŏm-mă	{ wŏl-kŭl-yĕ-ră (9) wŏl-koo-jă (10) }	mĕr-koo	kă-tĭ-lō-ă
Karanya ...	wŏr-kĕr-dĭ	kŏl-lō-ră	boom-bă-bă-rō	kă-pool-yō	pâ-rou-lĭ	wŏm-mă	{ pâ-rĭ-pă-ră (9) kă-rĭng-ă-ră (10) }	mĕr-kō	koo-yĕr-kō
Pitta-Pitta...	{ wă-kĕr-dĭ wŏ-kă-lă }	kŏl-loo-ră	kă-lĕn-jĭ	kĭ-bĭl-yō	pâ-rou-lĭ	{ wŏm-mă koon-dă-ră (13) koon-rĭ-mă-ră (13) }	{ pă-ră-pă-ră (9) kă-rĭng-ă-ră (10) }	mĕr-koo	{ kă-tĭ-lō-ă (9) nĭng-ō (10) }
Miorli ...	wă-kĕr-dĭ	kŏl-lō-ră	gĕ-lŭn-jĭ	kĭ-bĭl-yō	pŏr-ō-ă-lĭ	koon-dă-ră	{ pĭ-rĭ-mool-kă (9) kă-rĭng-ă-ră (10) }	mĕr-kō	nĭng-ō
Goa ...	wă-kă-nă	koo-rĕl-lă	gĕ-lou-rō	bĕn-dō-ră	jĕ-rō-ă-lĭ	koon-dă-ră	pă-rĭ-pă-ră	wŏl-kă-dō	tĕ-ră-pă-jĭ
Woonamurra	wŏr-kă-rŭn	{ moor-rŭn kă-răm-bō-lă }	gĕ-lou-rō	wŏl-lă-dō	jĕ-rō-ă-lĭ	jĕn-yŭr koon-dă-ră (6), wŏl-gĕr (7) koo-rĭ-mă-ră (8)	mŭm-boo-ră-pă-rĭ	wŏl-kă-dō	jou-tŭn
Mitakoodi ...	wŏm-mĕ-răn	koo-lŏr-ă	gĕ-lă-rō	wŭl-lă-dō	jĕr-rō-ă-lĭ	jĕn-yŭr	mŭm-boo-rō-pă-rĭ	wŏl-kă-dō	{ jou-tŭn (9) mĕl-lĭ (10) }
Kalkadoon...	ō-rŭn	{ kŏl-lō-ră yŭ-wĭ-ră }	gĕ-lŏr-ō	{ jĭ-bŏl-ō tŭl-pŏ-pă-rĭ (1) }	{ jĕr-rō-ă-lĭ koo-lă-mă-rĭ (3) }	{ tō-ŭl, tă-kō-yŭn mĕl-kĕ-ră ă-tĕr (4), pă-rĭ pă-rĭ (5) }	mŭr-ră-rĭ	wŏl-kă-tō	{ ō-bŭn (9) ō-loo-yŭn (10) }

(1) Black duck.   (2) Cf. "foot."   (3) Another kind of pigeon.   (4) Water snake.   (5) Carpet snake.   (6) Green snake.   (7) Black snake.
(8) Carpet snake.   (9) Large species.   (10) Small species.   (11) Large river-iguana.   (12) Large mountain-iguana.   (13) Sect. 48g.

53.—Fauna and Flora—*continued*.

Tribe.	fish (in general).	spider.	common house-fly.	mosquito.	ant.	short meadow-grass.	pituri.
Walookera ...	*nĕr*-mĕ	*poo*-mă-tă	wă-nă-mă	*ŭl*-yĕ-rĬ	*noo*-lă	*ŭl*-lō	*mă*-jă
Yaroinga ...	*ĕr*-pŭng-ă	*yŭm*-bă	*ă*-mŭng-ă	yoo-*wŭn*-yoo	chĕk-tĭl-yă	*tĭn*-jă-*ră*	nĕ-ĕm-pă
Undekerebina ...	*yĕr*-păng-ă	*ĕm*-bă	*ă*-mŭng-ă	you-*wŭn*-yă	*yĕr*-ră	tŭn-jă-*ră*	ŭn-dă-kŏr-ă
Ulaolinya ...	{ *koo*-pă, *kŭm*-bo *kŭm*-bo	mĬl-yă-*roon*-dĬ-jă	{ *mŏ*-kĬ, koo-*tŭn*-jĕ-rĬ	*tĭn*-oo-Ĭ	*tĭ*-tă	*kool*-yŭ-rō	*pĭ*-tŭ-rĬ
Wonkajera ...	*kō*-pĕ	*kŭr*-ră	koo-*nŭn*-jĕ-rĬ	moo-*rool*-kă	*tă*-tă	*kō*-kă-pĕ	
Karanya ...		*kŭr*-ră	*koon*-jĕ-rĬ	*koon*-tĬ	*tĭ*-tă	*pō*-kă-ră	tĭ-*rŭm*-bō-lă
Pitta-Pitta ...	*kō*-pĕ (9)	*kō*-pō	{ *mŏ*-kĬ, *oo*-nō (1), koo-*nŭn*-jĕ-rĬ	{ *nŏ-rool*-kă, *ool*-lō (3)	*tă*-tă	*pō*-kă-ră	tă-*rĕm*-bō-lă
Miorli ...	*wĭ*-kă-rĬ	*mŭn*-dă-ră	*mŏ*-kĬ	*koon*-dĬ	*tĭ*-tă	*pō*-kă-ră	
Goa ...	{ *pă*-tă-pă-lō, *wŏr*-kă-nĬ	*tă*-mă-rō	*nĬ*-moo-nă	boong-*kĭn*-yă	*wă*-tō	*pŏ*-kă-ră (4), *yŭk*-kō (3), *poon*-jō-lō (5)	
Woonamurra ...	*bŭl*-bĬ	*koon*-mō-rō	*mĭlg*-nă	*mĕ*-gi-ă	*wĭ*-dō	*poon*-jool	
Mitakoodi ...	*bŭl*-bĬ	*kō*-bō	*mĕlg*-nă	{ *mĬ*-kĬ-ă, *băng*-gō *băng*-gō (2)	*wă*-tō	*kă*-tăr	[wanting]
Kalkadoon ...	*wŏr*-kă-rĬ	*kō*-pō	*mĕlg*-nă	*mĬ*-kă	*ĭ*-tĬ	*kă*-tăr	*mō*-dă

(1) Sand-fly. (2) A bee. (3) Also = hair of head. (4) *Cf.* Goa *pŏ*-kō-yō = hair-louse. (5) = hair-louse. (6) *Cf.* Pitta-Pitta term for "hair of head." (9) Sect. 43*a*.

54.—Other Objects of Nature.

Tribe.	sun.	moon.	star.	night.	fire.	water.	river, creek.	mountain, hill, rock, stone.
Waloobera ...	boo-mǎ-tǎ	bǐ-lǐ-moon-dǔng	mǎ-ě-nǐ	joo-ǔl-lǎ	mǎ-nǔl-ǎ	koo-chǐ-ǒ-kō ǒ-kō (¹)	yá-rǎ	wǔǎ-tǎ
Yaroinga ...	woo-jǐ-lǎ	ǔl-kǔn-tǎ	ǔn-jě-rǎ	yoong-wǎ	ǎk-kǎ-pǎ	{ quǎ-jǎ ǎ-bǔng-ǎ (¹) }	ǔ-rǎ	{ ǔr-woo-dǎ oo-di-tǎ }
Undekerebina ...	gǔn-yǎ	ǔl-kǔn-tǎ	oon-tǎ	yǔng-wǎ	wǐ-rǎ	quǎ-jǎ	ǔ-rǎ	á-pǒr-tǎ
Ulaolinya	wǒl-kǎ-ěn-jě-rǐ	jǐ-bǎ	jǐn-pǐ	koon-doong-ǎ	mǎ-kǎ	koo-tǎ	kǔǔl-lǎ	{ poor-ǐ (⁶) bǔǔl-ki bǔǔl-kǐ }
Wonkajera	wǒl-oo-kǎ	{ chǐ-bǎ jǔng-ǐ }	děng-kō	koon-doong-ǎ	mǎ-kǎ	koo-tǎ	kǔǔl-lǎ	poor-ǐ
Karanya...	wǒl-kǎ	jǐ-bǎ	jǐn-hǐ	yǎ-kǐ-ě yǎ-kǐ-ě	mǎ-kǎ	{ kǔl-lǎ-mǎ-rě-ǎ (¹) ǔp-pō }	pǎ-rǎ-pǐ	tá-pō
Pitta-Pitta	wǒl-kǎ	{ chǐ-bǎ (¹⁰) jǔng-ǐ }	chǐn-bǐ (¹⁰)	{ ǔ-mó-lō yě-kǎ yǎ-kǎ-yě }	mǎ-kǎ	{ koo-tǎ pǎǔ-lǎ (¹) kǔǔ-tǎ-mǔl-lǎ (⁹) }	{ pǎ-rǎ-pǐ kǔǔl-lǎ }	{ tǎ-pō, mǔl-lǒ-rō (⁸) nǐ-rǐ-wǐn-nǐ kǒ-kō-toon-gō (⁷) }
Miorli ...	wǒl-kǎ	jǐ-bǎ	jǐn-bǐ	ǔ-mō-lō	mǎ-kǎ	{ ǔp-pō koo-rǐ-ǎ (¹) (⁹) }	pǒ-rǎ-pǐ	nǐ-rǐ-wǐn-nǐ
Goa ...	toor-rō	nǔl-jǐ	ǔ-kō	wǐn-tǎ	oo-lǎ	kǎ-mō	pǒ-rǎ-gō	koonǐ-gō (⁵)
Woonamurra ...	kǔm-bǎ	kǎ-kǎ-rǎ	yó-kō	kǎ-bǐ-jǐ	pǐ-yō	koo-nō	mǒng-gǎ-lǎ	bǒ-grǐ
Mitakoodi ...	kǔm-bǎ	koo-nō koo-nō	ǔ-kō (⁴)	kǎ-bǐ-jǐ	yǔng-ō	yǔp-pō	mǒng-kǎ-lǎ	{ bǒ-grǐ moor-kō }
Kalkadoon ...	{ wǐn-nǎ-gǎ pǐn-jǎ-mō }	{ jǐ-bǎ toon-dǔǐ }	jǎr-kǎ	{ wǎ-dǔng-gǎ ǎ-rǎ-nǐ-yǐn }	ǒ-jǐtn	kō (⁵) (²)	kō-ǎ (⁹)	{ ǔn-dě-ǎ pǒr-tǎ }

(¹) Rain.   (²) Also = a small creek, etc.   (³) Also = rain.   (⁴) Cf. Mitakoodi term for "eye."   (⁵) Cf. Goa, etc., terms for "stone-knife."

(⁶) Cf. Ulaolinya term for "stone-knife."   (⁷) Cf. Pitta-Pitta, etc., term for "back, dorsum."   (⁸) Cf. Wonkajera term for "back, dorsum."

(⁹) Cf. Goa, etc., term for "back, dorsum."   (¹⁰) Sect. 43c.   (¹¹) Sect. 43a.

55.—Weapons, Utensils, etc.

Tribe.	shield.	boomerang (in general).	spear (in general).	wommera.	stone-knife.	fighting-pole.	koolamon.	dilly-bag.	net (fish).
Walookera ...	mi-ŭng-ŏr-ă	too-ŭl-lY	tĭ-ĕl-lY	yŭm-mă-ră	wŭl-tă	kă-nŭng-ō	I-tŭng-ō	yŭn-nă-goo-nă	wī-ĕ-chī-ă
Yaroinga ...	ŭl-goo-tă	ĕ-lā-lă	{ĕ-chă-tă[1] / ĕ-lĭn-yă[2]}	ă-mă-ră	ŭng-guă-dĭ-jă	wŭl-tă	mă-ră	boong-gŏr-ă	{quă-ră[6] / kă-nŭng-ă-ră[7]}
Undekerebina	ŭl-kō-tă	ĕ-lā-lă	yĕ-rĭ-chă-tă	ă-mă-ră	ĕn-quă-ră-jă	ŭt-năm-mă	oort-nă	ĕn-dŭng-ă-mă	kō-ă-ră
Ulaolinya ...	tĕr-rŏng	wŏr-ră	yĕ-jĕ-ră	ŭm-mĕ-ră	{ŭl-loo-kă / poor-I[13]}	koo-koo-rō	pŭl-lă	poong-koo	tŭng-ă
Wonkajera...	tĕr-rŭng-ō	wŏr-ră	ĕ-jĕ-ră		koo-yă	{nă-wă-ră / woo-jă woo-jă-rī}	pŭl-lă	boong-ō	tŭng-ă
Karanya ...	koon-bă-ră	tĕ-ră	nă-roo-ă	kă-rŭn-mĕ	wŏm-mĕ	{kō-kō-rō / wă-ră wă-ră}	kă-kī-lă	pă-tă-jĕ	mă-lī
Pitta-Pitta {	koon-pă-ră[14][16] wŏr-ră	bĭ-bă-poo-rō[15]	{nă-roo-ă / mă-kō-wă-tă}	kă-rŭm-mĭn	koo-yă	kō-koo-rō	{tă-kă[5] / koor-dō[4] / koon-pă-ră[14]}	bĕr-dă-jĕ	{mă-lī[6] / yĕ-pī[7] / mōk-wă-rī[8]}
Miorli ...	koon-bă-ră	jĕ-lă jĕ-lă	mool-chă	mŏr-ō	kŭng-gă-rI[12]	wă-rĕn-jă	kă-lă-pō	bĕr-dă-jĕ	mă-lī
Goa	koon-pă-ră	kool-kă	{moor-ĭ-jă / ktŭn-dŏr-ă}	moor-jă	kŭn-kŭr-I[12]	wă-rĕn-jă	{wĭng-ă-ră[9] / oom-bō[10]}	{poong-gō / koon-yă koon-yă}	{mō-kō-ă-rĭ[6] / yĕn-dĭ-lă[11] / poo-lă-roo[11]}
Woonamurra	koon-bă-ră	blĭ-dă-rō	tă-boon	ŭl-mĭn	kŭl-bō	tăl-lĭm-bĕ-rĭ	yĭng-gō	koon-yă koon-yă	moo-nă
Mitakoodi ...	mĭ-tă	yŭl-kă-bă-rĭ	koong-gŭn	ŭl-mĭn	{kŭng-gă-rĭ[12] / ktŭm-bō[13]}	tăl-lĭm-bĕ-rĭ	nŭng-koor	[wŭ-ră-kă]	{moo-nă[6] / bŭl-lĭn-yă[0]}
Kalkadoon...	mĭ-tă ytŭm-boo-roo	yŭl-kă-bă-rĭ	yō-kō	ŭl-mĭn	wō-yĕn	{wă-ră wă-ră / koo-lăng-ă-ră[3]}	chĕr-tō	{wō-tă / tou-ă-tă}	{wŭn-tō[5] / yŭl-pI[7]}

(¹) Little spear.　(²) Big spear.　(³) For women only.　(⁴) Big variety.　(⁵) Small variety.　(⁶) Fishing-net.　(⁷) Emu-net.　(⁸) Pigeon-net.
(⁹) For women.　(¹⁰) For men.　(¹¹) Head-net.　(¹²) For "shield" and "koolamon."　(¹³) Goa term for "rock," etc.　(¹⁸) Cf. Ulaolinya term for "mountain, rock."
(¹⁴) Cf. Pitta-Pitta terms for "shield" and "koolamon."　(¹⁵) Sect. 43e.　(¹⁶) Sect. 43g.　(¹⁷) Sect. 43m.
(¹⁸) = rather, a flint-flake before being made into a knife proper.　See sect. 149.

56.—Numerals.   **57.—Abstract Ideas.**

Tribe.	one.	two.	three.	four.	big mob, etc.	good.	bad.	big, large.	little.
Walookera ...	ār-gō-loo	kŏt-yă	pă-pō-lă	kŏt-yă kŭ-ră ār-gō-loo	kŏt-yă kŭ-ră ār-gō-loo	mō-kă	koong-yŏr-ă	pĕr-tă	tou-ĕr-ĭ
Yaroinga ...	â-woon-yĕ-ră	ŭt-tĕ-ră	wŏr-ĭt-ă	wĕrk-ă	ăn-gĕ-ră / â-mŏr-nă	moo-rŭng-ŏr-ă	ŭk-kŭng-ă	ĕl-quă	ŭk-kŭl-yă
Undekerebina	â-wŏn-yĕ-ră	ŭt-tĕ-ră	wŏr-ĭt-ă	ĕr-k-nĭ-ră	ŭr-r-pĭ-nă / noo-kă	mă-rŭng-ŏr-ă	ĭn-dĭ-jă	yĕl-quă	ŭk-kŭl-yă
Ulaolinya ...	goon-yă-lă	pă-koo-loo	pă-koo-loo goon-yă	ŭn-ĭt-tă	pă-rĭ	koo-yŭng-ō	mŭn-nă	wĭm-mă	jă-bă-lă-dĭ
Wonkajera...	goon-yă-lă	pă-koo-loo	pă-koo-loo goon-yă	nĭŭn-tă	pă-rĭ / noo-kă	gŏo-yăng-ō / pĭl-lă-rĭ	too-tĭ-mă	wĭm-mă / pĕr-kĭl-lĭ	jă-bō
Karanya ...	oo-roo-roo	pă-koo-lă	pă-kuo-lă(ng)-oo-roo	pă-koo-lă / pă-koo-lĭ	pă-rĭ	koo-yŭng-ō	pĭ-lĭ-ŭ	tŭ-ă-rĭ (1)	mŭn-lă-tĕ / tă-ĕ-ō
Pitta-Pitta...	oo-roo-roo	pă-koo-lă	pă-koo-lă(ng)-oo-roo	pă-koo-lă / pă-koo-lă	pă-rĭ	koo-yăng-ō / mĭ-ĕr-lĭ	mŭn-nă	tŭ-ă-rĭ (1) / pĕr-kĭl-lĭ / mŭng-kŏr-ă (2)	tĭ-ĕ
Miorli ...	oo-roo-roo	pă-koo-lă	pă-koo-lă-wŏt-ĭ-ră	pă-koo-lă / pă-koo-lă	ró-pō / mŏr-rĭn-dĭ	koo-yŭng-ō	jŭng-gă	mŭng-gŏr-ă	jă-bă-bō
Goa	koo-rŏn-yō	oo-ră	oo-ră-păn-tă koo-rŏn-yō	oo-ră-păn-tă / oo-ră-păn-tă	toong-ă	mŭn-yō / koon-jŭng-i-ă	wâ-ră-kŭt-tō	bĕ-ŭl-lă	nĭ-ou-ool-yă
Woonamurra	ĕ-nĕr	koor-tō	pĭlă-gă-ră ĕ-nĕr	pĭlă-gă-ră / pĭlă-gă-ră	pŭng-gō	mŭn-yō	mŭd-dĭ	măr-dō	chă-lō
Mitakoodi ...	pĕ-koon-dĭtl	koor-tō	ō-mĭn	ō-mĭn	ō-mĭn	mŭk-ktl	mŭt-tĭ	mă-dō	chă-lō / wŭl-kŭt-jă-kă-jă-koo-ro
Kalkadoon...	ĭ-ĕr	lŭ-ă-dĭ	mŭt-tă	mŭt-tă-nă	mŭt-tă-nă	chă-kă-mō / poo-tŭr	yĕ-lou-ră	ŏt-kŏr-ĭ (1) / you-tĭn	kŭt-yă-kō-lō

(1) Long, tall.   (2) Large in size, or quantity.

58.—Family Relationships [6].

Tribe	Pitta-Pitta, etc.	Kalkadoon.	Mitakoodi.	Miubbi [7].	Woonamurra.	Goa.	Wommin [8].
brother	{ŭ-tĭ / wŏŏng-ĭ [1]}	{tă-pō / ŭng-gō-lō [2]}	{nă-boon / boo-gŭl [2]}	{nă-boon / bŭ-jă-mŏn [2]}	{yŭb-bă / bō-gă [2]}	yŭp-pă	ŭ-rŭng-ă
sister	{kă-kō [10] / wŭng-ĭ [1]}	bō-ă	{moo-nă / too-rō-gō [3]}	koo-lă-mō	moo-nă	kă-mĭ	wŭŭ-nă
mother	ŭm-nă	nă-dō	mĕ-rĭ-gă	yă-kō-ră	mĕ-ră	yŭng-ă	yŭng-tĭn
mother's brother	ŭl-lō	bō-bĕ	ŭm-mĭn	nŭm-mĭn	kă-nă	kŭng-ă	bō-bĭ
father	ŭp-pĕ-rĭ	kō-lă	yŭ-tō	moo-jō	yŭŭ-dō	koo-pă	yŭp-pă-nă
father's sister	jŭm-mĭ	ŏrt-yĕr	kŭn-doon	kŭn-doon	koong-ĭ	kō-yĕ	pŭm-mă-nă
sister-in-law	chă-tă [10]	koong-ĭ	nŭŭ-tĕ-ă	nŭŭ-tĕ-ă	nŭŭ-tĕ-ă	păr-gō	pă-pĭn
brother-in-law	yŭŭn-dĭ	mō-tŭng-ō	chă-lĭn	moo-lă	chă-lĭn	nŭŭ-tĭ-nă	bŭŭ-jĭn
husband	nō-pō	ŭ-kō-tă	pĭn-jŭ				bŭŭ-jĭn
wife	{nō-pō / pŭn-dĭ-ră}	mō-jō	păn-yă	boo-loon	poo-ltĭl		pĕr-kō-nă
father's father, son's son	jĭ-ŭng-kă	mō-jō	poo-ltĭl	boo-loon	poo-ltĭl		poo-ltĭl
mother's father	ŭt-tă-nă [9]	chă-jĭ	tĭ-nŭm-boo-roo	bō-bō	mŭn-jĕ-ă		păn-jĭ
father's mother	ŭt-tă-nă	pă-pĭ	pă-pĭn	pă-pĭn	pă-pĭn		pă-pĭn
mother's mother, son's daughter	kŭn-yĭ-nĭ [10]	mō-jō	kŭm-mĭn	gŭm-mĭn	kŭm-mĭn		kŭm-mĭn
man's mother-in-law	g'ŭm-bĭ [4]	wă-poo-tō	wŏp-poo-tō [4]	mŭm-mĭ			
woman's mother-in-law	kă-lă-rĭ [5] [10]	wă-poo-tō	wŏp-poo-tō [5]	mŭm-mĭ			
son, daughter, brother's son, brother's daughter	{ŭt-tă-pĕ-ŭk-kă [9] / ŭt-tă-rĕ-ka [9]}	koong-gō-yō	ŭn-bŭn	nŭn-bŭn	kă-tă-gō	kŭn-dō	kŭn-dō
sister's son, sister's daughter		ŭl-lō	nĭ-tĭl	nĭ-tĭl	too-tĭn-nĭ		too-wŭn-nă

[1] Younger brother, younger sister. [2] Younger brother. [3] Younger sister. [4] Also, woman's son-in-law. [5] Also, woman's daughter-in-law.

[6] Sect. 59. The Family Relationships as expressed in the languages of the Upper Georgina Districts are unfortunately not given here, owing to the fact that at the time of my visit to those parts, I was ignorant of their existence, and therefore made no special inquiries concerning them.

[7] [8] See General Index. [9] Sect. 43k. [10] Sect. 43k.

CHAPTER III.

SOCIAL AND INDIVIDUAL NOMENCLATURE : CLASS SYSTEMS, &c.

CONTENTS.—Section 59. Introductory. 60. Patronym. 61. Gamomatronym. 62. Paedo-matronym. 63. Heteronym. 64. Geneanym. 65. Genealogical Tree in the Pitta-Pitta Language. 66. Aboriginal and European Relationship-Equivalents. 67. Autonym. 68. Climanym. 69. Summary of Nomenclature. 70. Similar Systems in other portions of Queensland. 71. Probable Interpretation of the Class-Systems.

59. Introductory.—The complex nature of this subject, and the difficulty usually encountered in rendering it intelligible, will be my excuse for offering such elaborate detail as follows. At the outset it must be remembered that every individual aboriginal is related or connected in one way or another, not only with all other members of his own tribe, but also with those of other friendlies perhaps hundreds of miles distant, the majority of whom he has neither seen, dreamt, or heard of. Unfortunately, in the white man's languages, there are no adequate words of suitable application to give expression to these connecting ties, and hence the various terms that will here be brought into requisition must be understood as having a far more extended range of signification than would ordinarily be applied to them among Europeans. Every male is primarily someone's brother, father, brother-in-law, or mother's brother, while every female is similarly someone's sister, mother, sister-in-law, or father's sister. But these terms, "brother," "sister," "father," "mother," &c., in addition to their usual and generally accepted signification of relationship-by-blood, express a class or group-connection quite independent of it. For instance, the aboriginal uses the one and the same term, *e.g.*, "mother," to indicate the woman that gave him birth, the sisters (virgin or not) connected with her by blood, and the dozens of women connected with her by class or group on a basis of classification to be presently expounded (sect. 63). The same thing holds equally true for "fathers," "sisters," "brothers," &c., of each commodity of which an individual may have perhaps a handful in the camp, and heaps elsewhere. The term "sister-in-law," as here used signifies any female member of the particular group or class from among whom a man is allowed to choose a mate: hence the one and the same appellative will include a man's wife, and her blood-sisters, as well as the multitudinous sisters—other women—of the same group (sect. 63). A "brother-in-law" has a correspondingly similar meaning. Among all these aboriginals it may be said that blood and class bear equal nominal significance.

60. The Patro-nym, or Tribal name: depending on the blood-father. Each person belongs to the same camp or tribe as his or her own blood-father. Thus, if a Pitta-Pitta man marries a Yunda woman, their child is Pitta-Pitta; on the other hand, supposing a Yunda male has a child by a Pitta-Pitta female, the youngster becomes a Yunda—the sex of the offspring being immaterial. Hence the name of the blood-father's tribe may be well designated as the patro-nymic of the individual.

61. The Gamo-matro-nym : the name depending upon the suitable marriage-union and the blood-mother. Every person in North-West-Central Queensland belongs to one of two classes, as follows :—

oo-tă-roo	or	*pá*-koo-tă	among the	Pitta-Pitta and their messmates.
oo-tă-roo	,,	*pá*-kŭt-tă	,, ,,	Mitakoodi.
woo-dă-roo	,,	*pá*-kŭt-tă	,, ,,	Miubbi.
ŭr-tă-roo	,,	*bŭr*-gŭt-tă	,, ,,	Roxburgh (Georgina R.) blacks.
woo-dă-roo	,,	*pá*-kŭt-tă	,, ,,	Woonamurra and Goa.
oo-tă-roo	,,	*mŭl*-lă-ră	,, ,,	Kalkadoon.

In the absence of a better etymological interpretation the resemblance at first sight of the above words to the equivalents of the Pitta-Pitta numerals for "one" and "two," respectively (sect. 36), is somewhat remarkable (*see* also sect. 62*f*).

[It may be noted that all the different appellatives mentioned in this chapter as being Pitta-Pitta are not limited alone to this particular tribe residing at Boulia, but equally refers to all the neighbouring friendlies occupying that tract of country which has been described in sects. 2 and 45 as the Boulia District.]

An Ootaroo can only marry a Pakoota, or *vice versâ*—that is to say, these two groups are exogamous; but the offspring follows the mother always. Thus, no matter its sex, the child of an Ootaroo mother becomes an Ootaroo, while that of a Pakoota mother becomes a Pakoota. This double signification of marriage-able-ness and of blood-mother-ship is intended to be expressed in the term—gamo-matronym—now applied.

62. The Paedo-matro-nym: the name particularising the blood-mother from her offspring. Every Ootaroo is either a *Koo*-poo-roo or a *Woong*-kō, while every Pakoota is either a *Koor*-kĭl-lă or a *Bŭn*-bŭr-ĭ: the etymological significa-tion of these four terms is not obtainable. If the blood-mother is a Koopooroo her offspring will be a Woongko, and *vice versâ*. If the blood-mother is a Koor-killa, her child is a Bunburi, and *vice versâ*—the sex of the offspring is again immaterial, the same four terms being applied equally to boys or girls, adult men or women, according to the particular one of the four groups of which they are members. Concerning this quartet of classes, a considerable amount of informa-tion is available, as follows:—

a. They are universal throughout the Boulia District among the dozens of different tribes occupying it; each tribe having these four identically-named divisions. Also outside this area, exactly the same terms are applied at Roxburgh on the Georgina River, among the Miorli and Goa people of the Middle and Upper Diamantina River, and among the aboriginals of the Cloncurry and Flinders Dis-tricts. In three other tribes of North-West-Central Queensland, with which I also personally became acquainted, these four groups are named as follows:—

TABLE I.

—	Kalkadoon.	Miubbi.	Workoboongo.
Koopooroo =	*Pă*-tĭng-ō	*Bă*-dĭng-ō	*Pă*-tĭng-ō
Woongko =	*Kŭng*-gĭ-lŭng-ō	Jĭm-mĭ-*lĭng*-ō	Jĭm-mĭ-*lĭng*-ō
Koorkilla =	*Mă*-rĭ-nŭng-ō	*You*-ĭng-ō	*Kă*-poo-dŭng-ō
Bunburi =	*Toon*-bē-ŭng-ō	*Măr*-ĭng-ō	*Măr*-ĭng-ō

Unfortunately, to the far west of the Boulia District, I omitted to gather information concerning the paedo-matronyms: at the time that I did have opportunities of conversing with the blacks of the Toko Ranges I was not suffi-ciently conversant with the Pitta-Pitta language to have even a tittle of suspicion of the importance of these four group-ships. Enough, however, has been stated to demonstrate their universality throughout North-West-Central Queensland.

b. Every individual, as soon as he or she arrives at the necessary age, is forbidden to eat—not necessarily to kill—certain animals, each paedo-matronymic group having its own particular group of things that are "tabooed." Notwith-standing very careful search, I can find no plants, trees, shrubs, or grasses, as prohibited. Upon this point these aboriginals appear to be extremely particular, and should one of them wilfully partake of that which is "tabooed," he is firmly convinced that sickness, probably of a fatal character, will overtake him, and that certainly it would never satisfy his hunger. Should such a delinquent be caught red-handed by his fellow-men, he would in all probability be put to death.

With regard to the food not permissible, it has to be noted that the lists of prohibited articles though constant for each tribe are not identical throughout North-West-Central Queensland for the corresponding paedo-matroyms: this fact appears to be well known enough among the more civilised and intelligent of the aboriginals

Among the Pitta-Pitta blacks and their messmates throughout the Boulia District, the Koopooroo are not allowed to eat iguana, whistler-duck, black-duck, "blue-fellow" crane, yellow dingo, and small yellow fish "with-one-bone-in-him":

the Woongko have to avoid scrub-turkey, eagle-hawk, bandicoot or " bilbi," brown
snake, black dingo, and "white-altogether" duck: the Koorkilla have to do without kangaroo, carpet-snake, teal, white-bellied brown-headed duck, various kinds
of "diver" birds, "trumpeter" fish, and a kind of black bream: the Bunburi dare
not eat emu, yellow snake, galah parrot, and a certain species of hawk.

Along the Leichhardt-Selwyn Ranges, the following dietaries are prohibited
by the Kalkadoon in their respective groups:—The Patingo (i.e., Koopooroo) do
not eat emu, carpet-snake, brown-snake, "mountain" snake, &c., porcupine,
wallaby, rat, opossum, and "mountain" kangaroo: the Marinungo (i.e., Koorkilla)
are not allowed to partake of pelican, whistler-duck, black-duck, turkey, "plain"
kangaroo (i.e., living on the plains), and certain kinds of fish: the Kunggilungo
(i.e., Woongko) are forbidden to eat emu, "mountain" kangaroo, wallaby, "sugar-
bag" (i.e., honey), porcupine, opossum, carpet, brown, and "mountain" snake, and
various fish: the Toonbeungo (i.e., Bunburi) must avoid whistler and wood-duck,
the "native-companion," rat, bandicoot, "plain" kangaroo, and carpet-snake.

In the Cloncurry District, with the Mitakoodi, the forbidden foods are in the
main—iguana, whistler-duck, and carpet snake for the Koopooroo; porcupine,
emu, and kangaroo for the Woongko; water snake, corella, eagle-hawk, black-duck,
and turkey for the Koorkilla; carpet snake and dingo for the Bunburi.

In the Flinders district, among the Woonamurra, the eagle-hawk and black
and brown snakes are principally prohibited to the Koorkilla; carpet snake and
emu to the Koopooroo; black duck and turkey to the Bunburi, &c.

On the Upper Diamantina the Goa Koopooroo avoid both emu and kangaroo.

c. The paedo-matronymic groups have also an important bearing at the first
and subsequent rites or initiation ceremonies which admit the individual to his or
her respective grade or rank in the social status. Thus the persons with whom
one may converse by speech or sign on certain of these occasions depends upon
these particular groups: so also does the choice of "bucks" in the general coition
to which, at her first initiation ceremony, the young woman is forced to submit
(sect. 305-6).

d. It has already been laid down (sect. 61) that an Ootaroo can only marry a
Pakoota, and vice versâ, that every Ootaroo is either Koopooroo or Woongko, that
every Pakoota is either Koorkilla or Bunburi. The members of these four
paedo-matronymic groups can be married as follows only, no other arrangement
being allowed, the rule being constant throughout the North-West-Central
Queensland district (sects. 323, 326).

TABLE II.

male.	+	female.	=	resulting offspring.
Koopooroo		Koorkilla		Bunburi
Woongko		Bunburi		Koorkilla
Koorkilla		Koopooroo		Woongko
Bunburi		Woongko		Koopooroo

Or, in the case of the Kalkadoons, the foregoing Table might be written:—

TABLE III.

male.	+	female.	=	resulting offspring.
Patingo		Marinungo		Toonbeungo
Kunggilungo		Toonbeungo		Marinungo
Marinungo		Patingo		Kunggilungo
Toonbeungo		Kunggilungo		Patingo

Or, with the Miubbi, it would read :—

TABLE IV.

male.	+	female.	=	resulting offspring.
Badingo		Youingo		Maringo
Jimmilingo		Maringo		Youingo
Youingo		Badingo		Jimmilingo
Maringo		Jimmilingo		Badingo

e. Domestic and private quarrels are generally settled or continued by members of the same paedo-matronymic group—*i.e.*, by the brothers or sisters, mother's brothers or mothers.

f. In spite of every inquiry I found no signs or passwords used to distinguish the individuals comprising one paedo-matronym from those of another: this is mutually made known by word of mouth. It will also be noted that when an aboriginal is asked what he is, he will almost always mention his paedo-matronym: only on subsequent interrogation will he state his gamo-matronym, thus giving one the impression that the latter is only of secondary importance. The etymological interpretation of the gamo-matronym suggested in sect. 61 is therefore quite within the realms of probability: indeed, in one of the local Normanton tribes, I could find no special terms for these two main primary divisions (sect. 70c), an absence which was also met with around Rockhampton and Gladstone (sect. 70d).

63. The Hetero-nym : depending on the particular paedo-matronymic group to which the individual belongs. It was shown in sect. 59 that every male is primarily someone's brother, father, brother-in-law, or mother's brother, while every female (virgin or matron) is someone's sister, mother, sister-in-law, or father's sister. This comes about as follows: The individuals belonging to the same paedo-matronym call each other " brothers " and " sisters," bearing in mind of course the reservations laid down at the commencement of this chapter, *i.e.*, whether related by blood or not; the members of the corresponding paedo-matronym (belonging to the same gamo-matronym) being " mother's brothers " and " mothers " to them whether related by blood or not. Similarly (in the opposite gamo-matronym) the members of the paedo-matronym into which they are allowed to marry are group-related to them as " brothers-in-law " and " sisters-in-law " (although not already married perhaps), while the individuals comprising the remaining paedo-matronym are called their " fathers " and " fathers' sisters," respectively, whether blood-related or not. Thus, throughout North-West-Central Queensland, every person holds one or other of these eight group-relationships to everybody else, the particular term of relationship varying of course with the particular paedo-matronyms to which the compared parties belong. It is owing to this circumstance of these particular names varying with the paedo-matronym that the adoption of the term " hetero-nym " has appeared suitable to give expression to them.

To show this arrangement the more clearly, the following table has been compiled, in which the lists can be read either vertically or horizontally. To learn from it the particular hetero-nymic group-relationship subsisting between any two people, no matter the tribe or tribes to which they belong, one has only to look along the horizontal line for the one person and down the vertical column for the other : where these intersect one has what is required.

TABLE I.

gamo-matronym.	OOTAROO.				PAKOOTA.			
paedo-matronym.	KOOPOOROO.		WOONGKO.		KOORKILLA.		BUNBURI.	
—	male.	female.	male.	female.	male.	female.	male.	female.
Koopooroo ...	brother	sister	mother's brother	mother	brother-in-law	sister-in-law	father	father's sister
Woongko ...	mother's brother	mother	brother	sister	father	father's sister	brother-in-law	sister-in-law
Koorkilla ...	brother-in-law	sister-in-law	father	father's sister	brother	sister	mother's brother	mother
Bunburi ...	father	father's sister	brother-in-law	sister-in-law	mother's brother	mother	brother	sister

The above English equivalents, then, with their additional significations already mentioned (sects. 59, 63), are the nearest approaches I can find for the following aboriginal heteronymic terms in the principal ethnographical districts:—

TABLE II.

District ...	BOULIA.	LEICHHARDT-SELWYN.	CLONCURRY.	(CANOBIE COUNTRY.)	FLINDERS.	(UPPER DIAMANTINA COUNTRY.)	(MULLANGERA, ETC., COUNTRY.)
Tribe ...	Pitta-Pitta and Messmates.	Kalkaloon.	Mitakoodi.	Miubbi.	Woonamurra.	Goa.	Wommin.
brother ...	tí-tí	tǎ-ŋō	nǎ-boon	nǎ-boon	yǎl-bǎ	yǎp-pǎ	ū-rǐnǧ-ǎ
sister ...	kǎ-kō	lǔ-ǎ	moo-nǎ	koo-lǎ nō	moo-nǎ	kǎ-mī	wǎl-mǎ¹
mother ...	ǎm-mǎ	mǎ-dō	mǔ-rǐ-gǎ	pǎ-kǎ-rǎ	mǔ-rǐ	yǎnǧ-ǎ	yǎnǧ-fm
mother's brother ...	ǎl-lō	lū-lǎ	ǎm-mīn	wǎm-mīn	kǎ-nǎ	kǎnǧ-ǎ	bō-bī
father	ǎp-pǎ-rī	kō-lǎ	yǎt-tō	moo-jō	yǎl-dō	koo-pǎ	yǎp-pǎ-nǎ
father's sister ...	jǎm-mī	ǒrt-yǐr	kǔn-doon	kǔn-doon	koonǧ-I	kǐ-yǐ	pǐm-mǎ-nǎ
sister-in-law ...	chǎ-tā	koonǧ-I	nǎt-tā-ǎ	nǎt-tā-ǎ	nǎt-tā-ǎ	pǎr-gō	pǎ-pīn
brother-in-law ...	yǎn-dī	mǎ-īnǧ-ō	chǎ-lfn	moo-lǎ	chǎ-lfn	nǎt-tī-nǎ	bǐl-jīn

In the case of the heteronyms "brother" and "sister," a distinction is sometimes made between those older or younger than the person speaking of them. In the Pitta-Pitta and cognate languages, a younger brother or sister is *wŭng*-ĭ, those who are older being designated as above: with the Kalkadoon, while *bō*-ă signifies both older and younger sister, the term *ŏng*-gō-lō indicates a younger brother: the Mitakoodi speak of a younger brother as *boo*-gŭl, a younger sister as *too*-rō-gō : the Miubbi call a younger brother *bá*-jă-mŏn, while *koo*-lă-mō is applied to both an older and younger sister : the Woonamurra speak of a younger brother as *bō*-gâ.

Hence, the preceding group-relationship Table I. of heteronymic (English) terms may be written for the Boulia District, with the Pitta-Pitta equivalents as follows :—

TABLE III.

paedomatronym	KOOPOOROO.		WOONGKO.		KOORKILLA.		BUNBURI.	
sex	m.	f.	m.	f.	m.	f.	m.	f.
Koopooroo ...	titi	kako	ullo	umma	yundi	chata	upperi	jummi
Woongko ...	ullo	umma	titi	kako	upperi	jummi	yundi	chata
Koorkilla ...	yundi	chata	upperi	jummi	titi	kako	ullo	umma
Bunburi ...	upperi	jummi	yundi	chata.	ullo	umma	titi	kako

In the Mitakoodi language of the Cloncurry District, the same table may be framed thus :—

TABLE IV.

paedomatronym	KOOPOOROO.		WOONGKO.		KOORKILLA.		BUNBURI.	
sex	m.	f.	m.	f.	m.	f.	m.	f.
Koopooroo ...	naboon	moona	ummin	meriga	chalin	nuttea	yutto	kundoon
Woongko ...	ummin	meriga	naboon	moona	yutto	kundoon	chalin	nuttea
Koorkilla ...	chalin	nuttea	yutto	kundoon	naboon	moona	ummin	meriga
Bunburi ...	yutto	kundoon	chalin	nuttea	ummin	meriga	naboon	moona

For the Kalkadoon of the Leichhardt-Selwyn Ranges the same would read—

TABLE V.

paedomatronym	PATINGO, i.e., Koopooroo.		KUNGGILUNGO, i.e., Woongko.		MARINUNGO, i.c., Koorkilla.		TOONBEUNGO, i.e., Bunburi.	
sex	m.	f.	m.	f.	m.	f.	m.	f.
Patingo ...	tapo	boa	bobe	mado	moungo	koongi	kola	ortyer
Kunggilungo ...	bobe	mado	tapo	boa	kola	ortyer	moungo	koongi
Marinungo ...	moungo	koongi	kola	ortyer	tapo	boa	bobe	mado
Toonbeungo ...	kola	ortyer	moungo	koongi	bobe	mado	tapo	boa

Finally, in the Miubbi language, Canobie country, our heteronymic table could be expressed as—

TABLE VI.

paedomatronym	BADINGO, i.e., Koopooroo.		JIMMILINGO, i.e., Woongko.		YOUINGO, i.e., Koorkilla.		MARINGO, i.e., Bunburi.	
sex ...	m.	f.	m.	f.	m.	f.	m.	f.
Badingo ...	naboon	koolamo	nummin	yakora	moola	nuttea	moojo	kundoon
Jimmilingo ...	nummin	yakora	naboon	koolamo	moojo	kundoon	moola	nuttea
Youingo ...	moola	nuttea	moojo	kundoon	naboon	koolamo	nummin	yakora
Maringo ...	moojo	kundoon	moola	nuttea	nummin	yakora	naboon	koolamo

As will be shown in sect. 65, the heteronyms may be occasionally supplanted by special geneanyms.

64. The Genea-nym: the name depending on the person's own true family connections (as understood among Europeans). The various terms denoting such relationship would, in English, comprise the following :—

a. In the contemporary generation : brother, sister, husband, wife, husband's brother, wife's brother, husband's sister, wife's sister, male cousin, female cousin. The translations into the various languages of the terms for brother, sister, husband's and wife's brother (brother-in-law), husband's and wife's sister (sister-in-law) have already been given in the heteronymic tables (sect. 63). No special names are applied to denote male or female cousins ; they are simply known by the particular heteronymic groups into which they fall—*i.e.*, either as brothers or sisters (if father's brother's-sons and -daughters, mother's sister's-sons and -daughters) or brothers-in-law or sisters-in-law (if father's sister's-sons and -daughters, or mother's brother's-sons and -daughters). (*See* cousin-ship, Genealogical Table, in sect. 65.) With regard to husband and wife, the Kalkadoon calls the husband *ŭ*-kō-tă, the wife bearing the name of a sister-in-law—*i.e.*, the group from which he is allowed to choose her ; the Mitakoodi name husband and wife respectively *pŭn-jĭl* and *pŭn*-yă ; the Miubbi and Woonamurra have nothing to express them further than as brother-in-law and sister-in-law ; while the Pitta-Pitta applies the word *nō*-pō to both, the term *pŭn*-dĭ-ră being retained only for a man's sweetheart, the wife of his own personal choice (not the one assigned him by the community). (*See* sect. 323.)

b. In the preceding generations: father, mother, a father's-brother, -sister, -father and -mother, a mother's-brother, -sister, -father and -mother, a man's mother-in-law and father-in-law, a woman's father-in-law and mother-in-law. The aboriginal equivalents for father and mother, father's sister, and mother's brother, have already been noted in the heteronyms (sect. 63, Table II.) : father's brother and mother's sister are called respectively by the same names as for father and mother (sect. 59). The reason why the terms uncle and aunt are avoided will thus be rendered intelligible : as I will next show, the words grandfather, grandson, nephew, with their female equivalents, are similarly studiously omitted.

In connection with the remaining terms of this category, it is curious to note that, in all these tribes, a father's father passes by the same name as a son's son, a mother's mother by the same as a son's daughter ; in some—*e.g.*, Pitta-Pitta—a man's mother-in law goes by the same name as a woman's son-in-law, a woman's father-in-law the same as a man's daughter-in-law. In all of these tribes a father's father is designated differently from a mother's father, and a father's mother differently from a mother's mother. The Pitta-Pitta, Kalkadoon, and Mitakoodi speak of a man's father-in-law by the same heteronymic term as a man's mother's-brother. Another curiosity is the existence of a mutual term for the relationship—unknown among us Europeans—between the mother of the husband and the mother of the wife. These particular connections as expressed by the different tribes may be tabulated as follows :—

TABLE I.

—	Pitta-Pitta. and mess-mates.	Kalkadoon.	Mitakoodi.	Miubbi.	Woonamurra.
Father's father (or son's son)	jĭ-ŭng-kă	mō-jō	poo-lŭl	boo-loon	poo-lŭl
Mother's father ...	ŭt-tă-nă	chă-jĭ	tĭ-nŭm-boo-roo	bō-bō	mŭn-jē-ă
Father's mother ...	ŭt-tă-nă	pă-pĭ	pă-pĭn	pă-pĭn	pă-pĭn
Mother's mother (or son's daughter)	kăn-yĭ-nĭ	mō-jō	kŭm-mĭn	gŭm-mĭn	kŭm-mĭn
Man's mother-in-law	yŭm-bĭ (¹)	wă-poo-tō	wŏp-poo-tō (¹)	măm-mĭ	koong-ĭ (²)
Woman's mother-in-law	kă-lă-rĭ (³)	wă-poo-tō	wŏp-poo-tō (³)	măm-mĭ	—— (⁴)
Man's father-in-law...	ŭl-lō (⁶)	bō-bĕ (⁶)	ŭm-mĭn (⁶)	tŭl-ār-mă (⁷)	—— (⁴)
Woman's father-in-law	ŭn-jă-koot-tă (⁵)(⁹)	—— (⁴)	mŭn-dă-rĭ (⁵)	tŭl-ār-mă (⁵)	—— (⁴)
Relationship between husband's and wife's mothers	ŭt-tă-kă-lō (⁹)	—— (⁴)	mă-koo-dō	—— (⁴)	wŏr-rĭng-ō-mĭ-kă-ră (⁸)

(¹) Also = woman's son-in-law.   (²) *i.e.* Heteronym = father's sister.   (³) Also = a woman's daughter-in-law.   (⁴) Unfortunately omitted to inquire.   (⁵) Also = a man's daughter-in-law. (⁶) Heteronym = mother's brother.   (⁷) Note the special term—*not* heteronymic.   (⁸) In the Wommin language *wŏr-rĭng-ō* is a son's son or daughter.   (⁹) Sect. 43*k*.

c. In the succeeding generations : son, daughter, son's son and daughter, daughter's son and daughter, brother's son and daughter, sister's son and daughter, a man's son-in-law and daughter-in-law, a woman's son-in-law and daughter-in-law. The translation of son's son and son's daughter, identical with father's father and mother's mother respectively, has just been dealt with : daughter's son and daughter's daughter have no special names applied to them beyond the ordinary heteronyms into which they fall—*i.e.*, brother-in-law and sister-in-law (*see* Table I., sect. 63 : also Table sect. 65). In all these tribes, son, daughter, brother's son, brother's daughter have no distinguishing terms, each language having but one word to describe them all : similarly, sister's son and sister's daughter pass by the same cognomen. Thus :—

TABLE II.

—	Pitta-Pitta, etc.	Kalkadoon.	Mitakoodi.	Miubbi.	Woonamurra.
Son, daughter, brother's son, brother's daughter	ŭt-tă-pē-ŭk-kă	koong-gō-yō	ŭn-bŭn	năn-bŭn	kă-tă-gō
Sister's son, sister's daughter	ŭt-tă-rē-kă	ŭl-lō	nĭ-ŭl	nĭ-ŭl	too-ŭn-nĭ

The term applied by a man to his daughter-in-law is often, *e.g.*, in the Pitta-Pitta language, the same as that applied by a woman to her father-in-law (sect. 64*b*). In the case of a woman's daughter-in-law, this individual is identical with a woman's mother-in-law among the Pitta-Pitta and Mitakoodi : by the Kalkadoon she is known as *ŭl-lō* (*i.e.*, sister's daughter, Table II., sect. 64), and by the Miubbi as *pă-pĭn* (*i.e.*, father's mother, Table I., sect. 64). Similarly, a woman's son-in-law is known by the same name as a man's mother-in-law among the Pitta-Pitta and Mitakoodi : by the Kalkadoon he is known again as *ŭl-lō* (*i.e.*, sister's son, Table II., sect. 64), and by the Woonamurra as *ŭn-bŭn*. In all tribes a man speaks of his son-in-law as his sister's son.

65. Genealogical Tree.—This table has been drawn up in order to show more graphically the connection of group and blood-relationship—*i.e.*, heteronyms, &c., and geneanyms—existing between one individual and all the others constituting a small tribal encampment, say, of the Pitta-Pitta blacks.   For the sake of convenience and simplicity the number of terms given is the minimum consistent with the proper elucidation of the different relations by which the central figure, Charlie, a Koopooroo male, would personally know and speak of them.   The diversity of English equivalents for identical aboriginal terms is very striking.   Where special geneanyms are present, the heteronyms are discarded : *e.g.*, a man speaks of his paternal grandfather as jiungka although he is primarily a titi (brother), a member of the heteronymic group into which he is born.

66. Aboriginal and European Relationship-equivalents.— From the immediately preceding and other tables we see now how "Charlie," our Pitta-Pitta Koopooroo male adult, can speak of any other member, not only in the camp, but outside of it, as being one or other "connection" of his as follows :—

paedomatromym	male.	female.	European equivalent.
	titi	kako	blood : -brother, -sister
	,,	,,	group : -brother, -sister
	,,	,,	father's brother's : -son, -daughter
Koopooroo	,,	,,	mother's sister's : -son, -daughter
	jiungka	kanyini	father's father, mother's mother
	,,	,,	son's : -son, -daughter
	ullo	umma	blood-mother's : -brother, -sister
	,,	,,	group-mother's : -brother, -sister
	,,	,,	father's : -sister's husband, -brother's wife
		,,	blood-mother
Woongko ...		,,	group-mother
	uttareka	uttareka	blood-sister's : -son, -daughter
	,,	,,	group-sister's : -son, -daughter
		unjakootta	son's wife
	yundi	chata	blood : -sister's husband, -brother's wife
	,,	,,	group : -sister's husband, -brother's wife
	,,	,,	mother's brother's : -son, -daughter
Koorkilla ...	,,	,,	daughter's : -son, -daughter
	uttana	uttana	mother's father : father's mother
		nopo	wife
	upperi	jummi	blood-father's : -brother, -sister
	,,	,,	group-father's : -brother, -sister
	,,	,,	mother's : -sister's husband, -brother's wife
	,,		blood-father
Bunburi ...	,,		group-father
	uttapeukka	uttapeukka	son, daughter
	,,	,,	blood-brother's : -son, -daughter
	,,	,,	group-brother's : -son, -daughter
		yumbi	wife's blood-mother

The Genealogical Tree of a male Koopooroo Pitta-Pitta Aboriginal, e.g., "Charlie."

gamo-matronym	OOTAROO.				PAKOOTA.			
paedo-matronym … …	KOOPOOROO.		WOONGKO.		KOOBKILLA.		BUNBURI.	
sex … … …	male.	female.	male.	female.	male.	female.	male.	female.
heteronym (with primary signification)	titi = brother.	kako = sister.	ullo = mother's brother.	umna = mother.	yundi = brother-in-law.	chata = sister-in-law.	upperi = father.	jummi = father's sister.

jiungka = paternal grandfather
kanyini = maternal grandmother
uttana = maternal grandfather
uttana = paternal grandmother
upperi = father
jummi = father's sister

umna = mother's sister
umna = mother
ullo = mother's brother
upperi = father

titi = brother
kako = sister
yundi = sister's husband
chata = brother's wife

"Charlie"
titi = group-brother
uttareka (1) = sister's son
uttareka (1) = sister's daughter
chata = group-brother's wife
uttapeukka (2) = brother's son
uttapeukka (2) = brother's daughter
upperi = father's brother
jummi = father's sister

ullo = wife's father
uttapeukka (3) = group-brother's son
uttapeukka (3) = group-brother's daughter
upperi = group-brother's son
uttapeukka (4) = group-brother's daughter
nopo = wife
yumbi = wife's mother

Generations immediately preceding, succeeding, and the contemporary generation.

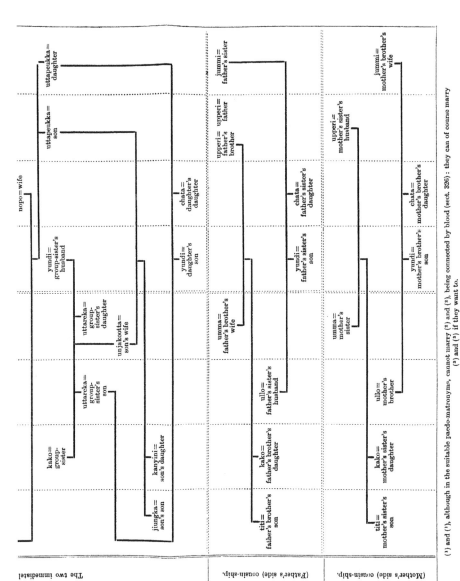

(¹) and (²), although in the suitable paedo-matronyms, cannot marry (¹) and (³), being connected by blood (sect. 326): they can of course marry (²) and (³) if they want to.

E

67. The Auto-nym: personal or individual name.

In the Boulia District the names applied to individuals are based for the most part upon physical peculiarities or objects of nature. Whether any connection is to be traced between parents and their offspring, so far as names is concerned, it is difficult to decide absolutely, though probably it would be negative ; in great measure this uncertainty on my part is due to the determined unwillingness on the part of survivors to mention anything concerning those deceased, their names, exploits, or other particulars (sects. 190, 289).

The names of women are given them at birth, and throughout life do not usually change; exceptions, however, are met with in cases where some physical defect or unusual habit is brought into prominence.

So-called " pet " names, *e.g.*, *poo*-koo-too (= a small ant crawling), *oo*-too (= small fish skimming the water surface), &c., are applied to young males, but these become dropped at the first of the initiation ceremonies (sect. 300, &c.), when, amid much ceremony, they receive their permanent names.

I have never met with two people bearing the same adult individual names. Some of these latter, with their meanings, collected in the Boulia District, are the following :—

a. MALE.—

Moor-ră-*wĭl*-ŭl-lĭ.—The one who is always cutting sticks (*cf.* moorra = stick).

Wŭn-jē-pĕ-rĭ.—He who always sits in the shade (*cf.* wunji-wunji = bough shed).

Mool-kō *mǎ*-rō.—Enduring as a stone ; (literally = stone-possessor).

Mŭr-ră-*pĭ*-tē-ă-mŭl-lĭ.—The angry fellow, the striker with the hand (*cf.* murra = hand, pite- = to strike).

Tēr-poo-lĭ.—He who has been speared through the thigh.

Chǎ-koo-lĭ.—One who has blood on him.

Chē-*koo*-tō-*koo*-tō.—Sticks his elbows out when walking.

Bĭl-kă-bŭr-ĭ.—Fish-eater (*cf.* bulkaberi = species of bream).

Rē-joo-pă-*rē*-ă.—One who is always chattering.

Poor-ĭ-chĭ-lĭ.—Makes the dust fly about in hot weather, when walking.

Yē-rŭng-ĭ-lĭ.—The tree-climber.

Jǎl-kĭ-lĭ.—He who can use the fire-stick.

Mŭl-loon-doo-mŭl-*lē*-lĭ.—The one who never greases himself (*cf.* mullo = sign of negation, oondamulle- = to grease oneself).

(*b*) FEMALE.—

Mĕl-*lĭ*-ĭn-ă.—A species of small pink flower.

Wĭ-ēr-pă.—Long-necked, like an emu.

Mē-lĕ-lă.—Slow, like a caterpillar on the ground (*cf.* mie = ground).

Pǎ-tă-*mǎ*-rō.—The " kopi " (*i.e.*, white plaster) possessor, and so " the one in mourning." Hence also applied to a widow or widower.

Yŭn-ă-ră.—The one who is always going away.

Choo-kă-*ŭng*-ă-lĭ.—A small kind of snake that moves about very rapidly.

Mŭn-dă-*wĭ*-ă-yă.—The woman who is always soliciting a man.

Bĭl-lă-*rŭng*-ō.—She who runs away when a boomerang is thrown.

Toon-toon-*dwē*-ă.—She who is always crying (*cf.* twinje = to cry).

Nēng-ă.—Skipping about like a little frog (*cf.* nengo = frog).

Mŭl-loon-dŭng-ō.—She who won't dip her feet in the water (*cf.* mullo = sign of negation).

Mē-lă-*oo*-tĕ-rĭ.—The woman with a good nose (*cf.* melya = nose).

68. To make the subject the more complete, I might include here the **Clima-nym**, the " step-ladder " or titular name of the individual, depending upon his social degree, his status on the social ladder. Details of the various steps,

F

ceremonies, or degrees over which a person passes to win these honours are given in sects. 300-315. For the present it will be sufficient to draw attention to the particular terms applied to the members of these degrees in certain tribes as follows :—

—	sex.	Pitta-Pitta, &c.	Kalkadoon.	Yaroinga.	Mitakoodi.	Woonamurra.
At first sign of puberty	m.	koo-ē-rĭ	koo-ē-rĭ	ō-wē-ă	{ kŭng-gĭ { kŭr-rŭng-gâ	gĭng-gō
	f.	mĭ-rĭ (¹)	{ wŏm-pă { ŭn-dō (²)	ŭl-lā-ŏk-ă	mŭng-gŭn	nŭng-gŭn
After 1st degree	m.	yŭp-pĭ-ĕ-rĭ	yŭp-pă-rā-rĭ	ŭr-goo-tă	yŭp-pĭ-ĕ-rĭ	yŭp-pĭ-ĕ-rĭ
„	f.	kă-nă-rĭ	·ē-ră-jĭ	ŭmb-bá	ē-ră-jĭ	ē-ră-jĭ
After 2nd degree	m.	kă-tĭ-kă-tĭ mă-rō	wō-brŭn-jĭ		ō-brŭn-jĭ	ō-brŭn-jĭ
„	f.	„	wŏl-loo-mă-ră		wŏl-lă-mă-ră	bŭn-yá (³)
After 3rd degree	m.	koo-koo-rĭ mă-rō	kŭn-tă-pē-ŭng-ō		nĭ-nĭng-ĭn-nĭ	mŭr-ŭk-kŭn-dĭ
„	f.	„	moon-tă-moon-tă		mŭr-ŭk-kŭn-dĭ	
After 4th degree	m.	mŭr-ŭk-kŭn-dĭ			mŭr-ŭk-kŭn-dĭ	
„	f.	„				

(¹) *Wă*-pă-rĭ among the Ulaolinya.   (²) Doubtfully correct.   (³) A full-grown adult woman.

69. In recapitulation, the complete nomenclature of any individual would be enumerated somewhat as follows :—

Patronym	e.g.	...	...	Pitta-Pitta, Kalkadoon
Gamo-matronym	„	...	...	Ootaroo, Pakoota
Paedo-matronym	„	...	...	Koopooroo, Woongko
Heteronym	„	...	...	Titi, Kako
Geneanym	„	...	...	Jiungka, Uttana
Autonym	„	...	...	Moorrawilulli, Melliina
Climanym	„	...	...	Yuppieri, Murukkundi

70. Similar Systems of Nomenclature in other portions of Queensland.—Outside the immediate districts (North-West-Central) under consideration, I have personally found similar systems of social and individual nomenclature among tribes living in other parts of Queensland.

(*a*) The *Pŭr*-gō-mă tribe, inhabiting the Palm Isles, a little to the north of Townsville.

Gamo-matronyms.—*Nă*-kă (=Ootaroo, sect. 61), *Tŭn*-nă (=Pakoota, sect. 61).

Paedo-matronyms (Naka=) Koopooroo, Woongko, (Tunna=) Koorkilla, Bunburi. (Identical with those given in sect. 62.)

Heteronyms (which it is well to compare with Table II., sect. 63)—

Brother	...	*kŭt*-tă		Father ...	...	*ă*-pō
Sister	...	*ŭp*-pă-rĭ		Father's sister ...		*kŭm*-mĭ
Mother	...	*ă*-kă		Sister-in-law	...	*kă*-ĕn
Mother's brother	*kou*-ă		Brother-in-law ...		*bŭl*-jĭn

Whence the heteronymic table (Table I., sect. 63) of Purgoma group-relationship equivalents can be written as follows :—

gamo-matronym ...	NAKA.				TUNNA.			
paedo-matronym ...	KOOPOOROO.		WOONGKO.		KOORKILLA.		BUNBURI.	
—	male.	female.	male.	female.	male.	female.	male.	female.
Koopooroo ...	kutta	uppari	koua	aka	buljin	kaen	apo	kummi
Woongko	koua	aka	kutta	uppari	apo	kummi	buljin	kaen
Koorkilla	buljin	kaen	apo	kummi	kutta	uppari	koua	aka
Bunburi	apo	kummi	buljin	kaen	koua	aka	kutta	uppari

Geneanyms (cf. sect. 64) :—

Husband, wife = expressed by the same heteronymic terms as brother-in-law and sister-in-law respectively.

Father's brother = father.

Mother's sister = apparently a new geneanymic term, $b\breve{o}l$-lŏng-gō.

Father's father, son's son = koo-pă.

Mother's father = $n\hat{a}$-jĭ. Father's mother = koom-bō.

Mother's mother, son's daughter = pă-pĭ.

Man's mother-in-law = wĭ-mĭn-gĭl.

Woman's son-in-law = pĭm-mō.

Man's father-in-law = kou-ă (i.e., heteronym, mother's brother).

Woman's father-in-law = tâ-rō.

Man's daughter-in-law, a man's sister's son or daughter = kŭp-pă.

Son = ĭn-dŭl.   Daughter = gē-ri.

(b) The Jou-ōn sub-tribe, with headquarters at Cooktown, travelling to the Laura, Maytown, and the Bloomfield.

Gamo-matronyms.—Chē-pâ (= Ootaroo, sect. 61), Jŭn-nă (= Pakoota, sect. 61).

Paedo-matronyms.—(Chepa =) Koopooroo, Woongko, (Junna =) Koorkilla, Bunburi.   (Identical with those given in sect. 62.)

Heteronyms (cf. Table II., sect. 63) :—

Brother	...	yŭp-pă	Father ...	...	ba-bă
Sister	...	kâ-nŭl	Father's sister ...		mō-kâ-gă
Mother	...	nâ⸱mō	Sister-in-law	...	chē-rŭl
Mother's brother	mō-kŭr		Brother-in-law ...		dŏn-yō.

Whence the heteronymic table (Table I., sect. 63) of Jouon group-relationship equivalents can be drawn up as follows :—

Gamo-matronym ...	CHEPA.				JUNNA.			
Paedo-matronym ...	KOOPOOROO.		WOONGKO.		KOORKILLA.		BUNBURI.	
—	male.	female.	male.	female.	male.	female.	male.	female.
Koopooroo ...	yuppa	kanul	mokur	namo	donyo	cherul	baba	mokaga
Woongko	mokur	namo	yuppa	kanul	baba	mokaga	donyo	cherul
Koorkilla	donyo	cherul	baba	mokaga	yuppa	kanul	mokur	namo
Bunburi	baba	mokaga	donyo	cherul	mokur	namo	yuppa	kanul

Geneanyms (*cf*. sect. 64) :—

Husband, wife = expressed by the same heteronymic terms as brother-in-law and sister-in-law respectively.

Father's father, son's son = *nă*-jĭ.

Mother's father = *ŭm*-mō.   Father's mother, son's daughter = *pá*-pĭ.

Mother's mother = *kŭm*-mĭ.

Man's mother-in-law = pē-*ŏrl*.

Son, daughter, a man's son's wife, a woman's daughter's husband = *ū*-mŏr.

Man's sister's son = jō-*i*.

Man's sister's daughter = *nŏr*-jŏr.

Man's father-in-law = *ō*-jŏr.

Woman's father-in-law = *mō*-kŭr (*i.e.*, heteronym for mother's brother).

(*c*) The *Wŏl*-lăng-ă-mă (originally from between Spear Creek and Croydon), one of the four tribes occupying the country in the neighbourhood of Normanton, Gulf of Carpentaria.

Gamo-matronym.—No term obtainable (sect. 62*f*).

Paedo-matronyms.—*Rā*-ră (= Koopooroo), *Răn*-yă (= Woongko), *ă*-*wŭng*-ă (= Koorkilla), *Loo*-ră (= Bunburi).

Heteronyms (which it is well to compare with Table II., sect. 63) :—

Brother	...	*ĕl*-ĭn-jō-kă	Father's sister	...	*loom*-bă
Sister	...	*kŏr*-pĕt-yă	Father	... ...	*mă*-ră *mă*-ră
Mother	...	*twŭng*-ŭl-wŭr-rŭl	Sister-in-law	...	*ŭn*-nĕl
Mother's brother	*woo*-lŭn-dŭn	Brother-in-law	...	*ŏrt*-mŭn-nă.

Whence the heteronymic table (Table I., sect. 63) of Wollangama group-relationships can be written as follows :—

Paedo-matronym	RARA (Koopooroo).		RANYA (Woongko).		AWUNGA (Koorkilla).		LOORA (Bunburi).	
—	male.	female.	male.	female.	male.	female.	male.	female.
Rara	elinjoka	korpetya	woolun-dun	twungul-wurrul	ortmun-na	unnel	mara-mara	loomba
Ranya	woolun-dun	twungul-wurrul	elinjoka	korpetya	mara-mara	loomba	ortmun-na	unnel
Awunga ...	ortmun-na	unnel	mara-mara	loomba	elinjoka	korpetya	woolun-dun	twungul-wurrul
Loora	mara-mara	loomba	ortmun-na	unnel	woolun-dun	twungul-wurrul	elinjoka	korpetya

Geneanyms (sect. 64) :—

Husband = *nŏr*-lă.

Wife = *tēn*-yă.

Father's brother = *yū*-wă.

Mother's sister = *bā*-ră.

Father's father = *á*-wŭng-ă-dă.

Mother's father = *chăng*-ă-dă.

Father's mother = *mē*-wă.

Mother's mother = *mā*-mă.

Son, daughter, sister's son, sister's daughter = *yĕng*-ŭl.

Son's son, son's daughter = *yá*-wă-nă.

Daughter's son, daughter's daughter = *goo*-nŭng-ă.

Brother's son, brother's daughter = *yĕn*-mŭn.

Man's or woman's mother-in-law = *tŏr*-rō-gă.

Woman's son-in-law or daughter-in-law = *wăng*-kă.

Climanyms (sect. 68) :—

			Male.		Female.
At 1st degree	...	...	kŏr-ăn-kŏr-ă	...	kŏr-mă-kă.
At 2nd „	...	...	dă-rĕ-kŏn-nă	...	bĕl-ĕn-bă-ră.
At 3rd „	...	...	ăp-mă	...	jŏr-ĭn-jă.
At 4th „	...	...	rŏm-ă-ră		

(*d*) Among the tribes around Rockhampton, Gladstone, and still further south, I have also met with similar systems of nomenclature—the gamo-matronyms being alone deficient. Particulars of these, however, I am reserving for a future work.

71. Probable Interpretation of these Class Systems.—From a consideration of Table II., sect. 62, it will be seen which paedo-matronymic groups are allowed to marry, and, comparing this with Tables I. and III. in sect. 63, the fact clearly comes into prominence that by the marriage-rule a man can only marry his (sister-in-law, &c., *i.e.*) chata, &c., while a woman can only marry her (brother-in-law, &c., *i.e.*) yundi, &c. But even then, as will be seen in sect. 326, these can only marry when they are not connected by blood : *i.e.*, when they do not happen to be true blood-cousins, or a father and his daughter's daughter, or a son and his father's mother. Over and over again have I both seen and heard the proposition laid down almost as a *sine qua non* that the various groups, classes, &c., have been devised in order to prevent consanguinity and incest : the more intimate, however, that I have become with the language and traditions of the aboriginals in the Boulia District and elsewhere, the more convinced am I that in these localities, at all events, this is not the case. The following three or four facts appear to be very strong arguments in contradiction to the generally accepted view :—

a. The marriage-rule, according to sect. 62*d*, which is common throughout North-West-Central Queensland does not *per se* prevent consanguinity. True blood-cousins fall within these otherwise intermarriageable groups, and yet they are not allowed to marry : similarly a man and his daughter's daughter, &c. (sect. 326 ; also Table, sect. 65).

b. The marriage-rule does in fact actually prevent the union of couples whom we know full well could not be possibly connected by any true blood-relationship whatsoever. For instance, a Koopooroo male at Boulia cannot marry a Koopooroo female belonging to a totally different tribe, say 150 miles distant, whom perhaps he or his family has never previously seen or mixed with : but of that same tribe he can marry a Koorkilla woman, and Koorkilla only. Again, as another example of the rule precluding marriage where again there is certainly no true consanguinity, is the fact that a man cannot marry the mother of his living or deceased wife. (He may have at least two wives, sect. 323.)

c. The marriage-rule, or rather its consummation, in the Boulia, Leichhardt-Selwyn, and Upper Georgina Districts, is totally disregarded at that most important of the ceremonial rites, the first of which every female has to undergo when ready to enter womanhood. The novitiate has here (sects. 305-308) to undergo promiscuous and general intercourse with all the "bucks" in camp, these gentry being members of any other paedo-matronym except that to which the woman herself belongs, and barring only her own father : should, in addition, any bucks be present from some other tribe, and yet belonging to the same paedo-matronym as herself, they are allowed to personally partake in the sexual orgie.

d. Group and blood-relationship is not to be distinguished : not only are similar terms applied (sects. 59, 63, 66), but the penalties for any infringement of the peculiar rights of either relationship are identical (sects. 238, 323, &c.).

What, then, is the interpretation of the various classes, groups, &c., mentioned in this chapter ? Let me answer this question as follows :—I am strongly of opinion that, independently of all questions of consanguinity, the paedo-matronyms upon which the marriage-rules depend (and which paedo-matronyms remain constant as compared with the heteronyms) have been devised, by a process of natural selection, to regulate the proper distribution of the total quantity of food avail-able. Thus the husband, according to his paedo-matronym (sect. 62*b*) lives on articles of diet different from those of his wife (or wives) : both of whom again are different from those permissible to their resulting offspring, which (sect. 62*d*) belong to a third paedo-matronymic group. Hence, to put it shortly, whereas in a European community with a common dietary, the more children there are to feed, the less will become the share for the parents, in this North-West-Central Queens-land aboriginal system, the appearance of children will make no appreciable difference in minimising the quantity of food available for those that give them birth. Any scarcity in the total quantity of all the food is met by a change of camping ground. A further circumstance that appears to lend great plausibility to this view is that, although practically identical terms and rules are followed through-out North-West-Central Queensland, the different animals, birds, fish, &c., "tabooed" by each paedo-matronymic group vary with each ethnographical district (sect. 62*b*). (For further information bearing on this matter of marriage, the reader is referred to sect. 320, dealing with the operation of "whistling" or introcision, where it will be shown that its ordinarily alleged object, that of limiting procreation, so as to equalise demand and supply, is untenable.)

CHAPTER IV.

THE EXPRESSION OF IDEAS BY MANUAL SIGNS:
A SIGN-LANGUAGE.

CONTENTS.—Section 72. Introductory. 73-74. Mammals. 75-76. Birds. 77-78. Reptiles. 79-80. Fish. 81-82. Molluscs. 83-84. Arthropods. 85-86. Plants. 87-88. Other Objects of Nature. 89-90. Individuals, Family Relatives. 91-92. Ornaments, Weapons, Implements, Utensils, Huts. 93-94. Number. 95-96. Locality, Direction. 97-98. Time. 99-100. Interrogation. 101-102. Simple Acts, States, and Conditions. 103-104. Complex Conditions, Abstract Ideas.

72. Introductory.—Although the signs collected together in this chapter can be spoken of as constituting a sign-language, it would be more correct to describe them as idea-grams, each sign conjuring up an idea, modified more or less by the context of the mute conversation. Thus, the sign for a boomerang may express not only the idea of the article itself, but also, according to the " run of the ' text,' " the idea of hitting or killing something by its means, or of swapping, manufacturing, or stealing it, &c. The sign of interrogation conjures up the idea of a question, but the nature of the query will depend upon what has gone before or is coming after.

The value of these ideagrams is apparent in the case of individuals travelling over country the spoken language of whose inhabitants they are ignorant of or only partially acquainted with; also, on the war-path or the chase, where silence is so essential an adjunct to success. For reasons difficult to estimate, their use is strictly enforced on certain special occasions, such as some of the initiation ceremonies (sect. 300, &c.).

I have personally proved the existence of these ideagrams for the whole of North-West-Central Queensland, this area being understood as comprising the various ethnographical districts known as the Boulia, Leichhardt-Selwyn, Cloncurry, Upper Georgina, and Flinders (sects. 2, 46-49); furthermore, on the Middle and Upper Diamantina they are also met with. From the fact that many of the indigenous aboriginals travel or go on the " walk-about " beyond these limits (sect. 224) there is every probability of these or similar signs being met with elsewhere than just mentioned.*

The various tribes from among which the following information concerning this subject of sign-language was collected may be tabulated as follows :—

Name of Tribe.	Country Occupied.	Abbreviation in Notes to the Illustrations.
Pitta-Pitta	Boulia District	P.P.
Boinji	Boulia District	Bo.
Ulaolinya	Boulia District	Ula.
Woukajera	Boulia District	Won.
Walookera	Upper Georgina District	Wal.
Undekerebina	Upper Georgina District	Und.
Kalkadoon	Leichhardt-Selwyn District	Kal.
Mitakoodi	Cloncurry District	Mit.
Woonamurra	Flinders District	Woo.
Goa	Upper Diamantina District	Goa

* Since the above lines were penned I have learnt of their existence among the Workia tribes, extending from the head of the Georgina waters to the McArthur River in Northern Territory.

Wherever in the notes to the illustrations the abbreviation referring to the tribe is placed in between parentheses, this will indicate that the particular sign, though actually sought for, has been found wanting; without the parentheses its general use has been confirmed. By this means it will the more easily be recognised that many of these signs or ideagrams are identical over large tracts of country, some of them being almost common throughout all North-West-Central Queensland : among such are the ideagrams for a dingo, kangaroo, large eagle-hawk, snake, fly, water, creek, adult man, mother, brother and sister, boomerang, hut, sunrise, the sign of interrogation, silence, by-and-by, anger, signs of affirmation and negation.

Of the various ideas that find expression through these signs may be mentioned those relating to animals, plants, and other objects of nature; to the various individuals constituting a camp or other family relationship; to weapons, implements, and utensils; to certain simple and complex states or actions; to number, place, interrogation, and to various abstract notions.

Although almost all the signs are executed with the one or other, or perhaps both hands, a few can be indicated by the head and face only, e.g., the ideas of "yea" and "nay," with corresponding head movements exactly after the European style, the sniffing of the nostrils to indicate the smelling of the wild-orange (sect. 86), the biting of the beard to express anger (sect. 104), the pouting of the lips towards the required quarter to show direction (sect. 95), &c. One or two signs can be expressed with the trunk, &c., e.g., the shrugging of the shoulders to denote doubt, interrogation, being a common example of the kind. Again, the greatest insult which it appears one woman can offer to another (among the Pitta-Pitta at least, and which is generally preliminary to mutual recriminations) is the protrusion forwards of the abdomen and exposure of the person simultaneously with the vibration of the knees and thighs one against the other, the heels being kept pretty close together.

Except, of course, where both hands are necessary to execute the required movement, it is immaterial which one, the right or left, is brought into requisition. In some cases the movement has a first and second, while in rare instances it may even have a third, position. In the illustrations the initial are distinguished from the final positions by having the lines indicating the latter dotted.

It may be mentioned that it was in these districts, some fifty years ago, that Captain Sturt made mention of the discovery of certain masonic signs among the aboriginals. So far as my limited knowledge of the craft allows, I have tested these people over and over again, repeatedly submitting them even to strict cross-examination, but have never succeeded in corroborating the gallant explorer's statement. I can only conclude that what he conscientiously believed to be aboriginal masonic signs are really the ideagrams which I am now about to describe.

73. Mammals.—That ubiquitous companion of the Australian savage, the dog and its half-brother the dingo, is clearly intelligible in the soft rounded toe-pads represented by the finger-tips in Fig. 1, while the animal's normal proclivities in "wolfing" up its food finds expression in Fig. 198. Among comparatively recently-introduced animals, the horns for a bullock in Figs. 4, 5, and the rounded hoof with corresponding motion for a horse in Fig. 2, are very clear: Fig. 3, perhaps not so evident, expresses more the pawing of the horse's foot. In the case of the rat, the motion of the head and nibbling action of the teeth are attempted with no small success in Fig. 6: the idea of digging up rats (or porcupines) from their burrows and striking them on the head with a waddy is utilised in Fig. 7. The porcupine has a curious habit of digging up the earth, and shovelling it laterally outwards as it were, an idea which is evidently intended in Fig. 8: the animal's spines are shown as the extended fingers in Fig. 9, while the pricking-up of its tiny ears is expressed in Fig. 10. With regard to the bandicoot, the long nose is evidently its strong point in more senses than one, if we are to judge by the comparatively large number of ideagrams devised to represent this particular organ. In Fig. 11 this is carried out by the finger moving forwards from the nasal organ of the signaller, and, without the latter, by means of the thumb (Fig. 12), or forefinger (Fig. 13), or bent-knuckle (Fig. 14) : other tribes look upon the big belly as the salient characteristic of the creature, and a corresponding ideagram is met with in Fig. 15. Only in one example, Fig. 16, are its underground burrowing habits brought into prominence. The opossum, or rather its claw-marks on the tree-trunks by means of which it is hunted and tracked, is represented in Fig. 17, where the two hooked and separated fingers indicate the two toes in the act of scratching on the bark : Figs. 18, 19 show the foot and toes similarly engaged, while Fig. 20 demonstrates the aboriginal hand in the act of twisting the animal's hair into twine. With regard to the paddymelon, one ideagram has some bearing upon its roundish elongate face in Fig. 21, while in another stress is laid upon its hop-like progression (Fig 22), or upon its slender toes (Fig. 23). A similar idea—the "hop"—is put into execution in Fig. 24 referring to the ordinary large kangaroo, also represented in Fig. 25 by the pricking up of its big ears when on the alert.

74. Notes to Illustrations.

Fig. 1. *Dingo, Dog.*—Finger-tips all touching top of thumb: flexion at wrist. Finger-tips represent the toe-pads. Among the Pitta-Pitta this sign represents more especially a small dog, as distinguished from a very large one (*see* Fig. 198). P.P., Bo., Ula., Won., Wal., (Und.), Kal., Mit., Woo., Goa.

Fig. 2. *Horse.*—Fingers closely apposed and all flexed at proximal joints with tips just touching palm : wrist flexed. Forwards and backwards movement from elbow to show the flat hoofs coming to the ground in rhythmic succession. Among the Boinji this sign, in addition, signifies a dog or dingo. P.P., Bo., Ula., Won., Wal., Und.

Fig. 3. *Horse.*—A somewhat similar sign to that of a dog, but instead of the flexion there is an inwards rotation at the wrist—a kind of "pawing." Mit.

Fig. 4. *Cattle.*—The horns of the beast are rendered prominent by the extended forefingers placed close to the front and side of the head. P.P., Bo., (Ula.), Und., (Mit.)

Fig. 5. *Cattle.*—The hand represents the head, while the movement forwards, upwards, and outwards signifies the curvature of the horn. Mit.

Fig. 6. *Rat.*—Forefinger fixed at an angle apart from thumb signifies the prominent incisor teeth : vibratory movement with fixed wrist shows the "nibbling" movement. P.P., Bo., Ula., Won., Wal., Und., (Kal., see Fig. 89).

Fig. 7. *Rat.*—The one hand is the animal's head : it is in the act of being struck with a stick, &c. Woo., Goa.

Fig. 8. *Porcupine* (Echidna hystrix). Forefinger held downwards, forwards, and slightly inwards : a lateral movement outwards to show the turning up of the soil. P.P., (Bo.), Ula., Won., Wal., Und., Kal., (Mit.).

Fig. 9. *Porcupine.*—All fingers and thumb slightly flexed and pretty widely separated—to express the "spears," *i.e.*, spines : motion forwards from elbow. Mit.

Fig. 10. *Porcupine.*—Tipping the ears backwards and forwards with the forefingers—an indication of the animal's little ears when alarmed, &c. (*Cf.* the Pitta-Pitta word nara-apari, where nara = ear.) (P.P.), Bo., (Mit.).

Fig. 11. *Bandicoot.*—Drawing attention to the animal's long nose. (P.P.), Bo., (Mit.).

Fig. 12. *Bandicoot.*—The thumb between the two fingers represents the long nose. Mit.

Fig. 13. *Bandicoot.*—The lengthy snout is here expressed by the extended forefinger: the thumb rests upon the side of this digit, and there is a vertical flexion at wrist. P.P., (Bo.), (Ula.), Won., Wal., (Und.), (Mit.)

Fig. 14. *Bandicoot.*—The same idea, but indicated with the knuckle of the proximal joint of the forefinger. Kal., (Mit.).

Fig. 15. *Bandicoot.*—The forefinger circles over the signaller's stomach, to show the comparatively big belly of the animal. (P.P.), Bo., (Mit.).

Fig. 16. *Bandicoot.*—Fingers somewhat separate, and extended; forward movement from elbow. The animal's toes digging into the ground. (P.P.), (Bo.), Ula., (Mit.), Woo., Goa.

Fig. 17. *Opossum* (Trichoglossus vulpecula).—The separated and hooked fore and middle fingers conjure up the idea of the double-claw mark on the tree-bark: movement of hand downwards. Kal.

Fig 18. *Opossum.*—Very similar to preceding, the two fingers touching each other only at their tips, where they meet the thumb: similar downwards movement. Mit.

Fig. 19. *Opossum.*—Hand in position depicted, with more or less rapid flexion at wrist: the clawing movement. Among the Ulaolinya blacks the thumb points upwards and outwards, and therefore, of course, does not touch the tip of fore-finger. (P.P.), Bo., Ula., Won., Wal., (Und.), (Kal.), (Mit.).

Fig. 20. *Opossum, Opossum string.*—The rolling of the fingers on the thumb —the idea of twisting the prepared opossum hair into twine (sect. 162). P.P., Woo., Goa.

Fig. 21. *Paddymelon.*—Circular movement made in front of and about the same size as the face: the animal's elongate roundish head. P.P., (Bo.), Ula., Won., Wal., (Mit.).

Fig. 22. *Paddymelon: Small Species of Kangaroo, &c.*—Fingers together and flexed, their tips with the thumb being all on same horizontal plane: flexion only at wrist—to show the comparatively short hop of the animal (*cf.* Fig. 24). Mit.

Fig. 23. *Paddymelon: Small Species of Kangaroo.*—Flexion of the first two fingers conjointly: indicative of the long foot. (Mit.), Kal.

Fig. 24. *Kangaroo: Any Large Species of Macropus.*—Both hands are held forwards with cupped palms down and bent fingers—the animal's paws: the movement consists in a short spring forwards—the big "hop." As often as not this ideagram is expressed with one hand only. P.P., (Bo.), Ula., Won., Wal., Und., (Kal., *see* Fig. 55), Mit., Woo., Goa.

Fig. 25. *Kangaroo: Any Large Species.*—Similar to Fig. 10, but instead of the forefingers denoting the small ears, the whole hand denotes the big ears turning backwards and forwards. (P.P.), Bo., (Kal.), (Mit.).

75. Birds.—All birds collectively, except those with something individually sufficiently distinctive, can be indicated by the flapping of either one or other hand, or both together synchronously—to call up the idea of flight, the beating of the wings. The variations in which the hand and fingers are held, the celerity and range of movement, &c., have all appreciable meanings, though as a matter of fact, these minute differences in such directions are almost inappreciable to the European eye. Figs. 26, 27, 28, 29, referring to birds in general, will give but a limited idea of them. Different from the ordinary run is Fig. 30, indicating the common brown hawk, with fixed and extended wing, swooping down upon, and up again with, its prey; so also the eagle-hawk, whose feathers are so prized for decorative purposes, is depicted by its big claws as the separated and " clawed " fingers clasping on its victim in Fig. 31, in addition to the ideagram representing the "circling" nature of its flight in Fig. 32. With the " flock "-pigeon again, besides the more or less peculiarly vibratory manner of its flight indicated in Fig. 33, the imitation of its capture by net is shown in Fig. 34. The emu, valued for both flesh and feathers, is shown by the toe-tracks in Fig. 35, the shape and motion of the long-necked head in Fig. 36, while an attempt has been made in Fig. 37 to illustrate the " wobbling " movements of the bird when running. With the turkey-bustard the characteristic side-to-side jerking motion of the head, the bird undisturbed, is expressed in Figs. 38, 39, 40. The pelican, or rather its immense lower beak, as might have been expected, could hardly have escaped notice: in Fig. 41 this is denoted by the hollowed hands resting horizontally from the protruded chin, in Fig. 42 by the flexed fingers twisted one behind the other, and in Fig. 43 by the hand ladling up an imaginary large volume of water. Cockatoos, parrots, galahs, &c., and all similar birds are represented by imitations of the beak or top-knot. Thus Fig. 44 affords a view of the upper and lower beak; the movement, a sudden extension forwards of the digits, indicating the top-knot feathers. In Fig. 45 the upper mandible alone is expressed by the hooked forefinger tapping on the upper gums or incisors. A "whistler" and certain other species of duck is notified either by the method adopted of capturing it, or the flattened nature of its beak, in Fig. 46. The idea of a black crow turning up the soil for food is expressed in Fig. 47. "Diver"-birds, "shag," and others with similar sub-aqueous habits are represented in Fig. 48 in the act of diving into the water and out again. The "native-companion" and the "spoon-bill" form an interesting couplet for comparison, the elongate beak in the former case being indicated by one finger solely (Fig. 49), or by two overlapping (Fig. 50), in the latter similarly by one finger (Fig. 51), or by two in close apposition (Fig. 52): the contrast between the vertical movement of the head in the case of the native-companion and the lateral movement in that of the spoon-bill is very striking.

76. Notes to Illustrations.

Fig. 26. *Bird: in general.*—Movement from elbow: to represent the beating, flapping, of the wings. P.P., Bo., Ula., (Und.), (Kal.), (Mit.).

Fig 27. *Bird: in general.*—Similar movement and idea. P.P., Bo., Ula., (Kal.), (Mit.).

Fig. 28. *Bird: in general.*—Similar movement and idea. (P.P.), (Bo.), (Ula.), Won., Wal., (Und.), (Kal.), (Mit.).

Fig. 29. *Bird: in general.*—Similar movement and idea. P.P., Bo., (Ula.), (Won.), (Wal.), Und., (Kal.), (Mit.).

Fig. 30. *Small hawk.*—The bird with fixed wing is swooping down and up again with its prey. P.P., Und., (Mit.).

Fig. 31. *Large Eagle-hawk* (Uroaltus audax).—The cupped palm and hooked fingers represent the claws: movement consists in the closure of these over its quarry. Among the Ulaolinya and Boinji blacks instead of the palm looking upwards, it is turned downwards. P.P., Bo., Ula., Won., Wal., Und., (Mit.), Woo., Goa.

Fig. 32. *Large Eagle-hawk.*—Expressive of the "circling" nature of the bird's flight. Mit.

Fig. 33. *Pigeon: "flock" and other species.*—Thumb, palm, and fingers all in the one same median vertical plane with fixed wrist: vibratile motion at wrist with simultaneous forward movement of forearm. P.P., (Bo.), (Ula.), Won., Wal., Und., (Kal.), (Mit.).

Fig. 34. *"Flock" pigeon, &c.* (Histriophagus histrionica).—The idea of turning over the net in the act of capture; the two hands are holding the long wooden handle (*see* sect. 137, Fig. 230). Woo., Goa.

Fig. 35. *Emu* (Dromaius novae-hollandiae).—The ring-finger is held down with the thumb, the three free digits indicating the bird's toes; the "tread" is represented by movement forwards of the arm with simultaneous flexion at the wrist. (P.P.), (Bo.), (Ula.), (Won.), (Wal.), Und., (Kal.), (Mit.).

Fig. 36. *Emu.*—Fingers fixed in flexed position and closely apposed, with thumb close to base of forefinger, and wrist flexed laterally: the arm and hand thus show the head and neck of the bird "nodding," the movement taking place at the elbow. P.P., Bo., Kal., Mit., Woo., Goa.

Fig. 37. *Emu.*—Here, there is indication of two legs: the movement—"wobbling" of bird's body and tail-feathers—is expressed by a vibratory motion at fixed wrist with simultaneous progression forwards. Palm of the hand is in median vertical plane. P.P., (Bo.), Ula., (Und.), (Kal.), (Mit.).

Fig. 38. *Turkey-bustard.*—Thumb touching top of forefinger, which, with the other closely apposed fingers, is semi-flexed and lies in a horizontal plane; sharp rotation at wrist. The side to side rotation of the bird's head. P.P.

Fig. 39. *Turkey-bustard.*—Similar movement to preceding. The bird's head is here expressed by the open hand and extended digits in a vertical median plane ; the hand is fixed in a flexed position with wrist. Mit.

Fig. 40. *Turkey-bustard*—Similar movement to preceding. The hand is held in similar position as Fig. 39, but the fingers are flexed into palm, with thumb—the beak—uppermost. Woo., Goa.

Fig. 41. *Pelican* (Pelicanus conspicillatus).—The closely apposed hands in a more or less cupped position are placed horizontally with the balls of the thumbs just touching the chin : the large lower " bill." (P.P.), Bo., (Kal.), (Mit.), Woo., Goa.

Fig. 42. *Pelican.*—The same distinctive feature represented by the fingers twisted one behind the other. (P.P.), (Bo.), Ula., (Kal.), (Mit.).

Fig. 43. *Pelican.*—Fingers semi-flexed, and fixed wrist ; rapid rotation inwards, with simultaneous movement of forearm slightly forwards and inwards. The idea of the bill "ladling" up the water, &c., in large quantities. P.P., (Bo.), (Ula.), Won., Wal., Und., (Kal.), (Mit.).

Fig 44. *Cockatoo, galah, parrot, &c.*—Fingers closely apposed and flexed—the upper beak : the idea of a top-knot is expressed by the subsequent sudden extension and separation of the digits. (P.P.), (Bo.), (Ula.), (Won.), (Wal.), Und., (Kal.), (Mit.).

Fig. 45. *Cockatoo, galah, parrot, &c.*—The beak is here indicated by the hooked forefinger tapping upon the upper gums or incisors. P.P., Bo., (Ula.), Won., Wal., (Und.), (Kal.), (Mit.), Woo., Goa.

Fig. 46. *Duck.*—The forefinger is brushed horizontally in front of the mouth. Two interpretations of this ideagram have been given me : one, expressive of the flattened and wide bill ; the other, indicative of the method of its capture by means of a slip-noose (sect. 140). Woo., Goa.

Fig. 47. *Black crow* (Corvus).—Fingers all clawed and separate : a swift rotatory movement at wrist : the idea of digging up the earth for offal, &c. (*see* Fig. 183). P.P., Won., Wal.

Fig. 48. *Diver-bird, "shag," &c. : anything that dives, to dive.*—The movement of diving down into the water, and out again, is evident. P.P., Bo., Ula., Won., Wal., Und., Kal.

Fig. 49. *Native Companion* (Grus australiasianus).—Flexion at wrist : the forefinger represents the long-necked head and beak of the bird moving vertically down into the water. P.P., (Bo.), Ula., Won., Wal., Und., (Kal.), (Mit.).

Fig. 50. *Native Companion.*—The neck and beak is here signified by fore and middle fingers, the former overlapped : movement similar to preceding. Kal.

Fig. 51. *Large Spoon-bill* (Platylea).—The finger, again giving the idea of head and beak as in Fig. 49, is now moved from side to side, at the elbow, in imitation of the bird's habit. P.P., (Bo.), Ula., Won., Wal., Und., (Kal.), Mit.

Fig. 52. *Large Spoon-bill.*—The two first fingers are put to the mouth, and moved forwards and downwards : the bird's flattened beak. (P.P.), Bo., (Kal.), (Mit.).

77. **Reptiles.**—Beyond the meaning of the quick side-to-side oscillatory or vibratory movements from elbow, with fixed wrist—the indication for rapidity of speed—with which the ideagrams for lizards, iguanas, &c., in Figs. 53, 54, 55 are executed, it is difficult to recognise anything characteristic unless it be in the long snout or tail. (*Cf.* the movements of these three with those of fish in Figs. 64-67.) In Fig. 56 is a representation of the clumsy, wobbling, twisted, side-to-side gait of the limbs in one of the larger varieties of iguana. Snakes in general are expressed by the forearm with closed hand in imitation of the body and head respectively, as in Figs. 57, 59, 60 : the position of the hand in the last-mentioned shows the characteristic movement of the animal's head protruding from out the surface when crossing water. In Fig. 58 the same reptile is indicated with the finger only, the simultaneous movements of the wrist and arm mimicking its

sinuous progression. A carpet snake is shown at repose in Fig. 61, with its head, the thumb, raised from within the centre of its coils. The fact of drawing attention to the colouration of the snout conveys the idea of a black-headed snake in Fig. 62. In the ideagram for a frog (Fig. 63), the "jump," coupled with the outstretched fingers (its toes), is unmistakeable.

78. Notes to Illustrations.

Fig. 53. *Lizards, Iguanas: any small species.*—Oscillatory motion at wrist—rapidity of animal's movements. P.P., Bo., Ula., Won., Wal., Und., (Kal.). (Among the Pitta-Pitta blacks the initial position of this ideagram also holds good for a particular fish, a species of black bream: the final, however, is a quick to-and-fro short lateral movement at elbow—see Fig. 64.)

Fig. 54. *Lizards, Iguanas: in general.*—Fingers and thumb all extended, and in close apposition: vibratory, &c., motion at wrist. Kal., Mit., Woo., Goa.

Fig. 55. *Lizards, Iguanas: in general.*—Forefinger tip and thumb touching, the remaining fingers being extended; similar movement to preceding. (P.P.), (Bo.), Ula., Won., Wal., Und., (Kal.), (Mit.). Among the Kalkadoons, any large kangaroo is represented by the same initial position, but the subsequent one consists in a wrist-flexion and forwards motion to express the amimal's "hop." (*Cf.* Fig. 24.)

Fig. 56. *Iguana: large species in general.*—The elbow, strongly flexed, is held out laterally on a level with the shoulder, the wrist rotated inwards: the idea of drawing attention to the wobbling twisting gait is expressed by the rotation of the wrist outwards. P.P., Bo., Ula., (Kal.), (Mit.).

Fig. 57. *Snake: in general.*—The closed fist and forearm express the head and body respectively: the course of the arm on same plane forwards, outwards, and backwards indicates the sinuous track of the animal. P.P., Bo., Ula., Won., Wal., Und., (Mit.), Woo., Goa.

Fig. 58. *Snake: in general.*—The forefinger here indicates the animal, while the wrist-rotation and simultaneous forwards motion of the arm express the course of its progression. Kal., Mit. (With the Kalkadoons this ideagram means rather any land snake in general as opposed to the ideagram of Fig. 60.)

Fig. 59. *Snake: in general.*—Finger-tips touching top of palm, which is held on a level with the face, palm turned towards signaller: the movement is more or less of an ellipse. (There is strong suspicion that this ideagram also often indicates a water snake—*cf.* Fig. 60.) (P.P.), (Bo.), (Ula.), (Won.), (Wal.), Und., (Mit.).

Fig. 60. *Water snake.*—Hand and forearm again signify the animal's head and body: the head is out of the water, and revolving from side to side as the creature swims along. Kal.

Fig. 61. *Carpet snake* (Morelia variegata).—The head, standing erect from within the centre of the coils, is shown by the thumb protruding from between the closed fore and middle fingers. P.P., Bo., Ula., (Und.), Kal., (Mit.).

Fig. 62. *Black-headed snake.*—The signaller is trying to draw attention to the black snout of the creature. P.P., Bo., Ula., Won., (Mit.).

Fig. 63. *Frog.*—The hand, with closed thumb and fingers, is thrust forwards and downwards, while at the same time all the digits are extended and separated: the jump with the webbed feet. P.P., Bo., Ula., Won., Wal., Und., Kal., (Mit.).

79. Fish.—With two exceptions, all the signs to denote fish—no matter what the initial position of the hand—are executed with a more or less rapid side-to-side oscillatory or vibratory movement from the elbow, the wrist being fixed: this serves to show the appearance which these creatures offer when observed through the ripples on the water-surface. (*Cf.* this movement with that already described in connection with lizards, iguanas, &c., sect. 77.) The various initial positions of the hand itself in Figs. 64, 65, 66, 67 have been described to me as signifying the tail, the fins, &c. In the case of Fig. 68, one of the two exceptions referred to, is to be seen the scraping off of the "scales" previous to being eaten, the idea being sometimes completed by the other hand—the fish itself—held close below : the other exception is Fig. 69, where the method of capture, &c. (sect. 129), is referred to.

80. Notes to Illustrations.

Fig. 64. *Fish.*—The shape of the hand, with finger-tips touching top of palm, represents the tail. The usual movement as just described. P.P., Bo., Ula.

Fig. 65. *Fish.*—Wrist at an angle with forearm, and all the digits extended and separate. Similar movement.   (P.P.), (Bo.), (Ula.), (Won.), (Wal.), Und.

Fig. 66. *Fish.*—Hand fixed at an angle sideways with the forearm, and flexed slightly backwards : the palm looks forwards and upwards.   Similar movement.   (P.P.), (Bo.), Ula., Won., Wal., Und., Woo., Goa.

Fig. 67. *Fish.*—Similar initial position as Fig. 66, save that the little finger alone is flexed on to the palm. Similar movement. (P.P.), Bo.

Fig. 68. *Fish : to prepare them, &c.*—Hand in more or less cupped position with fingers semiflexed and in close apposition : flexion takes place at wrist, the arm remaining in fixed position. The idea of scraping the scales off (in the case of a big-sized fish especially) previous to eating. Among the Pitta-Pitta aboriginals the ideagram is completed by sometimes holding the other hand out horizontally underneath, to show the actual animal. P.P., (Bo.), Ula., Won., Wal., (Und.), Kal.

Fig. 69. *Fish : to capture them, &c.*—The closed hand is brought up to the mouth, which is closed upon it sharply, when the hand is withdrawn, and a wave made of it. This represents the aboriginal biting the back of the fish's head, to kill it, previous to throwing it on to the river bank—whence it can be collected at leisure—the fisherman remaining in the water to catch more. (Sect. 129.)

81. Molluscs.

— The fresh-water mussel, an important ingredient of the aboriginal menu, is cleverly illustrated in Fig. 70, with the two overlapping fingers—the shells—rocking from side to side as the animal makes its progress along the mud. In Fig. 71 each hand represents a shell, the "hinge" being at the thumbs. In Fig. 72 each finger is a shell working on an imaginary hinge extending from the thumb-tip to the fork between the fore and middle fingers.

82. Notes to Illustrations.

Fig. 70. *Fresh-water mussel.*—Forefinger tucked under middle finger, ring and little finger flexed into the palm : position of thumb immaterial. Slow out-and-in rotatory motion at wrist, to imitate the "rocking" of the animal. P.P., Bo., Ula., Won., Wal., Und., (Kal.), (Mit.)

Fig. 71. *Fresh-water mussel.*—The thumbs remain stationary, as the hinge, while the fists, as the two shells, open outwards. Kal.

Fig. 72. *Fresh-water mussel.*—The two finger-tips of the fore and middle fingers remain in contact with the thumb-top, while the former digits become separated in their lengths at the proximal joints : each finger is a shell working on an imaginary hinge.

83. Arthropoda, &c.

—There are certain small flies which form quite an interesting group among themselves in connection with the expression of ideas by signs : thus the circular or lateral flight, as the case may be, of some of these little wretches is well portrayed in Figs. 73, 74, while the region which they may particularly affect or annoy is shown in Fig. 75 by a sand-fly alighting on the eye. Again, the methods adopted by the victim in obtaining relief from the scourge can be seen in Fig 76 with a mosquito suddenly crushed by the palm of the hand, or deftly caught in Fig. 77 between the finger and thumb, or, in the case of a small sand-fly (Fig. 78), being picked off with the finger-nail, or with some larger member of the same fraternity being brushed away from either side of the face in Fig. 79. I nowhere found any ideagrams directly intended for a honey-bee, though those for the "sugar-bag" itself—*i.e.*, the honey—are common: one of these

(Fig. 80) signifies the idea of its viscosity, while the other two (Figs. 81, 82) are expressive of the means employed in obtaining it. Remaining insects requiring notice are the edible caterpillar represented in Figs. 83, 84; the former showing the animal in *statu quo*, the latter in the act of being devoured. Ideagram Fig. 85 is intended for a hair-louse being squeezed between the thumb-nails—a practice not unknown among more civilised peoples. A cray-fish is indicated by the claws opening and shutting in Fig. 86.

84. Notes to Illustrations.

Fig. 73. *Any small (house) fly.*—The tip of the forefinger serves to indicate the small circles which the insect flies in. (P.P.), Bo., (Kal.).

Fig. 74. *Any small fly.*—Fingers slightly flexed, and rapid lateral movement —in imitation of the insect's flight. Mit.

Fig. 75. *Any sort of (sand) fly.*—The two fingers are in the act of catching the sand-fly which has alighted on the eye. Kal.

Fig. 76. *Mosquito.*—The cupped palm and fingers coming down with a quick and sudden rush upon the doomed creature : either done on the opposite arm or upon one of the thighs. P.P., (Bo.), Ula., Won., Wal., Und., Kal., (Mit.).

Fig. 77. *Mosquito.* With a swift forward movement the thumb and forefinger are just about to pounce upon it. The other fingers remain closed. (P.P.), Bo., (Kal.), (Mit.).

Fig. 78. *Sand-fly.*—The hooked forefinger is scraping up the minute creature which is supposed to be biting into the flesh: performed upon opposite arm, or upon a thigh. P.P., Bo., Ula, Won., Wal., Und.

Fig. 79. *Any small fly.*—The idea of brushing away from off the sides of the face the insect which is hanging about there. P.P., Bo., Ula., Won., Wal., Und., Woo., Goa.

Fig. 80. *Honey : (a honey bee).*—Its distinctive physical characteristic, its viscosity, is expressed by the circular motion imparted to the stick or finger to prevent its dropping off, somewhat after the fashion in which a European would twirl the spoon when taking treacle, &c., from out the tin on to a plate. P.P., Bo , Ula., Won., Wal., (Und.), (Kal.), (Mit.).

Fig. 81. *Honey.*—Where the tree which bears the comb is too massive or too tall to be cut down, the aboriginal will climb it by means of "nicks" cut alternately into either side, so as to form successive steps (sect. 118) : this is the idea proposed to be conveyed here. Kal., Mit.

Fig. 82. *Honey.* One way of learning whether the tree trunk is hollow, and therefore likely to contain a " sugar-bag," is to sound it by tapping with the fingers (sect. 118) : this is what is being done now. Woo., Goa.

Fig. 83. *Small Caterpillar, "grub," &c.*—Represented by the little finger alone extended. P.P., Bo., (Ula.), (Und.), (Mit.).

Fig. 84. *Large Edible Caterpillar, "grub."*—The hooked forefinger, the animal itself, is drawn from the side of the mouth upwards over the cheek. The insect's head, not being eaten, is in the act of being pulled off (sect. 119). P.P., Bo., Ula.

Fig. 85. *Hair-louse.*—The insect is in the act of being squeezed between the two thumb-nails. P.P., Bo., Kal., Mit., Woo., Goa.

Fig. 86. *Cray-fish.*—The forefinger and thumb opening apart from each other represent a " claw." P.P., (Mit.).

85. Plants.

— Only those with an economic value in the eyes of the aboriginals are represented by signs. Certain of the illustrations draw attention to the manner in which the plant, fruit, &c., is gathered or collected: the plucking off of the wild-orange from its branches in Fig. 87, the digging up of the yams in Figs. 88, 89, and the care necessary in pulling up the radish-like "witooka" root in Fig. 90, without breaking it, are all characteristic. Other series of ideagrams indicate methods of preparation or treatment, previously to being eaten, such as—the rubbing off of the husks of the " mungaroo " seeds between the finger and thumb in Fig. 91 ; the rolling into threads of the flax fibre, subsequently to soaking, along the surface of the thigh in Fig. 92 ; the shaking out or scraping off of the " pig-weed " seeds in Figs. 93, 94, 95 ; the operation of pounding the " nardoo " in Fig. 96. Similarly with ordinary grass-seed, the various stages in its preparation are all unmistakable: the shaking of a plant into a koolamon in Fig. 97, the grinding with a stone in Fig. 98, and the licking off of the subsequent mixture from the fingers in Figs. 99, 100, require but little further elucidation. The tying-up of the " wild-rice " into bundles, when first collected, is shown in Fig. 101. " Pituri " is represented not only during the process of mixing previous to chewing in Figs. 102, 103, but also in its completed stage when, as a small roll, it is kept in position behind and above the pinna of the ear in Fig. 104.

86. Notes to Illustrations.

Fig. 87. *Wild Orange.*—The marked odour of the fruit is represented by the nostrils in the act of " sniffing"; this is the complete ideagram among the Pitta-Pitta blacks. With the Ulaolinya there is the addition of the hand plucking down the fruit. The Undekerebina have a variation in plucking it down as just mentioned, and then, apparently, biting a piece off. The Kalkadoons express this ideagram by the movement of the hand only, the palm of which may be turned up or down. P.P., (Bo.), Ula., Und., Kal., (? Mit.).

Fig. 88. *Yam : a yam stick.*—The idea of digging the root up with the spatulate-tipped stick (sect. 158). P.P.

Fig. 89. *Yam.*—The act of digging up the root with a stick, and corresponding movement of arm and hand. (Among the Kalkadoons this ideagram expresses anything which is dug up out of the ground with a stick, *e.g.*, rat, &c., see Fig. 6.) Kal. Mit.

Fig. 90. " *Witooka* " (Boerhaavia diffusa).—The edible root of this plant is slender, brittle, and shaped much like an ordinary long radish, the fingers are in the act of pulling it very carefully out of the soil (sect. 113). With the Ulaolinya aboriginals the forefinger is half extended, the thumb being closed on the remaining fingers : there is a similar movement. P.P., Bo., Ula., Won., Und., Kal.

Fig. 91, " *Mungaroo* " (a species of nut-grass, sect. 113).—Winnowing the husks off the seeds between thumb and forefinger by rolling the former vertically upon the latter while moving horizontally. The movement itself is somewhat slow. P.P., Bo., Ula., Und., Kal., (Mit.).

Fig. 92. " *Native-flax* " : *a net : to make a net.*—The flax, after soaking, is rolled backwards and forwards along front and side of thigh : pressure during each " roll " is exerted alternately on palm or ball of thumb and length of the fingers (sect. 124, 153). Among the Boinji and Undekerebina blacks the other hand is held up with a twisting motion in the digits, to indicate the further extremity of the newly manufactured piece of twine. P.P., Bo., Ula., Und., Mit.

Fig. 93. " *Pig-weed* " (Portulaca oleracea).—The thumb and fingers are holding a twig of the plant, and by means of a shaking movement at the wrist dropping the seed into a koolamon (sect. 109). P.P., Bo., Ula. (Und.), (Mit.).

Fig. 94. *Pig-weed.*—Same shaking movement at wrist as in preceding, but the plant held somewhat differently. Kal.

Fig. 95A.B. " *Pig-weed.*"—Rubbing or scraping off the seeds from a bunch : two slight variations in the way of imitating the movement. Woo., Goa.

Fig. 96. " *Nardoo* " (Marsilea).—The palm of one hand with a nardoo-stone (sect. 155) is beating on and along the dorsum of the other in " measured time and slow" : the " pounding" of the seed between the two stones to crush the hard shells. P.P., (Mit.).

Fig. 97. *Seed-food, in general.*—The grass-tufts, held in the hands, are undergoing a rapid shaking of their seed into the koolamon lying below. P.P., Bo., Ula.

Fig. 98. *Seed-food, in general.*—The way in which the two hands are held when pressing upon the flat "pappa" stone and grinding the seed with a fore-and-aft movement (sect. 154). Kal., Mit.

Fig. 99. *Seed-food, in general : to eat.*—During the process of grinding, some of the "mess" gets stuck on the fingers. Here the forefinger is being drawn across the two lips, which are licking away any of the sticky mixture adhering: in the second movement any particles left are being jerked back on to the grindstone. P.P., Bo., Ula., Won., Wal. (Und.).

Fig. 100. *Seed-food, in general : to eat.*—The fore and middle fingers, well in the mouth, are firmly held there by the suction of the lips, and thence are drawn out slowly downwards: the mouth sucks off anything that may be sticking to them. (Compare with preceding.) Among the Pitta-Pitta this ideagram expresses the act of eating, especially any sticky stuff, *e.g.*, seed-food, &c. P.P., (Bo), (Ula.), (Won.), (Wal.), Und.

Fig. 101. *"Mokomurdo," "Wild-rice"* (sect. 111).—The plant is being tied up into bundles, when ripe enough, as soon as collected. Mit.

Fig. 102. *"Pituri"* (Duboisia.)—The forefinger is being pressed forwards from behind the thumb in the act of mixing up the pituri with ashes, &c., during its preparation previous to being made up into a roll (sect. 147). Kal.

Fig. 103. *Pituri.*—The same idea as in preceding, but a somewhat different position—rubbing the forefinger on the thumb. Mit., Woo., Goa.

Fig. 104. *Pituri.*—The "roll" of pituri when not in use—*i.e.*, being chewed—is kept behind and above the pinna of the ear (sect. 147). The forefinger is brought round forwards and downwards from behind the ear to signify this. P.P., Bo., Ula., Won., Wal., Und.

87. Other Objects of Nature.—These are somewhat limited, the "lapping-up" of water for drinking or for splashing over the body in Fig. 105, the flowing river or creek of Figs. 106, 107 as a "wave" of the arm, and the open hand with corresponding movements to denote the convexity of a hill or mountain in Figs 108, 109, being all that have been met with. (The rising and setting sun, &c., will be dealt with under the ideagrams relating to Time, in sect. 97).

88. Notes to Illustrations.

Fig. 105. *Water : to drink, &c.*—This ideagram shows the manner in which the aboriginal laps up the water, handful by handful. P.P., Bo., Ula., Und., Won., Wal., Und., Kal., Mit., Woo., Goa.

Fig. 106. *River, creek, &c.*—Elbow flexed and raised with arm, forearm and hand on same horizontal plane, fingers semiflexed, executing a more or less rapid movement in imitation of the flowing water, the hand being turned upward at its completion (? the source). The Mitakoodi have a similar representation, but the digits are more extended, and no upward movement at the termination. Among the Goa and Woonamurra, the Mitakoodi variation signifies a *large* creek, &c. P.P., Bo., Ula., Won., Wal., Und , (? Kal.), Mit., Woo., Goa.

Fig. 107. *Waterfall, spring, small creek.*—The extended hand is rapidly drawn backwards and downwards, as an indication of the torrent of water rushing down. Woo., Goa.

Fig. 108. *Mountain, hill.*—The hollowed hand, with slightly flexed and separated digits, is made to fit over the imaginary convex surface—the mountain, &c.—by means of a rotation at the wrist. P. P., (Kal.), Mit.

Fig. 109. *Mountain, hill.*—The hand in its initial position is raised over the level of the head, to express the idea of height, the subsequent elliptical movement of arm denoting its natural configuration. Mit.

89. Individuals, Family, Relatives, &c.—Any adult man, a father, &c., is signalled by means of the beard, a sign of manhood, as in Fig. 110 ; while any adult woman, a mother, &c., is represented by her development of breast, as in Figs. 111, 112, 113. A husband or wife is indicated by a tapping of the buttock

G

(Fig. 114) to express the idea of their occupancy of, or rather their sitting down in, the same hut. Satisfactory explanations for a woman, as regards venery, in Figs. 115, 116, are wanting, although the universality of the former ideagram is very marked ; they may have something to do possibly with the idea of sleeping or lying down. Venery is suggested in Figs. 117, 118, and its consummation expressed in Fig. 119. The sign for a brother or sister (Fig. 120) is a tapping of the shoulder, expressive of the fact that they have both been carried on the same spot. A little child is denoted by the idea of diminutiveness in Fig. 121, by its " babbling " in Fig. 122, by the source of its origin in Fig. 123, and by the fact of its " thinking-all-the-same " (as its parent) in Fig. 124. The " doctor," " medicine-man," &c., is shown (Fig. 125) in the act of pointing or insinuating the dreaded " bone" (sect. 264) ; Fig. 126 suggests his mystical power of removing the same evil after it is believed to have been maliciously inserted into the victim's body (sect. 263) ; while Fig. 127 is emblematical of his cutting a person's throat, the one hand holding the neck in position, while the other is doing the damage.

90. Notes to Illustrations.

Fig. 110. *Adult man : a father.*—The chin, or beard if present, is held in the closed hand while a slight rotatory movement backwards and forwards is exerted at the wrist. The beard of course is the sign of male adolescence. The Mitakoodi attach an additional signification to this ideagram as '' one's own flesh and blood," &c. P.P., Bo., Ula., Won., Wal., Und., Kal., Mit., Woo., Goa.

Fig. 111. *Adult woman.*—Circular movement of the cupped hand to express the rotundity of the fully-developed breast. Mit.

Fig. 112. *Mother.*—Resting the inner edge of the hollowed hand against the chest—the act of supporting the heavy milk-laden breast. Mit.

Fig. 113. *Mother.*—Depicted by a picking at or pulling of the nipple. P.P., Bo., Ula., Won., Wal., Und., Kal., (Mit.), Woo., Goa.

Fig. 114. *Husband, wife.*—The flat hand is made to smack the buttock in order to conjure up the idea of both mates sitting down, &c., in the same hut. With the Woonamurra and Goa tribes the tapping takes place on the middle and outer half of the thigh, and possibly suggests the position of the legs during copulation (sect. 320*d*). P.P., Bo., Ula., (Und.), (Kal.), Mit., Woo., Goa.

Fig. 115. *Woman : in general.*—The fingers are but loosely closed on to the palm which looks towards and up to the signaller's face : flexion of wrist alternately backwards and forwards—a sort of " shaking" movement. No satisfactory explanation of this ideagram is forthcoming. A comparison between it and that of Fig. 202 (to lie down, &c.), affords ground for thinking that the above expresses the idea of lying down, for copulatory purposes especially, as it is only the female who assumes this particular position under those circumstances ; possibly it is a modification of the Mitakoodi variation of Fig. 119. P.P., Bo., Ula., Won., Wal., Und., (Kal.), (Mit.).

Fig. 116. *Woman : in general.*—Instead of the palm being turned towards speaker's face as in the preceding, this position is now assumed by the back of the thumb : the shaking movement takes place from the elbow vertically. Kal., (Mit.).

Fig. 117. *Woman : Copulation.*—The forwards and backwards flexion of the middle finger is a very suggestive invitation : the palm may be turned up or down, in fact, in any position. P.P., Bo., Ula., Won., Wal., Und., (Kal.), (Mit.).

Fig. 118. *Woman : Copulation.*—The little finger takes the place of the middle finger in preceding : the ideagram is completed by a rotation inwards and upwards—a half-screwing motion. Woo., Goa.

Fig. 119. *Woman : Copulation.*—The thumb on the third finger leaves the first two free which, held in a more or less clawed position, represent the two thighs and knees. Among the Mitakoodi the ideagram is similar, but the palm turned upwards instead of downwards, and a slight fore-and-aft flexion at the wrist : possibly Fig. 115 is a modification of this variation. Kal., Mit.

Fig. 120. *Brother, sister, &c.*—The tapping of the shoulder here indicates that all the brothers and sisters have been alike carried on the same parent's shoulders (sect. 330). P.P., Bo., Ula., Wou., Wal., (Und.), Kal., Mit., Woo., Goa.

Fig. 121. *Child, infant, &c.*—The forefinger defines a small circle on a horizontal plane—the idea of diminutiveness. With the Boinji aboriginals all the fingers together take part in the small circular movement, while among the Undekerebina only the forefinger takes part in it, but instead of the circle, it performs a short vertical-like movement. P.P., Bo., Ula., Und., (Kal.), (Mit.).

Fig. 122. *Child, infant, &c.*—The two first fingers are tapping upon the protruded lips to express the infant's "babbling." Kal., (Mit.).

Fig. 123. *Child, infant, &c.*—Tapping with the finger-tips upon the abdomen to draw attention to its source of origin. Woo., Goa.

Fig. 124. *Child—one's own flesh and blood: mother-in-law.*—The closed hand and thumb tapping upon the forehead, the idea of "think-all-the-same" in the case of one's child; its interpretation for one's mother-in-law was not obtainable. P.P., (Bo.), Ula., (Kal.), (Mit.).

Fig. 125. *Doctor, &c.*—The medicine-man, &c., is in the act of "pointing" the dreaded "bone"-apparatus held between the thumb and forefinger (sect. 264). P.P., Bo., Und., (Kal.), (Mit.).

Fig. 126. *Doctor, &c.*—The mouth being well opened, the back of the tongue is touched with the forefinger. This ideagram draws attention to one of the mystical attributes of the medicine-man, &c., in being able to remove by suction from the invalid's body the "evil-bone" into his own mouth (sect. 263). (P.P.), Und., (Kal.).

Fig. 127. *Doctor, &c.*—The one hand, stationary, has seized the victim by the neck, and has got him down : the other passes rapidly forwards, downwards, and outwards, executing the imaginary damage required. P.P., (Bo.), (Kal.).

91. Articles of Manufacture: Ornaments, Weapons, Implements, Utensils, Huts, &c.—These are all enumerated by ideagrams, according to any striking peculiarity in their design and manufacture, or dependent upon their method and manner of use. Thus, in the cases where any special ornament happens to be worn : the two hands in the act of tying up the waist (Figs. 128, 129) afford an idea of a belt ; in the position of encircling the neck and fixing it up behind, represent a necklace (Fig. 130) ; of being slipped over the head produce a very fair notion of some chest ornament (Fig. 131) ; while the drawing up of the supporting-string over the opposite shoulder in Fig. 132 gives us a dilly-bag, which is also expressed through the sense of a receptacle in Fig. 133. According to the method of manufacture, three interesting ideagrams for a grass necklaec are to be seen in Figs. 134, 135, 136. Dependent upon their method of use, a very complete and intelligiole series is to be found among fighting weapons : a stone knife being pulled out of its sheath in Fig. 137, or gashed deeply into an adversary's buttock, &c., in Fig. 138, or slicing off a piece of wood, &c., in Fig. 139 ; a boomerang just at the moment of its leaving the hand, Fig. 140, or while in the act of "circling" in Fig. 141 ; a spear under corresponding conditions of just being let fly, &c., in Figs. 142, 143, 144 ; a fighting-stick is held in position ready to deliver a blow in Figs. 145, 146, and to receive one in Fig. 147 ; a tomahawk is doing its work in Figs. 148, 149. A shield held in position by the handle is indicated in Fig. 150 ; the convexity of the face of the weapon is expressed by the opposite hand in a concave position tapping upon it in Fig. 151. Notions of convexity or concavity are again to be seen in the case of a "koolamon" in Figs. 152, 153, the same vessel being expressed through another channel, the method of carrying, in Figs. 154, 155, 156, 157. The same ideagram for the native flax-plant of Fig. 92 is utilised to represent a net, the object which is most commonly manufactured from it, though, to prevent any misconception, the actual in-and-out movement of the shuttle is imitated in Figs. 158, 159. In the case of huts or "gundis" the two main-bars fixed together at their apices— the primary scaffolding, so to speak, of the hut—is represented in Figs. 160, 161, while the framework generally is indicated in Fig. 162.

92. Notes to Illustrations.

Fig. 128. *Waist belt.*—The two hands are in the act of winding the hair-twine (sect. 183) round the waist. P.P., Bo., Ula., Und., (Kal.), Mit., Woo., Goa.

Fig. 129. *Waist belt.*—The encircling of the waist by the belt is indicated by the movements of the two fingers. Kal.

Fig. 130. *Necklace: the wearing of one.*—The two fingers indicate the encircling of the neck and the tying of the ornament at the nape. With the Mitakoodi, Woonamurra, and Goa only one hand usually is used. P.P., Bo., Ula., Und., Mit., Woo., Goa.

Fig. 131. *Chest-ornament.*—This ideagram shows the putting of the "loop" over the head, so as to let the ornament hang from over the shoulders. P.P., Bo., Ula., Und.

Fig 132. *"Dilly" bag* (sect. 153, &c.).—The "moving" hand is putting the string supporting the bag upon the shoulder of the fixed arm and closed hand. P.P., Bo., Ula., Won., Wal., Und., (Kal.), Mit.

Fig. 133. *"Dilly" bag.*—The idea of a cavity or receptacle, the two hollowed hands being placed close together in the form of a cup. Woo., Goa.

Fig. 134. *Grass necklace: its manufacture.*—The fixed hand is holding the grass-reed, from the extremity of which the moving hand, with a mussel-shell, is cutting off in quick succession the individual pieces which are subsequently to be threaded (sect. 179). P.P., Bo., Ula., (Mit.).

Fig. 135. *Grass-necklace: its manufacture.*—Similar idea to proceeding, but here the one forefinger represents the grass-reed which is being cut off by the stone-knife, the other forefinger, with a rapid saw-like motion. Kal., (Mit.).

Fig. 136. *Grass-necklace: its manufacture.*—Similar idea as in Fig. 135, but the stone-knife represented by the entire hand. Mit.

Fig. 137. *Stone-knife.*—The lower hand is holding tightly the bark-sheath in position, while the upper hand is pulling out the flint-blade (sect. 257). P.P. (Bo.), Ula., Won., Wal., Und., (Kal.).

Fig. 138. *Stone-knife.*—The hand, clasping the stone-knife firmly, is slashing it round into the back or buttock of the adversary (sect. 238). P.P., Bo., Kal., Mit., Woo., Goa.

Fig. 139. *Stone-knife.*—The one hand represents the blade cutting into the other, whatever article that may be, *e.g.*, wood. Ula., Mit.

Fig. 140. *Boomerang.*—The remaining fingers being held down by the thumb, the forefinger is curved into the shape of a boomerang; a sharp, external rotation at the wrist indicates the weapon just at the moment when it is about to commence flight. Among the Goa and Woonamurra tribes the remaining fingers are only loosely flexed into the hand; there is also more of a "sweep" with the forearm. The Pitta-Pitta, Boinji, and Ulaolinya aboriginals have the little finger open and curved as well; perhaps something to do with the carrying, manufacturing, or bartering of these weapons in pairs (sect. 240). P.P., Bo., Ula., Won., Wal., Und., Kal., Woo., Goa.

Fig. 141. *Boomerang.*—Hand strongly flexed laterally inwards at wrist; the hand and arm thus together represent the weapon: a sort of "sweep" with the forearm to indicate the circle of flight. Mit.

Fig. 142. *Spear: Wommera-spear.*—This ideagram shows how, when the wommera is held between the fore and middle fingers, the spear glides between the forefinger and thumb; the movement expresses that of the spear just being let fly (sect. 253). (P.P.), (Bo.), (Ula), (Won.), (Wal.), Und., (Kal.), (Mit.), Woo., Goa.

Fig. 143. *Spear: Wommera-spear.*—The extended forefinger represents the wommera: inwards rotation at wrist, except among Mitakoodi, where there is movement forwards but no rotation. P.P., (Bo.), (Ula.), Won., Wal., (Und.), Kal., Mit., Woo., Goa.

Fig. 144. *Spear: Hand-spear.*—The ordinary hand-spear just in the act of being thrown (sect. 247). P.P., Bo., Ula., (Kal.), Mit., Woo., Goa.

Fig. 145. *Fighting-pole* (sect. 255).—The two hands are in their relative positions of holding the weapon and moving it up and down. Among the Kalkadoons the same ideagram denotes a stone tomahawk. (P.P.), (Bo.), (Ula.), (Won.), (Wal.), Und., Kal. (Mit.).

Fig. 146. *Fighting-pole: Stone Tomahawk.*—An imaginary blow through the air downwards, forwards, and inwards: the hands held in position depicted are striking a side-blow. With the same tribe a stone tomahawk is expressed by the same sign, but only the lower hand used in its execution. Mit.

Fig. 147. *Fighting-pole.*—The hand, with palm towards face, is closed over the stick which he moves from side to side in the act of warding off his adversary's vertical blow. Among the Boinji tribes the knuckles, instead of pointing upwards, look forwards as in Fig. 145. P.P., Bo., Ula., Won., Wal., (Und.), (Kal.), (Mit.).

Fig. 148. *(Stone-) tomahawk.*—Fingers in close apposition, and together flexed at right angles with the palm: the digits represent the blade (sect. 258). The movement, a sudden rotation at the wrist, indicates the blade falling. P.P., Bo., (Ula.), Won., Wal., Und., (Kal.), (Mit.).

Fig. 149. *(Stone-) tomahawk.*—The two hands extended and placed close together, are moved from the elbow sharply, to express the idea of the blade falling. (P.P.), Ula., (Kal.), (Mit.).

Fig. 150. *Shield.*—The hand at the handle (sect. 254) is holding the weapon in position. (P.P.), Bo., Ula., (Kal.), Mit., Woo., Goa.

Fig. 151. *Shield.*—The upper hand is holding the handle on the posterior flattened side of the weapon, while the lower hand is moulding and tapping itself upon the anterior convex surface (*cf.* Fig. 200). P.P., (Bo.), (Ula.), Won., Wal., Und., (Kal.), (Mit.).

Fig. 152. "*Koolamon.*"—The idea of the hollow hands, placed together at their finger tips, is to give expression to the concavity (or convexity) of the wooden vessel (sect. 148). Kal.

Fig. 153. "*Koolamon.*"—Similar idea as preceding, but only one hand is used, and a rotation at the wrist: the expression of rotundity, &c. P.P., Bo., Ula., Won., Wal., Und., (Kal.).

Fig. 154. "*Koolamon*": *to carry one on the head.*—The hands are placed, palms upward, upon either side of the head to balance the vessel which is carried there. (P.P.), Bo., Ula., (Kal.).

Fig. 155. "*Koolamon*": *to carry one on the head.*—One arm only, held above the vessel, is keeping it in position. Kal.

Fig. 156. "*Koolamon*": *to carry one at the side.*—The palm of the hand, together with the forearm, is maintaining the vessel close against the hip and flank. P.P., Bo., Ula. (Won.), (Wal.), Und., (Kal.).

Fig. 157 "*Koolamon*": *to carry one at the side.*—Similar idea as preceding, but in this case the act is represented just previously to the arm being shifted to support it Kal., Mit., Woo., Goa.

Fig. 158. *Net: to make one* (see also Fig. 92).—The fixed hand is holding the net in process of manufacture, while the other is imitating the movement of weaving. P.P., Kal.

Fig. 159. *Net: to make one.*—The forefinger tapping on the open palm is said to represent the "mesh." Mit.

Fig. 160. *Hut: to construct one.*—The two curved forefingers are brought downwards and inwards, so as to touch each other: these fingers indicate the two curved sticks which, firmly driven into the ground at their bases, are fixed together at their apices, thus constituting the scaffolding or "back bone" to which all the other timbers are attached (sect. 159). Among the Mitakoodi the action of the ideagram is reversed; it commences with the two fingers touching and then opening outwards. P.P., Bo., Ula., Won., Wal., Und., (Kal.), Mit.

Fig. 161. *Hut: to make one.*—Similar idea as in preceding: the two super-posed hands are the two sticks fixed at their apices. Kal.

Fig. 162. *Hut: to make one.*—The general convexity and timbering is indicated by the fingers of both hands being interlocked. Woo., Goa.

93. Number.—In addition to actual enumeration on the digits, the idea of a "big mob, a large number," is represented by the utilisation of them all—the notion of these constituting the whole lot. In Figs. 163, 164, both the open hands are used, in Fig. 165 only one, the want of the other being supplied by the side-to-side rapid motion. Fig. 166 shows a slight contrast in that both half open hands are made to circle one around the other, giving rise to the idea of a whole lot running up, being jumbled up, together, the idea of number in a collective sense.

94. Notes to Illustrations.

Fig. 163. *Large number: a lot.*—The two hands with palms held up towards the signaller's face—the idea of all the digits, the whole lot of them. P.P., Bo., Ula., Won., Wal., Und., (Kal.).

Fig. 164. *Large number, &c.*—Same idea as preceding; but fingers separated, and backs of palms towards signaller's face. Kal., Mit., Woo., Goa.

Fig. 165. *Large number, &c.*—Oscillation of open hand with palm facing the signaller. Among the Pitta-Pitta aboriginals, the dorsum is turned towards the signaller, and expresses the idea of a "big mob on the walk-about." P.P., Und., (Kal.).

Fig. 166. *Large number, all-together-in-a-body.*—Hand half-closed: the idea of the whole lot, all being jumbled up together. P.P., Bo., Ula., (Kal.). (*Cf.* Fig. 180.)

95. Locality and Direction.—These ideas are all expressed on lines very similar to those in vogue among Europeans: *e.g.*, the beckoning of a "come here" in Fig. 167, the waving of a "go away" in Figs. 168, 169, 170, or a "go along round" in Fig. 171, together with the curt indication of direction or propinquity by means of the thumb or forefinger in Fig. 172. Direction is also indicated by a pronounced pouting of the lips towards the required quarter.

96. Notes to Illustrations.

Fig. 167. *Hither!*—The idea of beckoning with the forefinger. P.P., Bo., Ula., Won., Wal., Und., Kal., Mit.

Fig. 168. *Thither!*—Antagonistic to the preceding, the position of arm and hand indicating required direction. P.P., Bo., Ula., Won., Wal., Und., Mit.

Fig. 169. *Thither!*—The flat of the hand down, and strongly marked flexion at wrist: the direction is expressed by the whole hand extended in its entirety. Woo., Goa.

Fig. 170. *Thither! There! A long way off.*—A longer sweep of the arm than in the preceding, and a "click" of the thumb and forefinger at end of the movement. Position of the arm and hand indicates the direction. Among the Pitta-Pitta blacks this idea is sometimes expressed by suitable position of the head with protruded lips.

Fig. 171. *Direction: Go along round! &c.*—The direction, where to go round, is indicated by the long sweep of the forefinger. P.P., Bo., Ula., Won., Wal., Und , Mit.

Fig. 172. *Place: Here! In this spot!*—The thumb acts as the indicator among the Wonkajera and Walookera (*cf.* the London costermonger with his thumb pointing over the shoulder): in remaining tribes, the forefinger usually. P.P., Bo., Ula., Won., Wal., Und., Mit., Woo., Goa.

97. Time.—The same notion of "Stay-where-you-are," in Fig. 182, also furnishes the idea of "Wait-a-bit" and so "By-and-by"; hence it happens that this ideagram is utilised for both purposes—position and time—though the direction in which the whole arm and hand would be pointing in the former case is, of course, subject to variation ; contrast this with the sign seen in Fig. 181. The idea of the sun rising above, or sinking below, the horizon finds itself well expressed in Figs. 173, 174, and hence we see the development of two fresh notions—sunrise, to-morrow, &c., on the one hand; and sunset, evening, night-time, &c., on the other. The moon is sometimes substituted for the sun, but with a slower movement; and thus moonrise, a month, &c., and similar expressions of thought signalled.

98. Notes to Illustrations.

Fig. 173. *Sunrise, a day : moonrise, a month, &c.*—The outstretched and cupped hand and fingers, by a slow flexion at the elbow, is moved up to the side and back of the speaker's head : the sun is rising slowly from the horizon. With the Kalkadoon tribes, the digits are all closed, except the forefinger, and the palm straight, not cupped : among the Woonamurra and Goa aboriginals, the digits are all closed. P.P., Bo., Ula., Und., Kal., Mit., Woo., Goa.

Fig. 174. *Sunset : night-time, &c.*—Antagonistic movement and position to the preceding : the sun sinking below the horizon. Same variations with Kalkadoon, Woonamurra, and Goa, as the preceding. P.P., Bo., Ula., Und., Kal., Mit., Woo., Goa.

99. Interrogation.

—This is indicated either in the ordinary European fashion of shrugging the arms and shoulders, or by a special movement of the arm and hand as in Fig. 175. In either case it is curious to note that with the Pitta-Pitta tribes the spoken word denoting doubt or interrogation is "kulli-kulli," a reduplication of the word denoting an arm. The nature of the interrogation will, of course, depend entirely upon the context of the dumb conversation.

100. Note to Illustration.

Fig. 175. *Interrogation.*—The fingers are loosely flexed, the movement consisting of a tossing of the hand outwards from the elbow, in a comparatively larger "sweep" than that represented in the diagram. Among the Kalkadoon, all th fingers are thrown open at the termination of the act ; among the Pitta-Pitta, only the forefinger. P.P., Bo., Ula., Won , Wal., Und., Kal., Mit., Woo., Goa.

101. Simple Acts, States, and Conditions.

—The expression of request or demand in the outstretched arm and open hand of Fig. 176, as well as the inculcation of silence in the movement of shutting-up the mouth in Figs. 177, 178, require no further elucidation. The same may be said of " Get out of the way" in Fig. 179, " Run" in Fig. 180, or "Stay where you are," " Sit down " in Figs. 181, 182. The act of covering with earth is represented in Fig. 183 : that which is covered—*e.g.*, excreta, &c.—is a development of the same idea. A corrobboree, music and dancing, is expressed in imitation of the men beating their boomerangs in rhythmic unison (Figs. 184, 185); or of the women clapping their opened hollowed hands upon the upper and inner aspects of the thighs (Fig. 186) ; or of the manner of raising the feet, the commonest step adopted by the performers engaging in the dance (Fig. 187). When the ways of making fire are understood, the blowing of the sparks and tinder in Figs. 188, 189, or the friction of the fire-sticks in Figs. 190, 191, 192, are perfectly intelligible. The same may be said of sleeping, Fig. 193 ; swimming, Figs. 194, 195 ; diving, Fig. 48 ; grasping or holding, Fig. 196 ; as well as the stealing of a woman from her lawful owners by dragging her away by the wrist, in Fig. 197. In the case of eating, any of the ideagrams referring to seed-food—the " daily-bread " of the aboriginal—can be made to do duty, *e.g.*, Figs. 99, 100 : an additional means of conveying the same idea is Fig. 198, the full hand being put up to the mouth, and returned empty. Water (Fig. 105) plays for drinking the same part that seed-food does for eating.

102. Notes to Illustrations.

Fig. 176. *Request, demand.*—The attitude of the outstretched arm and open hand is very definite. P.P., Kal., Mit.

Fig. 177. *Silence: be quiet!*—The slightly open hand is moved pretty quickly up to, round, and down again from the mouth : as it passes the mouth the hand is closed, and in that position completes the movement. P.P., Bo., Ula., Won., Wal., Und., Kal., Mit.

Fig. 178. *Silence: be quiet!*—The flat of the hand is held over the open mouth : it is then quickly turned forwards, downwards, and outwards. Woo., Goa.

Fig. 179. " *Get out of the road,*" &c.—The plane of the palm and extended fingers held vertically, is pointed forwards : the movement of the forearm outwards from the elbow signifies the idea of brushing something aside. Mit., Woo., Goa.

Fig. 180. "*Run !*"—Both fists closed and circular movement with each : the feet hurrying onwards. Mit. (*Cf.* Fig. 166.)

Fig. 181. " *Stay where you are : sit down,*" &c.—The hand is held out towards the necessary quarter, and the bidding the person stay there by means of a gentle fall of the arm. P.P., Bo., Ula., Won., Wal., Und., Kal., Mit.

Fig. 182. " *Sit down*": *by-and-by* : "*wait a bit.*"—Thumb on the closed fist : a sharp vertical movement from the elbow. (No holding outwards of the arm as in preceding.) P.P., Bo., Ula., Won., Wal., Und., Kal., Mit.

Fig. 183. *To cover with earth : corpse, excreta,* &c.—The idea of shovelling earth over the dead body, fæces, &c. Somewhat of a rotation inwards. (*Cf.* Fig. 47.) P.P., Kal., Mit., Woo., Goa.

Fig. 184. *Corrobboree.*—The two boomerangs (*see* Fig. 140) are being tapped together to keep the time. Among the Ulaolinya and Kalkadoon aboriginals, the two little fingers are not used ; with the Mitakoodi all the fingers of each hand are used, the one hand similarly tapping on the other. P.P., Bo., Ula., Kal., Mit., Woo., Goa.

Fig. 185. *Corrobboree.*—The same idea as in the preceding, but the two fore-fingers alone used, the hands kept apart, and alternate rapid outward and inward rotation at the wrists. P.P., (Bo.), (Ula.), Won., Wal., (Und.), Kal.

Fig. 186. *Corrobboree.*—This ideagram represents the method of beating time adopted by the gins (sect. 198) ; the hollowed hands placed one above the other are made to resound upon the crutch of the legs. P.P., Ula.

Fig. 187. *Corrobboree.*—Raising each hand alternately to indicate the commonest form of dance—the alternate raising of each leg (sect. 195). P.P., (Bo.), (Ula.), (Won.), (Wal.), Und.

Fig. 188. *Fire : to make one.*—The mouth is blowing upon the smouldering ember held in the hand, which remains stationary. (P.P.), (Bo.), (Ula.), (Won.), (Wal.), Und., (Kal.), Mit.

Fig. 189. *Fire,* &c.—Mouth is blowing upon the smouldering ember held between the fingers and thumb : vibratory movement of forearm from elbow. P.P., Bo., Ula., Won., Wal., (Und.), (Kal.).

Fig. 190. *Fire,* &c.—The two hands held closely, one above the other, are rubbing the more or less slanting firestick forwards and backwards across the horizontally placed one lying below (sect. 157*b*). (? P.P.), (Bo.), (Ula.), (Won.), (Wal.), Und., (Kal.).

Fig. 191. *Fire,* &c.—Similar idea as in preceding, but here the hands are held, one around the other, overlapping. Woo., Goa.

Fig. 192. *Fire,* &c.—Another form of firestick to the two preceding (sect 157*a*). The vertical component is being twirled backwards and forwards between the two firmly extended hands. P.P., Kal., Mit., Woo., Goa.

Fig. 193. *Sleep.*—The side of the head, with eyes shut, resting upon the hollowed hand. P.P., Bo., Ula., Won., Wal., Und., (Kal.), Mit., Woo., Goa.

Fig. 194. *Swimming.*—Both hands, on a horizontal plane, imitating natatory movements. P.P., Bo., Ula., Won., Wal., Und., Kal., Mit.

Fig. 195. *Swimming.*—The one hand, with palm in a vertical plane, is thrust out directly forwards, and slowly redrawn. Woo., Goa.

Fig. 196. *To grasp, catch hold of, &c.*—The outstretched hand pulled backwards and upwards, being simultaneously closed. P.P., Bo., Ula., Won., Wal., Und.

Fig. 197. *To grasp, to steal a gin.*—The idea of dragging her away by the wrist. Kal., Mit.

Fig. 198. *To eat : food, &c.*—The closed hand is put up to the mouth, and then redrawn pretty quickly in a downwards and forwards direction, when the palm shows forwards: the idea of the full hand, being put up to the mouth, whence it is returned empty. From the idea of thus bolting the food, the same ideagram is in addition used among the Pitta-Pitta aboriginals to express "a large dog" (*cf.* the English idiom of "wolfing up one's food"). P.P., Bo., Ula., Won., Wal., Und., Kal., Mit.

103. Complex Conditions, &c. Abstract Ideas.—Anger is represented by a biting of the ball of the thumb in Fig 199, or, if more convenient, by the lapping over of the beard into the mouth and holding it there between the teeth: another means of expressing anger, &c., is by the idea of hitting or striking, as in Fig. 200. Illness, sickness, disease, &c., is expressed in various ways. The practice of smearing blood over the body of the patient (sect. 283) is indicated in Fig. 201 ; on account of the complaint usually necessitating the patient's lying down or going to sleep, we find the ideagram Fig. 202 doing duty under both circumstances ; also by the pressing of the hand to the side, as in Fig. 203, a sufferer *in extremis*—a dramatic trick practised among even European people ; and, to express a fatal issue, the stiffening of the legs after death in Fig. 204. In loss of memory, forgetfulness, &c. (Fig. 205), attention is drawn to something having gone into the head, through the ear, but which is not willing to come out again—it is therefore being picked out with the fingers : in Fig. 206 a somewhat similar notion is expressed with the forehead. The true interpretations of the ideagrams for " yes" (Fig. 207), "no" (Fig. 208), "good" (Figs. 209, 210), " bad" (Fig. 211), I have not succeeded in obtaining from among the aboriginals whence I learnt them. Nevertheless, the similarity of Fig. 210 and the expression adopted by a European child patting itself in the sense of self-satisfaction, goodness, &c., is interesting ; while an explanation of Fig. 211 may possibly be found in a comparison with Fig. 204, death from a non-physical (*i.e.*, aboriginally unapparent) cause being always looked upon as a punishment for crime committed (sect. 279). The ideagrams indicative of two of the articles of faith, &c., though arbitrary, are recorded in Figs. 212, 213.

104. Notes to Illustrations.

Fig. 199. *Anger : intention of fighting, &c.*—The biting of the ball of the thumb. The same intention can also be expressed by the signaller holding his own beard between his teeth. It is possible that both these variations may be but reminiscences of the times when enemies were eaten after battle. (*Cf.* the biting of the lip in the case of a European ; also the expression of a man having " hair on his teeth.") P.P., Bo., Ula., Won., Wal., Und., Kal., Mit., Woo., Goa.

Fig. 200. *Anger : intention of fighting, &c.*—The dorsum of the one hand rapping sharply upon the hollowed palm of the other : the idea of punching, hitting, &c. P.P., Mit. (*cf.* Fig. 151).

Fig. 201. *Sickness : a sick person.*—A rubbing of the chest and breast slowly up and down in a more or less circular movement with the flats of the hands : an imitation of the method adopted in times of sickness of rubbing human blood over these same parts (sect. 283). In both these tribes, sickness, &c., can also be expressed in imitation of the treatment (sect. 283) in taking the sweat with each hand alternately from the opposite armpit, and either smelling them or rubbing them over the affected parts. P.P., Und.

Fig 202. *Sickness : to lie down : to sleep.*—Fingers loosely closed, palm towards signaller's face, and to-and-fro flexion at wrist. Kal.

Fig. 203. *Sickness: a seriously sick person.*—The cupped hand is pressed well into the flank, the trunk being at the same time time flexed laterally: the hand supports the side which is just going to fall over. (*Cf.* the similar European sign.) P.P., (Bo.), Ula., Won., Wal., Und., Kal., Mit.

Fig. 204. *Sickness: moribund: a corpse.*—The hand, palm up, held horizontally, with forefinger and little finger fully extended: the idea of a dead person with the legs stiffened out. (*Cf.* Fig. 211: a corpse has already been referred to in Fig. 183.) Woo., Goa.

Fig. 205. *Forgetfulness, loss of memory, &c.*—Picking at the centre or lobe of the ear with thumb and forefinger: the idea of bringing forth that which was originally put into it. (Compare the Pitta-Pitta word narapoonga—*i.e.*, to forget—where nara = ear.) P.P., Mit., Woo., Goa.

Fig. 206. *Forgetfulness, loss of memory, &c.*—Hand in corresponding position over brow as a European in deep thought: motion of the hand forwards and downwards. Similar idea as the preceding. Kal., Mit., Woo., Goa.

Fig. 207. *Yes! all right! &c.*—The fingers are loosely hooked at the proximal joints: a single vertical flexion from the elbow. P.P., Bo., Ula., Won., Wal., Und., Kal., Mit., Woo., Goa.

Fig. 208. *No! negation, &c.*—Hand towards signaller's face with the fingers conveniently flexed: a sudden movement downwards with simultaneous rotation inwards, the fingers being at the same time extended and separated. P.P., Bo., Ula., Won., Wal., Und., Kal., Mit., Woo., Goa.

Fig. 209. *Good: person or thing.*—Thumb working more or less circularly upon the middle and forefingers: the hand may often be pointed in the direction of the person or thing referred to. P.P., Bo., Ula., Won., Wal., Und., (Kal.), (Mit.), Woo., Goa.

Fig. 210. *Good: person (?or thing).*—Patting of the lower portion of the breast with the flattened hand. Compare the expression of a European child patting itself in self-satisfaction. Mit.

Fig. 211. *Bad: person, or thing.*—The extended fore and little fingers are pointed at the person or thing indicated, palm up or down. In addition to this ideagram, the Woonamurra and Goa have a variation: the fore and middle fingers widely separated and extended do the pointing. Compare this with Fig. 204, the ideagram for sickness, a corpse, &c.: sickness and death from a non-physical (*i.e.*, aboriginally unapparent) cause being always considered a punishment for crime committed (sect. 279).

Fig. 212. *Ghost* ("Moma," sect. 260).—The idea of the big snout being held in the hand and drawn over the head to get it out of the way. P.P.

Fig. 213. *Water-sprite* ("Kanmare," sect. 260).—Represents the snake-like individual swimming away along the surface of the water above which its head is protruded. (*Cf.* Fig. 60.) P.P.

CHAPTER V.

THE SEARCH FOR FOOD. PITURI.

105. Throughout the Boulia District all **Seed-Food** has the generic term of *pap-pa* applied to it : the following, with their Pitta-Pitta names, unless otherwise stated, are some of the varieties utilised.

106. The *ya-ra-ka* "star-grass" (*Eleusine ægyptiaca*, Pers.). A sufficient quantity having been collected—a woman always preparing all plant food—it is more or less broken up with the hands, next brushed into a heap, and then put into a circular hole in the ground (Fig. 214). Within this hole, about 12 inches in diameter and 7 or 8 in depth, the woman stands : pressing alternately one foot upon the other (Fig. 215) she exerts a sort of rotary motion into which she throws all her weight, with the result that the grass upon which she treads becomes more and more disintegrated, the seed itself gradually working its way to the bottom. To throw all her weight upon the legs, she either supports herself on a sort of tripod of forked sticks erected in front of her, or else, when it happens to be handy, some low-lying limb of a tree. From the hole the seed is transferred to a koolamon, any of the larger sprigs, &c., are removed with the fingers, and the rest winnowed with the breath or a current of air : it is now clean enough and ready for grinding on the pappa-stone (sect. 154). This is effected by a more or less forwards and backwards movement, the position of the operator being shown in the illustration, Fig. 216. During the grinding process the seed is moistened with water, and as each handful is adequately ground it is smeared over the edge of the slab into a koolamon ; when sufficient of this pasty mass has been prepared, it is roasted after the manner of a "damper," though sometimes it is eaten raw. Whatever opinion may be expressed as to the taste, it is always, as might have been expected, extremely gritty ; indeed, the flattened "ground-down" appearance of the crowns in the teeth among all these aboriginals must, in great measure, be ascribed to the sandy nature of their seed-food.

107. The *ka-too-ra* (*Sporobolus actinocladus*, F. v. M.) reminds one of the Ayrshire Downs Barley-grass. This is cut down, tied into small bundles, taken down to the nearest water-hole, and dipped under just for a minute or two : the bundles are next laid out to dry in the sun for a quarter-of-an-hour or so, but to prevent the process taking place too rapidly, especially on a very hot day, they may be covered over with some other grasses or bushes. When the moisture has been sufficiently removed, each bundle is firmly held by the stalk-portion with one hand, while the head-portion is gently brushed over and squeezed with the other, the seed so loosened being allowed to fall into the water contained in a koolamon beneath (Fig. 217). The water is drawn off subsequently by tipping up the vessel, and so letting the fluid escape through the interdigital spaces of the hollowed hand (Fig. 218) : the seed itself is then dried again before being ground and made up into a damper.

Another grass similar to the katoora, but much larger, is the *ya-ka-pa-ri* (*Sporobolus Lindleyi*, Benth.) : its seeds are prepared by an identical process.

108. The seed of the coolibar (*Eucalyptus bicolor*, A. Cunn.) also constitutes a staple article of diet, when grass-seed is scarce : locally it is known as *ka-ra-pa-ri*. With a hooked stick some terminal branches of this tree are pulled down and, just as they are, spread out to dry on a piece of ground cleared for the purpose. Here they lie, according to the heat of the sun, for half-a-day, a day, till sunset, or the following morning. The ends of the branches are then all collected together, and the seed obtained by damping the distal extremities and brushing them off into water, as in the case of the *katoora*. Before the ultimate drying, however, the coolibar seed is kept for a couple of hours or so in water, which during this time is repeatedly changed, so as to remove all traces of the "gum." After being ground on the pappa-stone it is eaten raw.

109. The "pig-weed" (*Portulaca oleracea*, Linn.), the *koo-ni* of this district may be eaten raw in its entirety, its taste very much resembling water-cress, or only its seed used. This latter is obtained by taking a goodly-sized bunch and rubbing it between the two hands held more or less horizontally (Fig. 219), the seeds dropping into a koolamon, and subjected to washing and grinding as before. It is eaten raw.

110. The hard-shelled seed of the "nardoo" (*Marsilea*), easily and speedily collected from the plant when growing in marshy swamps, is pounded and broken up with a special stone, the "nardoo"-stone (sect. 155), previous to grinding.

111. In the Cloncurry District, among the Mitakoodi, the *jil-qroo bur-i* (*Sporobolus indicus*, R. Br.), closely allied to the *katoora* and *yakapari* of the Boulia District, is prepared by similar process. Pig-weed, known as *tun-ga-ra* or *tal-lo* (Woonamurra *ya-ma-ri*, Goa *kun-go-yi*), and a species of "star-grass" called *tin-dil* (*Panicum decompositum*, R. Br.) are also treated the same, but neither nardoo nor coolibar seed is eaten up here. "Wild-rice" or *mo-ko-mur-lo* (*Oryza sativa*, Linn.), is prepared as follows :—After gathering, when the seeds are ripened, it is tied up in bundles and dried (sect. 86): the heads of these bundles are beaten on a piece of ti-tree bark, and the seeds falling out are collected and winnowed, subsequently ground, and cooked like a damper. The seeds of the water-lily, *too-lum-bool*, and of the *Portulaca napiformis*, F. v. M., or *ka-re-dil-la*, are also eaten, but, as their roots are more commonly partaken of, these plants will be referred to in sect. 114.

112. In the Leichhardt-Selwyn District, the Kalkadoon eat various forms of grass-seed under the name of *kun-yel*: pig-weed, or *poon-jo*, and the wild-rice are also common dietaries.

113. The following are some of the **Edible Roots** met with in the Boulia District :—The *wi-too-ka* or *win-nu* (*Boerhaavia diffusa*, Linn.), a peppery sort of small "yam," something like a radish, is found everywhere, is pretty brittle, and has to be plucked out of the ground somewhat carefully (sects. 85, 86) to prevent snapping : it is eaten roasted. Other yams, *ka-la-ra*, are dug up with a special stick (sect. 158) and eaten cooked or uncooked. The root of a species of water-lily, *pe-ta-bur-i*, known to me as growing at Wandetta and Idamea Lakes, on portions of the Burke River, on Tooleybuck Station and elsewhere, tastes not unlike a potato after roasting. *Mung-a-roo* is the root of a kind of "nut-grass" growing to a height of about 6 inches from the ground on soft sandy flats, having knobby or almost globular roots about one-sixth of an inch and more in diameter; the husks are removed ordinarily by a rolling between the fore-finger and thumb (sect. 86) or occasionally between the open hand and the thigh : eaten raw or roasted.

114. In the Cloncurry District, the Mitakoodi also eat several kinds of roots, either roasted or raw. There are two species of edible waterlily root, the one, *un-dul*, with a smooth-surfaced root, the other, *lin-da*, with a hairy surface : it is the seed, *too-lum-bool*, of the former variety only (sect. 111) which is eaten. Among yams, four at least are relished : the short-rooted *ma-la-ga* (*Vigna lanceolata*, Benth.), and a long-rooted one, *wol-le*, growing on sandy ground ; a third variety, *ur-ruk-ki-un*, thriving on the mountain ranges; and a fourth small one, called the *koo-jo*, identical with the *witooka* of Boulia, which can be found pretty well everywhere. The *ma-kor-a* is identical with the *mungaroo* of the Boulia District; the roots of the *ka-re-dil-la* (sect. 111) are also very commonly eaten.

115. In the Leichhardt-Selwyn District, the Kalkadoon eat the Boerhaavia-root, known locally as *wa-roo-po* (the *witooka* of Boulia), the "nut-grass" root or *to-ko* (*mungaroo* of Boulia), and various species of yams, *ng-ga*.

116. I have no personal knowledge of **Fungi**, mushrooms, &c., as articles of diet in these districts. However, Mr. Coghlan, of Glenormiston, a careful observer, says that just on the western side of the Mulligan a sort of truffle, with a yellowish flesh after roasting, appears to be a delicacy. This, he tells me, is very difficult to find even with the practised eye, a small undulation on the surface of the ground being its only indication: when once it has pushed its way through it rapidly gets "bad" through exposure to the sun.

117. Fruits and Vegetables.—Throughout North-West-Central Queensland the "wild orange" (*Atalantia glauca*, Hook., Pitta-Pitta *woom-bun-ye*, Kalkadoon *in-pa-ka-to*, Mitakoodi *kun-doo-tul*), "emu-apple," (*Owenia acidula*, F. v M., Mitakoodi *el-din*, *oo-ro-ka*), wild-currant (Mitakoodi *kung-ga-pa-ri*, *yul-boong-go*), several kinds of vine, caper, trefoil, and numerous berries and peas for which there are no European equivalents are all eaten. Indeed, it is difficult under this heading to know what is refused.

118. Flowers and Honey.—The blossoms of the "blood-wood" (*Eucalyptus corymbosa*, Sm.), and Bauhinia-trees at Glenormiston, and of the ti-trees (*Cordyline*, Comm.) at Roxburgh, are sucked for the sake of the sugar or honey contained.

Honey or "sugar-bag," as the more civilised aboriginals call it, is found throughout the North-West-Central Districts, especially along the river courses, except perhaps the Upper Mulligan, and obtained by one or other of the following methods. Its locality in the particular tree is tracked: during the winter-time, by watching carefully for the minute pellets of dung lying on the ground around the butt; in the summer months, by observing the bees going in and out of their nest; and at occasion by putting the ear down to some natural orifice at the base of the tree, and listening for the insects' hum and buzz. The trunk is often tapped lightly with the fingers (sects. 83, 84) or with a stone for indications of a hollow core: a likely situation for a nest. When the nest has been discovered, the limb may be removed bodily, or the tree climbed: the latter measure can be effected by cutting nicks or steps alternately higher and higher on either side of the trunk, and stepping from one on to the other (sect. 84, Fig. 82). To remove the honey from out of the cavity either the hand or a stick is inserted: this is swept round and round to prevent the glutinous mass from dropping off, somewhat after the style of a spoon with some thick syrup on it (sect. 84, Fig. 80). A bee is known as *ool-lo* in the Boulia District, *bung-go bung-go* in the Cloncurry: honey in the latter is *koong-ga*.

119. Insects and Crustaceans.—Certain species of ants (for local names, see sect. 53)—a green variety among the Mitakoodi—are eaten raw: the individual stands or stamps upon an ant-bed from which these creatures will run up his legs and thighs, and get scraped or swept off as fast as they come up. Smaller kinds of grubs and caterpillars, especially those found on the grass (*ka-pa-ra*, both of the Boulia and Cloncurry Districts) may be eaten raw and whole: the larger varieties, found in trees, (*ka-lo-rung-or-o* of the Boulia) are usually roasted, the heads not being eaten (sect. 84, Fig. 84), or may be dried in the sun, and put away for future occasion. Crayfish (Pitta-Pitta *koon-da-chi*, Mitakoodi *pe-kool*) are also relished.

120. Molluscs.—The freshwater mussel (*Unio*), which is a very common article of diet is roasted in its shell, whole. It is tracked usually by feeling for it in the mud with the feet. The Mitakoodi call it by three different names: *pe-je* or ·yung-un when obtained from water-covered mud, and lul-ka-rin when got out of dry mud. The Pitta-Pitta, Wonkajera and Kalkadoon apply the terms too-rool-ka, too-roo-ka, koo-joo-roo respectively to express the animal.

121. **Frogs** are eaten everywhere, and partaken of, roasted. In the Boulia District three kinds are eaten: the big bull-frog, ta-ral-ko, from 4½ to 5 inches long; a smaller variety, koon-pa, about 3½ inches, and a still more diminutive species ne-ma-ka, about 2½ inches long. True green-frogs do not appear to be used as articles of diet. These creatures are dug up from their burrows, the particular surface indications and tracks being well-known to them, by means of yam-sticks, &c., in hard ground, or with the hands in sandy soil. The two kinds of frogs which the Mitakoodi eat in the Cloncurry district are the jou-un or larger, and the nel-li or smaller variety.

122. **Lizards** are usually caught while running along the grass; **Iguanas** are generally dug up from out of the ground. The iguana-burrow is not vertical, but sloping, and very often in close proximity to some tree. These, like all the remaining animals and birds, to be successively mentioned, are eaten roasted. (sect. 156.)

Crocodiles (Mitakoodi pa-mi-te-ra) are hunted by the Workoboongo in the upper reaches of the Leichhardt, with hand-spears: it must be remembered in this connection that the reptiles (Philas Johnstonii) found up here are of much smaller size than those (Crocodilus porosus) found lower down the river.

123. **Snakes** are sometimes found in an old iguana-hole or in burrows of their own. The aboriginals will eat a snake when killed by themselves or others : as to any avoidance whether the animal has previously bitten itself or not appears to be a myth on the part of the Europeans.

124. **Fish** are caught by various methods and contrivances, the most general throughout North-West-Central Queensland being with special nets. The material of which these nets are manufactured is some form of plant-fibre, e.g., native flax, (? Linum marginale, A. Cunn., Pitta-Pitta ka-lo) woven on a pattern identical with that in use by Europeans (sect. 153). The wooden needle, over a foot long, with a small lump of cementing-substance at either end, has no "eye" in it, the twine being just wound on and off as required : in the Boulia District, this needle is called the ka-kum-bo-le. No wooden mesh is used in their manufacture, the regularity and uniformity of each loop being dependent upon the skill of the maker. The size of the net-mesh varies, some nets having theirs larger or smaller than others : about an inch and a-half to two inches is a fair average. The sides of the smaller nets are rounded off so as to allow for the "concavity," when on the stretch. The smaller nets reach from 6 to 12 feet in length, the larger from 50 to 70 or 80 feet, the width varying proportionately from about 2 to 6 or 7 feet : for decorative purposes, they may be painted with transverse bands of alternately red and yellow ochre. The longer nets are not to be too often met with, and would appear to be brought to these parts by the Miorli boys, on the Diamantina, who make them. In the Boulia District it may be stated generally that when fishing in shallow water the smaller-sized nets are brought into requisition : when in deep water, the larger ones. With the former, where three or four may be used in conjunction, a long thin stick is attached along the sides of each, not only to keep them open, but also to allow of their being the more easily handled. Two men start into the water from the river-bank, with the net between them (Fig. 220, A) followed successively by another and another pair, and perhaps a fourth (B, C, D), each couple coming up from behind so as to overlap the one immediately preceding, and together forming a gradually more and more enclosed space, into which the "beaters" (K), from the front are driving the fish. The chief objection, if such it may be considered, to employing the small variety of net in this manner, is that so many people are as a rule required to assist. The Boulia District aboriginals, who make these smaller nets, call them ma-li : the Kalkadoon, who obtain them by barter, wun-to.

With the long nets, only two people are necessary, though more may lend a hand, who work it after the manner illustrated in the diagram (Fig. 221). A and B are the two individuals in charge of the net Z, with pole at each extremity, the net lying parallel with the river-bank, a few feet from its edge. A swims out with one end of the net, sweeping along the water to the extent of almost a quarter-circle, until he reaches C, a point about opposite to B. B now slowly swims along the bank, which he hugs pretty closely, while his companion, making another and larger sweep, joins him at D, a spot about another 50 or 60 yards onwards, may be, from the starting point, where they land. Another method of using the long net is for two swimmers to take it straight across the width of the stream. The Miorli men who make these nets, as already mentioned, on the Diamantina, do not bring them into the district under consideration much further north than Marion Downs. I have neither seen nor heard of any weights, sinkers, &c., being used, their object being replaced by the fisherman holding down the extremity of the side pole under water with the big toe.

In the Cloncurry District the Mitakoodi use the smaller kind of net, the *moo-na*, which is usually obtained in barter from the Woonamurra. It is from 8 to 10 feet long by 3 to 4 feet wide, the sides being rounded off as before, and the mesh being about 2 inches. Along all four edges are fixed four curved sticks bound together at the corners, those on the two longer sides being sometimes made of two pieces braced together at a very open angle. Four or five of these nets are generally used at a time (as in the diagram Fig. 222), each individual holding two nets more or less on the flat under water, one with either hand. These boys move together in line from the river-bank to some distance out, their companions circling round, splashing about, and driving the fish into the nets, which are then raised horizontally from the surface. Another kind of net which the Mitakoodi use, similarly obtained from the Woonamurra, is the *bil-lin-ya*. It is about 3 feet or a little more in height and about 20 inches in width, having two strongly curved sticks, fixed loosely at their extremities, attached along the sides (Fig. 223). The fisherman goes into the water, usually its shallower parts, and quietly and slowly gropes along with the net held there in front of him by the sticks : thus, like a folding purse he encloses in his net any fish that may pass in through his open thighs or round his flanks.

125. Independently of nets, another contrivance for catching fish, and one greatly adopted after floods when the waters are going down, is the building of a dam or weir right across the stretch of water. These dams, which may be used again and again, season after season, constructed of rocks and stones, have "breaks" in them (AA in diagram Fig. 224) through which the water rushes on to platforms (BB) built immediately below: these platforms, also on a foundation of and surrounded with stone, are covered with boughs and a top layer of grass which in between its meshes catches the fish as they are carried over the breaks with the receding waters. Instead of, or sometimes in addition to, the platforms, a *mali* net may be fixed up with two sticks on the lower side of the breaks, and so catch them as in a large bag. These stone dams have been met with, so far as I know, only in the Boulia District.

In the Cloncurry, Woonamurra, and Leichhardt-Selwyn Districts an artificial movable dam formed of grass, bushes, &c., is worked as follows : In a pretty shallow water-hole, the whole diameter is blocked by all the gins from the camp taking up their positions close together side by side, progressing forwards on their hands and knees, and pushing thick bundles of grass tussets and leafy boughs in front of them (Fig. 225) : a " grass " dam is thus formed which shifting onwards and onwards drives the fish before it close on to the banks, where they are easily killed and caught.

126. The practice of poisoning the water by special plants and capturing the fish as they rise to the surface is met with in the Cloncurry and Woonamurra Districts. The Mitakoodi use the *too-ta* (*Tephrosia astragaloides*, R. Br.), a blue-flowered shrub growing about 3 or 4 feet high. Its leaves are crushed and bruised, and whole bundles-full thrown into the water-hole which may be waist-deep and 20 to 30 feet in diameter ; in the course of a quarter or half an hour the fish come up to the surface where they are knocked over by the hunters. In the Cloncurry, Woonamurra, and Leichhardt-Selwyn Districts, especially with large

water-holes, numerous leafy boughs and branches of "gum-tree" (Mitakoodi, *joo-a-ro*) are utilised for a similar purpose. The whole camp of blacks working at it, will start throwing these in first thing in the morning ; during the day the water becomes darker and darker and strongly-smelling until by the following morning at sunrise when it is almost black, the fish all lie panting at the surface and are easily caught, The simple "muddying" or "puddling" of the water by the feet, in small shallows, and hitting the fish as they come up with a stick, is a procedure common throughout North-West-Central Queensland.

127. Though the probability of the method is likely, I have not met with any spearing in the Boulia District ; it is certainly in vogue among the Cloncurry and Flinders District aboriginals. Thus, going into still and shallow water, the Mitakoodi will, with a lot of splashing and noise, spear the fish as they shoot past. In running water or in flood time, the natives take up their position on an over-hanging trunk or branch. On the Upper Leichhardt River, as is mentioned in sect. 252, spearing with foreign-made and specially constructed spears was found to be practised.

128. On some portions of the Georgina River, and in certain other creeks, the aboriginals will grope carefully along the mud and so transfix with their feet a sort of "cat-fish" to be found there.

129. A common way of killing fish is to bite into them deeply just at the back of the head; this is very frequently done by a fisherman before he is ready to leave the water, and who thus makes sure that on throwing the fish already caught on to the river bank, there is no chance of their skipping back into their native element (sects. 79, 80).

Fish are carried home to camp, &c., by passing a thin twig through the gills and mouth, the hook at its extremity—a shoot cut short—preventing the creature from slipping off.

130. Emus are trapped by being driven into nets with or without palisadings and enclosures ; caught in pit-falls ; surrounded and mustered in mobs ; tracked and speared ; or hunted with dogs.

131. Emus generally make for the water-hole day by day along the same track, coming either at early morn or mid-day. The hunters, having noted these tracks, will wait in ambush and allow the bird to pass down on its way to water, but while drinking will sneak round and silently as well as expeditiously rig up the emu-net some 30 or 40 yards behind the creature and right across the tracks. Since the emu usually spends some time at the water-hole, the fixing up of the net is not necessarily quite so hurried a performance as might have been expected, though it can be placed in position within a very few minutes. All being ready by the time the bird returns, the hunters will suddenly emerge from their hiding-places, and as the bird rushes headlong (any diversion from the path being prevented by the men stationed in suitable positions), drive it into the net, where it becomes entangled, and, with boomerangs and nulla-nullas, soon despatched. This method of emu-hunting is practised throughout all the ethnographical districts of North-West-Central Queensland.

The general appearance of two of these nets, as made in the Boulia district, is shown in the diagram, Fig. 226. The names given to the constituent parts are those applied by the Pitta-Pitta natives. These two nets were fixed up in position for my special inspection, close to the Boulia camp, in well under five minutes. A B C D are the strong terminal supports, *ma-kun-ye*, between 4½ and 5 feet long, fixed firmly into the ground. E E E are the slender intermediate supports, *tin-ja* (*cf.* sect. 241), about 8 or 9 feet long, forked at their upper extremities, which support the top-string of the net on the stretch, and lightly planted into the ground at an angle. X X X is the net itself, the *yel-pi*, made of flax-rope about ⅜ inch in diameter, and with meshes about 12 inches by 9 inches, the top ones hanging like curtain-rings from a top-string F, the *u-wun-na*, attached to the terminal posts. Each knot is called a *ma-ti*. By means of the intermediate supports on the top-string, the net in some places touches the ground from a height of quite 7 feet. The distance between A and D, the space enclosed by these two nets, was over 120 feet. The Mitakoodi obtain their emu-nets by barter from the Kalkadoon.

In the weaving of the net, no true needle whatever is used, both this and the mesh-stick being substituted as follows (Fig. 227) :—The former is replaced by the thick cord being rolled as required upon a twig or two about 18 inches long : the place of the latter is taken by the maker's foot which keeps each successive mesh, as it is netted, perfectly firm and regular by pulling on it with the back of the ankle. The net, as it is gradually completed bit by bit, is wound round a spear implanted firmly into the ground.

132. Sometimes a long alley-way (Pitta-Pitta *yel-ka yel-ka*) is built up in a convenient situation with bushes, boughs, and saplings intertwined : one end of this is closed in with the emu-net, while the other is left open and divergent. Its general shape is shown in the diagram (Fig. 228). Close to the opening, and about midway between the two sides, are the hunters who, concealed under cover of some bushes, &c., start imitating the emu's "call." The bird coming up, in answer to the sound, struts along either side of where the men are in ambush : the latter, rushing out, making a sort of wheeling movement and, once getting behind the creature, have no difficulty in driving it before them along the alley into the net where it becomes entrapped. The "call," a sort of "drumming" sound is imitated by blowing into a hollow log some 2½ to 3 feet long, from which the inside core has been burnt so as to form an aperture about 3 inches in diameter : when in use, the tube is held close to the ground in which a slight excavation has been made. These "call-tubes" are met with throughout North-West-Central Queensland. The alley-ways I only know of being employed in the Boulia district.

133. On the sandhills round above the Hamilton River in the Boulia District, a deep pit is dug during the middle of the day in close proximity to some wild vine bush, emu-apple tree, &c., and, to avert suspicion, the excavated sand removed to a considerable distance. The mouth of the pit is carefully covered in with light boughs and saplings hidden up with sand and not visited again until the following morning, by which time a bird, coming after the fruit, will probably have fallen in. The same method of single pitfalls is employed among the Kalkadoon along the Leichhardt-Selwyn Ranges. At Roxburgh, Carandotta, and in the Upper Georgina District generally, pitfalls were used in the old days, but such methods are now dying out.

From Mr. Coghlan, of Glenormiston, on the Georgina River, I have the following account of the "multiple" pit-falls to be met with on that station :— Arrived at the hunting-ground frequented by the emus, the men make a more or less circular fence or enclosure with trees, bushes, and saplings about 60 feet in diameter. Along this fence some half-dozen gaps are left, and at each of them a pit is sunk (Diagram Fig. 229, P.) about 2 or 3 feet wide and 4 feet deep, the mouth being cunningly concealed with boughs and grass. In the centre of the circle a bigger hole is dug, similarly masked by bushes, into which three or four men can crouch. With the "call-tubes" they imitate the emu's call, and the birds making for the direction in which they hear the sound, come up to the fence and run along it to the next gap where they fall unsuspectingly into the pit. Sometimes there are external wings to the circular fence also with gaps. The same enclosure may be used for three or four years in succession, the birds being hunted by this method during the pairing season.

134. In the Boulia District, on occasion, when a mob of emus happens to come within the neighbourhood of a camp, all the men and women may assist in surrounding and mustering them like cattle, subsequently driving them down to the nearest water-hole, where they are killed with nulla, boomerang, or spear.

135. In the Cloncurry District the Mitakoodi's commonest plan of catching emus is to sneak up to them while feeding and spear them with a heavy wommera spear. To prevent the bird seeing him the hunter covers himself with bushes,

H

and holds others in front of him: to prevent the bird " smelling" him, he gets rid of the perspiration from under the armpits and from between the thighs by rubbing these parts with earth.

At Roxburgh, and higher up the Georgina, emus may be hunted with dogs, the latter always making for the bird's neck.

136. In the Boulia District **Turkey Bustards** are either caught with a grass-hopper and noose (*cf.* sect. 140) fixed to the extremity of a long thin switch held by the hunter, who gradually creeps forward unobserved enveloped in boughs and bushes, or else quietly surrounded in the open. In the latter case, numerous fires are simultaneously raised in more or less of the line of a circle right round the group of unsuspecting birds, which, dazed with the smoke and din, are rushed upon and easily knocked over with boomerangs, nulla-nullas, &c.

137. "**Flock**"-**Pigeons** *(Histriophagus histrionica)* along the Burke, Georgina, and other rivers, where they can be met with in thousands, are caught in small-mesh nets of a particular shape, the *mok-wa-ri* of the Pitta-Pitta language. The upper edge of this net is attached along its whole length to a long thin curved stick, the handle of which is free, and held by the hunter when all is in readiness: its lower edge, about 10 or 12 feet in length, is about 3 feet longer than the upper, and when in use fixed along its entire extent into the ground by means of little forked twigs. The diagram in Fig. 230 is intended to explain this more graphically. A small artificial water-hole A, about 6 feet long and 2 or 3 wide, is made parallel with, and at a little distance from, the main channel B, where the birds have been noticed to usually alight: this miniature lake is effected by a scooping up with the hands, and, what with the sandy formation of the soil, it quickly fills with beautiful clear water. When in the late afternoon the birds come down to drink they will in all probability make for it, thinking it to be a new hole, and its water fresher. The hunter knows this, and lays his net quite flat upon the ground, with the lower edge fixed close to that side of the artificial water-hole further removed from the creek: he hides himself in a crouching position under some bushes and sand close enough to have full control of the long handle. The pigeons settle down in time, walk on and over the net, and collect on the miniature lake where they " sit" the water like ducks. As soon as the individual in ambush thinks the opportunity suitable, he revolves the net around its fixed axis by a very swift movement of the arm and wrist, thus enclosing the unsuspecting birds beneath.

A similar but smaller *mokwari* net is used by the Mitakoodi in the Cloncurry District, not only for flock pigeons, but also for galah parrots and other birds: the handle, however, is more curved, and the lower edge of the net itself only just a little longer than the upper. The artificial water-hole is not necessarily made near a river, but usually anywhere in the open. A small excavation is made, 18 inches to 2 feet in diameter, and filled with water carried in big koolamons, &c. The gin comes forward and fills the hole as it dries up: as she retires, the birds of course think the coast is clear and come down to drink, when they are easily caught by the hunter, who is lying concealed all the time half-hidden underground, and covered with bushes. This method is adopted especially in the summer months when all the natural water-channels have dried up.

On the head-waters of the Georgina, the Workia and Yaroinga tribes bring down flock-pigeons by throwing a hook-boomerang into the middle of a mob of them.

138. The green " shell-back" ("love"-bird or " budgeregar") and other similarly **small birds** are caught with net and alley-way at Herbert Downs, Glenormiston, Roxburgh, Carandotta, &c.—*i.e.*, in the Boulia and Upper Georgina Districts—by a method which the diagram Fig. 231 is intended to illustrate. Stretching from some water-hole D, two long divergent palisades A B are built: these are made with thick bushes, saplings, and twigs about 8 or 10 feet high, and 40 or 50 yards long. The space C C C in the narrower portion of the alley is cleared of trees, &c., those in the diverging portion E E E being left untouched. In the very early morning a number of men sneak up towards the trees, and with loud shouting and every kind of noise will suddenly commence throwing sticks and boomerangs into them. The birds, being thus driven from their roosts by what they think to be hawks, fly low and in a direction opposite to whence the noise proceeds, but not being able to penetrate the bushes forming the palisade, make straight for the water-hole, where they are intercepted in scores by a fine-meshed net F F held up by two men standing just in front of it.

139. Corellas (*Licinetis nasica*), **Galahs** (*Cacatua roseicassila*), **Cockatoos, &c.**, are entrapped on the water in the late afternoon, at Roxburgh, Carandotta, &c., in the Upper Georgina District. The hunter, after tying numerous grass twigs and leafy boughs round his head, neck, and face, which are thus completely concealed, swims out to some log or "snag" projecting just out of the water, and supports himself there by its aid, with only his head out. As the birds come down to drink they fly round the bushes, and alighting on the log, &c., are easily caught by the legs, pulled under the water, their necks wrung, and stuck one after another in the hunter's waist-belt.

Another and very common method throughout North-West-Central Queensland of catching these and other birds which fly in mobs, is to throw a light boomerang into their very midst when on the wing.

140. Ducks, Cranes, Diver-birds, and others, if not caught in the nesting-season by sneaking upon them unawares, may at other times be noosed with a long slender stick to the extremity of which a feather-quill with slip-noose (Pitta-Pitta *nun-te-ri*) is attached. The hunter, concealed with leafy bushes tied round his head and face, waits patiently in the water for his prey, which, paddling along the water, soon comes into suitable position for the loop to be slipped over its neck. In the Boulia District at least, this method is employed.

141. The **Pelican** (*Pelicanus conspicillatus*) is caught as follows in the Boulia District:—At that portion of a creek or water-hole which the bird is known to frequent, the hunter will be sitting in the water in ambush under cover of the bushes or suitable overhanging tree, &c., and throwing empty mussel shells one after another to some considerable distance on the water. The bird, thinking that these are fish "jumping" on the surface, comes closer to see; at the same time the individual concealed, and still otherwise immovable, taps the water with his fingers to mimic the fishes splashing. The pelican, more and more convinced of the plenteous supply of fish in and around these very same bushes, &c., swims more into danger, and when arrived close enough is either hit with a boomerang or sometimes even caught by the hands.

In the Upper Georgina, at Headingly, &c., pelicans are caught at night when asleep on the river banks. The hunters, their bodies greased with ashes, and heads covered with bushes to conceal themselves the better in the darkness, will noiselessly swim up to the unsuspecting creatures and despatch them with boomerangs, nullas, &c. The Kalkadoon, in the Leichhardt-Selwyn District, often sneak upon these birds in the daytime.

142. All birds are roasted whole; in the larger kinds, the skin is subsequently removed by making a longitudinal incision down along the centre of the back, and thus turning the creature inside out, as it were.

143. Bandicoots, "Porcupines," "bilbi-rats," &c., are tracked and dug out of their holes in the ground. This "bilbi" (a doubtful locally-aboriginal term) is really a bandicoot—*Peragale lagotis*, Reid.

144. The **Opossum** (*Trichoglossus vulpecula*) is now rarely met with in the immediate vicinity of Boulia. Elsewhere it may be caught either in the daytime or at night by moonlight: in both cases by climbing the trees with, if necessary, "steps" cut alternately on either sides of the trunk. In the daytime the presence of the animal in the particular tree is determined by the nature of the double-claw marks; in the moonlight by actually seeing the creature, one man climbing up while another waits below as it is driven down.

145. Kangaroos and similarly large marsupials are hunted in various ways. They may be tracked and sneaked upon during the extreme midday heat, and caught while resting in the shade by means of a wommera-spear or boomerang. In rainy weather, and over boggy soil, they are run down with dogs. In other cases they may be caught in nets, which are quickly rigged up along their beaten tracks to water with exactly the same contrivance and method as that employed in catching emus (sect. 131). Occasionally they may be driven into an enclosure formed of three nets fixed in the position somewhat of the three sides of a square (Fig. 232) the hunters, having previously determined upon the locality where the kangaroos are encamped, will drive them into this enclosure with the assistance of numerous "beaters" stationed in such manner as to compel the animals running into the required direction.

146. Dingoes are tracked up on very hot days over the sandhills, and are then speared.

147. Though not an article of food, a few notes concerning **Pituri** (*Duboisia*) will not be quite out of place here. If all is well, pituri arrives in Boulia in the rough about the beginning of March. By "in the rough" is meant the condition, very much like half-green half-yellow tea with plenty of chips, in which it is conveyed in the dilly-bags for barter, &c. The pituri shrub itself flowers about January. The supply for the Boulia District is obtained in the neighbourhood of Carlo (*vel* Mungerebar), on the Upper Mulligan. As a matter of fact, the plant grows further eastwards than this, though in scattered patches only—*e.g.*, about sixteen miles westwards of Glenormiston head station ; a patch of it is also said by the Mitakoodi aboriginals to be growing in one of the gullies at Cloncurry, on the Rifle Mountain (where the old target-range used to be). From Boulia and Marion Downs, from Herbert Downs and Roxburgh, messengers are sent direct to the Ulaolinya tribes at Carlo with spears and boomerangs, "Government" and other blankets, nets, and especially red-coloured cloths, ribbons, and handkerchiefs to exchange and barter for large supplies of the drug. On its advent at Roxburgh the pituri may travel partly up the Georgina and partly along the ranges to the Kalkadoon, who may supply the Mitakoodi with it, but very little gets further eastward. From Boulia it is sent up the Burke, and so through the Yellunga and Kalkadoon, again carried to the Mitakoodi, or may be forwarded on to Warenda and Tooleybuck. Marion Downs sends it *via* Springvale, &c., to the Middle Diamantina, whence it may go up as far as Elderslie and Winton, very little, if any, ever reaching the Thomson River.

Arrived at its destination, the pituri is prepared for use as follows :—After roasting in the ashes the pituri-chips become pliable, so as to be easily bent, and are then wetted with water if in large quantity or with the mouth if in small, and teased up with the fingers so as to remove all the bigger pieces. Some leaves of a certain species of "wattle" (Pitta-Pitta *poo-ka-ti-ka*), or of gidyea when the former is not obtainable, are next heated over the fire, and then burnt, the ashes being retained. The pituri in its moist state is now mixed with these ashes on some smoothed surface, a "pituri-plate," koolamon, &c., and worked with the fingers into small rolls, about 2½ inches long by ⅜ inch diameter, which "quids" are now ready for chewing. Sometimes the quid is teased up with some threads of native flax to give it compactness and intercoherence, as it were. When not being chewed, these rolls are carried worn above the top of the ear, the position being indicated in the ideagram Fig. 104, sect. 86. At Quarmby, I learn that the Kalkadoon will often prepare their tobacco in similar manner to the pituri, which is made into a quid with certain gidyea leaf ashes for chewing.

Among the aboriginals themselves everywhere as great a craving appears to exist for pituri as alcohol for Europeans, a fact which is put into practical and economical effect by drovers, station-managers, and others. Mr. Reardon, the manager of Carlo (1895), tells me that when on the Mulligan the supply of tobacco runs out the aboriginals will smoke pituri in their pipes. Pituri is certainly never used in any of these districts for contaminating the water-holes with the object of drugging the birds and animals drinking therein.

Some of the native names for pituri will be found in sect. 53.

CHAPTER VI.

DOMESTIC IMPLEMENTS AND UTENSILS.   FIRE STICKS AND YAM STICKS.
HUTS AND SHELTERS.

148. The **Koolamon,** or elongate wooden trough (Fig. 233), with rounded extremities, is manufactured out of the same material and in the same localities as the shield, and travels in exchange and barter along identical routes (sect. 254). When made from the "cork," or "coral" tree (*Erythrina*, Linn.), &c., they are cut out straight away, two, three, or four at a time, like the shields, into the particular shape required, and then finished off with the native chisel (sect. 149). Where the wood does not lend itself to "splitting,"—*e.g.*, the coolibar—a trunk or limb is selected as near as possible to the required shape—*i.e.*, having a slight bend in it—ultimately to become the outer convex surface of the vessel. The proper length is next cut off the tree, and what will be its ultimate concave side slightly burned, so as to make the subsequent scooping-out with the chisel so much the easier; when roughly got into shape it is steeped in water, may be some days, wound round with twine to fix its permanent contour, and then finished off again with a chisel. Koolamons usually show a longitudinal fluting, and may be coloured red or black. They vary greatly in size from under a foot to over two and a-half in length, and up to 9 or 10 inches in width, and are either convex or slightly flat-bottomed. They are carried either on the head, or at the side or back of the body; in the latter cases, supported by a cord passed over the opposite shoulder assisted, as often as not, with the arm (Fig. 234). Some of the names applied to these wooden vessels are given in sect. 55.

149. The **Native Chisel,** one of the most useful tools in the possession of the aboriginals, and universal throughout North-West-Central Queensland, is not used for purposes of exchange or barter. It consists of a smoothed and rounded piece of wood up to 2 feet in length and thick in proportion, generally made of gidyea, and bent into the shape of an arc (Fig. 235). At either end of this wooden handle is a piece of flint-flake (Pitta-Pitta, *koo-ya*; Mitakoodi, *kum-bo*) firmly secured in position with cementing substance: it is this sharp little stone which is responsible for the fluted ornamentation so commonly found upon the other weapons, &c. Of recent years, one of these flints has been substituted by a portion of disused shear-blade (Mitakoodi, *o-lun*), barrel-band, or other form of iron ground down and rounded off to the required shape, and with this modification the implement is most commonly now found. It is, in its entirety, a cutting, shaving, and scooping tool, a true chisel, and used with both hands, moving towards the operator as shown in Fig. 236. The verb expressing the action of this instrument is *puk-ka-* in the Pitta-Pitta language : the name of the implement itself is at Boulia (Pitta-Pitta) *koom-pa-ta* (sect. 43*g*), at Glenormiston *puk-kang-i*, at Lake Nash (Yaroinga) *el-bil-la* and *jor-je-ra* : of these two last-mentioned terms, the former is the larger variety of implement for "cutting in the rough," while the latter is the smaller kind used especially for "finishing off." The Mitakoodi and Kalkadoon call the weapon by the same name as that applied to it at Boulia : sometimes the Mitakoodi speak of the whole instrument as *o-lun*, after its shear-blade tip (see *ante*).

150. The **Native Cementing Substance,** of which so much is said in connection with various weapons, &c., is manufactured throughout North-West-Central Queensland with the possible, though doubtful, exception of the Leichhardt-Selwyn District. In the Boulia and Upper Georgina Districts it is called *kun-ti*, and obtained either from the "porcupine" or "spinifex"-grass (*Trioda*, R. Br.). The plant is gathered in large quantities, broken up into small pieces with the fingers, and still further disintegrated and pounded with stones: it is then rolled over and over, pounded upon a heated flattened stone, and so with the sticky matter in it, rendered down into a dullish brown-black pasty mass, which, soon hardening, is put by for subsequent use. No water, wax, or other ingredients are used in its manufacture. It remains remarkably hard and firm, and only requires heat to soften it again. The Kalkadoon would seem to obtain some of the *kunti* which they require at Buckingham Downs, whither it is brought Boulia-way. The Mitakoodi of the Cloncurry District can also make a cement with similar materials and methods, though the usual substance which is brought into requisition on the north of the ranges is the gum of the "beefwood" tree, *Grevillea striata*, R. Br., *Stenocarpus salignus*, R. Br. (Mitakoodi, *toong-ga-ro*). This, after being collected, is roasted over a fire, and then, when melting, allowed to run out below on to a sheet of bark: after cooling, it is only just warmed again, beaten upon, and hammered, and while still pliable mixed up with powdered charcoal. It hardens on cooling, and only requires heat to soften it again.

151. Artificial Bending and Straightening of Timber.—The aboriginals throughout all the different ethnographical districts both know and practise various methods of bending or straightening timber, either when already cut or in the rough. Thus, a dry heat in ordinary sand, a moist heat from burning freshly-gathered gum-leaves, or moisture in general, such as soaking in water, is employed for bending any of their wooden implements into shape as required. In order to maintain and preserve the timber in the position attained by one or other of the preceding processes, the whole is covered thickly with grease and fat, saurian or mammalian.

152. Water-bags.—For the conveyance of water over long distances, water-bags (Fig. 237) used to be manufactured whenever and wherever this commodity was scarce, such as along the Leichhardt-Selwyn Ranges, and also on the ranges on the other side of Carlo. They were formerly made at Boulia, but what with the far better canvas water-bags obtainable from the whites, their manufacture both here and elsewhere has long ago ceased. They are as rare now in these particular districts as the complete stone-tomahawk. Made from kangaroo, paddymelon, or opossum, the skin is cut all the way round, high up in the neck, the front-paws and tail removed close to their bases, and the whole skin pulled away inside out from the carcass: it is subsequently tanned with bloodwood gum. The front paw and tail-hole openings, together with those of the natural passages, are closed by means of a bone or wooden peg pierced through opposite edges, below which some strong twine or tendon is wound: tears in the skins may also be seen mended with pegs supported by a figure-of-8 twine, reminding one very much of the surgeon's fixing of a "hare-lip pin." Finally the two hind legs are tied together, so as to act conjointly like a strap which may either be slung over a shoulder (Fig. 238) or carried in the hand. What was once the neck of the animals forms now the mouth of the bag: the tanned side of the skin is inside. The water-bag is called *nil-pa* by the Pitta-Pitta, *nor-lo* by the Kalkadoon.

For the conveyance of water between short distances, *e.g.*, the creek and the camp, a koolamon may be used: this will often be carried on the head, and the spilling of the fluid markedly limited, almost prevented, by laying small twigs of leaves upon its surface.

153. Dilly-bags are made somewhat after the manner of a satchel, in such a way that, when empty, the two sides lie one upon the other perfectly flat. They vary between a square and a boat-shape, all intermediate forms being discoverable (Fig. 239, A B C). The larger kinds—and the larger are mostly navicular or inclined to be so—measure over 30 inches along the upper edges: these are carried on the back, invariably by women, by means of a cord or string attached to the opposite ends of the opening slung over one or other shoulder, the base of the bag being supported by the corresponding arm turned up behind. The mouth of the dilly-bag may be of the same extent as the upper edge, as in the smaller and square kind, or much smaller as in the larger and navicular variety. The material employed in their manufacture is "white-fellow's" twine and blanket-thread, opossum string, human hair mixed with twine, &c., or plant-fibre (*i.e.*, flax twine). When made from the usual Government blankets, the threads are carefully picked out and sorted, the bluish-gray and black ones being respectively utilised for patterns: in other kinds of blankets, the red and yellow may be similarly sorted, and the bag woven in various linear-coloured stripes. Otherwise the whole receptacle may be stained or painted uniform red. If opossum string is used, human-hair twine is often mixed with it. The plant-fibre is that obtained from the beautiful yet common blue-flowered native flax (Pitta-Pitta *ka-lo*). Another plant, which unfortunately I have not had opportunities of identifying, was formerly employed for the same purpose by the Boulia blacks, who used to fetch it in from Carlo, Marion Downs, Cooraboolka, &c., where it might be seen growing on the sandhills to a height of about 2 feet, with yellow flowers; they called it *mun-ji*. So again, on the northern side of the Selwyn Ranges, are other kinds of flax-plants; but, for the same reason, I must again plead my excuses for not acquainting myself with their true botanical names. I have come across no cases up here where a true tree-bark fibre is utilised in the manufacture of any utensils, &c.

The *kalo* flax is worked up as follows:—The plant is collected into thick bundles, up to 4 and 5 feet long, and each tied round with string, the whole being then immersed in water for several days, with rock or stones on top to prevent its being washed away. Its fine outer skin is next stripped off the stems, one at a time, and beaten up and teased out until such time as it becomes quite soft, when it is sun-dried and rolled into skeins or bundles about a couple of feet in length. As the individual, who is sitting in the squatting position (Fig. 240), wants to work it up, he pulls out of the skein a piece or two, some 3 or 4 inches long, and moistening it either with his mouth, or dipping it into some water provided in a koolamon at his side, places it crossways on his thigh; another and another thin and small length is picked off, treated similarly, and placed side by side upon the thigh, along which all three or four are rolled backwards and forwards with the open hand, until by twisting and rolling these few thin sets of shreds become a single composite one. When the next piece of composite thread is in similar manner made up from its three or four simple components, it is placed end on end (not sideways, of course) with the first-made composite one, and by a little rolling manipulation of the fingers, intertwined with it: a piece of about 7 or 8 inches is now obtained. By a repetition of this process the length of the newly-manufactured twine is gradually increased, while, what is already made and completed, is rolled up into a ball. When two such balls have been made, the moistened strings from each, *while twisted in opposite directions*, are in similar manner rolled into one, in these relative positions, the double plait so formed being wound up as manufactured into a third ball, and in this last condition it is ready for use. It may be stated here that any increase in the thickness of the twine, when required, can be effected to any extent by this method of doubling, with the simultaneous rolling or twisting of each of the two strings in opposite directions.

There are three kinds of mesh to be found in the weaving of a dilly-bag. The most common, what may be called the "type," is that marked A in the diagram (Fig. 241): rarer forms are the "hair-net" B, and its modification, the "twist" C. The type-pattern may be alone used in the weaving of the bag throughout, and under such circumstances it would be pretty safe to infer that it had been made by women, who do not usually weave the other forms of mesh. The hair-net pattern has been so described because of its identity with what is met with in that particular article of dress (sect. 168), which can certainly only be made by males: there are generally two or three rows of this mesh connecting the type with the twist pattern surrounding the mouth of the bag. No dilly-bags made in their entirety with the hair-net or twist pattern are discoverable: these particular meshes would seem to be only subsidiary to the type one: The making of the bag starts with the thin strip, constituting ultimately its lower edge, around and along which the remainder is woven step by step. Unfortunately those, the smaller varieties, which I have watched in the process of manufacture, were in the hands of women, who invariably used an ordinary darning or small packing needle to get

the thread in and out with : what kind of a needle, if any, is used in areas outside
civilising influences, it is impossible for me to say. In this connection it is
interesting to note that in the Cloncurry District I was assured over and again by
Mitakoodi blacks that it has only been of late years (*i.e.*, since their childhood
days) that woven dilly-bags have put in an appearance in those parts at all, and
that their women have learnt to make them from their eastern and southern
neighbours, the Woonamurra and the Goa : they can well call to mind the grass
(*i.e.*, plant fibre) dilly-bags which used to be made there, but of which, at the time
of my visit, none were procurable, though their particular name *koon-ya koon-ya*
(both Mitakoodi and Woonamurra) was remembered. Again, it was only in the
Cloncurry District that I frequently observed a form of bark envelope or
receptacle, known locally as the *wa-ra-ka*. It is formed of two separate longish
pieces of ti-tree bark, one placed above and the other below the particular article
or articles it is wished to enclose : the edges of the one are next turned up over
those of the other, and the whole bundle tied up with string wound round and
round from end to end. In the various districts some of the local names applied
to dilly-bags are given in sect. 55.

154. **Grindstones** are met with throughout North-West-Central Queensland•
Each set consists of a movable stone and a fixed slab upon which it is
rubbed and pressed : both made from a kind of sandstone. The movable one
is round, flattened, with thinned edge, and about 5, 6, or more inches in diameter
(Fig. 242) ; it is pressed with both hands (sect. 106, Fig. 216) backwards and
forwards, each change in direction being accompanied by a sort of preliminary
half-circular movement at the wrist (sect. 86). The slab, beyond its general
elongate shape, is more or less irregular : the upper grinding surface, however, is
invariably comparatively flattened. The movable stone is known as the *wa-ko* in
the Boulia and Upper Georgina (certainly at Roxburgh), and as the *koo-e-la* in the
Leichhardt-Selwyn and Cloncurry Districts : the fixed slab is called *ja-ra ja-ra* in
the Boulia District. The particular material of which these grindstones are made
is found only in the country around Walaya and along the Toko ranges, where
the natives cut, hew, and grind it into the required shapes and bring them for
barter either to Carandotta or to Roxburgh. At Carandotta they come into the
possession of the Kalkadoon and other tribes living along and north of the
Leichhardt-Selwyn Ranges. At Roxburgh they start on their journey down the
Georgina River, branching off at Glenormiston for Carlo and the Upper Mulligan,
or at Herbert Downs for Boulia, whence, *via* Springvale, they may reach the
Middle Diamantina. It seems almost incredible that some of these large slabs
should be carried such immense distances : but then, the poor women of course
are the beasts of burden.

155. **Nardoo-stone.**—In connection with the preceding may be mentioned
the nardoo-stone used in the Boulia and Upper Georgina Districts. It is a sort
of boulder-pebble (Fig. 243) ground more or less into the shape of an oval with
flattened upper and under surfaces, and just big enough to be clutched firmly
with one hand. It is only used for pounding or hammering the hard nardoo
shell with (sect. 86). There is no nardoo-stone, or for that matter any nardoo,
in use among the Kalkadoon or Mitakoodi ; it therefore does not travel into the
districts occupied by these tribes for the purposes of exchange or barter. By
the Pitta-Pitta tribes at Boulia this stone is called *mur-ra-too-no* (*cf.* Pitta-Pitta
murra = hand, *toue-* = to strike) ; at Glenormiston and Roxburgh it is known as
por-ri (*cf.* Ulaolinya and Wonkajera *poor-i* = rock, stone, &c., in sect. 54).

156. **Baking Ovens.**—It will be noticed in the accounts of the different
animals and birds utilised for food, that they are all eaten roasted—that is,
cooked on the ashes. A modification of the process, it may almost be called
"baking," is effected as follows, and may be met with throughout North-West-
Central Queensland :—A pretty large fire is made and a number of biggish-sized
stones rendered as hot as possible : at the same time a hole is dug close alongside
and some of these hot stones put in to line it. The "meat," whatever it is, is
now put in and covered over with another layer of hot stones, to be followed by

a "hide" of some sort, and a final covering of mud, the whole constituting a kind of primitive bake-house.   It is used especially for any very large sized piece of flesh, emu, kangaroo, bullock, &c.

157. Fire Sticks.—Throughout North-West-Central Queensland two methods are adopted for kindling fire, though the second to be described is perhaps commoner along the Upper Georgina.

a. Twirling the stick between the flattened palms.   A very dry piece of wood is selected, a little nick or concavity cut into it, and fixed with the legs or feet lengthways on the ground in front of the operator (Fig. 244).   Another long stick of the same material is taken, like it perfectly dry, and its roughly-sharpened extremity placed vertically upon the nick already cut on the fixed piece.   The vertical one is now twirled, rolled backwards and forwards, as rapidly as possible, between the flat opened palms, the hands all the time being pressed gradually and firmly downwards.   The smoke, followed by a spark or two, soon appears : with some very dry grass and a little " blowing " this is soon fanned into flame.

b. Rubbing one stick over another like a saw (Fig. 245). The fixed piece of the preceding is here replaced by a piece split at its extremity into which a wedge (*a*) is placed so as to allow of some fine dry grass, &c. (*d*), being placed and firmly clutched in the fork (*c*) so produced.   Across the edges of the split, a more or less deep notch (*b*) is cut, along which another piece of wood with an angular edge made to fit, is rapidly rubbed forwards and backwards.   The horizontal piece, what with the attrition, becomes pulverised and heated at the notch, so that sparks soon arise and catch on to the grass which thus becomes ignited.

As a rule, these fire-sticks (Pitta-Pitta *toor-kin-je*) are thrown aside or discarded after use : they are made only as they are wanted, and in these districts are certainly not to be seen carried about for future use.   The particular timber of which they are made would appear to vary, though the root portion is said to be usually requisitioned : it is said to be a kind of " box-wood," at other times "lavender"-wood (Glenormiston), sometimes " wild-orange "(Leichhardt-Selwyn District), &c.

158. The true **Yam-stick** is a thin, roughly-cut, light stick, on an average about 4 feet in length, with a flattened tip (Fig. 245A), and is essentially a woman's implement.   It is used for digging up yams and other roots, shifting the ashes (whence its extremity may often be seen charred), and other domestic purposes. It is called the *ka-la-ra* (sect. 43*b*) in the Boulia, *tan-de* in the Cloncurry District, and is met with throughout all the ethnographical districts under consideration. It must on no account be confounded with the two-handed fighting pole (sect. 255).

159. Huts and Shelters.—In the Boulia District three kinds of habitation are constructed, each of them designed for different purposes, and all possessing various points of interest : these are the *koo-rou-i*, the *un-na-kud-ye*, and the *win-ji win-ji*, to give them their Pitta-Pitta names.

The *kooroui*, originally designed for withstanding rain, but now devoted to indiscriminate use, is almost always constructed on a piece of high ground, any little hillock or mound, so as to ensure the more rapid dispersal of the water. Building operations are commenced with two naturally more-or-less bent saplings stuck at an angle well into the earth to a depth of 8 or 10 inches and fixed at their apices by the interlocking of the fork or forks in which they are cut (Fig. 246, A B).   These two primary supports pass by the name of *wun-da-roo* (signifying the back-bone or vertebral column) their lengths varying according to the size of the hut required, the summit of which on an average is about 4 feet and upwards from the ground-level.   On either side, resting up against the *wundaroo*, are numerous secondary sticks, called the *prin-na* (*i.e.*, legs) placed more or less parallel with one another and fixed into the ground below in the position required : these "legs" constitute the frame-work over which the hut-wall is built (Fig. 247, A B).   Along the intervals between the *prinna*, and these intervals may form no inconsiderable spaces, are placed and intertwined some light bushes, the foliage downwards, these being followed by tussets of grass, then a coating of mud, and lastly another layer of bushes : the layer of mud, requiring both time and skill, is often omitted. The ground-space enclosed by the hut-wall is more or less circular in the smaller varieties, somewhat elliptical in the larger. To allow for an entrance or *te-ra*, the *prinna* are omitted over the larger portion of the base end of one of the *wundaroo*, and should subsequently the rain beat in here, the aperture is just covered in with an armful of bushes thrown up in front of it. Sometimes a *kooroui* is built with an entrance at each extremity, and especially is this the case with the larger-sized huts, so that from whichever quarter the rain may come, it can always be easily blocked. The level of the ground inside is not purposely lowered, though what with constant use and treading upon, it often gives one this appearance.

The *unnakudye* is designed especially for warmth, and for use in the winter months. A flat-bottomed hole is dug into the ground to a depth of about 1½ feet, or even more, the rather elliptical outline of its sides forming the limits of the habitation to be erected over it, the bottom of the excavation forming of course the actual floor. The scaffolding of *wundaroo* and *prinna* is next built in. Wet grass is now collected and wedged into the spaces intervening between the *prinna*, and mud covered on ; the mud thus moistened soon becomes hardened and, by means of the grass, fixed in place. A ring of wet mud about a foot in width is then placed round the edges of the entrance, for which it forms a sort of artificial door-frame, and at the same time gives it rather an ornamental appearance. On completion a big fire is kindled inside in the corner opposite the door, with the result that by sundown, when the embers are removed, the place is quite warm enough to sleep in.

Strictly speaking, the *winji-winji* is any temporary bough-shed for protection from rain should it suddenly come up, and is but lightly built of grass and bushes. A very common form is to have it attached to the hut with a view to shelter the fire which is usually kept burning there just outside. The two *wundaroo* of this kind of *winji-winji* are built as high as, or higher even than those of the attached habitation (Fig. 248), and the *prinna*, instead of being fixed vertically, are kept in position more or less horizontally one above the other by being stuck into the vertical interspaces surrounding the original entrance-way. Individuals pass in and out of the *kooroui* or *unnakudye*, as the case may be, on either side of the fire. Another form of *winji-winji* which I have noticed on the Birdsville road, some three or four miles from Boulia, is where the boughs and saplings rest on a tree-trunk with a marked natural slope, the trunk acting the part of a *wundaroo* (Fig. 249).

So far as the district around Boulia is concerned, the use of bark as a wall-covering is unusual in the construction of any variety of hut : whether this is directly due to scarcity of timber it is impossible to say. It must be borne in mind also that the advent of the European with his accompaniments has been productive of certain appreciable changes in the construction of these aboriginal habitations. Thus, at Boulia in particular, to obviate the trouble of finding and cutting suitable lengths of timber with the orthodox forked extremities the *wundaroo* may be occasionally seen manufactured with timbers spliced at the apices, and bound with rope. Again, the facility with which a hide can be obtained all over this cattle country is gradually making itself more and more apparent in the supplanting of the mud and grass wall-coverings by skins. The most interesting change of all, however, is the gradual and marked disappearance of the *unnakudye* form of hut with the introduction of clothes and Government or other blankets. Finding that they can obtain protection from cold with the aid of such coverings, the aboriginals are dispensing more and more with these particular structures, which entail no inconsiderable amount of time, toil, and patience in their making ; the change itself, owing to such civilising influences, has not been a sudden but a gradual one, the depth of the floor below the ground surface having been slowly decreased, while the height of the hut above ground has been correspondingly increased. It is only due to state that Mr. Craigie, of Roxburgh, had originally noticed this gradual modification in height and depth during a stay out west of sixteen or seventeen years : its explanation was given me by the Pitta-Pitta aboriginals.

Though the entrance of the hut is generally made on the side opposite to the quarter whence the prevailing winds rise, a "break-wind" is often constructed on one or both sides of the door-way so as to protect not only the fire itself but also the individuals who may choose to be squatting down in the open around it. The structure itself, the *wul-lo-a* or *yung-ko* is about 2½ to 3 feet high, and composed of light leafy saplings fixed into the ground and intertwined with others and grasses placed crossways.

It remains to be noted that, while the koolamons, dillybags, boomerangs, &c., of the occupants may be kept, when not in use, on the ground outside or inside, or allowed to lie upon or against the roof of the huts, all spears are always stuck vertically into the walls with their butt-ends downwards, probably to prevent them being trodden upon or otherwise injured.

The relative positions of the huts, &c., at a main camping-ground will be referred to in section 228.

160. In the Cloncurry District, among the Mitakoodi, a hut or gundi is called a *yin-bur*. It is built after the same style as the *kooroui* of the Boulia District, so far as the general scaffolding is concerned, the intervals being filled in with tussets of grass, &c., but the whole is usually covered with sheets of bark kept in position by the agency of heavy boughs resting on top (Fig. 250). The gundi floor is apparently flush with the ground-surface : at any rate, no earth is certainly dug out of it. Any of the sticks, primary or secondary, forming the framework of the hut are known as *ta-li*.

161. In the Leichhardt-Selwyn District the Kalkadoon name a hut *wul-li-be-ri* (*cf.* Pitta-Pitta term *wul-lo-a*). It is built very much like the second variety of *winji-winji* mentioned as being met with at Boulia. Either a markedly-bent tree-trunk or a low-lying horizontal branch is utilised against which to fix the vertical saplings and boughs (Fig. 251) : the latter, of course, are wider apart below than above, where they practically touch. Where these sticks (*koong-ga*) are fixed into the ground a mound of earth is collected all round, which forms the limit of the surface-space to be enclosed : from this ring of earth is piled up bundle upon bundle of grass, bushes, &c , twined and intertwined among the slanting sticks, which are thus assisted in maintaining their position. Occasionally, bark may be seen superimposed in addition.

CHAPTER VII.

PERSONAL ORNAMENTATION AND DECORATION. MURAL PAINTING, &c.

162. Method of Working-up the Hair.—The hair of the head—and especially is this the case with the males—is dressed with grease after growing a certain length, and put up very much after the style of the throms in a mop-broom. This facilitates not only its removal when required for subsequent use in making hair-twine, but also prevents its becoming too closely matted together.

The method of procedure for making hair into twine, only practised by the men, is as follows:—The hair is cut off, throm by throm, as it is required, cleaned, and teased out very much after the manner of horse-hair for a cushion: in this condition it is loosely wound round a stick, the whole then moistened, and when dry the "skein" removed and put aside. A fine thin stick, Pitta-Pitta *ming-ko*, a sort of "crochet-needle," about 1 foot long and ⅛-inch in diameter with a short wooden barb attached to its lower extremity by means of "cement," is next brought into requisition (Fig. 252). With this instrument rolled backwards and forwards between the thumb and forefinger of the one hand, the varying lengths of hair, sorted, arranged, and rolled by the moistened fingers of the other hand, become one single thread, into which another and another length is successively entwined; as this thread is produced it is wound on to the needle, off which the barb prevents it slipping, and when some few feet of it have been made it is unwound and rolled up into a tight ball.* Two such balls are now taken and put into a koolamon containing water, and the twine from each fixed to the lower end of the ming-ko stick: the two strings are now twisted separately along the thigh, as in the case of native-flax (sect. 153), each in opposite directions. and in these relative positions they are together wound on the wooden needle, the resulting double-twist hair-twine being soon ready for use. Though I have not had the opportunity of watching the process of "spinning" opossum-hair, I am informed that it is very similar to what takes place in the case of human hair.

163. Decoration and Ornamentation of the Head.—The decoration of the head involves a consideration of the following ornaments: feather-tufts or "aigrettes," kangaroo and dingo bones, tooth-ornaments, artificial "whiskers," head-nets, fore-head nets, fillets, circlets, spiral-bands, the wooden cross-piece, and handkerchiefs.

164. Feather Tufts.—Feather-tufts or "aigrettes" are formed with various birds' feathers tied on to a small sprig, which is stuck indiscriminately here and there into the hair: among birds so utilised are the emu, eaglehawk, pelican, turkey, crow, &c. These feather-tufts are very generally used in times of rejoicing, at corrobborees: they may sometimes be stuck into the waist-belt either at its side or back, or may be fixed under the armlets. Common throughout North-West-Central Queensland. On the Upper Georgina I met with "bilbi"-tails put to similar use.

165. Knuckle-bones.—"Knuckle" and similar bones from the kangaroo or dingo, and up to about 2½ inches in length, are fixed with cement by string to the tuft of hair over the temporal region, whence they dangle one on each side in front of the ears. In the Boulia and Upper Georgina Districts.

---

* Just like a white woman makes a ball of a woollen skein.

166. Tooth Ornaments.—The "tooth"-ornament, Pitta-Pitta *mil-ka*, is formed of two kangaroo (rarely dingo) teeth fixed into a more or less oval-shaped base (Fig. 253). The base is made of spinifex or beef-wood cement, having a small aperture through which a small lock of hair from over the centre of the forehead is passed and thus fixed: the ornament is hung so that its tip rests midway between the eye-brows. Sometimes it is made to hang from a forehead band instead. Though used by both sexes at corrobborees and other festive occasions, it is manufactured, by men only, in the Upper Georgina, Leichhardt-Selwyn (Kalkadoon *yer-ra-ra*), Cloncurry (Mitakoodi *yer-rang-gul*), Upper Diamantina, and portions of the Boulia Districts: it is not made at the present time at Marion Downs, nor on the Mulligan, Lower Georgina, nor middle Diamantina Rivers.

167. Artificial Whiskers.—The Mitakoodi women and little boys for "flash" purposes wear an ornament, an artificial "whisker," formed of locks of hair cemented together at one extremity by means of beef-wood gum : such a *wol-la-koo-ja* is attached on either side to the temporal hair in front of the ear, and hangs to a length of about 2 inches below the jaw.

168. Head-net.—The *kool-poo-roo*, its Pitta-Pitta name, is a sort of netted cap with circular ring at the top (Fig. 254) from around which the body of the net is woven, the pattern of the stitch being shown in the diagram (Fig. 255) : the twine used is made of flax-fibre, &c., coated thickly with red-ochre grease. The use of this netted cap is to prevent the hair (when being cultivated to an adequate length for subsequent requirements) from dangling over into the eyes. It is manufactured, by men only, in the Boulia and Leichhardt-Selwyn Districts : its Kalkadoon name is *kun-ta-ma-ra*. Another form of head-net, an undoubtedly modern innovation, is made by the women, though not necessarily worn by them alone, after the manner and of same mesh as a fishing net, with a conical " blind " extremity.

169. Forehead-net.—The forehead net, the *mi-ri mi-ri*—a name common throughout North-West-Central Queensland—is a spindle-shaped piece of fine netting quite a foot long (Figs. 256, 257) worn over the forehead so as to keep the hair well back, the two strings passing above the ears and tied together at the back of the head. It is really an exquisite piece of workmanship, woven after the style of an ordinary fishing-net, though no mesh-stick is used : when it is borne in mind that, in some examples, each individual mesh is only about $\frac{1}{8}$-inch in size, its regularity calls both for wonder and for admiration. When lying on the flat, the total depth of this ornament averages about 2 inches, but it can be stretched to between $4\frac{1}{2}$ and 5. The material used in its manufacture is either human hair, ordinary flax-fibre, or opossum-twine : with the two latter a correspondingly larger-sized mesh is of course employed. The *mi-ri mi-ri* is one of the badges of the last of the initiation ceremonies (sect. 313) in the Boulia District, and can be worn by both men and women, subsequently to that stage, at all times, whether corrobboree or not. It is made by males only.

170. Fillets.—The opossum-string fillet (Figs. 258, 259) is made of four separate circlets of opossum-twine bound together flat by means of four "ties," with the result that a band-like ornament, over a foot long, consisting of eight closely apposed strands, is produced : the extremities of this composite band are looped into the two tying strings to be knotted at the back of the head. Upon making a closer investigation into the strands the opossum string is seen to be closely wound spirally round a central human-hair core, while, so far as the " ties " have been examined, these are always made of plant-fibre. The strands, as well as the ties, are greased with red ochre : all opossum string ornaments indeed are invariably coloured red. This fillet has been observed sometimes as being worn like a necklace in the Boulia District, and both as a necklace and armlet in the Cloncurry District : it is still manufactured in the former, but rarely now in the latter, and may be worn by either sex any time subsequently to the first of the initiation ceremonies (sect. 300). Its Pitta-Pitta name is *moong-ka-la*, the same as applied to some other opossum-string ornaments : in the Mitakoodi language it is the *cha-bo* of the Leichhardt-Selwyn District where exceptionally it used sometimes to be made of rock-wallaby hair.

In the Boulia District a dingo-tail may sometimes be worn over the forehead, like a fillet, and tied by strings at the back: sometimes feather-tufts may be stuck, and so supported in position, underneath it.

The band-fillet, though strictly speaking not an aboriginal ornament, might nevertheless be mentioned here, it being so very common throughout all these districts. Instead of the net, &c., any thin strip of linen, calico, or riband, especially anything of a red colour, passes over the forehead, and is tied behind. Fixed in it may be the usual feather-tufts, or even, as I have seen at Glenormiston, some small wooden pegs which, cut and curled at their upper ends, gave rise to the appearance of a sort of tiara or diadem.

171. Circlets.—There are two varieties of the ring or circlet (Pitta-Pitta *moong-ka-la*, Mitakoodi *up-poo-la-ra* or *wop-poo-la-ra*), according as they are single or double: both are made with opossum-string. In the former case, according as the central core is thick or thin, around which the string is spirally and closely wound, the diameter varies for different examples (Fig. 260). In the latter, the two circlets are fixed together with two ties, at places more or less opposite: when measured out each ring in its continuous length is about 16 inches. As usual, coloured red and greased.

172. The Spiral Band, the *kul-go* of the Mitakoodi, but hardly ever made now, and extremely rarely met with, is a long strip of opossum skin, with the hair left on, about 7 or 8 feet in length, and about ⅜-inch in width. This used to be made out of an opossum skin by starting from about the centre of the back, and cutting out concentrically round and round, the strip being subsequently stretched and dried (Fig. 261) Starting from just above the ears, it was wound round the head, and ostensibly served to keep the hair from falling over the eyes and face: both men and women wore it, and were in the habit of removing it at night.

173. Wooden Cross-piece: Handkerchiefs.—The *ta-ka-le* wooden cross-piece, which I have met with in the Boulia and Cloncurry Districts, at corrobboree times only, is described in sect. 310.

The red and other handkerchiefs, obtained originally from civilised centres, and then bartered from tribe to tribe, throughout North-West-Central Queensland, are commonly worn by the aboriginals as articles of head-dress (Fig. 261A). The handkerchief is folded diagonally, and the two extremities of the fold tied in a knot over the forehead: under the knot a knife, pipe, &c, may be carried, while the angle falling over the back of the head and neck serves to protect these parts from the heat of the sun.

174. Ornamentation of the Face.—Throughout the North-West-Central Districts the entire face may be smeared with greased yellow or red ochre, or else decked with transverse bands of white (Fig. 275), as in the country round about Boulia. This white (? Pigeon English "*ko-pi*," Pitta-Pitta *pa-ta*) is a sort of gypsum, which is first of all burnt, and subsequently immersed in a comparatively small quantity of water, so as to make a viscid mass which dries hard like plaster of paris.

175. Piercing of the Nose.—The piercing of the nasal septum is practised everywhere, by both sexes, at any time of life, and voluntarily, to "make him flash-fellow": there is no compulsion about it, and certainly has no special signification. It is made with any sharply-pointed bone, and the wound kept open for a few days with a piece of stick which is shifted and dragged upon at intervals. The nose-pin (Pitta-Pitta *mel-ya per-kil-li* = nose big-fellow"), up to 9 or 10 inches long, is either a turkey, pelican, kangaroo, or emu bone: when these are not handy, a grass-reed, green cockatoo feather-quill, &c., can be used.

176. Piercing of the Ears.—Alone among the Mitakoodi of the Cloncurry District, and then only with some of the older men, ear-holes are sometimes present. Piercing which, in reply to inquiry, was practised pretty commonly in past times, is never done nowadays: a kangaroo bone is said to have been worn.

177. Avulsion of the Teeth.—The knocking out of the two central upper incisors is practised among the Boulia District tribes as follows :—The gums all round the teeth to be extracted are loosened with the thumb and finger nails: this loosening is then aided by biting hard into a stick held transversely in the mouth for a good ten minutes or so. The patient in squatting position, with head raised, now holds the stick vertically behind the two to be extracted, and pushes it firmly upwards and forwards while a friend hammers away with a wooden chisel driven by a heavy stone for a mallet (Fig. 262). The whole operation is thus over from beginning to end within a quarter of an hour, and all soreness is said to disappear by about the third day. In the Upper Georgina District, among the Yaroinga, the patient lies on his back with head touching the ground, while his friend takes a stick which he presses against the teeth to be removed (these having been previously loosened with the finger-nails), and hammers on it until they are broken out. This custom of avulsion is common throughout North-West-Central Queensland as well as up and down the Diamantina, though it is gradually dying out : it is a mutilation which is perfectly voluntary, may be practised by both sexes, and most certainly at the present time has nothing whatever to do with any of the initiation ceremonies. That it has been in vogue for ages past is probable from the fact that in none of the languages of these districts, as pointed out in the philological section (sect. 3), are there a *th, v, f,* or *s,* sounds which require these teeth for their proper enunciation.

178. The Beard.—In the Boulia District the beard is often tied close to its base with a piece of twine to make it look " flash," both at corrobboree-time and on other occasions (Fig. 263).

179. Grass Necklaces.—Necklaces in North-West-Central Queensland are mainly of two kinds, according as they are manufactured from grass-reed or opossum-string. The reed necklace is manufactured everywhere, and usually by the women. It is the badge of the " first " degree (sect. 300), whence it can be worn subsequently, and on any occasion, by both male and female : the same name of *ko-nu-pa* is applied to it in the Boulia, Leichhardt-Selwyn, and Cloncurry Districts. The most ordinary form of this ornament is represented in Figs. 264, 265. The main portion of the necklace may be considered as consisting of an upper and lower belly joined together with twine or thread at their extremities, these two joining strings being each again looped into a tying-string ; the two latter together fix the ornament at the nape of the neck. Each belly consists of numerous threads, two dozen and more, on which are beaded the grass-reed bugles cut into lengths of from about $\frac{1}{2}$ to $\frac{5}{8}$-inch and over : these reed-beads are cut out with either the sharp edge of a mussel-shell (Boulia, &c.) or a stone-knife (Kalkadoon country), the exact procedure being depicted under sect. 91, 92, illustrating the sign-language. Some of the beads may have one or two rings cut into them.

The second variety of the reed-necklace (Fig. 266), first noticed at Glenormiston, and subsequently in a few examples at Boulia and at Cloncurry, is made of a single belly, the extremities of which, being strengthened with twine, &c., are looped directly into the tying-string. The tying-string, as in all these necklaces, may be of any material, from a shred of moleskin to a piece of hair-twine.

The third kind of necklace, manufactured certainly by both Kalkadoon and Mitakoodi, consists of one endless beaded string (Fig. 267), about 12 to 16 feet in its continuous length, rolled up into a thick loop so as to make two bellies of it, the extremities being attached to tying-strings. It can also on other occasions be worn as a coil wound round and round the neck.

180. Opossum-string Necklaces.—The true opossum-string necklace (Fig. 268) as will be seen from a study of the diagram (Fig. 269), consists of a main supporting string, in itself more or less composite, from which hang some dozens of secondary strings somewhat after the manner of a fringe : these secondary strings are in reality formed of one continuous length, which, successively twisted upon itself and around the main-string, produces the fringe-like appearance. The length of each hanging-twist is about 4 inches.   In those cases where the supply of opossum-string is deficient, the red worsted obtained from out of a blanket may be sub-stituted.

The opossum-string necklace, Pitta-Pitta *moo-na-mul-ya-ri*, Kalkadoon and Mitakoodi *mi-ta-mi-ko*, is manufactured in the Boulia, Leichhardt-Selwyn, and Cloncurry Districts, usually by women ; it is coloured red, and primarily intended for use at corrobborees.   When made somewhat larger than usual, as is sometimes the case in the Boulia District, &c., it may be worn by women as an apron, hanging from the hips.

Another form of necklace, and manufactured of the same material, was met with at Glenormiston, and Roxburgh : this is made after the style of the single-bellied variety of grass necklace, with all the opossum-hair strands fixed at either extremity to the tying-strings.   One specimen which I obtained from the latter station was manufactured after the same plan, but, instead of opossum-string, the cotton threads pulled out of an old sock were brought into requisition, while the tying-strings were made of twisted moleskin.   The opossum-string fillet referred to in sect. 170 has been already noted as being occasionally used as a necklace : the same may be said of the dingo-tail.

181. Armlets, Anklets, Body-cords.—Opossum-string armlets and anklets, Pitta-Pitta *moong-ka-la*, in the form of rings, are met with everywhere : in times of corrobboree, feather-tufts, &c., may be stuck into the former.   In the Cloncurry District, armlets are either single—*i.e.*, made of one string, Mitakoodi *jum-mul ;* or multiple—*i.e.*, made of three or four, Mitakoodi *mul-la-ri*, and then almost identical with the *chabo* (sect. 170).   Body-cords of opossum-string have been now and again observed in the Boulia District, but beyond the way in which they are worn by the leaders on the fighting expeditions of the Pitta-Pitta aboriginals, nothing particular is noticeable : a loop thrown over the head hangs loosely upon the chest.

182. Chest Ornaments.—The chest ornaments in these districts are mainly of the claw and shell varieties.   The former is made from the claws of the large eagle-hawk, two being attached moon-shape-like into a piece of black cement : two of these double-claw hoops may be attached to the same neck-string (Fig. 270).   The claw is brought to Boulia from the north, both from down the Georgina River, and down the Burke and Wills : its Pitta-Pitta name is *ming-ka-ra* (= a nail, claw), and its Kalkadoon *pe-ko* (= a nail, claw).

The shell ornament is a concave piece of white shell (a species of *Melo*) cut into more or less the shape of an oval, about 2 to 2½ inches in its longer diameter, and fixed either by a small drilled aperture, or a piece of cement, to the neck-string (Fig. 271).   It is met with in the Boulia District, which it enters *via* Spring-vale, &c., from Diamantina Gates and Cork, whither it is brought by the Goa blacks of Elderslie : the Goa have themselves obtained it both at the headwaters of the Diamantina, Kynuna, &c., from the Mitakoodi and Woonamurra, and around Hughenden from the Yerundulli, the latter having bartered it from the Woonamurra on their own account.   These Upper Flinders and Cloncurry District aboriginals (*i.e.*, the Woonamurra and Mitakoodi) get possession of it from the Nouun blacks at Mullangera, to whom it was originally brought by the Karunti, &c., people living around Normanton.   At Boulia the shell is occasionally but irregularly seen worn on the forehead like a kangaroo-tooth ornament.   In the Boulia District this shell-ornament is known as the *koo-lin-je-ri* : in the Clon-curry and Flinders as the *che-ka-ra* (*cf.* the *che-ka-la-ri* pearl-shell phallocrypt, sect. 184).   At Roxburgh, and south of that station, as well as elsewhere, I have observed this shell ornament being imitated by grinding and chipping down pieces of broken chinaware.

It may be noted that the *woraka*, referred to in sect. 286, is sometimes worn as a true chest ornament, though its primary use is as a charm against certain illnesses.

183. Waist-belts, Aprons.—Waist-belts, aprons, &c., are made either of human or opossum hair-twine.

The human-hair belt, found throughout North-West-Central Queensland, is known as *wa-koo-la* in the Boulia, *wun-ni-qa* in the Leichhardt-Selwyn, and *u-ro-do* in the Cloncurry District. It is one of these ornaments allowed to be worn by both sexes subsequently to the first initiation ceremonies (sect. 300); the men usually don it continuously from this time forwards, but the women only at corrobborees and other special occasions, though not necessarily even then. It consists of a long piece of double-plaited hair-twine wound round and round the waist, so as to form a thick belt or band: the thickness resulting may be gauged from the fact that a comparatively small example in my possession when unravelled measured a length of over 26 yards. The end of the hair-twine is often attached to a little wooden peg which, by its speedy recognition, enables the wearer to start unravelling all the more readily. This hair-belt, into which a stone-knife, pipe, &c., is often to be seen stuck, may not be removed from the body for weeks, perhaps months, at a time; its very nature precludes it from getting rotten through moisture, &c.

Throughout the Boulia District, in times of corrobboree and other occasions for rejoicing, certain ornaments are fixed or rather suspended from this hair-belt in the case of males only; to give them their names, as used by the Pitta-Pitta tribe, these are the *ping-ka-ra*, *til-ya-ri*, *koom-pa-ra*, and *che-ka la-ri*, though from what actual sources these terms have been derived it is impossible to say. The *pingkara* is a bunch of eagle-hawk feathers tied tightly round at their shafts into the form of a "feather-duster" and attached by the quill end on either side of the belt so as to dangle over each hip (Fig. 275, 294, &c.); it is called *wun-pa* by the Mitakoodi, who let it hang down in the central line behind instead of at the sides. The *tilyari* is a similarly bound bundle of emu feathers, but fixed behind so as to fall between the fold of the buttocks. The *koompara* and *chekalari* will be dealt with in the next section.

The larger-sized example of opossum-string *moonamulyari* necklace has already been noted (sect. 180), as occasionally worn by the women in the Boulia District in place of an apron.

What may be termed an opossum-rope waist-belt (Mitakoodi *moon-do-lo*) is met with in the Cloncurry and Flinders Districts. It is in the form of a ring, upwards of an inch in diameter, through which the wearer has to squeeze to get it on, the outer circumference of the belt running up to 37 inches and more. It is made of a thick skein of fibre (Fig. 272A) acting as a sort of core, around which a single external strand of opossum string, fibre, &c., is wound transversely. A pattern representing areas of black bands is worked in with hair-twine in this external layer. In the smaller varieties of belts (those for females) the internal core or skein may be made of human-hair twine instead of fibre. The belt is worn by adult males at corrobboree time only, by women at any or every occasion, and by young boys at any time previous to reaching the first stage of social rank (sect. 303). In the case of a woman's belt, there are usually a few opossum-string tags, a thin fringe as it were, hanging down from it in front (Fig. 272B).

184. Phallocrypts.—"Phallocrypts" or "penis-concealers," only used by the males at corrobborees and other public rejoicings, are either formed of pearl-shell or opossum string.

The *che-ka-la-ri* (see *che-ka-ra*, &c., in sect. 182, and *ker-ka-la* in sect. 272) is a flat, more or less oval, piece of pearl-shell of varying size, from 3 to 4 inches in length, fixed with cement to a human-hair-string which in turn is attached to the middle of the belt in front, so as to cover in the privates. This pearl-shell which I have only met with in the Leichhardt-Selwyn, Upper Georgina, and Boulia Districts, comes into these parts from the headwater country of the Georgina River, though from which portion of the coast it is originally brought I have not been able to discover.

The *koom-pa-ra* (*cf.* the Pitta-Pitta term *koon-pa-ra*, a shield) is the Pitta-Pitta name for the opossum-string form of phallocrypt (Fig. 273A) manufactured on exactly the same plan as the *moonamulyari* necklace (sect. 180) which is subsequently

I

wound in a spiral round itself (Fig. 273B), and fixed in this position, so as to form a kind of tassel, and coloured red. It is hung from the waist-belt in the middle line in front on occasion of corrobboree and other public ceremonials: sometimes it is used in the hand as a kind of fan, or duster, to brush the flies away from the face, &c. It is manufactured in the Boulia, Leichhardt-Selwyn, and Cloncurry Districts, and by males only: the Kalkadoon name is *mon-a-ro*, the Mitakoodi one *toong-ga*. The Mitakoodi under the same name of *toong-ga* possess a phallocrypt in the form of two tassels made of opossum-string, joined by an intermediate portion which suspends the article from the waist-belt (Fig. 274): the individual threads of each tassel are upwards of, and sometimes over, a foot in length, each thread being looped upon itself. The *tin-jin-na* is the Pitta-Pitta name for a sort of miniature *koompara*, which I have met with only in the Boulia District, and peculiar in that, instead of being attached to the belt, it is fixed to the pubic hair: it is made after the same plan and with similar material as the larger variety, though only about 2 or 2½ inches in length, but at corrobborees, &c., when it is worn, it may be painted white—the only occasion on which an opossum-string ornament is coloured otherwise than red.

It is needless to point out that with both sexes the privates are only covered on special public occasions, or when in close proximity to white settlements.

185. **Painting and Feathering of the Body.**—The ordinary painting of the body as practised in time of general warfare is referred to in sect. 238. Throughout North-West-Central Queensland, at corrobborees, or just for the sake of appearing a bit "flash," certain transverse and semi-lunar bands of white paint, Pitta-Pitta *pa-ta*, or greased yellow and red ochre may be daubed on: a good example of the white ornamentation is shown in Fig. 275—a Pitta-Pitta adult male in full "flash" costume. On similar occasions, and other public rejoicings, and also at any time, the women throughout the Boulia District may adopt a greased yellow or red tri-linear pattern: this is put on by means of the three first fingers dabbed simultaneously on the paint, and then smeared sinuously along the limbs, both upper and lower, and more or less transversely across the trunk. The females look upon themselves thus decorated as being in the height of fashion: the particular marking itself, the *koo-di-ja koo-di-ja*, is noted in the female corrobboree decorations (sect. 193) as well as in the ornamentation of the ornate boomerang (sect. 241). This grease colour painting must not be confounded with the general smearing of the body and limbs with fat; the latter practice is only adopted in times of sickness (sect. 284) or to relieve the fatigue and languor consequent on a long and tiresome journey—on no other occasions.

"Feathering" of the body is in vogue throughout all these ethnographical districts, but limited to corrobborees and to men only. "White" feather-down required for this purpose is obtained from duck, wild turkey, &c.: it can be made "red," when this colour is wanted, by dusting the feathers over with greased red ochre, which has been previously pounded up by means of a nardoo-stone. These two sets of feathers (no yellow ones are made) are put by and retained in respective dilly-bags, koolamons, &c. A sufficient supply of blood, obtained by the ordinary bleeding process (sect. 283), is collected into any convenient receptacle—anything, from an old disused jam tin to a piece of curved bark or a koolamon; this blood, by means of rag or feathers tied to the end of a stick, is painted over the required surface, which has been previously deliminated with its "kopi" pattern, and dab after dab, just a pinch, of feather-down put on—this remaining in position with the coagulation. Sometimes the whole day may be thus occupied in preparing for the night's festivities, but no women or children are ever allowed to watch the procedure.

186. **Mutilations, Flash-cuts.**—The "flash"-cuts, scars, or mutilations on the trunk and limbs, other than the sexual (sect. 316, &c.), the mourning (sect. 289, &c.), and the fighting (sect. 238, &c.), will now be considered: these are met with in both sexes throughout North-West-Central Queensland. As a rule they consist of numerous transverse scars cut across the trunk from about the level of the nipples to the navel, and a few, from one to three, longitudinal cuts along

the top and front aspect of each shoulder (Fig. 276) ; using Pitta-Pitta terms, the former marks are spoken of as *ti-pa-do*, and the latter as *moo-too-roo*. These positions are the ones adopted most commonly in all the ethnographical districts, but additional ones may occasionally be found, as on the upper portions of the chest (Figs. 277, 278) and on the back. Thus, among the Mitakoodi especially, on the back are five or six pairs of small cuts on either side of the vertebral column from the loins up, and intervening between these may be found two or three pairs of longer bands coming right round the flanks to join those in the front (Fig. 279). Again, here and there may be found additionally small dots scattered irregularly on the arms and back. Among the Yaroinga tribe I have noticed a couple of transverse scars on the upper arms just below the orthodox longitudinal shoulder ones.

Flash-marks in these districts, whatever may have been their original signification, have certainly at the present day no connection with any of the initiation ceremonies: they are optional, and their infliction is certainly dying out, so far as the numerous examinations enabled me to judge, more rapidly in the females than the males. The results also of my various inquiries into any pictorial or other hidden signification proved fruitless. Flash-marks can be recognised from all other scars, not only by their same constant position on the body, but from the fact that they are invariably raised more or less artificially, in some cases quite a quarter of an inch, above the surrounding surface: to the naked eye these scars appear to be of cicatricial tissue, yet sometimes containing traces of pigment, quite smooth, and having rounded edges. The actual procedure of elevating these scars I have not had opportunities of witnessing, and the explanations and descriptions offered me appear unsatisfactory: to judge, however, from what I have observed in the making of the raised dots (see subsequently) there is ground for believing that some particular idiosyncrasy in the skin itself is responsible for the peculiarity. In all cases the initial incision appears to be made with a sharpened flint or glass-chip along a previously marked charcoal or "kopi" line: the account of what follows varies. At Boulia the aboriginals tell me that bits of " pig-weed" plant are rubbed well into the freshly-made wound for upwards of a quarter of hour, and that the nature of the elevation depends upon whether the particular individual has a "tight" or a "loose" skin: the picking at the wound with the fingers is also subsequently adopted at intervals to make it " jump-up." At Glenormiston and at Roxburgh a quantity of bird's or other blood was said to be put on the incision so as to increase the size of the clot. A Yaroinga boy told me that among his own people the wounds are rubbed into with charcoal.

At Cloncurry, the aboriginals assured me that feather-down is first of all put on to cause coagulation, that is, to prevent the blood running off, and left there for two or three days until such time as the wound gets rotten and the " yellow muck " (*i.e.*, the pus) runs out: the latter is next removed by rubbing fat into it, and the wound "grows himself then." The dotted, elevated scars on the arms I have witnessed being made among the Mitakoodi as follows:—The individual takes a small cold piece of charcoal, about ⅓ or ⅝ inch in height, and places it on the spot where he intends the flash-mark to be: he then puts a light to the top of the charcoal which, after the preliminary flame is extinguished, goes on glowing until the base is reached, thus letting it burn out to a white ash, with the simultaneous scorching and destruction of the subjacent skin. In two or three days the " pimple " of cicatricial tissue begins to form. These flash-marks are said to remain for a good many years, but eventually decline : what lends colour to this statement is that, as a rule, the scars among the older men are apparently not so strongly elevated as those in the younger people. In marked contrast with all the preceding flash-marks, are the usual non-elevated fighting scars, which may be met with in the males on the back of the shoulders, the flanks, the buttocks, and lower masses of flesh—the only parts one is allowed to tackle in duelling with stone knives (sect. 238). These scars, of which many a man is proud to possess at least one or two, can be distinguished from the true " flash "-marks by their comparatively large size, irregular direction and outline, non-elevation, and general asymmetry.

187. Mural Painting, Art, and Draughtsmanship.— The only two localities where examples of mural painting have been met with, to my knowledge, in these North-West-Central Districts are on Oorindimindi Station, and at a small water-hole on the old Normanton road, about six miles from Cloncurry. At the latter, these consist of a saurian type of figure, varying from about 12 inches to over 6 feet in length, and hence possibly representing a lizard, an iguana, or crocodile, painted in red ochre upon the blocks of granite. I counted seven or eight of these figures in January, 1896. They are nearly all weather-worn, and except under very careful scrutiny the majority of them would pass unnoticed: the best-preserved and one of the largest, over 6 feet long, is that under an overhanging ledge of rock represented in Fig. 280, which, in addition, is distinguished from all the others by holding what could very well pass for a stone-tomahawk. The local aboriginals knew nothing of these paintings or their signification.

In Glenormiston country, yet on the Toko Ranges, Mr. J. Coghlan, the station manager (1895), informed me that up in one of the caves he came across a circle of about 18 inches diameter cut pretty accurately in a piece of solid rock: it may be mentioned here that the representation of a circle is only met with on ornaments and implements coming from, and to the west of, the Upper Georgina Districts.

The ornamentation of the various boomerangs, letter-sticks, &c., will be referred to in their respective sections.

As examples of draughtsmanship, three drawings, all of them first attempts, are given. Fig. 281A drawn by an adult woman at Glenormiston, represents her idea of any man in general; while Fig. 281B is a fair representation of a goat: Fig. 282, sketched by a Pitta-Pitta male, depicts one of the figures (Fig. 296) in the "Molonga" corrobboree referred to in sect. 199.

So far as colour is concerned, all the tribes concerned have distinct names for red and yellow (ochre): blue very often is confounded with black, so far as nomenclature is concerned, although their visible differences are appreciated.

CHAPTER VIII.

RECREATION: CORROBBOREES, SPORTS, AND GAMES.

188. The Corrobboree (Pitta-Pitta *wun-ni*, Ulaolinya *won-ni-na*, Kalkadoon *wa-ma*, Undekerebina *wun-tun-ya*) consists of singing (Pitta-Pitta *wun-ka-*), accompanied by dancing (Pitta-Pitta *e-cha-la-mul-le-*) and accompaniments: throughout North-West-Central Queensland the performance has certain features in common.

189. (A) Time of Performance.—The corrobboree commences at sunset and may be continued until sunrise, the whole performance being extended sometimes over three, four, or even five nights consecutively. Exceptions to this rule of night performance are some unimportant local dances, or one danced by the women only, or the corrobboree for bringing up rain, &c., and those dependent upon certain of the initiation ceremonies: to these particular last-mentioned ones, described in sects. 294-297 and in chap. XIII., the following notes do not refer.

190. (B) Authorship and Plot.—Anybody may "find," *i.e.*, compose a corrobboree, and more often a "doctor" as not: sometimes it is alleged to have been found in a dream. The corrobboree may be held just for the sake of the amusement that is in itself afforded, and beyond the repetition of some simple statement or assertion may have no meaning whatsoever behind it (*see* Boulia songs in sect. 196): on the other hand, as on the Upper Georgina, at Roxburgh, Carandotta, and in the Cloncurry District, &c., a sort of pantomime relating to some event of individual interest or tribal importance may be enacted. Thus I have known where the climbing of a tree after honey, the stealing of cattle (the "horns" represented in Fig. 292) by blacks with the tracking and shooting of the marauders, or again, the rescue of a European by three aboriginals in the late floods (which had actually occurred) was staged with full histrionic powers and accoutrements. I have not come across any songs or dances dealing with the prowess, life-history, battles, &c., of any individual deceased: indeed, not in any way to refer to the dead appears to be an understood rule among all these tribes (sect. 67).

191. (c) May be Taught and Carried to other Tribes.—Corrobborees may be taught and conveyed from one tribe to another. Like articles of exchange and barter, corrobborees may travel in various directions and along identical trade-routes and markets (sect. 229). When taught to one tribe, the latter may take it on to the next, and so on, the visitors being paid in blankets or other presents in return for the instruction imparted. Sometimes picked men may be sent to a distant tribe just for the sake of learning one: from Boulia to Herbert Downs or Roxburgh, from Cloncurry, *viâ* the Upper Diamantina, to Cork, &c. It may thus come to pass, and almost invariably does, that a tribe will learn and sing by rote whole corrobborees in a language absolutely remote from its own, and not one word of which the audience or performers can understand the meaning of. That the words are very carefully committed to memory, I have obtained ample proof by taking down phonetically the same corrobborees as performed by different-speaking people living at distances upwards of 100 miles apart; as, for instance,

in the case of the *Molonga* performances, to be subsequently dealt with, where it
had already passed through at least three separate and distinct camps (sect.
199). This same Molonga also affords a good illustration of the distance and
time taken by one of these dances in its peregrination. Whether the Workia, of
the Georgina headwaters and Northern Territory, invented it themselves or only
received it from others, it is impossible for me to say : nevertheless, from them it
travelled to Camooweal and Lake Nash, whence the Headingly men, the Yaroinga,
brought it down to Carandotta, where it made its appearance for the first time in
1893. Hence, it branched along in three directions : westwards, to the Toko
Ranges, to Carlo, and down the Mulligan ; eastwards, along the Leichhardt-
Selwyn Ranges, including Mount Merlin, Buckingham Downs, &c., and to
Cloncurry ; southwards, to Roxburgh and Glenormiston, at both of which localities
it appeared at the end of 1894, and so to Herbert Downs and Boulia, where it
arrived in 1895. From Boulia, it travelled on the one hand, *viâ* Marion Downs
down the Georgina, making for the Lower Diamantina, and, on the other, *viâ*
Springvale for the "Gates," Davenport, and Cork on the Middle Diamantina, where
it was met with at the beginning of 1896. Even at Roxburgh all traces of the
meanings of the words had been lost by, or rather were unintelligible to, the
individuals singing it.

192. (D) **Performers.**—Adults of either sex may take part in the dancing, but
as a rule women only perform in the daytime. Men may occasionally join in these
day-light ones, but in such circumstances are never blood-feathered (sect. 185) :
they are only grease-painted.

193. (E) **Dress and Decorations.**—Each tribe appears to have its own particular
designs and decorations so far as the accoutrements and paraphernalia are concerned (*cf.* the various articles of attire described in Chap. VII.), the newly
invented corrobboree-song in each district consisting in the main of a new song in
an actually old "dress": of course when it is one that has been imported the
accompanying new "dress" is adopted. Blood-feathering (sect. 185) is invariably
used in the male costumes, but never in the female. The following illustrations
represent typical local costumes of the Boulia District :—

Fig. 283. *Male.*—On the top of the head are fixed two light sticks at right
angles, tipped at their extremities with white-owl or corella feathers: this ornament
is the *ta-ka-le.* Over the *miri-miri*, or forehead-net, are stuck a few vertical white-
feather bands. The face, trunk, and limbs, as far as the wrists and ankles, are
covered with red-ochre grease. Two charcoal spirals reach from the forehead to just
below the knees, one spiral passing in front, and the other behind the trunk: also, two
semi-ovals of charcoal over the front and side of each elbow. The remaining white
stripes, running parallel with the charcoal ones, consist of feather-down put on in
the usual way with blood (sect. 185). The "get-up" is completed with a human-
hair waist-belt, a *koompara*, a bunch of emu or eagle-hawk feathers (the *tilyari*
or *pingkura*) hanging over the fold of the buttocks, and a bunch of singed leaves
tied on to the ankles and wrists. The object of these singed leaves (used only by
the men) is to cause a rustling or crackling noise when dancing. The "leaders"
in the dance are not to be distinguished, so far as dress is concerned, from the
other performers.

Fig. 284. *Male.*—May be adopted even during the same performance,
indiscriminately with the preceding, than which it is said to be easier to properly
design. Instead of spirals, the bands are vertical, and the two main charcoal ones
are each composed of two closely apposed ones.

Fig. 285. *Male.*—Sometimes a design with transverse instead of vertical
stripes may be noticed : the easiest of all to manipulate. It consists of thick
charcoal bands on the upper chest, stomach, and limbs, filled in between with
red-ochre grease and white feather-down. Singed leaves on wrists and ankles as
before.

Fig. 286. *Male.*—Is a rare variation, practised more in the old days than
now. A charcoal band encircles the body from one shoulder over the opposite
hip : the rest filled in as before.

Fig. 287. *Female.*—A very common pattern. Excepting the feet and hands, the whole body is first of all greased with red ochre, and the subsequent ornamentation put on, by means of the three fingers, with yellow ochre according to the pattern shown. This tri-linear marking is the *koodija-koodija* mark of the boomerangs (sect. 241). The number of transverse series across the back varies. The only ornaments used are the *moonamulyari* apron-belt, and some grass-blades fixed with any coloured band, &c., across the forehead. Singed leaves are never used in the decoration of the women.

Fig. 288. *Female.*—Used especially in corrobborees danced by women only. The body is first of all covered with greased red-ochre, and then the white stripes are put on with " kopi," and the black ones with charcoal. To the *takale* head-piece, a number of " bilbi"-tails are suspended : the remaining articles worn are the apron-belt and grass-blades as before, together with a human-hair or opossum string held between the two hands.

Figs. 289, 290, represent two male costumes in charcoal and " kopi" from a Cloncurry District corrobboree at Clonagh, which had arrived there from the Diamantina, *viâ* Kynuna.

194. (F) Dancing Ground, Dressing Room.—The corrobboree is always held at some distance from the main camping-ground. The sexes prepare themselves for the dance, and this may occupy the greater portion of the day, in separate localities, the one not being allowed to watch the other: furthermore no individual is permitted to watch the " dressing" of either, unless he or she shall have previously witnessed that same performance. When, however, the respective toilettes are completed, the performers will betake themselves to what may be called the " green-room," at all events what would correspond to it among more civilised communities, whence they emerge or whither they retreat according as their presence is required or not during the course of the performance. In the Boulia District this green-room consists of a sort of bough-shed formed of long boughs placed slantingly so as to rest upon each other at their apices (Fig. 291): it is known to the Pitta-Pitta as the *duk-ka duk-ka* (*cf.* Pitta-Pitta *tuk-ka*=to stand), to the Mitakoodi as *jil-bi.* There is always at night a fire between audience and performers, affording more or less sufficient illumination to see by.

195. (G) The Dance.—With the males, the dancing consists in the main of a stamping movement of the feet, raised alternately and rhythmically to the time beaten on the boomerangs, &c., by the audience : during this movement the thigh is raised almost horizontally. Another fairly common movement of the lower extremities is a slight genuflexion, accompanied with a vibratory out-and-in motion of the knees, while the feet are close together. Occasionally one foot may be placed over the opposite knee (a common position of rest), and a hopping kind of a step introduced. The opened, closed, and other positions of the upper limbs vary, of course, in great measure with the different implements, sticks, &c., that may be brought into requisition. Sometimes the ground is struck with the flat of the hands. With the females, the movements of the lower limbs also present great variety : that of the vibration of the knees would seem to be the most usual. The upper extremities, if not otherwise employed with a corrobboree string, &c., are commonly maintained in such a manner that the hands rest on the top of the buttocks, while the elbows, sticking out at the sides, are rhythmically drawn backwards and forwards. In many dances the women never turn their backs on the audience, even when retiring to the dressing-room. The performers may dance singly, in pairs, in Indian file, indeed in almost endless initial positions ; they are invariably led by one or sometimes two "masters of ceremonies" or " leaders," who may be distinguished occasionally by an extra feather-tuft on the arm, &c. : the Pitta-Pitta blacks call this leader by terms signifying the " father," or " old man," the remaining dancers being the " children." Beyond an occasional shout or " whoop " the dancers, certainly while dancing, do not participate in the singing.

196. (H) The Words of the Song.—The singing is carried on by the audience, including both male and female portions of it, and in its simplest form consists of the repetition over and again, somewhat after the manner of a chant, of some simple statement or assertion. In the indigenous, that is, pure Pitta-Pitta songs at Boulia, there is undoubtedly a variation both in pronunciation and inflexion from the ordinary every-day language, a variation which might certainly be regarded in the light of poetical or musical license.

Thus—

mŏl-lō-rō-chĭ-*á*-nă pŏr-*á*-kĕ *nŭng*-kĕ, ought grammatically to be mŏl-lō-rō-ē-nă *pá*-koo-lă nŭng-*kĭ*-ă
= mountain-alongside-of two (people) sit-down.

Again—

kō-tă *nēn*-yă mŭn-kă-*rĭn*-nĭ, should be in ordinary conversation *koo*-tă *nŭn*-yâ-tĭ, &c.
= water belonging-to-me (is) clean.

Or—

wŏr-pĭl-lă-ng *nēn*-yă koo-nă-*mŭl*-yă-rō yăk-kă-yăk-*kŭng*-ĭ, should read *wŏr*-pĭl-lă *nŭn*-yâ-tĭ, &c., the *ng* being euphonic (compare Pitta-Pitta *pakoolangooro*, sect. 36).
= hook-boomerang belonging-to-me mud digs-up.

Other Boulia District songs are—

yĕr-tă *yĕr*-tă   ē-rĭ-*tē*-chă
= grass-tops (make) bough-shed.

mă-lă-kă *nēm*-pă kâ-rĭl-pŭl-*lē*-ă
= dog (and) slut are-jumping, &c.

The first verse of the song gives the name to the particular corrobboree: *cf.* the European's "Pater Noster," "Alphabet," &c. (sect. 199).

197. (J) Music of the Song.—Unfortunately the actual harmony of the music I have not been able to decipher: to my unmusical ear the cadences seem always identical, a sort of wail commencing with a sudden rise and ending with a slow prolonged fall.

198. (K) Beating of the Time.—The audience squat upon the ground, usually in rows (in the Boulia District) ranged one behind the other, like the seats in the old form of theatre-pit. The men sit in front, the women and children behind, while the dogs are scattered anywhere around. Occasionally the audience is divided into two groups, side by side, one for each sex. Both sexes, as has been already mentioned, carry on the singing and both beat time, the men alone doing this with two boomerangs, one held in either hand, made to strike one another on the flat: the women clap the open hand on to the crutch of the thighs, and thus produce a loud reverberation (Fig. 293). In the Leichhardt-Selwyn and Cloncurry Districts, the women, instead of striking their thighs, occasionally employ a sort of drum or small pillow made of opossum skin, &c., filled with feathers, rags, &c., upon which they bang with the flat of the open hands: in the Mitakoodi language the name of this pillow is *pi-ka-bur-ra*. To tintinabulate with boomerangs is called, in the Pitta-Pitta, *moolka-lo wunka-linga*—*i.e.*, to sing with the sticks; the clapping of the hands, in the same language, is *poor-pa-le*. What with the barking of the dogs, the clapping of the hands, the beating of the boomerangs, the chanting of the song, and the stamping of the dancers—the weird and uncanny appearance presented by the costumes and the different attitudes only lit up by the intervening fire, all help to produce a scene which requires an abler pen than mine to describe.

199. (L) The Molonga Set of Corrobborees.—An account of this dance, together with the stage directions as far as they could be followed and understood, may not prove uninteresting here as indicative of the powers of memory that are exercised in reciting a song the delivery of which takes upwards of five nights for its completion. Here and there I will show how slight the variations are that may occur over the distance of ninety miles which separate Glenormiston from Boulia: the wonder is increased when it is remembered that the words are sung in a language of which the singers of both localities are entirely ignorant. This same corrobboree also draws into prominence the various changes of costumes throughout, and the introduction of certain salient features which distinguish the "boss" or "leader of the dance" from the others : remaining points of interest are the introduction of various implements only to be subsequently destroyed, and the different attitudes assumed by the trunk and limbs.

The place of origin and peregrinations of this particular corrobboree, as far as they could be traced, have been already referred to in sect. 191.

The meaning of the word *Molonga* (*cf.* Pitta-Pitta *mo-ma*) is difficult to interpret in European fashion. It hardly corresponds with our conception of the "devil," and yet at the same time it does signify an evil-doer from whom mischief may be expected. He is invisible to ordinary mortals unless it be to the "doctors," and in general appearance is believed to be something like the central figure in the fifth night's performance. When on his depredatory excursions, on the warpath, &c., *Molonga* is said to tie up the toes on each foot and hitch them up with string to their respective knees : another string is similarly fixed to each heel and attached to the back of the knee in corresponding fashion. The object of this tying-up is to necessitate the gentleman's walking only on the under-surface of the instep, with a view to obliterating all the tracks, and so it comes to pass that his presence is not detected, except of course to the favoured few. [It must be remembered that this particular conception of the evil-one in question is peculiar to the Workia and Upper Georgina tribes : the Pitta-Pitta blacks have different ideas concerning him.] Supposing the performance of this particular corrobboree were not to be properly executed, *Molonga* would revenge himself by raping the women and putting some of the men to death.

The green-room shed is here replaced by a large bush, built somewhat after the manner of a haystack, but made of boughs, saplings, and leaves closely interlaced. This *moy-er-jo* is about 4½ to 5 feet high, and more or less dome-shaped: the performers slink into and out of view from behind this, while the various implements, &c., required in the dance are stuck into it when not in actual-use, and where they may be left throughout the whole length of the five days' entertainment. It separates the actors' portion of the corrobboree ground from that occupied by the women and children : should a female ever trespass too close to or beyond this spot, or gaze upon any of the corrobboree sticks otherwise than when exhibited during the performance, she would be sure to fall sick, and in all probability die. On each occasion of my witnessing this *Molonga* dance, the *moyerjo* was built on the right-hand side (from the audience) of the central fire, in such position as to screen the sun just setting from the spectators.

It is only men that dance this particular corrobboree, the leader or "boss" (there may be two of them) of each evening's performance being substituted by another or others on subsequent nights.

a. The First Night's Performance.—There are two leaders here, distinguished from all the others by two red bands across the face and forehead and curled prolongations over each shoulder from the main vertical trunk ones : they also alone wear a feather-tuft stuck into each armlet (Fig. 294, 295). The red and white colours on the face, trunk, and limbs in all the accompanying figures are composed of dyed feather-down stuck in with human blood. The head-piece, shaped like a straw bottle-envelope, is formed of grass tied round with hair-twine, and tipped with a more or less elongate "kopi"-covered portion formed from the quills of a bundle of emu feathers. From the human-hair belt hangs a bunch of eagle-hawk feathers on either side, and a *koompara* or else a pearl-shell in front. On the ankles and lower shins are tied some gum or coolibar leaves which have been previously singed (sect. 193) over the fire.

The forked stick is tipped with white feathers. At sunset the male portion of the audience take their places in the front rows (sect. 198), and tingling their boomerangs sing kŭn-*jăn*-jă *pŏr*-ō-nō-mĭl-lă, at the sound of which the women put in an appearance and sit down behind them. [The words of all these songs were taken down always the following day, in the presence and with the assistance of the very same individuals who sang them the night before.] The performers slink up one by one from behind the *moyerjo*, and as each one comes forward, his advent being accompanied with an extra quick tintinabulation of the boomerangs, he dances the foot-stamp, half-squats, vibrates thighs and knees, and retires: he advances again and repeats the process. All the performers in succession thus make their preliminary bow before the "footlights," and then the corrobboree proper commences—

DANCERS.	AUDIENCE: SINGING.
All performers dancing the foot-stamp, and with hands on the forked stick held horizontally forwards, the crutch being on the neck (Fig. 296) ...	wŏl-lă *koor*-pă-nă koo-*loo*-loo *wă*-roo (this first verse giving the name to this particular evening's dance).
The leader alone	mē-ŭn kŏr-*ăn*-nă *lĭn*-jă-roo-ĕ-rĭ. „ „ wĕ-ăt-yŏr-ĭn-nĭ.
All together, but without the sticks, which have been stuck into the moyerjo	wŏl-lŭn kŭl-prŭn-nă *wĭnt*-yō-lă-prŭn-nă. „ „ wĭn-jĭn-jă *wĭn*-jō-lă-prŭn-nă.
At completion of the figure	ă-*mĭl*-kĭ-prŭn-nă ă-*mŭn*-kă-doo-dō *loo*-too-tō-mŭr-rō. *loo*-too-tō mă-*rō*-lă *bĭn*-jĭ bĭn-*jō*-lă.

A spell is now given to the dancing, and the musicians sing the following three verses, in which some of the dancers may come round to the front to join, while the women retire to a distance to prepare the tea or supper. Of course, each verse is repeated over and over again, and hence takes an appreciable time in its delivery—

pool lă *mă* ră *kă* lă ră kă-*lă* ră.
lĭn-jă „ „ „
lĭn-jă *noo*-nă „ „

The evening meal having been partaken of, the performance is resumed, and the forked stick is again brought into requisition; but this time it is held only with one hand, alternately the right and the left—

DANCERS.	AUDIENCE: SINGING.
All together	*lĭp*-pĭp-prĭn-*pō*-ĕ-jō mĭn-gă-rō-ă-rĭ.
The leader alone	nī-ă mĭn-kă *răl*-lĭ-lă.
All together	*wĭn*-tū wŏl-lă *koor*-pă-nă.

Dancing is over now until the following morning, but the singing is kept up all night before the fires until sunrise. Two women beat time with the flat of the hand upon the crutch of the thighs, &c.; one relieves the other so as to get a snatch of sleep. Some of the audience may continue singing all the night through, but as a rule they rest each other occasionally. The following are a few of three or four dozen verses sung throughout the watches of the night: they were taken down both at Glenormiston and at Boulia, 90 miles apart, where I heard them rendered by different tribes—

AT GLENORMISTON	AT BOULIA
(but sung by Roxburgh boys).	(sung by the local Pitta-Pitta).
mŭn-nŭn-kō-*bī*-lă kŭn-kŭn-*gŏr*-ĭl-ă.	mŭn-nŭn-kō-*pī*-ō-lă, etc.
kŏr-*ĭn*-jō-bă-nĭl-lă yŭng-ă *yŭng*-ă-ră.	kŏr-*ĭ*-chĭ-bă-nĭl-lă ō-*rŭng*-ŏr-ă.
kool-kŏr-*ă*-nĕl-lă *lă*-jō-jĭ-nĕl-lă.	*kool*-kŏr-ă-nĕl-lă *jă*-joo-nĕl-lă
nĭ-rŭng-*ĭ*-ră „	nă-rŭng-oo-*ă*-ră „
etc., etc.	etc., etc.

At the first streak of sunrise, the corrobboree dance is resumed by one individual only (Fig. 297) with a pair of fluted boomerangs (sect. 242), and blood-feathered as in the illustration. The accompanying song, which gives the dance its name, is koo-*lă*-rĭ *pŭn*-tă pŭn-tă-*nă*. Everything is now over for the day.

b. The Second Night's Performance.—At sunset the preliminary song and double bowing of each performer takes place just as it did the night before. The dancers are all dressed alike (Fig. 298), similar to the "boss" in the previous evening's performance, but have an additional red circular patch on the forehead. The corrobboree implement here is a tight roll made of skin, linen, rags, &c., and wound pretty tightly round with string: it is about 18 inches long—

DANCERS.	AUDIENCE: SINGING.
All together, and with the rag-sticks	{ *koon*-jĭn-jĭn *mĕl*-lă wŏl-lŭm-*boo*-mă-ră; the name of this night's dance.
The leader alone	{ meun korunna, etc. meun korunna, etc.
All together, but without the rag-sticks, which have been stuck into the *moyerjo*	{ wollun, etc. ... wollun, etc. ... } as on previous night.
At completion of the figure	{ amilkiprunna, etc. lootooto marola, etc. ... ...

Subsequently the musicians, while the women are preparing the tea, sing again the three verses—

poolla, etc.
linja, etc.
linja, etc. just as before.

After supper, the dancing is resumed with—

All together	lippipprin, etc.
The leader alone	nia minka, etc.
All together	wintu, etc.

Singing is kept up all night, and at the first sign of dawn one single performer dances to *kŭr*-ră *pŭt*-yă-*pŭt*-yă *koo*-tă-ră *mŭl*-lă. He is dressed like the individual who danced the "koolari punta" the morning before, but his face is wholly white, there being no bars across it (Fig. 299). He holds a singed leaf-bunch in either hand, which he raises alternately up and down.

c. The Third Night's Performance.—On the top of the head-piece is a charcoal ornamentation formed of two or three concentric circles around a central spot, and between two parallel bands joined behind: this circular mark (Fig. 300) is known to the Pitta-Pitta as *u-ron-goo-to*. The "leader" (Fig 301) can be recognised by a transverse bar instead of a circular patch (Fig. 302) on the forehead, while the two vertical bands on the trunk are split up into several more or less rectangular patches. The implement consists of a long stick with a bunch of singed leaves and twigs tied at each end. The corrobboree commences as usual at sunset, but starts with all the performers sitting round in a semi-circle; then the music commences, and the gins are called—

DANCERS.	AUDIENCE: SINGING.
Performers all squatting— sticks all pointing down to left ...	{ *woo*-room pō-*loo*-loo kâ-too-lŭm-*bá*-nă: the name of this night's dance.
sticks all pointing down to right (Fig. 301)	{ *woo*-room pō-*loo*-loo koo-jē-lâ-*prŭn*-nă
Performers all standing— sticks horizontal (Fig. 302) ...	{ *ná*-ră *ná*-ră jē-mŭn-*ká*-ră
sticks removed to *moyerjo*	{ wollun, etc. wollun, etc. amilkiprunna, etc. lootootomarola, etc. } as on first night.
at completion	

The musicians again sing the same three songs, during the preparation for supper, as on previous occasions—viz , "poolla," &c.

After tea, the dancing recommences with—

Performers squatting ...	{ wooroom polooloo katoolumbana „ „ koojelaprunna	} as at commencement of entertainment.
Performers standing ...	nara nara jemunkara	

This is followed by the all-night singing, and then at sunrise the "koolari punta" corrobboree is again repeated with similar costume as on the first morning, but two people, instead of one, take part in it.

d. The Fourth Night's Performance.—The two "leaders" and other dancers are all dressed the same (Fig. 303), except that the former wear feather-tufts in the armlets. There is the same "circle" design on the head-gear as of the night before. The corrobboree stick is between 2 and 3 feet long, made of bundles of grass and flax, and bound lengthways with human hair-twine, and then finished off by being wound round transversely with the same material : sometimes it may, in addition, be decorated with three or four narrow rings of white or white-and-red feather-down.

At sunset, the male musicians commence singing "wooroom polooloo," &c., the same song as the night before, and the gins put in an appearance. The performers now emerge from behind the *moyerjo* in indian file, the two "bosses" being respectively first and last. As they advance forwards, stamping rhythmically, and sticks all pointing down to (performers') left, the audience sing "*yŭng-ŭn-jŭng-ŭn-jŭ wŏl*-lŭm pool-*mŭ*-rŭ," and when the last one comes into view, the real corrobboree commences with—

DANCERS.	AUDIENCE : SINGING.	

The sticks are changed from left to right and back again alternately: two jerks with each.	⌠ wĭn-tĭ *mŭ*-kō-lŭn-nă ků-pō-*lŭl*-lă-pâ (the name).
	  „ „ ků-rĭn-ĭ-*ŏr*-ă.
	  „ „ *pŭl*-tĭ-ă bâ-*nŭ*-ră.
	 ⌡ loo-kă-pă-*tŭ*-nă „ „	

Sticks put into *moyerjo* … …	⎰ wollun, etc. ⎱ wollun, etc.	⎱ as on previous
At completion … … …	⎰ amilkiprunna, etc. ⎱ lootooto marola, etc.	⎰ nights.

The same three verses, " poolla," &c., are again sung during the preparation of supper, and after the meal has been partaken of, dancing is resumed with—

winti makolunna kapolullapa
   „   „   kariniora.
   „   „   pultia banara.
lookapatara   „   „

as at commencement of the evening. The singing as usual goes on again all night, and at sunrise a performer, costumed as on the second morning, dances the " kurra putya," &c.

e. The Fifth, and last, Night's Performance.—The central figure of this entertainment, *Molonga* himself (Fig. 304), is greased with red ochre on the forearms and thighs, and is the only person throughout the whole corrobboree who is feathered on the back. This pattern on the back consists of a median (seen at Boulia, Fig. 305), or unilateral (seen at Glenormiston, Fig. 306) circle from which the design more or less radiates in the former case, but which becomes somewhat concentric in the latter : both "costumes" are said to be quite orthodox and correct, though the Glenormiston one, being more difficult to " draw," is not so often attempted. *Molonga* carries a long feather-tipped spear, and numerous white feathers stuck into his hair, but wears no leaf anklets. With regard to the other dancers (Fig. 307), their head-gear instead of being cone-shaped is flattened from before backwards (sometimes made on a foundation of a disused bent jam-tin) : the two leaders are distinguished from the others by the transverse white bars on the main vertical red trunk-bands, and the feather tufts on the armlets.

At sunset the male musicians appear first as usual, and sing " wooroom polooloo katoolumbana" (as on the third night), when the women join in, and the performers advance one by one and make their obeisance, as on the first night. The corrobboree itself, while all are dancing with alternate open and closed arms, commences with—

pĭl-ĭl-ă-*roo*-lă wŏt-yă-*rŭm*-brĭn-ă (the name).   Then
pā-ŭm-pā-*ŭm*-bĭ mĕt-yĕ-kō-*lŭ*-ră
gā-lā-*wĕr*-nă wŏt-yă-*chŭ*-ră-nă
   „   „   wŏt-yă-*wŏt*-yă-ră

The dancing being temporarily over, the evening meal is prepared, but on this occasion there is no " poolla," &c. ; after supper the musicians sing, accompanied by all the performers dancing—

ŏr-ă-kĭ-mă-*nĭl*-lă mŏl-lă-mă-*nĭl*-lĭ.

„   „   ŏl-loor-*má*-nĭ.

Suddenly, the great event of the evening appears, amidst the shrieking and shouting of the excited audience, in the person of *Molonga* himself, who rushes in at them from the darkness in front as if about to spear them : he retires and then advances again to feign another attack.   The excitement having subsided on his final disappearance, the singing proceeds with—

koo-too-lă pă-rĕn-jă-*rĕn*-jă

kŭn-tĭ-ĕn pō-*loo*-loo wŏl-lŭm-poo-*má*-ră

kâ-*rá* pâ-*tá*-pâ-*tá* lâ-pâ-rĭng-*ká*-ră.

wĭn-nă-*ná*-ră prĭn-jŏl-*pŏr*-ŏn-jō.

Singing is again kept up all night, but on this particular evening a sort of premium or reward in the shape of extra food, &c., is held out as a bait to keep the men up and singing, the one who holds out till sunrise winning it.   At sunrise the whole series of performances is brought to a close by one performer (Fig. 308) dancing " kurra putya," &c. (as at the second morning's entertainment), but instead of the leafy bushes he holds an oval-shaped flat piece of wood in his hands, which he sways from side to side.   This implement, which is covered with feather-down on both sides, according to pattern, is intended to depict the female genitals.

The dance being now completed, the women and children retire while the *moyerjo*, together with the head-dresses, forked and other sticks that have been used during the preceding five nights, &c., are all consumed by fire.   The sun is well up over the horizon now.

200.   Fables, Tales, and Legends.—How far the following fables are traditional it is impossible to say.   The women, and those men who are lazy, that is, who are always loafing around the camp, are the best hands at telling them : a man in the full vigour of mental and bodily physique looks upon it as womanish and childish, almost derogatory, to know anything concerning them, and will almost invariably refer to his gin when any such matters are inquired of.   The large majority of the stories refer to animals with human attributes, and in this connection it is well to remember the traditional superstition throughout all these districts, of those extremely remote times when all the birds and quadrupeds were blackfellows (sect. 39) : furthermore there is almost invariably some attempt made at explaining any physical peculiarity or conformation.   The following tales were obtained all in the Boulia District :—

201.   (A)   The Water-hen and the Emu.—An emu was hatching her eggs in close proximity to a small water-hen, who was also engaged in the same interesting occupation.   By-and-by both birds proceeded to walk along the grass for something to eat, and in the evening returned to their respective nests.   The same thing happened next day.   But on the following morning, the water-hen got up somewhat earlier than usual and went her way.   The emu happening to see her neighbour's eggs, said, " Hullo ! big-fellow eggs all same like mine, me take him," and shifting from her own nest, sat upon them.   As the afternoon drew on, the water-hen returned home, and when she saw the emu appropriating her eggs, began growling, but being so much smaller a bird could not use force to turn her away.   So she built a large fire, and threw all the ashes over her opponent, who thus got all her feathers browned : in retaliation, the emu threw her antagonist into the flames, and burnt her legs for her, which resulted in their turning red.

202.   (B)   The Galah-parrot and the Lizard.—One time, there was a row between the galah and the lizard.   The lizard took up a chisel (sect. 149) with which he cut the bird upon the head, the result being that his " top-knot " jumped up like a wood-shaving, and the blood streaked down over his neck and breast (the red mark): the galah, however, revenged himself by getting a lot of the "prickly bendii" or "burr," and sticking it all ever the lizard's back, so as to form the warty growths there.

203. (c) The Opossum and the Wild (or Spotted) Cat.—The opossum and the spotted cat went away in different directions to collect pappa-seed. The opossum climbed up a coolibar-tree, got his from the pods (sect. 108), and then returning home was just in the act of preparing it on the grindstone, when the cat came back empty-handed. "My word!" said the latter, when he cast eyes upon the seed that was being ground, "good-fellow pappa-seed. Where you get him that one?" Now the opossum of course was not anxious to tell whence he had obtained his supply, so he gammoned a bit, and said "Oh! I get him along big rough bushes on ground." The cat, believing what he heard, broke a lot of bushes down, and placed the fragments on the stone, but of course they were no good, and as the opossum would not let him have any, poor pussy had to go to bed hungry. Exactly the same thing happened next day, the opossum returning with proper coolibar-seed, and the cat with the bush-tops: again, in reply to inquiry, the opossum told a lie, and while he managed to have a good feed the cat was obliged to starve. On the following morning, both animals started out again to collect food, but the cat instead of going off in an opposite direction watched his opportunity when his companion was out of sight, and stole the coolibar-seed which the opossum had left in his koolamon: having duly ground, tasted, and eaten it, he remarked, "This more better." When the opossum arrived back in camp, he saw his koolamon empty, and expressed his suspicion by stating, "Here! you been steal pappa-seed belong me?" "No," replied the cat, "pappa belong me all round about." After some preliminary growling they began to fight, the opossum got the worst of it and his ham-strings cut, with the result that his "heel" became very prominent, while the cat got his fur spotted with the seed.

204. (d) The "Laughing Jackass" and the Blackfellows.—Two blacks were hunting up a big mob of emus, and having got everything ready in absolute silence, were just about to drive them into the net (sect. 131), when one of these jackasses burst out laughing, and frightened the emus away. Of course the blacks were very wild at having lost their intended prey, and therefore killed him. The bird now always laughs at their failure in catching emus.

205. (e) The Snake and the Fish.—A snake and a fish had a fight: the former turned out victorious, and as a punishment made his victim carry his skin (the scales) and bones (dorsal-fin) on his back.

206. (f) The Red-tit and the Brown-tit.—[The red-tit, Pitta-Pitta *moo-na-tim-pi-el-la*, is about 2 to 2⅓ inches long with red head and breast: the brown-tit, Pitta-Pitta *tin-er-ta*, of similar size, is a brown bird living among the porcupine-grass.] "Come and catch kangaroo," said the brown to the red-tit; the latter said, "No! me go look out for *witooka* (sect. 113), and then me go along camp." On their return after a successful expedition in both cases, the red-tit wanted to exchange some of his *witooka* for kangaroo-flesh, and asked his friend to partake of some, but the only reply he got was, "No! me no eat him—me get him guts' ache.' When the brown-tit had finished his meal, he hid what remained of the kangaroo-flesh up in a tree, and cleared the ground all round the butt, so that even if the red-tit had stolen some he would have recognised the thief by his tracks in the sand around (sect. 225). By-and-by the red-tit began to think, "What me do?" so he proceeded to the sand-hills, where he saw some emu-tracks, and having dug four or five pit-falls close up against some wild-grape vines (sect. 133), gathered a few *witooka* roots, and returned with them to camp. It was night-time now, and still being keen on getting some kangaroo-flesh, the red-tit again offered the brown-tit some of his *witooka* in exchange, but being refused, retired to rest very much disgusted. Early the following morning, however, the red-tit went to have a look at his emu-traps, and finding them full of emus, cooked and skinned them: what flesh he could not eat, he brought back to camp close alongside the particular tree where the kangaroo meat had been placed. His mate soon saw him, and recognising the emu-flesh said, "Hullo!

you been catch him emu ?   Here! give him me.   Me give him you kangaroo."
But the red-tit having now the advantage said, " No ! me no want him tuck out
now.   Might get long ears" (like a kangaroo, sect. 74, Fig. 25), and to aggravate
him still more proceeded a second time to the sand-hills only to return with still
more emu-flesh, and again point-blank refused to barter, reiterating, " No ! no !
me might get him long ears and long tail, too."   And though the brown-tit gave his
assurance that he had himself already eaten two kangaroos and had noticed no special
growth either in his ears or in the lower part of his back, the red-tit would not
come to terms.   Of course, as might be expected, they soon both got into a
temper, and began to fight, the brown one with a kangaroo-tail, and the red one
with an emu-leg : the scrimmage lasted a long while, the red-tit getting his head
and breast besmothered in blood, and the brown-tit having his head and beak
battered into its present shape.

207. (G) The Two Fishermen.—Two blackfellows, a Yunda and a Pitta-Pitta,
having made some nets went fishing in the Booloo-Booloo water-hole [on the " 15-
Mile Creek" branch of the Hamilton River, where the Winton road crosses it, about
15 miles from Boulia, sect. 226].   By-and-by, *Mul-ka-ri* (sect. 260) said to them,
" You go along other fellow water-hole.   Me want him this one water-hole myself."
So they turned round and made tracks for Parapijori [= Parapituri Water-hole on
the Georgina River—sect. 226), and as they were drawing near their destination
saw a lot of hawks flying about (sect. 225) : thus they knew that some one was
already camped there.   Nevertheless, they went on, and as soon as they reached
the water-edge recognised a large mob of blacks on the other side of the river.
The latter shouted out, " Hullo! you two-fellow! what name?" (= what
do you want ?), and got for answer, " Me two-fellow look out pish (= fish, sect. 3).
Leave him little-fellow place.   Me two-fellow only got him small net."   The
necessary permission having been granted, the two visitors went out into the middle
of the water-hole and driving their hosts away, got all the fish for themselves and
returned to Booloo Booloo.   When *Mulkari* asked them where they had got such
a fine haul, they told him a lie and said, " Oh ! from little fellow water-hole, very
muddy," so that he should not guess the exact spot.   Soon afterwards our two
visitors again went to Parapijori, and did exactly the same thing : they turned the
whole crowd of friendlies away, caught all the fish, and told a similar tale to
Mulkari on their return.   They played this trick so often, that at last the Parapijori
boys got into a temper and said, " Me altogether-fellow kill him that two-fellow " :
they therefore stuck some hook boomerangs (sect. 224) point upwards into the
mud at the bottom of the water, and taking care to cast their nets earlier than
usual, caught all the fish, and hid them behind some bushes.   By-and-by, the two
fishermen came up as usual, and noticing the tracks, exclaimed, " Hullo ! you
been catch him pish this morning,? " in answer to which the crowd replied, " No!
me altogether-fellow no been catch him pish this morning.   Big mob pelican and
shag been playing about here and catch him all pish," and words to that effect.   So
the pair went into the water, upon permit being granted, hunted the others away
as before, but of course on this occasion caught no fish at all.   At last when their
patience was exhausted, the Pitta-Pitta said to the Yunda boy, " You go dive
down," but the latter excused himself on account of his wearing a large head-net
(sect. 168).   After a bit of wrangling one of them eventually dived down, and as
he remained below the surface rather longer than customary, his mate, wondering
what had happened, dived down too : directly both were out of sight, all the Parapijori
men jumped in, and having drowned them both, stuck them on to the hook-
boomerangs in the mud at the bottom.

208. (H) The Porcupine and the Eagle-Hawk.—A porcupine and eagle-hawk
were fighting one day : the latter had a lot of spears which he stuck into the porcupine (the bristles), but by way of punishment he was made to eat raw meat.

209. (J) The Black Crow and the Hawk.—A black crow and a hawk had a
fight.   The hawk succeeded in knocking his adversary over and rolling him in the
charcoal, whence his black plumage : he himself got punished, however, by being
made to eat putrid meat.

210. (K) The Hawk and the Bower-bird.—There was a quarrel between a small hawk—the species with a "dirty brisket"—and the bower-bird : the hawk got the worst of it. So the hawk thought he would steal his opponent's young ones and eggs, but going to the nest could only find grass and stones there (*i.e.*, the play-ground) : he therefore left a snake in the enclosure which bit and killed the bower-bird when he came home at night.

211. (L) The Moon.—A long time ago, when the blackfellow was a turkey, he damaged his foot and ankle very badly, and asked a gin, a cockatoo-parrot, where the nearest water-hole was. She said, "No water here." He then asked a green parrot if he knew where the water was, and as the foot was becoming more swollen, requested him furthermore to cut it open, but the green-parrot said he couldn't do it. He thereupon successively appealed to a crow, a black-fellow doctor, an eagle-hawk, the moon, a white-fellow doctor, and even the evil-one himself, to render him the necessary assistance : but they one and all said they couldn't undertake the job. As a last chance he begged of the earth-grub to give him relief : the latter said he would, and thereupon bit into the swollen flesh, bored his way deep into the diseased part, sucked all the putrid matter out, and cured the patient. A large corrobboree was therefore held, and the galahs, storm-birds, white and black cockatoos, butcher-birds, magpies, bower-birds, together with the opossums, porcupines, bandicoots, &c., all took part in it. And while the turkey and the earth-grub together with the clouds and skies shifted their position (for the latter had until then always remained on the surface of the ground) the whole party began singing "there goes our brother up." And of course both animals stayed up there. But so that the people below should always remember what a good physician he had proved himself to be, the earth-grub sends a moon regularly every month to bear him in mind, for the moon is a brother of his, and, like him, bores his way out of the ground, rises up again on high, sinks once more and dies. He has plenty of brothers, this worm, and so he sends a different one, a moon, every month. [N.B.—That it is a different moon every month is a common belief among these aboriginals.]

212. (M) The Galah-parrot and the Opossum.—A galah and an opossum, each having tomahawks, were fighting one day, with the result that they both got very much damaged : the parrot got his neck and breast all cut open (red plumage), while the opossum received a black mark on his snout.

213. The "Come-back" or "Return" Boomerang (Pitta-Pitta *ma-ke* or *wop-poo-ro ma-ro*, Yaroinga *ung-qub-pi-ja-ul-ve-a*, Mitakoodi *pe-eng boo-na*, &c.) is a toy which, compared with a fighting boomerang, is always lighter, much smaller, and varies in shape from a comparatively strong angle to something approaching a half-moon, the knee or bend being always in the centre. Sometimes it is cut down from one of the other kinds of boomerang that has been damaged or broken. If coloured at all, it is smeared with charcoal : it may often be ornamented, but there is no rule or uniformity in the gravings, of which some of the designs may be very quaint (*e.g.*, emus with net in Fig. 309, iguanas in Fig. 310). No further definitive description can be offered. The return boomerang is never used as a recognised article of exchange or barter: that is to say it does not travel, and is manufactured just as occasion requires. It is strictly a man's toy, and is used in different ways as follows :—In the Boulia District, five, six, or perhaps more men will stand in Indian file, each individual with raised arms resting his hands on the shoulders of the one in front: another of the playmates, standing by himself at some distance ahead and facing the foremost of the file, throws the boomerang over their heads, and as it circles round they all follow it in its gyration, the game being for any of them to escape being hit, each taking it in turn to throw the missile (see bird's-eye view in Fig. 311). Among the Yaroinga tribe on the Upper Georgina, they often try and arrange to make up two sides, the object being for a member of one team to hit an individual of the opposite group. In the Cloncurry District, the Mitakoodi fix a peg into the ground, and the one who can strike or come nearest to it with the boomerang when it falls to the ground is declared the best man.

It might be pointed out here that any kind of fighting boomerang can be more or less thrown in such manner as to "return" or "come-back," making one single complete, or perhaps two incomplete, revolutions from the starting-point. This particular toy variety, however, can make three, or sometimes even four, complete gyrations, each whirl being antagonistic (*i.e.*, reversed in direction) at a lower level, and smaller, than the one immediately preceding (see the diagrams of the bird's-eye and side-views of its flight in Figs. 312 and 313 respectively).

214. The Toy "Throwing-stick" is a thin rounded straight stick, usually gidyea, with an elongately knobbed extremity (Fig. 314), the whole varying from about 12 to 20 inches in length : it reminds one somewhat of a nulla-nulla (but very much attenuated), the larger varieties having even a similar name.   At Boulia, Marion Downs, and Glenormiston, the shorter kind is known as *boom-bo*, in the Leichhardt-Selwyn District as *koom-po*, and in the Cloncurry as *jim-ba-do* : in the Boulia District the larger variety is called *moor-ro* (*cf.*, Pitta-Pitta *mor-ro*, a nulla-nulla, sect. 43*f*) and in the Cloncurry, *min-jo*.   Held at the thinner end with the arm thrust well back from the shoulder, the smaller toy is thrown from a distance of 2 or 3 yards up and against the fringe of some overhanging bushes or leafy branches, or even against some thick foliage held up by a companion : immediately upon striking the obstacle so interposed, the stick shoots through the air, knob foremost, and with greater impetus to a distance quite one and a-half to twice as great than would otherwise be traversed.   The larger toy is similarly employed, but is thrown downwards against a tussock or low-lying bush, whence it shoots along or close to the surface of the ground.

Throughout North-West-Central Queensland is to be met another toy similar to the preceding, and known, certainly in the Boulia and Cloncurry Districts, by the same name—the *kun-di kun-di* (sect. 43*g*).   It is thick, rounded, from 18 to 20 inches in length, pointed at both extremities, but strongly bent (Fig. 315), indeed approaching nearest in shape to the boomerangs met with around Birdsville (sect. 242) : one can hardly help suspecting, in fact, but that this toy is a stage in the evolution of the boomerang from the nulla-nulla or straight throwing-stick.   It is held, convex side forwards, firmly in the hand, and simultaneously pressed close against the extended forefinger : it is thrown downwards against a log or thick branch lying on the ground, from which it rises into the air in a straight direction, revolving in its flight on a more or less horizontal plane.

215. "The Whirler."—The "whirler," "whirring-stick," "roarer," &c., of one's boyhood days is met with throughout North-West-Central Queensland : (Pitta-Pitta *pril-ling-a*, Roxburgh blacks, *mer-pul-li-mung-i*, Yaroinga *un-mun-ja*, Kalkadoon and Mitakoodi *pi-ri pi-ri*).   It is made of a flattened piece of gidyea or other timber, cut into a spindle-shape, into one extremity of which a hole is drilled with a sharpened emu-bone (Fig. 316).   By means of the aperture, this whirler is attached to a piece of string fixed to the end of a small stick ; with the latter held in the hand the "roarer" can be made to rapidly revolve, the flat surface as it catches the wind, giving rise to the noise (Fig. 317).   The smaller whirring boards are about 4 inches in length, and have no gravings on them, though they may sometimes be red-ochred : they are used as toys or playthings indiscriminately by either sex and at any age.   The graved and larger varieties, 7 to 8 inches and more, are brought into requisition at certain of the initiation ceremonies (sect. 301, Figs. 318, 319), while among the Yaroinga tribes they may be put to the special use of love-charms (sect. 325, Fig. 320) : both these last-mentioned would appear to be always kept away from the view of women.

216. The Ball.—Three kinds of ball-game are to be found in these districts : the "catch-ball," "stick-and-stone," and "spin-ball," the two former of which are certainly indigenous, the last being imported within recent times.

a. The catch-ball is played everywhere by both sexes, and either singly, or with sides, throwing it from the one to the other, the individuals trying to intercept it while still off the ground.   From the fact of the players jumping up to catch it resembling the antics of a kangaroo, the Kalkadoons sometimes describe this game as the "kangaroo-play."   The ball itself is made of a piece of opossum or kangaroo hide, or some rags, &c., tied up with opossum-string or hair-twine.

K

b. Stick-and-stone I only know of being practised in the Boulia District where it is spoken of by the Pitta-Pitta blacks as *poo-cho poo-cho tou-e-mul-le-a* (*cf.* Kalkadoon *poo-cho poo-cho*, the name for a spin-ball, and Pitta-Pitta *tou-e-mul-le-* the reflexive form of the verb *tou-e-* to hit, or to strike). It is played among the men, with from four to six individuals on each side, the two groups standing at a distance of from 15 to 20 yards apart : the members of each group, all armed with a stick, stand one behind the other, a space of 3 or 4 feet separating them. The game consists in alternately throwing a stone in the rough and of convenient size from one side to the other, each individual trying to intercept it with his stick as it skips or rolls before him on the ground.

c. The spin-ball is a round ball of about 1 to 1½ inch diameter, made of lime, ashes, sand, clay, and sometimes hair, rolled into shape either between the hands or the folds of a blanket, and subsequently baked, thus making it smooth and hard : it may subsequently be painted with red or yellow-ochre. The ball is spun by being pressed between the fore and middle fingers (Fig. 321) upon either a patch of smooth hard ground, or more usually upon a flat board, sheet of kerosene-tin, &c. Played by men and women, two or even three at a time ; the one whose ball spins longest wins the stake, which is often a wax-match or two ! The game can also be played by the participants taking sides, each backing individual members against its adversary's. It would appear to have been introduced into these parts from the Lower Diamantina River, within but very recent years, coming up the Georgina *via* Bedouri : it does not seem to have reached, or to be known, to the Mitakoodi as yet (1896). The spin-ball is called *jil-lor-a* at Boulia, *po-po-jo* at Glenormiston and Roxburgh, *poo-cho poo-cho* in the Kalkadoon country, and *un ni dup-it up pa* at Headingly and Lake Nash.

217. The Skipping-rope.—Among the Northern Mitakoodi and Grenada Kalkadoon, a sort of skipping-rope, *too-ri too-ri*, is made from the long roots of the Bauhinia or of the big white-gum growing near the water's edge : the rope is held by two play-mates, who swing it backwards and forwards—they do not circle it.

218. "Hunt the Eye" is played as follows :—On a small piece of level sandy ground, a circular space of from 2 to 2½ feet in diameter is roughly marked out, and carefully smoothed over with the hand. Round this ring members of either sex and any age may be squatting, and all eyes being closed at a given signal, one amongst the number will hide some small object beneath the sand which the others will now set upon discovering. The object hidden is the lens of a rat's, opossum's, or small kangaroo's eye, removed after cooking ; indeed, the Kalkadoons speak of this as the *mil-ti* or "eye"-game, though, as a matter of fact, anything different from the constituents of the subjacent soil, *e.g.*, seeds, &c., and of comparatively minute size, say, ⅛ to ¼ inch in diameter, may be used for the purpose. The players start looking for the hidden object by picking up a pinch or two of sand at a time, and letting it sift slowly through the fingers. Another way of playing the game is for the original hider, while the others have their eyes open, to take up handful after handful of sand and sprinkle it here and there rapidly over the circular space : he watches his opportunity, and lets the object to be hidden fall with the sand. "Hunt the Eye" is common throughout all the different ethnographical districts.

219. "Hide and Seek" is also a very commonly played game, even by adults. There may be as many as three seekers in it, these covering their eyes with the hands, or putting their heads, with eyes shut, close to the ground while the others hide themselves. If they cannot find those who are concealed, they often make a whistling sound as a sign of defeat.

220. "Smoke-Spirals" are played thus :—Any leaf, piece of light bark, or even a mussel shell, by means of a peculiar motion of the wrist and arm, can be thrown in such manner into the smoke rising from an ample fire as to ascend with it like a spiral. There are different ways of holding the article in question, the most usual being represented in Fig. 322 : the wrist is rotated outwards at the same time that the fore-arm is jerked sharply forwards and downwards the object leaving the hand just at the completion of the movement. Another method of throwing the leaf into the smoke is to hold the leaf between the fourth and fifth digits, as in Fig. 323, and with a motion of the fore-arm similar to that in the preceding rotate the wrist inwards : the Kalkadoon among whom I have noticed this way of jerking it, speak of this game as *pi-ri-jo-rong-o*. A far easier and commoner method of throwing the leaf is to make the firmly extended fore-finger of the one hand act as a sort of spring on the other (Fig. 324), the leaf at the moment of release being shot at an angle into the smoke.

221. Mimicking Animals and Birds.—The mimicking of animals and birds forms an important category in the diversions with which the aboriginals of these districts may amuse themselves in their leisure hours. Emus and kangaroos can be very well imitated ; the former especially at even a short distance might easily be mistaken for the genuine article (Fig. 325). The mimic's arm and hand represent the bird's neck and head, his own head and back being covered with a blanket (a Queensland Government one probably), the extremity of which he tilts up, with a bunch of feathers in his hand perhaps, to indicate the tail Or again, a whole party may be bathing together in the river, and while some may be imitating the actions and " calls " of various water-birds, others will hunt and try to catch them. The most interesting and perhaps most general of all these " imitative " games is the drawing of different animal and bird-tracks in the smoothed sand, by means of the fingers, finger-nails, palms, small sticks, &c. : after making several of these artificial tracks they will finish up with a European boot-print, making it about 10 or 12 inches in length, and then burst out laughing at its ludicrous size. It will subsequently be noted that given a fairly-sized camp, the foot-print of each adult may be recognised by the others (sect. 225).

222. Coursing.—A form of " coursing " is practised in the Leichhardt-Selwyn District as follows :—A wallaby, dingo, rat, &c., having been previously caught with a net, is kept alive and in captivity by means of a strong twine attached to one of its legs. When all the players are ready, and in position, the animal is let go, and must be caught with the hands only, no sticks, stones, or boomerangs being permissible in its recapture.

223. Pit-throwing is a game played by the Kalkadoon. Any fairly-sized bone, often a human shin, is slung by means of attached twine over an emu-net into a pit or hole excavated on its further side. Considering the great distance often intervening between the thrower and the excavation, great skill is apparently necessary in making the bone fall into the hole without touching the net.

CHAPTER IX.

TRAVEL, TRADE, AND BARTER. THE SO-CALLED "LETTER" OR "MESSAGE-STICK."

CONTENTS.—Section 224. The "Walk-about." 225. Signs and Signals on the Road. 226. Names of Water-holes, Camping Grounds, &c. 227. The Points of the Compass. 228. Arrangements at the Camping Ground. 229. Trade Routes ; 230, in the Boulia District ; 231, in the Upper Georgina District ; 232, in the Leichhardt-Selwyn District ; 233, in the Cloncurry District. 234. Transmission of Customs, Beliefs, and Language by means of these Trade Routes. 235. The So-called Letter or Message-sticks. 236. Notes to Illustrations of these Sticks. 237. How a Message-stick is put into Use.

224. The "Walk-about" is perhaps, in its ultimate results, one of the most important institutions in vogue among the aboriginals, and yet one on account of which their white brethren will, as often as not, hold them up to ridicule and contempt. To the settlers it is considered in the light of an excuse for a holiday or for shirking the work upon which the blacks would otherwise be employed : surmises that in some cases may be perfectly correct. In the majority of instances, however, this walk-about is but part and parcel of the great trading or bartering system which is more or less continually going on throughout the various districts. Certain trade-routes laid down from time immemorial along their own or messmates' country are followed by the members of a tribe or tribes, along which each knows that he is free to travel unmolested : these routes, of greater or less extent, are rigidly adhered to. The opening of the local market, so to speak, may take place at the instance of one of the elders or " bosses " at one of the larger camps, *e.g.*, Marion Downs, Fort Constantine, &c., where instructions are issued as to when to leave, whom to go, what to take, and what to return with. In smaller and less frequented encampments, *e.g.*, Boulia, the peregrination may commence when any fresh pituri is seen knocking about for sale, this being a pretty certain indication that their neighbours elsewhere must all be on the walk-about themselves. It also often happens that an individual will start on the road for business on his own, or friends' account, whenever the inclination suits.

The recognised routes invariably, and for reasons readily intelligible, run along water-courses and water-holes ; taking all in all it may be stated that owing to the ordinarily scanty supplies of this commodity during the summer months, the walk-about usually takes place sometime during the winter ones. The length of time occupied on each journey varies with the distance of course, from a few weeks to several months, and cases are not unknown where the blacks will travel all one winter before reaching their destination, will spend the summer, the dry season, there, and then return the following winter.

225. Signs and Signals on the Road.—In connection with these peregrinations certain methods are adopted for indicating the road or denoting the traveller's presence to friends and fellow-tribesmen in front or behind : such are the smoke-signals, finger-posts, foot-prints, geographical names, terms for cardinal points, &c. Smoke-signals and signal-fires are known to have been recognised and answered at distances upwards of ten miles apart. A variation is sometimes made in "breaking" the smoke so as to make it rise in quickly succeeding columns : these smoke-breaks are made by lighting an ordinary fire in the open, but alternately covering and removing with leafy boughs in rapid succession. "Smoke-rings" at Birdsville and the surrounding district are said to be produced by igniting some bushes placed inside a hollow log fixed up on end, on the top of of which a piece of bark is placed, this being quickly slipped off in the same horizontal plane, and as speedily replaced when a "ring" is wanted : I have observed nothing like this, however, around Boulia. In response to inquiry, it would appear that no special information can be conveyed by these smoke-signals beyond the actual presence there of the person or persons making them. Though outside human control, yet forming a very distinctive sign at long distance of the presence of a camping-ground, are the numerous small brown hawks which will follow in the wake of the travellers for miles and miles : in the early days, these feathered scavengers have often proved the means of giving the aboriginals away (sect. 207). To show any deviation from the main-track, a finger post, in the shape of any small stick, tussock of grass, &c , is stuck in the direction to be pursued into a small mound of sand, earth, &c., two or three inches high, erected on the roadway. Sometimes the somewhat similar plan is adopted of placing at intervals of every 200 yards or so, a tussock of grass pulled up by the roots: not so much to act as a director but rather to ensure for those following that the route pursued is the correct one. Mr. Wienholt tells me that on Warenda and around the Hamilton River generally, what he believed to be a form of a track-signal, in the form of two boomerangs placed crosswise on the flat, used frequently to be met with when the blacks were in the neighbourhood. The most definitive forms of track-signal, however, are the actual footprints of the party preceding ; and in this connection it may be noted that in each camp many an individual's footprint is known and remembered, very much in the same way that a European can often recognise certain hoof-marks belonging to particular horses of his. At Boulia, when a black proposes leaving camp for a few days, and is unwilling to take with him all his belongings, little enough though they are, he will go to some neighbouring and not too much frequented spot, leave his impedimenta there, and on the surface around clear a circular space, upon an extra well-smoothed portion of which he will plant an imprint of his foot: this impress being well known to his mates, he can rest assured that the property will remain intact during his absence (sect. 206). No evidence has been forthcoming, at all events in the Boulia District, where it was carefully inquired for, that the track is ever indicated by any cuts, marks, &c., on the trees.

226. Names of Water-holes, Camping-grounds, &c.—At the chief encampment, the central camping-home of each tribe, there is a name for every landmark, or what can possibly be used as such, in the vicinity: each sandhill, mountain, water-hole, river bend, stony ridge, gully, bigger-sized tree, indeed anything and everything out of the ordinary has a special name applied to it. During my visit to Roxburgh Downs I was shown a fairly-sized water-hole, the portions of which are described at least under seven different names. The importance of water both in the neighbourhood of camp and along the different lines of travel will explain in some measure how it happens that, except in the case of a mountain or some markedly elevated ridge, all geographical location is indicated among these different peoples by words denoting creeks, rivers, water-holes, lakes, or springs. It thus comes to pass that the head stations, townships, &c., of the white settlers, which have been built on sites selected for exactly similar reasons, have all their aboriginal equivalents in the names of their adjacent water-holes, thus:—

Boulia	...	*Bool-yo.*	Fort William...	*Tou-er-el-la.*
Buckingham Downs	...	*Wol-ul-ta.*	Glenormiston	*Wor-ka-pa.*
			Grenada ...	*Ti-ba-ri-pul.*
Chatsworth	...	*Mo-a.*	Herbert Downs	*Wun-de-ra.*
Clonagh	...	*Bil-li-bung-gul.*	Leilavale ...	*Woong-ool.*
Cloncurry (also River)	...	*Pi-mur-ra.*	McKinlay (township)	*Yal-la-kud-ye.*
Dalgonally	...	*Ya-ko-in.*	Roxburgh ...	*Munq-a-la.*
Devoncourt	...	*Ka-ta-ga-un-ji-ing-o.*	Springvale ...	*Bo-nin-ji.*
Eddington	...	*On-da-roon-doo.*	Ulolo ...	*Ma-chi-rung-i-rul.*
Fort Constantine	...	*Lun-ta-or-gul.*	Warenda (creek)	*Wa-rin-ta.*

The following are the names of some rivers and water-holes :—

Corella or Williams R.		*Ka-ra-la.*	Paripituri W.H.	*Pa-ra-pi-jor-i.*
Fullarton R.	...	*Ma-ka-bur-i.*	Rockies W. H. (on the Upper Burke River)	*Wool-kun-ni.*
Hamilton R.	...	*En-ji.*		
Hamilton W.H.		*Boo-loo Boo-loo.*		
McKinlay R.	...	*Ya-ra-ri, Kul-ye-a.*	Williams R. ...	*Kul-poo-roo.*

The remainder are a few names of mountains :—

Table Top Mn. (Cloncurry)	*Ya-ra Ya-ra.*	Mount Datson (Warenda)	*Gop-pa Gop-pa.*
Black Mountain (Cloncurry)	*Oo-ro-lo.*	and two neighbouring hills	*Nin-ma-roo, Boo-doo-wa-ri.*

227. The Points of the Compass.—In addition to geographical nomenclature, directions can be further indicated by the cardinal and intermediate points, which are here given for the Boulia and Cloncurry Districts.

			PITTA-PITTA AND MESSMATES.			MITAKOODI.
North	...	...	*ti-nung-a-ra*	...	...	*yuk-koo-be-ri.*
South	...	...	*wor-ka-ra*	...	...	*mun-ta-ba.*
East	...	...	*te-ri-wa*	...	...	*koong-ga-ri.*
West	...	...	*kul-ka*	...	...	*roong-ka-ri.*
North-east	...	...	*u-ro-mo-ko*	...	...	*kud-yi-li.*
North-west	...	...	*mul-ka*	...	...	*kool-bil-la.*
South-east	...	...	*too-che-ra*	...	...	
South-west	...	...	*u-lor-a*	...	...	

228. Arrangements at the Camping-ground.—On the road a man will travel by himself, unlike a woman, or in company. If women are present, they bring up the rear with the children, well-stuffed dilly-bags and other possessions, the men at some distance ahead carrying their own fighting weapons. As the different parties reach their ultimate destination, they take up their quarters or build temporary huts around the visited, their hosts', camp upon that side of it in the direction whence they came. Thus, in the Pitta-Pitta camp at Boulia, if all arrangements were properly carried out, the Miorli visitors from Springvale and the Diamantina would settle down on the eastern side of the Boulia-ites, the Yunda and Yellunga folk on the north, the Marion Downs people on the south, &c. From the fact that a comparatively large number of people of both sexes may be congregated at the various camps and swapping-grounds, pleasure is often combined with business, new corrobborees are performed and taught to others, or perhaps old ones exchanged, a general holiday made of it, and the relaxation thoroughly enjoyed. When acquaintances meet, men and men, there may be a hand-shaking, but whether this is indigenous or a habit derived from the whites I am unable to say. Instead of for sorrow, tears may be made to flow, among the women-folk, for very gladness. Thus, a not uncommon form of greeting, say, after some years' interval, between mother and daughter, among the northern Kalkadoon of Quamby, &c., is for the elder woman to take any heavy stick, a fighting-pole, and, digging into the top of her head, rub it in there until the blood comes, crying and sobbing as much as she can: the daughter from behind is all this time putting her arms round the old woman's waist, and when she thinks that her mother has given way sufficiently to her feelings will forcibly take the stick away.

229. Trade Routes.—In the following notes relative to the trade-routes, markets, &c., of some of the more important tribes of North-West-Central Queensland, difficulty is here and there experienced in locating their chief home or head-encampment owing to there being perhaps no station homestead marked near enough on the maps to indicate accurately its geographical position: further-more, the alienation from the aboriginals of their hunting-grounds, the hostility of some of the station-managers, stockmen, &c., and other causes, have of late years concurred, and still concur, in making appreciable changes in the lines of travel. Information has been collected concerning the "markets" of the Boulia, Upper Georgina, Leichhardt-Selwyn, and Cloncurry Districts, and in this order it is proposed to deal with them.

230. (A) In the Boulia District, Pitta-Pitta blacks will travel *via* Herbert Downs to Glenormiston, and then either on to Carlo or to Roxburgh, returning the same way to Boulia or Marion Downs. This is the route adopted when pituri is required: the plant (sect. 147) grows in the neighbourhood of Carlo, whence some of it is already taken over to Roxburgh *via* the Toko Ranges. This same tribe, the Pitta-Pitta, together with the Boinji and Yellunga, may also go along the Burke and Wills Rivers to Buckingham Downs, Chatsworth, and Devoncourt to return with spears and koolamons: others, in company or not with Kalkadoon people, may continue their journey along the ranges to Rochdale and Carandotta, returning home down the Georgina *via* Herbert Downs and Parapijori, exchanging Government blankets, pituri, human-hair belts, "bilbi"-tails, &c., for shields, stone-knives, opossum twine, human-hair twine (sect. 162), and hand-spears. The Yunda people will visit Boulia, Marion Downs, Cooraboolka, Springvale, Diamantina Gates, and following the river up to Kynuna and Dagworth, may sometimes call in at McKinlay, and return home *viâ* Devoncourt and Chatsworth : these take or collect on the road pituri, spears, opossum-twine, and boomerangs for the Yellunga, Kalkadoon, and Goa, obtaining in exchange stone-knives, spears, &c. The Weelko, Kwokwa, and others, starting from Marion Downs, &c., travel up the Georgina as far as Headingly, returning *viâ* Gordon's Creek, Walaya, Toko water-hole, and Glenormiston : they barter all sorts of spears, ornate boomerangs (sect. 241), Government blankets, &c., for lunga-lunga (sect. 242) and hook-boomerangs (sect. 244), leaf-shaped wommeras (sect. 253), and long single-piece spears, painted shields (sect. 254), pearl-shell, eagle-hawk feathers, grind-stones (sect. 154), &c. The Miorli, from the neighbourhood of Springvale, may take a road up the Diamantina as far as Cork, and, until a few years ago, or perhaps still, cut across even to Acheron Creek, Tocal, and down the Thomson to Carella, returning by the same route : they exchange lunga-lunga and hook-boomerangs, shields, pituri, Government blankets, and other commodities obtained at Boulia, Marion Downs, or Cork, for bigger shields, yellow ochre, flat-tipped single-piece hand-spears, red handkerchiefs, shirts, and "white-shell" (sect. 182). The Ooloopooloo, Yunnateunnea, Tinka Tinki, Koonkoolenya, Dunga-Dungara, Rukkia, and others (all south of Boulia) may travel down the Georgina River as far as Cuttaburra and L. Machattie, when they make their way across through Karkori and Toorikungora to Birdsville, whence they return up the Diamantina to Monkira, and back home again *viâ* St. Albans and Cluny : just at the present time Davenport Downs is not visited, as they are not too friendly with the Miorli men who would be met there. They take koolamons, shields, spears, kangaroo teeth (sect. 166), Government blankets, pituri, grind-stones, red-ochre, &c., for which they obtain other blankets, human-hair belts, "bilbi"-tails, white plaster (kopi), &c.

231. (B) In the **Upper Georgina District**, the Yaroinga have trade relations on the north with the Workia, whom they meet at Lake Nash, Austral Downs, and Camooweal, and from whom they get pearl-shell, eagle-hawk feathers, stone-knives, large koolamons, human-hair belts, &c., in exchange for spears, hook and simple boomerangs, white-man's knives, blankets, shirts, trousers, as well as pituri, small (coolibar) koolamons, emu-feathers, &c. On the south, the Yaroinga are in communication with the Undekerebina natives of the Toko Ranges, who come up to them either direct to Gordon's Creek, or else indirectly, up the Georgina, *viâ* Glenormiston : the Toko people come with pituri, opossum-twine, blankets, &c., and take back ochre, boomerangs, stone-knives, human-hair belts, &c. Again, in another direction, on the east, along by Rochdale, &c, the Yaroinga barter with the Kalkadoon, Yellunga, &c.

232. (C) In the **Leichhardt-Selwyn District**, the Kalkadoon, said to be the most savage of the aboriginals under consideration, travel southwards but very short distances outside their own immediate country. They come down from their high-land home to Camooweal, Headingly, &c., to meet the Workia and Yaroinga ; to Fort Constantine to see the Mitakoodi ; and to Buckingham Downs, &c., to visit the Yunda, Yellunga, and other Boulia District tribes. At the Georgina River markets, the Kalkadoon exchange lunga-lunga boomerangs, stone-knives, human-, opossum-, kangaroo-, and wallaby-hair (in the rough), koolamons, short wommera-spears and long gidyea ones—for blankets, human-hair twine, other boomerangs and spears, nulla-nullas, fighting-poles, grindstones, red ochre, dilly-bags, grass necklaces, hook-boomerangs, and shields. To Buckingham Downs, Chatsworth, and, until a a short time ago, Noranside, the Kalkadoon bring similar articles to those taken to the Georgina ; but in this case they return chiefly with pituri, fishing-nets, &c.

233. (D) In the **Cloncurry District**, among the Mitakoodi, with head encamp-ment at Fort Constantine, some five markets may be noted, to each of which they take for barter the following articles (with their Mitakoodi names) :—Yellow ochre (*pa-ro, moo-loo moo-loo*), red-ochre (*ji-ring-er-i*), a bluish probably-copper stone (*wom-mu-ji-mun-ji*), large koolamons for carrying water, women's opossum-twine

waist-belts, fighting-poles, shields, hand-spears, "whitewood" boomerangs, &c. In exchange for these commodities they get: at Mullangera, from the Nouun tribes, the shell-wommera with its corresponding spear (*ta-poon*), and white-shell (*che-ka-ra*) chest-ornament which has been already obtained by barter from the Karunti through Croydon, &c., from Normanton, &c.; at Eddington and Dalgonally, from the Woonamurra, fishing-nets (*moo-na*), other kinds of wommeras and spears, and the forehead net (*mi-ri mi-ri*); at Canobie, from the Mikoolun, similar articles to what were obtainable at Mullangera; at various points on the Leichhardt-Selwyn Ranges or at Fort Constantine, from the Kalkadoon, flax-twine, human-hair belts, opossum-string waist-belts, ochre, &c.

234. **Transmission of Customs, Beliefs, and Language, &c.**—This system of inter-communication, necessitated by exchange and barter, is one to which far too little importance appears to have been attached by European writers. In the case, for instance, of implements, stress has hitherto been laid on the particular locality whence they have been collected, rather than upon the particular tribe or district which originally manufactured them. The presence in camp at Boulia of opossum-hair and eagle-hawk feather ornaments (both of which creatures are almost extinct in the neighbourhood), mother-of-pearl and other marine shells, as well as two curiously barbed spears (which I knew from previous evidence and descriptions could only have come from one of the Northern Territory coast tribes), led me on step by step to the inquiry as to how these articles, as well as others, reached their destination. The outcome of these investigations was that the various recognised trade routes were gradually learnt, and the commodities bartered at the different swapping-grounds enumerated. Mention has already been made (sect. 228, &c.) how that comparatively large numbers of people of both sexes may be congregated sometimes at these local markets. Thus it happens that ideas are interchanged, superstitions and traditions handed from district to district, and more or less modified and altered in transit, that new words and terms are picked up, and that corrobborees are learnt and exchanged, just like any other commodities. I have repeatedly obtained proofs of similar customs, beliefs, corrobborees (sect. 191), &c., holding good among tribes separated by miles of country which, except through the medium of others, had certainly not within the white-man's memory ever been in communication. Thus, tribes occupying territory at opposite extremes, and beyond them also, of a large district like North-West-Central Queensland are brought into contact through the inter-mediation of others: indeed, so far as philology alone is concerned, it is matter for wonder that there are comparatively so few, where we might have expected so many, words with common-root stems among tribes undoubtedly speaking absolutely different languages. Again, there is reason to believe that for future pioneers and settlers into the far western, and what is still believed to be arid, country, a knowledge of these aboriginal lines of travel or trade-routes might prove of great value, since only along them would there be a chance of finding water. Out beyond the Toko Ranges, over large areas still awaiting exploration at the hands of Europeans, the Undekerebina men, who were encamped at Glenormiston during my visit there, assured me of certain definite routes which they had themselves followed—they knew all about the Central telegraph line in the sister colony, which some of them had seen. Furthermore, it is quite within the realms of probability that a careful study of the aboriginal trade-routes throughout the various colonies (as in the analogous examples elsewhere of the migrations of animals and birds) would throw no unimportant light upon that much-vexed question as to the source of origin of the Australian aboriginal—whence he came to be where he is now found.

235. **Letter or Message Sticks.**—Circumstances often arise which may prevent an individual setting out for the "swapping-ground" or local market, and in such cases he may send a substitute or agent together with a so-called letter-stick to do business for him. This letter or message stick is called *ka-lor-i* by the Pitta-Pitta tribes, *kool-bo* by the Mitakoodi, and *koong-ga* by the Kalkadoon: in the last-mentioned language this word signifies a piece of wood of any description (*e.g.*, sect. 161). The stick is usually a piece of wood, gidyea, ti-tree, or any other convenient, coloured perhaps black, red, or yellow, from two to four or more inches in

length, cut to various shapes from flat to round, and incised with various marks or patterns: occasionally, if the sender is in a hurry, or too lazy to manufacture one, it may consist of some peculiarly-marked twig in the rough, a *plain* piece of wood cut to shape, a small bundle of rags tied round and round with hair-string, twine, or cotton, &c. It means nothing more than a sort of brand or mark belonging to an individual who, so long as he is able to recognise it again, or others for him, can vary it at will in shape, size, or design: in other words, two which happen to be totally unlike, may be accompaniments of the identical message. More than anything else, the stick acts as a sort of guarantee of good faith, to show there is "no gammon," and may at times act as a safeguard or passport over otherwise hostile country: there is nothing on it in the form of a communication which can actually be read, the substitute or messenger invariably carrying the message by word of mouth. The messenger is in all cases an adult man, never a woman, and a person, such as a brother, &c , whom it is known can be trusted. With regard to the particular shapes and designs of these message-sticks, there are traces of similarity even over large areas of country. In the Boulia District they are flattened, generally thinner at the edges than elsewhere, rounded or more or less pointed at the extremities, and incised only with straight lines. These straight lines are cut either parallel with, at an angle, or across each other, and represent quite arbitrarily anything which the manufacturer chooses, from a mountain or a river to a station homestead: sometimes, the comparatively large size of the head station or chief encampment has been attempted in an extra number of lines or cross lines. The back of the message-stick bears the same or similar design as the front, or else is covered with "flash" marks, to make it look "pretty fellow"; these marks have no other meaning whatsoever, alleged or implied. In the Leichhardt-Selwyn District, the Kalkadoon letter-stick bears usually a design of a phallic nature (Fig. 333); sometimes the beard is represented. In the Cloncurry and Flinders Districts nothing distinctive in the designs was recognised. The following illustrations will give some idea of these letter-sticks, and the messages, which were discoverable by me personally from the actual transmitter, it was intended should be simultaneously conveyed.

236. Notes to Illustrations.

Fig. 326. Made by a Pitta-Pitta (Boulia District). *Obv.*: "Come up for a corrobboree." *Rev.*: "Quick! hurry up."

Fig. 327. Made by a Boinji (Boulia District). To be forwarded to wherever any of his mates may be staying. *Obv.*: To tell him to come up to the meeting-place. *Rev.*: Covered with "flash" marks. The obverse was "read" from below up. **A** = sandhills, **B** = sandy creek, **C** = sandhills—these three together representing *Ka-ti-min-ji-li*, the particular spot where the Boinji have their head camp—**D** = country round about Marion Downs, **E** = plains and flat open country, **F** = *Te-di-boo*, the "five-mile" yard from Boulia, **G** = River Hamilton, **H** = "where we meet" —at a spot belonging to Warenda country.

Fig. 328. Made by a Boinji. Forwarded to Carlo when pituri was required. *Obv.*: **A** = all the mountains and creeks round about Marion Downs, **B** = Marion Downs station. *Rev.* is incised with flash-marks.

Fig. 329. Made by a Karanya (Boulia District). *Obv.* and *Rev.* identical. The message to be conveyed was: "All you fellows belonging to Bedouri, &c., come up to Boulia for blankets, or a corrobboree," &c. **A** = Bedouri, **B** = Breadalbane, **C** = Cooraboolka, **D** = Marion Downs, **E** = Boulia.

Fig. 330. Made by a Karanya. Similar message to preceding, but the people of different districts addressed: **A** and **C** = localities unmapped, **B** = Headingly, **D** = Carandotta, **E** = Roxburgh, **F** = Glenormiston, **G** = Herbert Downs, **H** = Boulia.

Fig. 331. Made by a Karanya. Forwarded when pituri was required. **A** = Pilliou Creek, **B** = Carlo, **C** = Glenormiston, **D** = Herbert Downs, **E** = Boulia.

Fig. 332. Made by a Miorli (of Springvale—southern border of Boulia District). He is sending a message to all these places, though far more are mentioned on the route than are indicated by the nicks: he "reads" it from below up. **A** = Monkira, Davenport, Diamantina Gates, Springvale, Brighton

Downs, Cork, Elderslie, Muckunda Creek, Pollygammon Creek, Niangiangi, Tooleybuck, Boulia, Herbert Downs, Glenormiston, Toko, Carlo, Mulligan River, Bedouri, Cluny, Karkori, &c., &c. **B** = two moons, **C** = one moon, **D** = two moons, **E** = river, **F** = drought, **G** = mosquitoes, flies, **H** = nardoo. The last four together constitute a representation of the meeting place. This stick has been coloured black.

Fig. 333. Made by a Kalkadoon (Leichhardt-Selwyn District). A hollow band as it were is cut round the centre. **A** = the beard (*yun-pul*), **B** = the vulva (*tin-ti*). The remaining marks are all ornamental, "flash:"

Fig. 334. Made by a (Grenada) Kalkadoon. Similar phallic marks as preceding.

Fig. 335. Made by a Kalkadoon. **A** = dead-fellows, **B** = boomerangs. Note the flash-marks (**C**) identical with those in Fig. 333. This stick is coloured red.

Fig. 336. Made by a Kalkadoon. *Obv.* and *Rev.* similar. Coloured with a black band.

Fig. 336A. Sent by a Kalkadoon boy from Gunpowder Creek to his gin (in the service of Mr. E. McDonnell) at Normanton, 1894. Note the unusual bifurcate shape. Message not known.

Fig. 337. Made by a Woonamurra (Flinders District). Coloured yellow.

Fig. 338. Made by a Mitakoodi (Cloncurry). The message intended to be conveyed is to the effect that the sender wants his spears, boomerangs, and shields forwarded, as an initiation ceremony is about to be held at the river (Cloncurry), and the addressee is to come and join.

237. How a Message-stick is put into Use.—The message-stick may be put into actual use as follows :—"Charlie," residing at Boulia, we will say, wants some pituri, but being employed at work from which he cannot be spared, or being sick, is prevented going for it himself: he therefore sends a brother of his, "Peter," to the nearest market, which in this case would be Carlo, to get some for him. Peter takes the stick which Charlie has just made, and journeying *via* Herbert Downs and Glenormiston arrives at his destination on the Mulligan River where, being asked his business, he says that he has come for pituri, and hands in the message-stick. In reply to questions he will mention who it is that has sent him—namely, Charlie of Boulia—and may be then informed by his inquisitor, " No, I can't let you have any. I have two or three letter-sticks here already, waiting for pituri, and I must serve them first. Go and ask that fellow over there." Approaching the person indicated, he is asked as before, what he wants and whom he comes from : having satisfied the vendor as to his *bona fides*, the latter takes charge of the stick and tells him he can supply him in a few days' time, Peter in the meantime making friends with some " brother" or " sister" in the local camp. A dilly-bag-full of pituri being at last forthcoming, it is handed over with the letter-stick (which the vendor has been taking careful mental note of, so as to recognise again), and Peter takes his departure back to Charlie at Boulia. Charlie, on receipt of the parcel, will now forward some boomerangs, spears, a Government blanket, &c., in payment : if he can get Peter to take a second trip all well and good, but if not, as is generally the case for such a journey, he gets another messenger with the goods and the identical message-stick as before. This second messenger arriving at Carlo, finds the vendor, and hands him over the goods together with the stick : recognising the latter the seller accepts the various articles in payment for the particular bag-full of pituri which he had parted with some few weeks previously, knowing now that he has been paid by the right party (probably personally unknown to him)—*i.e.*, the sender of the original stick. But supposing he never gets paid, or does not receive what he considers to be sufficient, he will bear the fact well in mind that Charlie of Boulia is a bad character not to be depended on, and take good care that neither he nor his friends have any dealings with him in the future. The seller, under circumstances such as have been just narrated, does not, as a rule, ask for the particular commodities he expects to exchange, each head-encampment having its own special and well-known line of goods. Instead of trade or barter, the letter-stick may be sent round with any ordinary message or private communication, as already mentioned in the notes to illustrations (sect. 236).

CHAPTER X.

THE MAINTENANCE OF LAW AND ORDER: FIGHTING, FIGHTING-WEAPONS.

238. The Maintenance of Law and Order: Methods of Fighting.—Among the Pitta-Pitta and other tribes of the Boulia District, the paucity of old men whose opinions and wishes would otherwise be respected and enforced, is very marked. Each individual, within certain limits, can do what he pleases. On the other hand, he has to reckon not only with the particular person injured, or his relatives, but also, in some cases, with the whole camp collectively. Thus the camp as a body, as a camp council, will take upon itself to mete out punishment in crimes of murder, incest, or the promiscuous use of fighting-implements within the precincts of the camping-ground: death, and probably the digging of his own grave, awaits the delinquent in the former case, while "crippling," generally with knives, constitutes the penalty for a violation of the latter. Private quarrels are arranged and settled somewhat on the following lines:—Supposing an individual considers himself aggrieved, an animated conversation ensues between the parties concerned, obscene language is freely used (sect. 333), the hand goes up to the mouth in the customary manner (sects. 103, 104), and all of a sudden, probably a boomerang is let fly, to be followed or replied by another or similar implement. Mutual friends, or their gins, will, in nine case out of ten, next intervene, and make an attempt at separating the pair: otherwise, they will each run for the nearest spear or anything handy, and throw it. Success may or may not attend the efforts of the peace-makers, but the truce, if one exists, is usually only temporary, for each combatant may have concealed in his waist-belt a stone-knife, which in close quarters can play terrible mischief. If the feud is going to develop into anything serious, both parties will probably betake themselves to a distance from camp. In fighting thus as the outcome of a private quarrel, there is actually, as a rule, no intention of killing, the risk, as will be shown further on, being too great. With two-handed swords, they would only aim at striking each other on the head: with spears, they would only make for the fleshy parts of the thighs: with stone-knives, they would only cut into the shoulders, flanks, and buttocks, producing gashes an inch or more deep, and up to seven or even eight inches long. In using the last-named implement, the one individual may grapple the other, standing or sitting, very much after the manner of a person wrestling (Fig. 339). Clasping his opponent with the one hand, he holds the knife in the other, and sticks it into one of the localities permitted; with a turn of the wrist he gives jag for jag, as a rule, not removing the blade from the wound. Accidents sometimes occur, and an incision is made unfairly—that is, outside one of the recognised spots: thus, during a fight with stone-knives at Glenormiston in 1894, "Toko Tommy," a visitor from the Undekerebina tribe, when remonstrated with for inflicting a very ugly cut into the back of his adversary's knee, excused himself by maintaining "Charlie, silly b——: he move him leg," insinuating by this remark that it was the fault of his opponent in shifting his position. The lying upon the back on the ground, a posture in which no lawful incisions with a stone-knife can be made, is the sign of defeat—that the combatant has had enough, and gives in. Even while a fight is going on, the gins belonging to the two individuals in combat, as well as others, may have a set-to among themselves not only with their tongues but with fighting-poles, &c., and what with the shouting and screaming of the women, the crying of the children, coupled with the cheering and yelling .of the other spectators, make veritably a temporary pandemonium of the scene.   At Glenormiston, the women coming up to join a fray give a sort of war-whoop : they will jump up in the air, and as their feet, a little apart, touch the ground, they knock up the dust and sand with the fighting-pole, &c., held between their legs, very like one's early reminiscences in the picture-books of a witch riding a broom-stick.   Before fighting commences, the combatants usually strip off even that little which they ordinarily wear.   As a rule they are very proud of these wounds received in fight, but they apparently only very rarely take steps to elevate them above the level of the surrounding surface, as in the case of the " flash" scars on the chest, &c. (sect. 186).

The fight between the two individuals being at length brought to a termination, steps are taken by the old men and elders to inquire into the rights or wrongs of the dispute.   If the victor turns out to be the aggrieved party he has to show good cause, as for instance that the man whom he has just taken upon himself to punish, had raped his gin, gave him the *munguni* (sect. 259, &c.), or wrought him some similarly flagrant wrong : under such circumstances, no further action is taken by anyone.   If, on the other hand, the victor happens to be the aggrieved party only in his own opinion, and not in that of those to whom he is answerable, and who do not believe the grounds on which he commenced the fight to be sufficient, he has to undergo exactly the same mutilations subsequently at the hands of the vanquished as he himself had inflicted : it devolves upon his "brother" to bring him back to undergo the punishment, though if a coward he may run away from camp, but he dare then never return.   Thus, in all these individual quarrels or fights, whatever injury may be perpetrated upon the vanquished, the latter, supposing he has justice on his side—and this is regulated by the general opinion of the elders in camp—has the opportunity always afforded him of retaliating by similar injury with similar weapon—" an eye for an eye, a tooth for a tooth."

It occasionally happens that party feeling runs very high, and perhaps the "brothers"—and there may be dozens of these (sect. 59) on either side—take up the quarrel, which may hence lead to the whole camp, men as well as women, joining indiscriminately in the general *mêlée*.   To prevent such occurrences, determined efforts are always made to nip a quarrel in the bud.

Sometimes, in the original duel, one of the combatants may be killed, and unless the survivor can show that he had sufficient provocation or cause, he will be put to death in similar manner, at the instance of the camp-council, and usually undergo the extra degradation of digging his own as well as his victim's grave. It may happen, however, that the person slain belongs to some neighbouring tribe, and consequently some time will elapse before the retribution falls, deservedly or otherwise, upon the slayer.   The deceased's friends, brothers, &c., when the news reaches them, will come up and demand the culprit, delivery of whom is usually given, considering that the request is generally backed by a formidable array of warriors.   The individual in question has now to stand single-handed the onslaught of his late victim's partisans—a sort of " running the gauntlet."   If spears are thrown he is allowed a shield wherewith to defend himself ; if fighting-sticks are employed he is given the use of one : sometimes by accident or design—*i.e.*, the judicious gift of various presents to the ringleaders in the latter case—he may stand the test successfully and escape with his life.   But the occasion now and again arises where not even with the actual death of the destroyer are the friends of the deceased individual satisfied : they may require delivery of another man to make up for their loss, as it were, and if refused will fight collectively, with the result that not unfrequently more or less are slain.   There are times when the homicide may get information privately concerning some expedition being on the road after him, but to his credit, be it said, he will very rarely try to escape : if courage should fail him, and he makes a bolt of it, he does so with the full knowledge of being ostracised for ever.   It was to guard against escape that in the old days, before the advent of the whites, the party seeking satisfaction would surround the camp at night-time (*see* inter-tribal warfare) and demand the man required at early morn: in those days also they might take summary vengeance on the whole camp, and destroy all the men, sparing only the women and children.

In the case of a man killing his own gin, he has to deliver up one of his own sisters for his late wife's friends to put to death, he personally escaping punishment; but supposing an individual takes the life of another's gin, his own will be forfeited. On the other hand, a wife has always her "brothers" to look after her interests. If two women fight, and one is killed, the survivor, unless, of course, proper cause be shown, would pay the death-penalty. Among the Kalkadoon, where a man may have three, four, or even five gins, the discarded ones will often, through jealousy, fight with her whom they consider more favoured: on such occasions they may often resort to stone-throwing or even use fire-sticks and stone-knives with which to mutilate the genitals. In the Boulia District, however, women fight among themselves on the same general principles as the men, using the smaller varieties of boomerang rarely, and fighting-poles generally: never with any other implements or weapons. The fighting-pole (sect. 255) is really a sort of thick heavy pole, often as much as 4 feet long on an average, and very cumbersome to wield, even when used in the orthodox manner by being held in the hands at one extremity and swung vertically over the head from behind forwards. The encounter progresses somewhat after this fashion (Fig. 340): One of the combatants with her hands between her knees, supposing that only one stick is available, ducks her head slightly—almost in the position of a schoolboy playing leap-frog—and waits for her adversary's blow, which she receives on the top of the head. The attitudes are now reversed, and the one just attacked is now the attacking party. Blow for blow is thus alternated until one of them gives in, which is generally the case after three or four hits. Great animal pluck is sometimes displayed, and though one of them may fall temporarily stunned, she will soon recover herself as ready as not to continue the fight; blood also may often be drawn. As a rule each woman has her own fighting-stick, but on occasion, as in the description above, only one may be handy, each taking her respective turn at it. Should a woman ever put up her hand or a stick, &c., to ward a blow, she would be regarded in the light of a coward. Men sometimes fight with this same weapon, and on similar lines, but usually adopt certain methods of defence (sect. 255). As in the case with the stronger sex, there is a subsequent adjustment of the rights and wrongs of the dispute, and, unless sufficient cause be proved, the victorious amazon will be similarly treated. A woman's quarrel may sometimes be taken up by her mother and brothers. Again, if a woman makes herself generally obnoxious in the camp, especially to the female portion of it, she is liable to be set upon and "hammered" by her fellow sisters collectively, the males on such occasions not interfering. Under no circumstances is fighting of any description whatsoever allowed in camp at night, and the whole crowd collectively will see that no infringement of this rule ever takes place: if people want to fight, they must go outside, and, when necessary, kindle fires to see by.

The fact will therefore be recognised that only in cases of major offences, murder, incest, physical violence, &c., is there an application of any code, and that in the form of the Mosaic one. The old men and elders act the part of "bosses," "kings," "judges," &c., in influencing aboriginal public opinion in these matters of enforcing domestic policy: a ripe old age constitutes the highest social status in the camp, and the one calling for the greatest respect. There is no single individual chief to direct affairs.

Only on one special occasion are the women allowed to chastise, and inflict punishment upon the men (sect. 310).

In the Boulia District, when engaged in inter-tribal warfare, a very rare occurrence now-a-days, the warriors are all painted as follows:—The face is entirely covered with "kopi," the same substance being also applied in the form of three wide circular bands on upper and lower limbs, and in the form of a boomerang from each shoulder to the middle of the waist-belt in front. They are all painted alike so as to be mutually recognisable: any of their allies, for the same reason, will be similarly ornamented. No particular attire is worn by those engaged in battle, except by the two leaders, who may have a thick opossum-string hanging from around the neck, hitched below to another passing round the waist : the head-dress of these two individuals also varies from the others (which are composed of white feather-down stuck on with mud), in that it consists of a large head-net or *koolpooroo* stuffed with grass, into which several shag's-tail-feathers are stuck. On such occasions of warfare a common procedure is to steal up to the enemy's camp in the dead of night and encircle it at the first ray of dawn by breaking up into two parties, each with a leader, one going round on the left, the other on the right, and meeting on the opposite side : as soon as the leaders, by means of their head-dress, recognise one another, they raise a shout which their followers take' up, spears are thrown into the area encircled, and the carnage commences.

239. Classification of Fighting Boomerangs.—There are at least four distinct kinds of fighting boomerang discoverable in North-West-Central Queensland ; the "toy" or "come-back" weapon has been already described in sect. 213. Features in common with all, are a general tendency to flattening of both surfaces, the upper being more or less convex though usually very distinctly so as compared with the under ; and a single more or less prominent bend or "knee" on the external convex edge—the bend (Fig. 351A) far from necessarily at the centre, dividing the weapon into a distal (free) and a proximal (handle) portion, the latter (Fig. 351C) being usually narrower than the former (Fig. 351B). According to their plan of construction, all boomerangs can be grouped into one or other of two classes, the simple or non-hooked, and the hooked, the former being again divisible, with reference to the graving, into the ornate, the fluted, and the plain. Among the tribes occupying the various ethnographical districts, fighting boomerangs are known by different names, as follows :—

	A. BOOMERANG (IN GENERAL).	B. BOOMERANG (IN PARTICULAR).			
		a. SIMPLE (NO HOOK).			*b.* HOOK.
		(i.) Ornate.	(ii.) Fluted.	(iii.) Plain.	
Pitta-Pitta, &c.		*ming-ka-ra ma-ro*([1])	*lung-a lung-a*		*chuk-ul-bur-ra*
Mitakoodi ...		*ro-ko-ro boo-na* ([1])		*pa-je-ra* ([2])	
Kalkadoon ...	See Names given in sect. 55.		{ *poo-ta poo-ta* ([2]) / *ta-roo-roo* ([2]) }	*ma-ra-bil-la*	*wol-loom-ba*
Walookera ...			*me-wul-la*		{ *wor-ra-dil-la* / *oo-ra-dil-la* }
Yaroinga ...			*ul-lo-da*		
Wonkajera ...					*wor-pil-la*

([1]) *See* sect. 8. ([2]) The name of the timber employed—*pa-je-ra* = gidyea, *poo-ta poo-ta* = white-gum.

240. Material, Manufacture, and Flight of Boomerangs.—The most common material, perhaps, of which these fighting boomerangs are made is gidyea (*Acacia homalophylla*, A. Cunn.), though other woods, such as mulga (*Acacia aneura*, F. v. M.), white-gum, &c., are often used, the name of the timber occasionally giving the name to the implement, as shown in preceding section. The weapon is originally cut out from the side of a tree-trunk *en bloc*, then gradually got into shape with a chisel, &c., and finally smoothed off with a piece of sharp-edged flint or glass. With wood of suitable grain, white-gum, for example, the original block may be split down and two boomerangs made of it. Any defect in shape, in the nature of a bend or twist, can be remedied by the various artificial means which have already been discussed (sect. 151). The mode of manufacture of the hooked variety varies somewhat from the preceding, the portion of trunk for its shaft being cut out at the same time with an adjacent branch or rootlet for its hook : a specimen in the Brisbane Museum, I believe, of the implement in the progress of manufacture illustrates this point pretty clearly. It is interesting to note that both in camp or on the walk-about, though an aboriginal may carry one spear, one shield, &c., he almost invariably has two boomerangs. If they have both been made by the same person they are very probably similarly marked: if he barters them, he will generally "swap" them only as a pair, though beyond the fact of two being required as an accompaniment for beating time at the sing-songs and the corrobborees, it is difficult to understand why this should so often be the case. All these fighting boomerangs are intended for throwing at compara-tively close quarters, and cannot by any deftness of hand be made to produce the complete gyrations possible with the "come-back" or toy varieties (sec. 213). When a boomerang is about to be thrown it is held at the extremity in such a way that the flattened under-surface rests on the palm while the thumb and finger-tops lie on the convex upper-surface ; the majority of these weapons, except the hooked varieties, can therefore be used with either hand, and the convex edge of the weapon at the commencement of flight, immediately it is let go, is therefore always on the outer side of the thrower' as compared with the median vertical plane of his body. Among the number of aboriginals examined for left-handedness, the proportion of such was found to be very marked, though in no case was any truly ambidextrous individual discovered—that is, no one who could throw the boomerang equally well with either hand.

The interpretation of the "hook" on the hooked variety was offered me by some Pitta-Pitta blacks as follows:—It appears that when warding off a blow from a boomerang of any description the defence consists in holding forwards and vertically any stick, nulla-nulla, shield, &c., that comes to hand, and moving it more or less outwards, right or left as the case may be, thus causing the missile on contact to glance to the one or other side. The hook is intended to counteract this movement of defence by "catching on" the defending stick around which it swings and, with the increased impetus so produced, making sure of striking the one attacked. The diagram, in the form of a bird's-eye view (Fig. 341), will perhaps explain the mechanism just described more clearly.

241. The Ornate Boomerang.—The ornate boomerang, which is always coloured black by means of charcoal grease, bears certain typical gravings on its upper convex surface only. In the old days, i.e., before the advent of the whites, this graving was effected by means of an opossum-tooth or sharp flint fitted into a suitable handle. At the present time, though this primitive method is still occasion-ally followed, it is being rapidly supplanted by iron in its various forms, obtained by filing or grinding down discarded shear-blades, springs, barrel-bands, knife-blades, &c., to the suitable shape required. This form of boomerang is manufactured throughout North-West-Central Queensland, except in the Upper Georgina District. Thus, along the watershed of the Cloncurry and Flinders, by the Mitakoodi, Woonamurra, and others ; in the Leichhardt-Selwyn District, by the Muntaba Kalkadoon ; in the Boulia District, &c., at Noranside, Boulia, Marion Downs, Warenda, Springvale, Davenport, Diamantina Gates, Brighton Downs, Cork, Elderslie, Kynuna, and Dagworth (i.e., on the Lower Burke, Hamilton, Middle Georgina, and Upper Diamantina Rivers), by the Pitta-Pitta and cognate tribes, the Miorli and the Goa. With a view to exchange and barter, the ornate boomerang from these localities is taken either a long way up or a short way down the Georgina River : in the former case it may branch off at Glenormiston both for the Toko Ranges and for the Carlo country, while in the latter it comes to its journey's end, so far as this district is concerned, by crossing westwards to the Upper Mulligan country in general. Varying somewhat in length, it measures from about 30 to 35 inches from tip to tip, and, if these be joined by a straight line, the greatest vertical distance between it and the extreme convex edge is from 4½ inches to 6½ inches. The width at the bend or knee, which is at the centre of the boomerang in the Boulia District weapons only, is always greater than at the extremities: in the Leichhardt-Selwyn and Cloncurry Districts, the proximal portions of the implement are markedly narrower than the distal (sect. 239). The ends or extremities may be rounded, oval, angular, &c., but no significance or importance is attached to this "finishing off" (Fig. 342), which is only executed for the sake of making the implement look more "flash." The edges are comparatively sharp. The preliminary smoothing-down on the upper surface is so well effected that the original chisel-marks cannot be recognised : on the under-surface these are now and again visible and perhaps sometimes are purposely left in this condition, as in the case of that manufactured by the Mitakoodi, so regularly and precisely are these flutings effected.

The ornamentation of this boomerang (which, as we have seen, is confined to its upper convex surface) will now be described, according as the gravings composing it extend the length or the breadth of the weapon, or fill up the intermediate spaces so produced.

The longitudinal figures, invariably present, and reaching from tip to tip, consist of straight lines, single or composite (Figs. 343, 344, A), and elongate ovals strung end on end : the former would appear to be absent in weapons manu-factured in or to the north of the Leichardt-Selwyn Ranges, by the Kalkadoon and Mitakoodi, for instance. The ovals, from their resemblance to things which they most nearly approach, may be spoken of as shuttles and festoons. The festoons, only found on implements made in and to the south of the Boulia District, are limited to the extreme edges of the weapon (Figs. 344, 345, B) : their interstices are filled up with parallel concentric lines, concavity outwards, so as to represent ripples on the water's edge, and hence in the Pitta-Pitta language are spoken of as the *nar-pi ming-ka-ra*, or river-bank marks. The shuttles (Figs. 344, 345, 346, C) are similarly filled in with more or less longitudinal lines, and are named as follows :—In the Boulia District, according to some native authorities, they are called *mol-lo-ro* or mountain-tops, but the general consensus of opinion is that they represent the large fishing nets folded up for purposes of transit, and hence are described as *ma-li ming-ka-ra* or fishing-net marks. In the Cloncurry District the shuttles, when their enclosed lines are strictly longitudinal as just described, are known as *gin-ja-la* or leaves; when inclined to a distinct slant (Fig. 347D) they are called *che-ka-ra* or white-shell (sect. 182) marks. In the Leichhardt-Selwyn District, I could obtain no local terms for them. As in the case with the longitudinal lines, there may be one, two, or even three strings of these shuttles running the length of the weapon.

The transverse figures (those stretching across the breadth of the boomerang) not met with outside the Boulia District, are limited to the markings at the extremities, and at the centre, though in either case they are not invariably present. The former, which are far more common, are constituted of from one to three or four more or less parallel lines (Figs. 343, 344, E), and known in the Boulia District as *tin-ja* (sect. 131) *ming-ka-ra* or handle-marks : they are met with again on the nulla-nullas (sect. 256) and fighting-poles (sect. 255), and are primarily intended to act as a support to prevent the hand from slipping. The central gravings which, commencing somewhat south of Boulia, at Springvale, &c., are most usually found on the Diamantina weapons, consist either of two lines placed parallel or crosswise : in the latter case (Fig. 349A-B) forming two triangles with apices in contact, the two areas enclosed being often subdivided into secondary spaces, each of which, independently of its neighbour, is filled with closely parallel lines. There is a similar subdivision into secondary spaces, &c., of the area enclosed by the two parallel lines (Fig. 348). It should be borne in mind that these central transverse gravings do not by any means entail bilateral symmetry on the complete design.

In the Boulia District, among the simpler interstitial figures—*i.e.*, those occupying the intervening gaps left by the preceding longitudinal and transverse ones—may be described the kangaroo (Figs. 343, 346, 347, F) and emu (Fig. 350G) toe-tracks, with their two and three digits respectively, called in consequence the *ma-choom-ba* and *kool-pa-ri* marks in the Pitta-Pitta language. Other marks are the following :—The *koodija-koodija* represents the female flash-mark of red or yellow ochre (sects. 185, 193) smeared over the thighs, legs, trunk, and arms, by means of the three middle fingers dipped into the paint: this "brand" which, by-the-by, is never spoken of as a snake, as might have been expected, is in exceptional cases cut across the entire width of the blade (Fig. 345H). The *koo-ding-be-ri* or single zigzag line is formed of circumflex accents, each made with two separate cuts, the style of the teeth in a saw: its native name would appear to have no other interpretation attached to it. The *ka-ta-pa ka-ta-pa* (Fig. 350L) and *me* (Fig. placed end on end with more or less regular precision (Fig. 350K), somewhat after 350M) marks are made with six and four separate incisions respectively; the former signifies a hornet or bee, the latter an eye. The *wer-koo* or cross-cut (Fig. 346N) is identical with that made on the thighs of near male-relatives in times of mourning (sect. 289): the same mark is also locally described sometimes as indicative of Marion Downs, situated, as it is, at the "crossing" of the two rivers, the Hamilton and the Georgina. It must not be forgotten that of all the preceding types of interstitial incisions it is exceptional to find more than two or three varieties upon a boomerang at one and the same time. In the Leichhardt-Selwyn and Cloncurry Districts the interstitial marks are limited to the kangaroo-toe type and the feather-pattern line. The former, up here, appears to have no further meaning than "two-fellow anything": the latter is composed of circumflex accents placed vertically and parallel (Fig. 350o), and is known as the *koon-ya koon-ya* (sect. 153), a grass-woven dilly-bag.

242. **The Fluted Boomerang** (Fig. 352) is not made at Boulia. Its home is beyond Noranside, at Buckingham Downs, Mount Merlin, Chatsworth, &c., and along the Upper Georgina, certainly as far as Lake Nash, and out westwards from this river along the Toko Ranges, and so into Central Australia: indeed this particular weapon may be said to be peculiar to the Leichhardt-Selwyn and Upper Georgina Districts. For purposes of exchange and barter, it travels both up and down the Georgina: in the former case branching on the way eastwards across to the Mitakoodi of the Cloncurry District, in the latter making its way to the Mulligan and the Burke, whence *viâ* Springvale it may journey both up and down the Diamantina. This weapon is invariably coloured red with ochre grease, and made either of gidyea or "white-wood." As a rule it is shorter by 2 or 3 inches than the ornate variety of the Boulia District, and, unlike it, the bend or knee, its widest part, is never exactly at the centre, while the extremities, or tips, without exception, are always rounded. The upper convex side invariably, and the lower flattened one very often, is completely covered with a distinct longitudinal fluting, each flute being about an eighth of an inch wide, though the width would seem to increase proportionally with the further north the locality of manufacture: in all cases, the fluting is always wider and coarser on the under than on the upper surface. At Bedouri, Birdsville, and on the Lower Georgina is manufactured a fluted and red-coloured boomerang which is long, thin, inclined to be pointed at the extremities, and is more or less rounded in section, though the tendency to flattening on the under surface is fairly marked: this weapon, the *pa-run-da*, is very rarely, and then only accidentaly, met with at Boulia, its route being in an opposite direction, southwards down the Diamantina.

243. **The Plain Boomerang**, with its surfaces perfectly smoothed, and coloured black with charcoal, comes from the Cloncurry District, where it is named after the gidyea wood of which it is made, the *pa-je-ra* (sect. 239.) Whether the Kalkadoon obtain this implement in barter from their Mitakoodi neighbours, or make it themselves, is doubtful, though the fact of their having a name of their own for it, the *ma-ra-bil-la* (sect. 239), renders the latter supposition a little likely. In reply to inquiry in the Boulia District, a "plain" boomerang is always looked upon in the light of one incompleted. The Cloncurry District plain boomerang averages between 29 and 30 inches from tip to tip, with the proximal end markedly narrower than the distal: it has no signs of a fluting, but in most cases the extremities are "angled" off for flash purposes.

244. **The Hook Boomerang** (Fig. 353) has the same destination as the fluted variety, which it resembles both in fluting and in colour: it is made chiefly in the Upper Georgina Districts by the Workia and Yaroinga especially. It differs from the fluted boomerang in the possession of a hook, the "ear" of the Boulia and Toko Ranges tribes, from 4 to 5 inches long projecting backwards, in the same plane, from the extremity of the shaft on the convex edge: this hook, about an inch or more wide at its base, tapers gradually to a blunt point, and bears a longitudinal fluting continuous with that on the main shaft. Furthermore, the shape

L

of the shaft contrasts markedly with that of all other boomerangs in its width, independently of the bend or knee (*not* its widest part), increasing progressively from the proximal to the hooked extremity. Its use has already been drawn attention to in sect. 240, while the various names applied to it are given in sect. 239. Besides being used as a fighting weapon, the Workia employ the hook-boomerang for throwing into flying mobs of flock-pigeons (sect. 137).

245. The Two-handed Sword is manufactured at Boulia, Warenda, Herbert Downs, Marion Downs, and south of this on portions of the Diamantina—*i.e.*, in the Boulia District only, so far as North-West-Central Queensland is concerned. It travels northwards, up the Georgina, where it is bartered for fluted and hook boomerangs, peg-tipped spears, and other things. Made from gidyea, and subsequently blacked with charcoal, it varies from $3\frac{1}{2}$ to over 4 feet in length. It is curved, though not so markedly, after the manner of a boomerang, which it further resembles in being wider at the middle than at the extremities; both surfaces are convex, one being very much more so than the other, and its tips are always evenly rounded. Only one side, the more convex, is ornamented with gravings which, according to the orthodox fashion, are of the following pattern :— This, in the main, consists of groups of parallel bars running lengthways with the implement, the number of separate groups varying from five or six to as many as a dozen (Figs. 354, 355, 356, 357, 358, A), and the number of contained bars from three to five or six: furthermore, each bar is itself composed of from three to sometimes half-a-dozen closely applied parallel longitudinal lines. Transversely cut gravings may sometimes be seen either at the centre of the weapon (Figs. 356, 357, 358, B) or else dividing off the separate groups of bars into compartments (Fig. 355c): generally speaking, these are either of an angular or curved type. At one or both extremities, handle-marks may be met with in the form of cross-cuts (Fig. 354D), dashes (Fig. 355E), or transverse lines (Fig. 356F). Any really curvilinear longitudinal incisions are extremely rare, if they ever occur : only on one occasion, at Roxburgh, on a disused and broken implement, did I see any traces of the festoons, shuttles, &c., met with on the Boulia District ornate boomerangs. Otherwise, than for these gravings, the two-handed sword or *un-ti-ti-ri* has a smooth surface throughout, unless we except the purposely or accidentally left slight longitudinal fluting on the less convex surface. From the fact that this weapon when in use is held at either extremity with both hands, the concave edge being the cutting one, the two surfaces cannot be spoken of as upper or under.

246. Spears.—In the Boulia District, when any extra good spear is made, or when one has been proved to aim true, &c., it is often ornamented more or less in its whole length with a very fine longitudinal fluting : such an one is not easy for white strangers to get hold of. Both here and elsewhere—*e.g.*, north of the Selwyn Ranges—spears may be painted with alternate red and white bars for flash purposes. No spears whatever are manufactured round Bedouri and down towards Birdsville : whatever are found there are brought in exchange and barter. The names for spears of any kind in general, throughout the different ethnographical districts, are given in the table in sect. 55. The different varieties of spears in particular (with their local terms) met with throughout North-West-Central Queensland will now be detailed.

247. The Acicular-tip Hand-spear.—The *ma-ri-mo* of the Boulia District (Fig. 359) is a hand-spear from 8 to 10 feet long, made in one piece, circular in section from butt to tip, which is tapering and sharply pointed : the butt also gradually tapers off. The material from which this spear is cut is either gidyea, "dead-finish" scrub (*Acacia farnesiana*, Willd., *Albizzia basaltica*, Benth.), a species of rosewood, &c. It is manufactured in the Boulia, Leichhardt-Selwyn, Cloncurry, and Flinders Districts, including the country around the Upper Diamantina from its very source. Occasionally, previous to fighting, some cementing substance, spinifex- or beefwood-gum, is stuck on in the form of a ring about $\frac{1}{4}$ inch thick at a distance of, perhaps, a couple of feet from the tip: into this band some iron nails, pieces of flint or glass, &c., may be found stuck This spear is bartered on the one hand northwards along the Upper Georgina, and on the other southwards along the Lower Diamantina. The Mitakoodi call it *me-ri-mo* or *ne-ri-mo*, the Goa *tun-doo-roo-la*. The position of the hand when in the act of throwing this and similar hand-spears is shown in Fig. 144, the weapon being balanced on the palm and along the length of thumb.

248. The Spatulate-tip Hand-spear.—The *tum-ba-ra* spear (Fig. 360) of the Boulia District, which, like the preceding, is a hand one, differs from it in having a spatulate, instead of a gradually tapering, tip: this blade, which locally undergoes modification both in shape and size, so far as comparative width (up to 2 inches) to length (up to 30 inches) is concerned, may sometimes be seen decorated with a bilinearly parallel and sinuous red pattern on a white background (Fig. 361A). The butt also tapers off somewhat. The weapon reaches to a length of about a foot shorter than the *marimo*, is similarly made in one piece of the same materials, and goes on transit along identical tracts of country. Among the Mitakoodi this spear is called *e-ra-ka-la* or *ji-ni-bur-i*: a curious fact in connection with the former name is that the same word in the Pitta-Pitta language signifies "flat," and in all probability refers to its spatulate tip. In this same tribe, the base of the blade may have a mitre-form pattern graved upon it (Fig. 361B). Here and there I have come across extra long examples of this spear, especially designed for killing cattle.

249. The Spatulate-tip Wommera Spear.—The *per-cha ma-ro*, literally signifying "peg-possessor" in the Pitta-Pitta language, is among the heaviest of the wommera-thrown spears. It is well over 8 feet long, and made of three pieces, which may be spoken of respectively as the butt, the shaft, and the tip. The shaft is the only portion of the weapon which is ever ornamented, if at all, with a longitudinal fluting, and is made of some particular wood, *e.g.*, mulga, which will give strength, weight, and stability: it is very firmly attached by splicing and the ordinary spinifex cementing substance, &c., with the butt, and only very loosely with the tip. The butt is made of any light kind of timber, *e.g.*, "cork" wood (*Erythrina*, Linn.), or a piece of pine when obtainable, and is intended to impart the proper direction required when throwing: at its free extremity is the small concavity for the wommera to fit into. The spatulate tip, between 16 and 17 inches long (Figs. 362, 363), on to one surface of which the rounded, almost half-moon-shaped wooden hook is firmly bound, is fixed loosely into the shaft for a twofold reason: to increase the difficulties of extraction when once the leverage is removed, and to prevent the butt or shaft being broken in view of its being required on a future occasion. The above explanations of the mechanism were given me by some Pitta-Pitta blacks. These spears are made in the Upper Georgina district from Glenormiston onwards; westwards, the Undekerebina use them; and eastwards, they may sometimes be met with among the Kalkadoon, who probably also make them.

250. Wommera Reed-spears.—The *li-bi-ja-ra* of the Cloncurry District is a reed-spear, very heavy and long, sometimes over 12 feet, and thrown with a wommera. It is composed of a butt and shaft. The butt, made of reed, takes up about half or slightly less than the length of the entire weapon: into its hollow (Fig. 364A) is fixed the thin gidyea shaft, the union of the two being strengthened with beef-wood gum and a few turns of tendon. The tip ends in a gradually tapering point, like the *marimo*. When in the act of being thrown with the wommera in one hand, the spear itself is supported on the other, which is extended forward.

The *ma-ba-na* is even thicker, longer, and heavier than the preceding, but otherwise of similar construction, and wommera-thrown. It used to be manufactured out Mullangera way, but is very rarely to be met with now anywhere; it was originally designed for the spearing of cattle.

The *ki-tu-ma* and *ja-loon*, also of the Cloncurry District, are both of them smaller, and comparatively lighter, varieties of the *libijara*; on an average they are about 7½ feet long, and thrown with wommeras. In the *ja-loon*, the reed-butt is almost twice as long as the gidyea, "dead-finish" scrub, or "needle-bush" shaft; with the *kituma*, the reverse is the case, the shaft being always very much longer than the butt.

The particular water-reed (*kin-di* in the Mitakoodi language) out of which the butts of these particular Cloncurry District spears are manufactured is not too commonly to be found; but as a rule is brought over from Woolgar and surrounding neighbourhood, where it is bartered for. A similar reed grows, perhaps, along the upper reaches of the Burke and Wills; at all events, the small *kun-dor-a* (so-called by the Pitta-Pitta aboriginals) reed-spear, which comes down from these rivers to Boulia occasionally (but which, unfortunately, I have not personally handled) appears to be identical with the *lituma* or *jaloon* of the Cloncurry tribes. Again, one or two hooks may be attached to any or all of these and the preceding reed-spears. This hook (*pril-ja* in the Mitakoodi language, *cf. per-cha* in the Pitta-Pitta) is cut out from "wild currant" bush, &c., about 4 inches long, in the shape of a slightly curved sort of thin pencil gradually tapering to a point at each extremity; it is fixed on to the very tip of the spear (Fig. 364B) with beef-wood gum bound round with tendon obtained from kangaroo-tail, emu-leg, or snake-neck. The second hook, when present, is fixed similarly a few inches below the first.

251. The Quartz-tip Wommera Reed-spear.—The *yun-ba-ra* wommera-spear is met with among the Northern Mitakoodi, whence it may be bartered to the Kalkadoon around Grenada and surrounding country; though it is sometimes made by the former, it is most commonly manufactured by the blacks around Sevannah. It reminds one very much of the *libijara*, being 11 feet long and upwards, with the reed-butt and gidyea shaft of about equal lengths, but differs in the get-up of the gradually tapering tip (Fig. 365), upon which are fixed with beef-wood gum some ten or twelve small chips of white quartz placed oppositely to another set, very much after the style of the teeth in a lady's small hair-comb. The Mitakoodi call this white quartz-stone *yung-un-da-ra*, whence another name for this spear is sometimes derived.

252. Non-indigenous Spears.—In addition to all the spears just described as being indigenous to North-Western-Central Queensland, there are others occasionally met with, especially on its northern and north-western confines, which come in through exchange and barter. Thus at Coolullah, on the Upper Leichhardt River (sect. 127), I met with certain hand-spears for catching fish, &c., bearing at their extremities barbed prongs of sharpened wood or filed iron-wire (Fig. 366): these belonged to some Karunti boys who had come down from the other side of Normanton. So again at Camooweal are found various forms of stone and barb-tipped spears of foreign origin which have reached their destination from more northerly and more westerly districts.

253. Wommeras.—The various names applied to the wommera in the different ethnographical districts are tabulated in sect. 55.

The wommera manufactured in the Boulia, Leichhardt-Selwyn, and Cloncurry Districts is of the nature of a thin, straight lath of gidyea, about 2½ feet long, ⅜-inch thick, and 1½ inches wide, the width (in the Boulia District) being pretty constant in its entire length. So far as the width of the shaft is concerned, it should be noted that as one travels northwards from Boulia into Kalkadoon and Mitakoodi country, this becomes markedly increased, up to 2 inches and more, at the centre as compared with the extremities (Figs. 367, 368). The thinner the lath, the better is the weapon considered. The surfaces are slightly and equally convex, but no graving or fluting has been noticed; sometimes a kind of decoration is produced by tying a string spirally round and colouring the parts, left exposed, over a fire. The free extremity is rounded off, while the opposite one is cut off at more or less of a right angle, and in the Boulia District two holes pierced or burnt in it (Fig. 369): when pierced, these holes are drilled with a sharpened emu or kangaroo bone, and by this means, and with tendon, &c., the peg tied on, its fixture being rendered still more complete by a subsequent covering of the usual cementing substance of spinifex or beef-wood gum. Outside the Boulia District, the peg is fixed on without any holes whatsoever, some tendon or twine with cement being used instead. It is this peg or hook (the *per-cha* again of the Pitta Pitta) which fits into the concavity at the butt-end of the spear. It may be noted that this wommera, the whirler (sect. 215), and the *chekara*-shell chest-ornament (sect. 182) are the only examples of aboriginal workmanship in these parts of the country, in which "drilling" is employed.   The weapon is handled by fixing it between the fore-finger and middle digit, clasping its free end on to the palm with the middle, ring, and little fingers, and at the same time guiding, or rather steadying, the spear between the fore-finger and thumb (Fig. 370).

Among the Northern Mitakoodi of Clonagh, &c., and Northern Kalkadoon of Grenada, &c., the following variety of wommera made of gidyea, iron-wood (*Acacia excelsa*, Benth.), &c. is very commonly met with, though not actually manufactured by them.   It differs from the preceding pattern in having a sort of haft to prevent the hand slipping off (Fig. 371): this haft, projecting at an angle from the same edge as the peg, is composed of a flattened ovate piece of beef-wood gum, about 3 inches or more in its greater diameter; a white piece of shell, the *che-ka-ra* (sect. 182) of the Mitakoodi language, with convex side outwards, is fixed on to both sides of it.   Occasionally, a smaller chip of similar shell is fixed into the cement at the peg-end of the weapon.   The width of the shaft is greater at the centre than at the extremities.   This form of wommera reaches its destination here through the Nouun tribe at Mullangera, who obtain the shell from the Karunti, &c., people at Normanton.   The *ta-poon* is the name (given me at Clonagh) of the spear belonging originally to this particular form of wommera, and which is bartered with it at the same time.

In the Upper Georgina District, certainly on the Upper Mulligan and Upper Georgina Rivers, and along the Toko Ranges, another kind of wommera (Fig. 372) is manufactured, totally different to the preceding lath-types: its particular name at Roxburgh among the Walookera tribe is *yum-ma-ra* (sect. 55).   The whole implement is very much shorter, just a little over 2 feet being a very fair average.   The shaft is flattened out in the shape of a leaf, slightly concave, both lengthways and crossways like a spoon, about 6 inches at its greatest width, and about $\frac{1}{4}$-inch in thickness: its concavity may be used as a "pituri-plate"—*i.e.*, to mix the pituri on—and traces of the greenish-yellow stains from this plant are very generally perceptible.   The shaft may be decorated further with a charcoal pattern of two parallel and sinuous lines, or with gravings in the shape of concentric circles; often a few transverse incisions are seen on the handle-end.   The handle is covered with the usual cementing substance, into the extremity of which (Fig. 372A) is stuck a little piece of flint, which constitutes a "sharpener" when the spear-tip becomes blunted.   At the opposite end of the weapon is a small half-moon-shaped peg (Fig. 372B), fixed on with tendon, &c., and cementing substance.   When in use for spear-throwing, it is clutched between the fore and middle fingers, &c., as in the manner already described, but the plane of the shaft is held vertically, so as to afford least resistance to the air in the movement forwards.   Sometimes, in close quarters, this wommera may be held by the handle and employed like a short single-handed sword: the nearest district where I have come across a true single-handed short sword is in the neighbourhood of Normanton, where the Wollangama call it *roonq-ka-ren*.   There are thus four different uses to which this "leaf" variety of implement can be applied: a wommera, pituri-plate, sharpener, and sword.   The Boulia District aboriginals cannot use this form of weapon for throwing spears.

254. Shields (for their various names, see sect. 55) are manufactured at Roxburgh and along the Upper Georgina, and in the Leichhardt-Selwyn and Cloncurry Districts: Noranside, in the Boulia District, is said to be the only locality therein where they can be made—*i.e.*, where suitable timber is met with.   For purposes of trade and barter, those from the Upper Georgina come down the river direct for the Lower Diamantina, a few branching off on the way from Roxburgh, &c., across country to the Toko Ranges, &c., or indirectly for the Middle Diamantina, *viâ* Boulia, Springvale, and Diamantina Gates.   Shields made in the Leichhardt-Selwyn and Cloncurry Districts may travel to the Upper Diamantina.

The timber employed in the manufacture of a shield is the "coral" or "cork"-tree (*Erythrina*, Linn.), or other soft and light wood, the name of the particular material sometimes being identical with that of the weapon, *e.g.*, Pitta-Pitta *koon-pa-ra* = cork-tree, shield, koolamon.

If the tree be a small one the required length of trunk may be cut off, and one shield made: if larger, it may be split longitudinally, and two of them made: whereas, if the trunk be of unusual size, four and even five may be cut out simultaneously by splitting. These shields are all cut somewhat after the same pattern, varying from about 22 to 26 inches in length, 7½ to 9 inches in width, and having the handle cut into the back (Figs. 373, 377, 378): the anterior surfaces are markedly convex both longitudinally and transversely (Figs. 374, 375), the degree of convexity varying inversely with the width, while the posterior are flattened or even slightly concave (Figs. 379, 380). A fluting is to be seen on both sides, though how far this is purposely or accidentally present in the Leichhardt-Selwyn and Cloncurry District examples, which in addition bear a superposed incised pattern, it is impossible to say.

The superposed pattern in the examples from those two districts consists of a sort of looped design on both sides, reminding one somewhat when seen at a distance, though the resemblance may perhaps be considered far-fetched, of the plaques on a tortoise-shell (Figs. 376, 377), occasionally, and additionally, there may be one or two transverse cuts above and below, while invariably the incisions constituting the design are subsequently filled in with red ochre. In the Upper Georgina and Boulia Districts, the pattern on the front is more complicated (Fig. 373, 374A.B., 375), a fluting drawn to special design: it might be described as composed of numerous lines running parallel with the two vertical edges of the weapon, the two series of curved flutes thus produced crossing in the middle line, and forming a more or less concentric shuttle-pattern around the central portion of the shield. The pattern on the back may occasionally be similar to the front, though usually it is in the form of parallel longitudinal straight lines. Both front and back may be further painted, especially when on the "walk-about" &c., with red and yellow ochre and charcoal, according to the pattern indicated by the fluting: on other occasions, the weapon may either be left uncoloured, or else be painted all over with the one pigment, especially when the supply of the other runs short. No interpretation as to the signification of the design was obtainable.

255. Fighting-poles.—It is a pity that the misnomer "yam-stick" (sect. 158) has so often been applied by Europeans to the two-handed fighting-pole, a weapon which has nothing whatever to do with the esculent in question: it is employed by both men and women, especially the latter, for fighting purposes only, and on the whole may be said to be not too frequently met with in the Boulia District. The different names which it receives are given in sect. 55. This fighting-pole (Fig. 384) is manufactured in the Boulia, Cloncurry, Flinders, and perhaps the Leichhardt-Selwyn Districts, and apparently does not travel much: if it does, the area of circuit is very limited. In length the weapon varies from about 4 feet to 4 feet 6 inches, in diameter it is sometimes over 2½ inches: each extremity tapers abruptly to a point. Being made from gidyea, mulga, "box," or other hardwood it is correspondingly heavy. In the Boulia District the surface is generally smoothed, though, if an "old friend," or the owner attaches particular importance to it, it may be covered with a longitudinal fluting: in the Cloncurry District it is invariably smoothed. Often, at one or both extremities, a few more or less parallel or looped bands may be incised to minimise the chance of the hands slipping (see handle-marks in sects. 241, 256). The Mitakoodi alone manufacture a comparatively thinner and much longer fighting-stick, longitudinally fluted, and coloured red: this is used by women only, and known as the *koo-lung-a-ra*. In making attack with the fighting-pole (with men) one end of it is clasped by both hands closely one above the other: in the defence, one hand is held at each extremity, the weapon being thus maintained either horizontally above the head, or more or less vertically at the side, right or left, as the case requires (sect. 238).

256. Nulla-nullas.—The manufacture of the throwing-stick or nulla-nulla (Fig. 385) is gradually dying out in the Boulia District where it is not employed for purposes of barter, though it is still pretty common along and to the north of the Leichhardt-Selwyn ranges. It is made from gidyea, coloured black with charcoal grease, and met with up to about two feet in length. The free end is enlarged and tapers to a point : a good one is usually incised with some circular bands at the handle (*see* handle-marks in sects. 241, 255), and a longitudinal fluting which reaches either to the tip or ceases abruptly about an inch from it.

The name applied to this weapon in the Boulia District is *mor-ro* : the Mitakoodi call it *ma-ro*. The nulla-nulla in these districts is not so much a "hand" instrument as a throwing implement—*i.e.*, it is used more for throwing at short distances than for hitting at close quarters.

257. Stone-knives.—The stone-knife consists of a chipped flint-flake blade fixed into a rounded or oval handle made of cementing-substance (Figs. 387, 389). The flake, varying from about two to over six inches in length, has from three (Fig. 388) to five or more facets (Fig. 387), an extra large one, as a rule, forming one side of the blade ; the whole knife is known by the same name as the blade. The cement-handle is either smoothed nicely off to fit the hollow of the hand, or else may be lengthened by the addition of a piece of wood (Fig. 390) : in the Boulia District the handle is spoken of as *kun-ti ma-ro*—*i.e.*, cement-possessor. Along with the implement there is very often a sort of sheath made of fine strips of bark longitudinally placed, wound round and round with opossum-string, and enclosing at its apex some emu-feathers which, projecting inwards, protect the knife-point (Fig. 386) : at Glenormiston and Boulia this sheath is called the *moon-ta-bil-la*. The flint stone from which the blade is made is obtainable along the head of the Burke and Wills Rivers, in the Leichhardt-Selwyn and the Toko Ranges, and Upper Georgina River, but not on the Mulligan. From the Leichhardt-Selwyn and Upper Georgina Districts, the stone-knife travels, for purposes of exchange and barter—(*a*) across to the Mitakoodi and Woonamurra, (*b*) to the Middle Diamantina River *viâ* Noranside, Boulia, and Marion Downs or Springvale, (*c*) to the Upper Diamantina *viâ* Kynuna. The names it receives in the various ethnographical districts are to be seen in sect. 55.

The stone-blade, certainly in the eastern portions of North-West-Central Queensland, owing to contact with a higher civilisation, is gradually being replaced by the iron, filed and ground down, obtained from disused shear-blades, barrel-hoops, &c ; the handle is also similarly undergoing modifications, a pretty common form being its encasement in the testicle-pouch removed from sheep, goat, or kangaroo.

258. The Stone Tomahawk (Fig. 391) used to be made years ago, previous to the advent of the whites and their more serviceable metal ones, by the Kalkadoon, Mitakoodi, &c., from a kind of greenstone obtained in the Leichhardt-Selwyn Ranges. I am informed on very reliable authority that at the present time (1896), at a spot called "Bora," in the close neighbourhood of the Bower Bird Gold Field, on the Upper Leichhardt River, are to be seen remains of one of the pits or quarries whence this particular stone was originally obtained. From descriptions given me by the older blackfellows I find that the stone-head itself used to be cut as follows :—A lump about the required size was first of all broken away, and parts chipped off here and there with another similar piece of rock until the necessary shape would be roughly attained. A whole day perhaps would be occupied in doing this, while another twenty-four hours would be required for the grinding down, with water, along another smooth piece of the same material until such time as the edge would be sharpened enough for use. Some of these stone-heads reach a considerable size, one in my possession, found in the neighbourhood of Boulia, measuring over 9 inches in its greatest diameter. It is very rare now-a-days to meet with one of these weapons in its entirety. The handles of the few in my possession are formed of a single piece of wood, bent at its middle, so as to form two limbs which together constitute the handle by being firmly bound above and below with opossum-twine, &c. ; the stone-head is fixed into the wooden loop with "spinifex" or beef-wood gum. I have not come across any examples where the stone is fixed into the fork of a limb. The Boulia and Glenormiston people speak of the handle as *chi-ri* or *wa-cha-ma*, the stone-head as *wul-lung-a-ra* or *ma-re-a* (the last term also signifying the implement as a whole) ; the complete weapon is known as *wa-ra-per-ta* among the Boulia tribes, as the *wa-rum-per-ta* by the South Kalkadoon.

CHAPTER XI.

DISEASE, ACCIDENT, DEATH. CANNIBALISM.

CONTENTS.—Sections 259-268. The Death-bone. 269. Death from Snake-bite. 270. Other Diseases and Accidents produced by the Death-bone. 271. Women-Doctors. 272. The Pearl-plate. 273. The Death-powder. 274. The Bone-pin. 275. Incurable Blindness. 276. Drowning. 277. Sudden Disappearance. 278. Mental Disease. 279. Belief in Death as a Punishment—a Future State. 280. Treatment of Non-fatal Snake-bite. 281. Fractures. 282. Chants and Dirges for Exorcising Ailments. 283. Smearing of Blood, of Perspiration; Drinking of Blood, of Seminal Fluid; Wet-cupping. 284. Smearing of Fat. 285. Poultices. 286. Amulets and Charms. 287. Medicinal Plants. 288. Clay-pills. 289. Burial in the Boulia District; 290, of a Murderer. 291. Burial in the Cloncurry District; 292, in the Upper Georgina District. 293. Cannibalism.

259. The Death-bone, or bone-apparatus, and its property of producing sickness and death, which, in the absence of sufficiently demonstrable causes, cannot otherwise be accounted for, is one of the most dreaded, as it is universal, of the aboriginal superstitions of North-West-Central Queensland, including the adjoining Upper and Middle Diamantina districts. The implement can be manufactured by the "doctor," "medicine man," or any other male individual, though were such an one to chance upon a specimen, not his own property, he would immediately wash and destroy it in case of its ever being employed to his own detriment: in the case of a woman, she would immediately fall sick were she to touch, or even to look at it. For descriptive purposes, the apparatus (Fig. 392) may be said to consist of a pointer (D) connected by string, &c., (C) with an elongate cylindrical receptacle (A B), the various terms applied to these component parts in different districts being tabulated as follows :—

—	Boulia District.	Leichhardt-Selwyn District.	Cloncurry District.	Upper Flinders District.
The death-bone as a whole	*mung-un-i* ([5]) *kum-bo* ([4])	*wa-to-ko* *mul-ta*	*mung-un-i*	*kul-ka*
The pointer	*te-ri*	*koong-ga* ([3]) *ka-te-bri-na*	*ka-te-bri-na*	
The connecting string ...	*win-ni-mun-na-ri*	*wul-koor*	*wul-koor*	
The receptacle	*tou-er-li*	*wo-bil*	*wo-bil*	
The "medicine-man," "doctor," &c., who knows how to employ it	*munguni ma-ro* ([1]) *kumbo ma-ro* ([1])	*too-a-run*	*munguni boo-na* ([2])	
To kill with it	*mun-da-*			

([1]) *Ma-ro*=sign of possession, &c. ([2]) *Boo-na*=sign of possession, &c. ([3]) Any stick, piece of wood (sect. 235). ([4]) A flint-flake, stone (sects. 290, 149). ([5]) This word signifies a bone of any sort in the Karanya dialect (sect. 52).

The pointer, from 3 to 5 inches in length, is made usually from one of the human forearm bones, or an emu bone, ground down from the blunt extremity to a gradually tapering point: among the Kalkadoon, the sharpened end of this pointer is fashioned into the shape of a fish-hook sometimes. The string itself is made of human hair or opossum-twine, &c., or both plaited together, and varies from 3 or 4 to as much as 12 or 15 feet in length : by means of cementing-substance, beef-wood or spinifex, according to the district (sect. 150), it connects the blunt extremity of the pointer with the internal surface of the receptacle base. The receptacle is formed generally out of a piece of human arm or shin bone cut to a length of 3 or 4 inches and hollowed or scraped out so as to form a kind of cylinder: a human bone, however, though most appreciated for the purpose, is not always at the moment obtainable, and under such circumstances may be substituted by a portion of a kangaroo's or an emu's leg bone, a bit of bamboo-cane, even a piece of an old gun-barrel, or a small sheet of tinware, &c., rolled on itself. One extremity, the base, of the receptacle is closed in with the usual cementing substance to which, passing down on the inside, the connecting string is attached. When the instrument is put into practice, it is the receptacle which encloses the victim's life-blood.

260. In the Boulia District, the doctors, medicine-men, or whatever they may be called, come to learn the art of successfully "pointing," *i.e.*, employing, the death-bone as follows :—

The individual will leave camp for three or four days, and subsist only on bushes, &c.—that is, practically starve himself : he gets more or less "cranky" and when in that condition sees *Mul-ka-ri*, who is pleased to make him a doctor by inserting certain small flints, bones, or gee-gaws in his "inside" (sect. 261). This is the most ordinary method. *Mulkari* is the supernatural power who makes everything which the Boulia District aboriginals cannot otherwise account for : he is a good, beneficent person and never kills anyone.

Other doctors obtain their powers through the instrumentality of *Kan-ma-re*, a huge supernatural water-snake with a mane-like head of hair. He it is who drowns people (and in this connection it is interesting to note the neighbouring Kalkadoon word *kan-da-jin*, to swim) ; the same reptile is spoken of as *tul-lo-un* among the Mitakoodi (*cf.* the Kalkadoon name for the person who uses this instrument, *too-a-run*). Supposing, now, that a man be fishing at the river-side, *Kanmare* may "point" at him a death-bone (sect. 264), of course at such a distance and under circumstances that he neither knows nor sees what is taking place. But by-and-by, as the night-shades begin to fall, he sees the dreaded monster undulating along upon the surface of the water, and runs as fast as his legs will carry him to the camp, where he recounts what has taken place. That night he goes to sleep as usual, but in the morning he feels sick. The sickness continues and becomes worse and worse. In from four to five days after the commencement of the attack, he is attended by some doctor, who removes from the patient's inside, by a process to be afterwards described (sect. 263), the pebble, flint, bone, &c., that *Kanmare* put there, with the result that the individual recovers and becomes a doctor himself. The bone so removed, the *kanmare*-bone, is a rather long one, and coloured dark : as usual, it is said to be sharpened at one extremity, and covered with cementing substance at the other.

Mo-ma, the ghost, or shade, or spirit of someone departed can also initiate an individual into the mysteries of the craft. It is he that haunts the graves of the dead : the Mitakoodi call him *Lim-bi-ja-koo-lun*.

Another method of initiating the doctor or *munguni-maro* is to put into the novice, by means to be subsequently considered (sect. 264), the identical "bone" removed (sect. 263) from the person in whom *Mulkari* or *Kanmare* originally placed it. This procedure may be effected on the individual when he is perhaps but a child, and as the years roll on he will suddenly blossom forth with all the powers peculiar to his profession.

In the Cloncurry District, among the Mitakoodi, it is the supernatural Being with immense eyes and very big ears, *Ten-gul-a-goo-lun*, who teaches the doctor how to use the *munguni*: when people are in camp at night he can be heard scratching on the timber and breaking off the branches. But when this individual is not convenient, and will not make himself patent, the man who wants to graduate as a medicine-man or *munguni-boona* (sect 259) has to travel all the way down the Diamantina, usually *viâ* Eddington, Kynuna, Dagworth, and Elderslie, as far as Brighton Downs perhaps, at a certain encampment of the Goa tribe, where he learns the art, as follows :—Having made a present of a shirt, blankets, &c., to his teacher, he is first of all put to death, next thrown into a water-hole for four days, and then on the fifth taken out, when a number of fires are lighted all round him, and his body thus smoked quite dry, with the object of getting all the water out, and so making him all right and quite alive again : he is now shown how to use the bone, and taught the, in this tribe, necessary songs to sing with it, his success in the art being now assured.

261. No matter the different methods by which "doctors" come to be what they are, all of these folk are co-potent: they can all not only cure, but also produce, sickness according to procedures which will be subsequently detailed. Beyond their occult powers in this connection, the doctors, except for certain articles which they keep about them, have nothing to distinguish them from the

other individuals in the camp: they engage in similar pursuits, enjoy no extra rights, they marry and may themselves get sick or die through similar agencies, in fact they may get hoisted on their own petards. The certain articles which they keep about them are small pieces of pointed bone, ordinary knuckle-bone, pebble, flint, quartz-crystals, gypsum, anything indeed at all striking or out of the common, which *Mulkari* or *Kanmare* is believed to have originally inserted into them (sect. 260), and which have thence been subsequently removed (sect. 263), the property of one doctor being thus capable, as a rule, of being distinguished from the stock-in-trade of others (*cf.* the term *kumbo maro*, sect. 259, where *kumbo* = flint, stone, &c.). Their owner will show these gew-gaws now and again, as the opportunity occurs, to other individuals and friends who, when the occasion arises (sect. 263), can thus recognise to whom they belong or who, at the time, can see in them a sort of guarantee as to the genuineness and respectability of the practitioner. Whenever a big mob of blacks happens to be collected at the camp, it is believed that the doctor always keeps his eyes and ears well open, and on such occasions never goes to sleep at night: he thus gleans heaps of information, and often discovers not only who it is that possesses a bone-apparatus, which has caught and bottled up someone else's life-blood (sect. 264), but also even at whom it has been pointed—*i.e.*, whose blood it belongs to—notwithstanding the fact that this may have been obtained from an individual in some other tribe living even a long way off.

The doctors of the tribe may be on friendly terms with one another, and may consult among themselves when necessary concerning whose blood has been, or is to be, taken—*i.e.*, at whom a death-bone has been, or is to be, "pointed." At heart, nevertheless, they do not trust one another; they are in reality a bad lot, and it is only a common fear which binds them together: without them, the effects of the *munguni* or death-bone would be harmless, sickness and death would consequently gradually disappear, and there would be a likelihood of the aboriginals living for ever. As a matter of fact, the other individuals in camp are usually, though not invariably, afraid to tackle them: I only know of one instance where an outsider, my own black servant, dared "point" the death-bone at a native doctor, the latter dying about a fortnight later, though the *real* cause of death I had no opportunity of verifying.

262. To explain the method of using the *munguni*, or "pointing" the apparatus for producing sickness or death, as adopted throughout the Boulia, Leichhardt-Selwyn, Cloncurry, and Upper Georgina Districts, it will be convenient to deal with each stage of the process in proper order, as follows:—(*a*) a person becomes otherwise-unaccountably sick, and consequently believes himself to be in some enemy's power—*i.e.*, to have been "pointed" at (sect. 264); (*b*) he finds out the doctor and particular enemy who made him ill (sect. 263); (*c*) he employs another doctor to retaliate upon his would-be destroyer (sect. 264-265); (*d*) he makes sure that his adversary is now equally so in *his* power (sect. 266-267); (*e*) so that mutual fear tends to break the spell, with a view to health and harmony being restored (sect. 268).

An individual becomes incapacitated through some chronic and painful illness which does not answer to the various aboriginal methods of treatment or materia medica: the illness weighs upon his mind, and after a time he becomes more and more confirmed in his conviction that someone has been "pointing" the munguni at him—*i.e.*, that a "bone," pebble, flint, &c., has been put inside him, and his blood removed (sect. 264). Such sickness, which I have had several opportunities of observing, is usually a kind of malaria, ague, rheumatism, &c, or some chronic form of venereal disease: in the last case, owing to the comparatively long incubative stage, any idea that it arises from sexual connection is not even dreamt of, so much so that syphilis, &c., is believed capable of being imparted by burying certain charms, &c. (sect. 274), in the ground. So rooted sometimes is this belief on the part of a patient, that some enemy has "pointed" the bone at him, that he will actually lie down to die, and succeed in the attempt, even at the expense of refusing food and succour within his reach: I have myself witnessed three or four such cases.

263. Fortunately for himself, however, the patient is not always so weak-minded as to give up all hope, but, at length recovering a bit, pulls himself together and determines upon finding out who it was that had wrought him the injury. He either asks a friend or relative, who possibly may mention the name of some poor wretch upon whom he (the friend) may have a " down," or else sees the imaginary culprit in a dream ; should both these means fail him he consults a " doctor." These three methods of inquiry have each their separate accompaniments. In the case where he learns the information required through the agency of a friend, he seeks the doctor's assistance, and by means of some sort of a present, such as a blanket, human-hair belt, &c., prevails upon him to " point" the bone at his alleged assailant (and get some of his blood in retaliation, sect. 264). It may happen, however, that the alleged culprit is physically more powerful or possessed of greater personal influence than the medicine-man himself, in which case the latter may decline the job, being fearful of the retribution that might follow should his action in the matter be subsequently discovered ; at any rate, in the long run a willing practitioner is obtained. If in a dream he recognises his enemy, or the doctor who lent assistance, he will perhaps go and fight one or both—if he thinks he can do so successfully ; he will not attempt to do either of them to death, but only just cripple them with knife, spear, or boomerang, and take measures in addition to have each of them " pointed " at with a bone in return. The reason of his not wishing to actually kill one or other is that so long as his own blood remains in the receptacle of the bone-apparatus in the alleged enemy's possession, and is not properly rinsed out with water (sects. 267, 268), his own life remains in danger.

Where corroborative evidence, by both preceding methods, is wanting, the injured individual will consult some medical friend of his, and, with the usual gift, ask him to discover his assailant, and possibly the name of his alleged enemy may be divulged straight away. More often, however, the doctor is not quite such a fool as to commit himself so readily, but exercises his power of removing from within the patient's body the actual bone, pebble, flint, &c., which the would-be murderer had invisibly inserted there (sect. 264). Having inquired where the bodily pains were most marked, or their effects still remain, he sets about rubbing or massaging the affected parts, perhaps at intervals rinsing his hands in water. He may also blow upon the patient's chest, take some water into his own mouth and spit it out again, probably to show that nothing is concealed therein, that there is no deception in fact, and may even apply his lips in the act of suction to that portion of the patient's anatomy most complained of. At any rate in a short time he certainly contrives, by a kind of sleight of hand, to get some sort of a doctor's gew-gaw, some of the stock-in-trade—bone, flint, quartz, &c. (sect. 261)—into his hand, or more usually into his mouth, which the patient, as well as any one else who may be present, implicitly believes he has managed to draw out from the part of the body affected. The exact manner in which this bone, pebble, &c., which has invisibly been causing all the mischief, is suddenly made to put in an appearance on these occasions is certainly very puzzling, even to Europeans : at any rate there it is, and the sick individual is now absolutely cured, though his life remains in danger, his life's " blood" being in the enemy's bone-receptacle. Now, the particular gew-gaw thus apparently removed from the person ailing must have been placed in the part complained of by some other and rival doctor. The present consultant therefore examines it most carefully and tells the patient to which member of the profession it belongs—that is, who did the actual mischief ; he says he will now try and find out which of the victim's enemies instigated the deed, but will require some little time to do so. The doctor in the meantime consults privately with his fellow-practitioners, and may suggest some personally obnoxious individual, but the latter may have some friends at court, and the idea is scouted : at all events, among themselves collectively in secret conclave they hit upon some poor wretch of a fellow who has perhaps and probably been lately causing trouble in the camp, and all agree in making him the scape-goat. The particular person having been selected, the doctor returns to his quondam patient and divulges the name of his enemy : the patient will not, however, fight him yet, not until he has got his would-be destroyer's life-blood similarly into his own possession (sects. 266, 267).

264. To do this, he must again employ the services of the medicine-man, who works his speciality, the bone-apparatus, after one or other of the following fashions, the procedure always taking place at night, when the individual to be made sick or to die is asleep. It is most important to remember that in all cases while the death-bone (sect. 259) is being "pointed," *the blood of the victim passes invisibly across the intervening space to the "pointer," and so along the connecting-string, into the receptacle, where it is collected : at the same time one of the doctor's gew-gaws, or stock-in-trade, bone, pebble, &c. (sect. 261), passes invisibly from the "pointer" to be inserted into the body of the victim, who thus contracts his sick-ness—in other words, the latter, in addition to losing blood, receives a dreaded bone, stone, &c.*

265. In the Boulia District the death-bone is "pointed" thus :—If single-handed, and he knows that he can get to within a short distance of his prey, the doctor fixes the cup or receptacle of the bone-apparatus upright into the ground, while the pointer, resting between the big toe and digit, is directed at the person selected, the connecting string being held in the hand, and never by any chance allowed to touch the earth (Fig. 393A).

Again, if single-handed, but the victim, owing to the position of his gundi or the presence of others, cannot be approached at short distance, a longer string is used : the receptacle is fixed to a stump or tree, while the pointer, which is held in the position of rest upon a forked stick firmly planted into the ground, is directed as required (Fig. 393B).

Of course it is always advisable for the practitioner to work the *munguni* by him-self, but sometimes, if in doubt or unsuccessful, he may call in the assistance of other medicos : in the former case he can keep the transaction secret between himself and his employer, whereas in the latter the evil business might leak out, the danger of such a contingency being, however, perhaps counterbalanced by the fact that the full responsibility is now shared with others. Should two of them be working the instrument, one holds the pointer and the other the receptacle. When three, four, or even perhaps five medicine-men are pointing the bone-apparatus, one holds the pointer, another the receptacle, while the remainder support the con-necting-string, which under these circumstances would be very much longer than the ordinary. Among those holding the string there may be some intimate friend of the proposed victim, and he, by means of a secreted flint, &c., may cut the twine while the performance is proceeding: if, on re-tying the string it again breaks (*i.e.*, is more probably purposely cut), the intended victim is spared. Though the others may have a shrewd suspicion as to which of their mates severed the cord, they find it wiser not to express any opinion publicly : they only recognise the fact that whoever did it was afraid of stating his convictions openly when the secret conclave (sect. 263) was held. Under such circumstances the doctor returns to his employer and explains how it was that his endeavours to obtain the required blood, &c., were unsuccessful : the employer can please himself whether he consults another medical man or not.

In the Cloncurry District, the manner in which the *munguni* is pointed by the Mitakoodi doctor is almost identical, both in procedure and results, with the method holding good in the Boulia District. The receptacle is clutched between the two knees, the string held in the hand, while the pointer, directed in the proper quarter, is made to rest upon a branch or stick in the manner indicated in Fig. 394. In low tones, so as not to notify his presence, he sings a dirge (the meaning of which he does not know) while pointing.

In the Upper Georgina District, the traditions of the bone-apparatus are upheld, with more or less variations, both among the Undekerebina and Yaroinga tribes. In addition to "pointing" by the ordinary method, the Yaroinga doctor "shoots" the pointer with a sharp push from the open palm of one hand along the prongs of a forked stick held in the other into the required direction (Fig. 395), his assistant, who has hold of the connecting-string, pulling the pointer back again as it falls : this procedure may be repeated a few times.

In the Leichhardt-Selwyn District, the Kalkadoon doctor usually employs another to help him "point," the one holding the pointer and the other the receptacle.

266. Having by some one or other of the above methods of "pointing" obtained the required blood (sect. 264) in the receptacle of the "bone-apparatus" the doctor puts into it the pointer, tip downwards, around the exposed butt-end of which and the otherwise open mouth of the cylinder he fixes a lot of the usual cementing substance so as to completely seal it: outside the whole concern he winds the connecting-string round and round. Though he will swear to his employer as to the presence and genuineness of the contained blood, it is difficult to learn whether the medical man has inserted some of his own, or that of some animal, or indeed any at all: he naturally takes every precaution, to maintain the deception, that no one shall actually see what he does enclose in the cylinder when sealing it. But the employer wants to make doubly sure that he really has the blood of his alleged would-be destroyer, and not that of someone else who may have been "pointed" at in mistake. He therefore, in company with the doctor who procured it, will in a few days' time, to avert suspicion, leave the camp after dark, and in some sequestered spot kindle a fire, over which they warm the bone-apparatus with its ghostly contents. Leaving the medicine-man to keep watch, he returns to camp, divulges his mission to no one, but enters into conversation with his alleged assailant on any ordinary everyday topic, watches most carefully to see if he is at all sick or not, and may casually get him to admit that he is feeling a bit tired or is a little out of sorts. This admission, simple as it is, constitutes ample proof of guilt under the circumstances, but the avenger says nothing, continues the conversation to allay even the slightest suspicion, parts with him on apparently friendly terms, and sneaks back to the doctor, to whom he narrates exactly what has taken place. Supposing that the wrong individua's blood has been "caught," i.e., an innocent person has been "pointed" at in mistake—and this is judged to be the case when not the slightest sign of sickness is discoverable—the medicine-man breaks open the top of the receptacle, which he rinses out and washes well in water, so as to allow of its being used again in another attempt.

267. But if everything is satisfactory, and the blood of the required culprit has been really (as is believed) obtained, the one in possession has only to warm the apparatus again over the fire to make his alleged, and now proven, enemy more sick; to destroy it in the flames to make him actually die; or to rinse it in water and rub fat of any description over it to put him all to rights again. He thus has his enemy completely in his power, and continues to make him sick—there is generally some ague, venereal, or chronic rheumatism, &c., about—but will not kill him—i.e., burn the *munguni*—for fear of his own life, which continues in danger so long as his own blood (which can be affected, for good or for evil, and by similar methods) remains in his enemy's possession.

268. After a longer or shorter interval, when the passions have subsided—and Time heals all things, even the quarrels of the aboriginal—the complainant will consider that he has punished his enemy sufficiently by making him so seriously ill. He will find some opportunity for making an explanation, and admit, more or less truly, that it was he, but only in retaliation, who "caught" and still possesses his blood: the owner of the latter will naturally, and most conscientiously, of course, deny the charge *in toto* at first, but when the strong array of facts is marshalled before him, admit it for peace and security sake, and invent or find perhaps some trifling excuse to justify his alleged original act of injury. They do not fight, being mutually afraid of each other, now that each is firmly believed to be in possession of the other's "blood," but settle the matter amicably, the mutual understanding being cemented by the alleged careful washing out and rinsing of the respective *mungunis,* one of which—the original alleged enemy's—is probably, and, of course, in most cases, not really existent.

269. Death from Snake-bite.—To account for a death from snake-bite—which apparently only rarely happens, and in such cases the purely natural cause and fatal effect are not reconciled— a variation in the superstition of the death-bone is brought into requisition. This modification in the procedure, though known throughout the whole Boulia District, is said to be only occasionally employed. By means similar to those already mentioned, proof is forthcoming that the receptacle of the bone-apparatus actually contains the particular person's blood required, but this time it is believed that the doctor has sealed up a small snake with it in addition : the implement is next smeared over with fat, and the predestinated victim allowed to go away from camp. The latter may depart as usual on some hunting expedition, and become fully occupied in the excitement of the chase, when he suddenly feels something at his leg or foot, and sees a snake just in the act of biting him. Strange to say, this particular kind of snake will now immediately disappear : it does not crawl into the ground, or hide under a stone like any ordinary ophidian would do, but actually vanishes away into space. Indeed, by this very process of invisibility the person bitten recognises that some enemy has been "pointing" at him the *munguni*, and that through this particular form of it he is sure to die ; nothing can possibly save him. He makes no effort, in fact, to apply a remedy, loses heart, gives way and dies (*see* treatment of ordinary, *i.e.*, non-fatal snake-bite, sect. 280). Supposing the gin of the thus snake-bitten individual to be present at the time of the occurrence, she will run back to camp as fast as she can go and tell one of the doctors. The latter, from a careful cross-examination as to the nature of the bite, the variety of the snake, and the condition of the patient, will soon gather all the information he requires, and then glance up at the skies to see if *Mulkari* is spitting or not : if, as he says, he does not recognise this supernatural Being expectorating from above, he tells her that some mortal must have got her husband's blood, using this particular form of the *munguni* to effect his purpose, and that it is impossible to save his life. Furthermore, at some future time, the doctor referred to will tell her who actually did the mischief : the widow will not learn this information perhaps for some months to come, but when she does she will tell her brothers and other kindred, who then take the necessary steps to avenge her husband's death.

270. Other Diseases and Accidents produced by the Death-bone.—Instead of inserting a snake in the death-bone receptacle with the required blood, certain doctors, and they only, can talk to the captured blood and tell it to kill the person from whom it has been taken, by lightning, by the fall of a tree, or to injure him by running a thorn into his foot, or inflicting upon him some vile complaint or disease.

At Bedouri, on the southern confines of the Boulia District, among the Ooloopooloo tribe, still another modification of the *munguni* is the *wul-loo-ka*, which is believed to be similar in mode and action, but can be used between very long distances. Thus, one of the Bedouri men may have a grudge against a Boulia black, and will tell a white or a blue crane, or even a pelican, to travel all over the intervening distance, and by "pointing" get the blood for him. Some time after, during the shades of night, the victim sees one of these birds in question and will throw a stick at it to drive it away, but the creature, being engaged in "pointing," will not budge for some little time; it will only fly away back to Bedouri when it has got a sufficient quantity of blood in the bone-apparatus receptacle. To make sure now that he really has possession of his victim's blood, the would-be assailant at Bedouri will send four or five other birds again to Boulia in order to glean the necessary information as to whether the individual upon whom he has sinister designs is sick or not : he is afraid to send the same bird by itself on the second journey in case it were to "gammon" him. This procedure is considered to be far more potent in its action than the ordinary form of *munguni*. Indeed, *Mulkari* invented this method originally, though he taught both systems to the Ooloopooloo men, whence the commoner process travelled all over the district : the secret of the *wul-loo-ka*, however, they have kept to themselves, and will on no account teach the details of the process to their northern neighbours.

271. Women Doctors.—Though a woman dare not handle or look upon a *munguni*, she sometimes knows and practises the "trick" of removing by mouth or hand (sect. 263) the particular gew-gaw which is alleged and believed to have been inserted, and to be prolonging the sickness, in the patient's body. She may herself be a doctor's wife or not, but on no account is she ostensibly allowed to join in the secret deliberations of the other medical practitioners. If she herself wishes to get possession of another woman's blood, she may prevail, if married, upon her husband, or, if single, upon her brother, to put her wishes into practical execution.

272. The Pearl-plate, like the death-bone, is made to account for various forms of sickness and death, which otherwise to the aboriginal mind would be inexplicable. It consists of a flat, more or less, triangular piece of pearl-shell, with rounded angles, measuring in its greatest length, from middle of base to the subtended angle, at which some cementing substance with a piece of hair-twine is attached, from 1½ to 2 inches (Fig. 396). Brought by the Workia tribes into North-West-Central Queensland to Lake Nash and neighbourhood, it reaches on the one hand the Leichhardt-Selwyn, and on the other the Upper Georgina District. The Kalkadoon, who call this implement the *che-ka-la-ri* (*cf.* sect. 184), employ it far more frequently perhaps than the *munguni*, and have introduced it among the Mitakoodi, who now practice it with the same evil intent. Through the Yaroinga, by whom it is named *ker-ka-la*, the Undekerebina tribe of the Toko Ranges has also come to learn its uses. The usual precedure is for the assailant to come, ordinarily at night-time, as close as possible to his intended and unconscious victim, to hold the implement by the cemented corner at arm's-length, and, through the air in the direction indicated, make two horizontal and two vertical passes: the former is considered symbolical of the cutting of the throat, the latter the ripping-up of the belly-wall. The Undekerebina, who apparently attach great importance to this particular mode of injury, take extra precautions lest any innocent or harmless person be hurt by the too great extent of the horizontal sweep, and will therefore hold up the other fore-arm (Fig. 397) to limit it: or, again, with a similar object in view, the performer will open his legs, tuck his head well down, and then put the pearl-shell into execution (Fig. 398), the lower limbs limiting the movement either to the right or to the left.

273. The Death-powder.—The Workia people, it would seem, are also responsible for the death-powder, the *mo-a-ri* or *moy-a-ri*, somewhat of the appearance of very white ashes which, placed anywhere in close proximity to where the victim is sleeping, under his blanket, &c., will kill him in no time. This practice prevails among the Yaroinga and the Kalkadoon: through the latter it has reached the Mitakoodi on the one hand and the Yellunga of Noranside on the other. In the Boulia District, Noranside is the only locality where it has been noted: the superstition is certainly not met with at Boulia. The Mitakoodi speak of the powder as the *mou-ar*, and so that the performer should not injure himself by contact he sprinkles it where required from out of a mussel-shell: the same tribe also use a reddish powder, *mung-gil-li*, with similar methods and design, but the exact composition of either material, which unfortunately I was never allowed to see, is unknown to me. In the neighbourhood of Normanton, outside this district, a specimen of this powder was found to be ground glass. There is suspicion that this particular superstition has its origin in the fact that in the stores on all these Western stations the large quantity of strychnine, the poisonous properties of which many of these aboriginals fully appreciate, is always coloured with ruddle—*i.e.*, red ochre—to minimise the chances of accident.

274. The Bone-pin or *chi-roo-ko* (in the Pitta-Pitta language) is another instrument, perhaps a development of the *munguni* "pointer," brought into requisition for producing venereal and other cognate disorders, fatal or not, which otherwise are inexplicable: the aboriginal has not yet learnt that these particular diseases are capable of transmission by sexual connection. Besides being used in the Boulia District, the *chi-roo-ko* is at present employed by the Yaroinga in the Upper Georgina, and by the Kalkadoon in the Lichhardt-Selwyn District, though I have only Pitta-Pitta corroborative evidence for the latter statement: a slight variation of it is certainly in vogue among the Mitakoodi of the Cloncurry District under the name of *je-go*. In its ordinary form, the *chi-roo-ko* consists of a short emu-bone from 2 to 2½ inches long, filed to a point—a small edition of the *munguni* "pointer"—or perhaps the beak of some long-necked diver-bird, having a little spinifex-gum attached to the base (Fig. 399). There are two methods adopted in its employment. If placed underground with the point up, but not visible, in the situation where the victim has been expelling one or other of the products of the emunctories, he or she develops some form of venereal disease, and subsequent rotting-away of the privates: if similarly placed in the gundi, or wherever else he

or she may be sleeping, it may cause such a disturbance of the general health as
to result even in death. The Mitakoodi make their *je-go* from a human arm-bone:
it is of about the same size as the *chi-roo-ko*, but with beef-wood gum at the blunt
extremity, and when in use is hidden anywhere underneath where the victim may
be sleeping. Both *chi-roo-ko* and *je-go* can be used by the medical as well as the
lay fraternity, but never by women. In all cases, the assailant may be discovered
as with the *munguni*, either by consulting a doctor or by revelation in a dream,
subsequent retaliation being effected by similar means : as soon as the implement
is removed from out of the ground, the sick individual makes a speedy recovery.

275. **Incurable Blindness.**—The development of blindness, when not explicable
by visible traumatic causes, is in the case of men accounted as a punishment, by
human agency, for a continued persistency in " catching"—*i.e.*, raping—married
women when alone and unprotected out in the bush. In the Boulia District, this
punishment of blindness or *me-puk-koo-re-a (cf.* Pitta-Pitta *me*, an eye, *puk-ka-*,
to cut, &c.) can be inflicted by anyone except a woman. The individual whose
honour has been sullied gets two of the incisor teeth of a young opossum and ties
them with twine, derived from the same animal, one to each of his little fingers,
on their inner aspects. So prepared, he comes into camp and squats down with
the chin resting on his closed hands (Fig. 400), taking up such position that he
can get a good view of the delinquent without exciting suspicion. He watches
his opportunity to get into line with the offender's eyes, and, without being noticed
of course, stretches forwards in required direction with both hands, one on a higher
level than the other, and with the little fingers (all the other digits remaining
closed) claws into the air at one eye (Fig. 401) : after a few seconds' interval
he shifts the position of his hands, the one which was on a higher level before
being now lower, and "makes for" the other eye with a similar clawing. After use,
the opossum teeth and string are destroyed by fire. The result is that, although
the culprit is totally unconscious of what has been done to his visual organs, his
eye-sight becomes subsequently affected, he gets quite and incurably blind, and
can see no more women to assault.

In the Cloncurry District, when the Mitakoodi want to " blind " a man, they
do it by " singing " only, casting over him a sort of spell, as it were.

276. **Drowning.**—Death by drowning is a phenomenon explained, in the entire
Boulia District at least, by means of *Kanmare*, the huge supernatural water-snake
already mentioned (sect. 260). For instance, when about to swim across any big
stream or river that he suspects or fears, the aboriginal will speak to this Being,
and express himself somewhat as follows :—"Do not touch me. I belong to this
country." But were he to cross even his own country's river with a stranger to
the district, it is possible that he might be engulfed. Again, whenever a big flood
comes up, it brings *Kanmare* in its wake, so that, supposing our traveller wants to
effect a crossing, he will only venture in up to his waist : if the water be too warm
he will get across either there or at some other spot : but if too cold, and he
persists in the attempt, he is sure to be caught by *Kenmare*—*i e.*, drowned.
Nothing can cure him or bring back animation.

277. **Sudden Disappearance.**—In the Cloncurry District any sudden disappearance (what Europeans would probably speak of as murder and concealment of
the body) is credited to *Mo-ki-pi-ung-o.* This individual, this " bogie-man," who
lives underground in the seclusion of the mountain fastnesses, is somewhat like a
blackfellow in appearance, but has some very long teeth with which he can easily
bite through a man's neck : he drags his victim into the " pit," where he finishes
by making a meal off him.

278. **Mental Disease.**—The same tribe, the Mitakoodi, have a belief that
" crankiness," mental disease, &c., is caused by a Being known as *Di-pung-un-ya.*

279. **Belief in Death as a Punishment—A Future State.**—In conclusion of the
immediately preceding sections, since all the above procedures are for the most
part looked upon by the aboriginals in the light of punishments for wrongs committed, death is on the whole regarded somewhat as a penalty. Were an

individual always to remain good, he would, barring the *munguni*, and "accident" of death by actual physical violence—*e.g.*, spear, boomerang, &c.—probably live for ever. It is only a child that can die " by itself." In his natural state, the fear of death is but as nothing to the savage ; he has a hazy notion of the corpse "getting older and moving about elsewhere," when he ceases to bring food and tobacco any longer to the burial-place (sects. 289, 291): he has no dread of future punishment, no hope of reward in another life. Among the Boulia natives, with whom I could converse in their own language, I am absolutely convinced that their belief concerning a future state is as represented : in other districts, when conversing on these topics, interpreters had of course to be made use of.

280. **Treatment of Non-fatal Snake-bite.**—I will now consider the various ailments or accidents, temporary in their nature, and trivial in their results, which to the aboriginal mind are considered as arising from simple every-day causes—*i.e.*, which have been induced without the intervention of the *munguni*, and are amenable to ordinary simple treatment. The most interesting of these is non-fatal snake-bite, the treatment of which in the Boulia District should be compared with the *munguni* variety of snake-bite (sect. 269) that invariably ends in the death of the person attacked. In this case, the sufferer would see the creature gliding away after it had bitten him, and would carefully watch the hole into which it hides: this he immediately blocks up, and makes a careful note of the exact spot. With his hair-belt, or any other convenient twine, he next ties two ligatures around the limb bitten, above and below the knee if on the leg, or above and below the elbow if on the hand, " to stop the blood come up ": if possible, he applies suction to the wound. His gin, or any other mate who may be present, would rush back to consult the nearest doctor, and returning, dig a largish hole in close proximity to where the accident took place, kindle a fire in it and heat some big stones and lumps of rock : when these have become sufficiently hot and the flames somewhat subsident, a lot of fresh leafy boughs and branches and leaves, sprinkled with water to prevent ignition, are placed on top. Upon this smoking mass of foliage the bitten individual now lies, and what with the smouldering embers and hot steam arising from the leaves he soon becomes enveloped in perspiration, falls asleep for two or three hours, wakes up refreshed, has a " spit," and is quite recovered. In the meantime, however, the medicine-man has not been idle, for he of course has had a share in the cure : when the messenger first came to report the accident, he would, after cross-examination, look up at the sky and declare that he could see *Mulkari* spitting, and that therefore the patient would be all right if he went under the prescribed treatment. Furthermore, the doctor himself comes to the place where the accident happened, is shown the identical spot where the snake lies imprisoned, digs it out, and lets it travel away a few feet before commencing to pelt at it with stones. During this process the snake gradually becomes smaller and smaller until, from an original length of 3 or 4 feet, it may dwindle down to 12 or 10 inches : the creature, thus rendered harmless, is carried back to camp, where the medicine-man, turning its skin half-way inside out while still alive, throws it into the water, and so makes an end of it. It is needless to say that no lay-man is allowed to witness the process of causing the ophidian to diminish in size. The blacks will admit that if an infant or young child is bitten by a snake it cannot usually be cured unless all the above performances are quickly gone through : if, for instance, the accident takes place three or four miles from camp, the little sufferer cannot possibly stand the delay like an elderly individual would. Among the Mitakoodi the treatment of ordinary snake-bite is very similar, but no " tricks " on the part of the doctor are brought into requisition : suction, with or without scarifying by knife or stone, and ligature, followed by sweating over heated leaves, especially if the particular species is believed to be a dangerous one.

281. **Fractures.**—With regard to fractured limbs, two to four sticks in the rough may be tied on a broken arm or leg, and left there perhaps for from one to two months : the value of the remedy is rendered inactive, however, by the fact that these splints are not of sufficient length to keep the adjacent joints at rest. At other times (*e.g.*, among the Mitakoodi), instead of splints, the limb may be

M

wrapped up in opossum skins, and tied tightly round and round with twine. The value of slings, crutches, &c., in these cases is unknown : if an arm is broken, it is supported by the hand of the opposite one ; if a leg, the patient is carried to camp and laid there, &c.

282. The various **Chants and Dirges for exorcising Ailments, inducing Sleep, &c.,** have been so handed down from one to another, both individually and tribally, that though some of the lay as well as the professional members of the community know several of them by rote, none of them understand their actual meaning : for instance, here is one used at Boulia, in addition to other remedies, for dispelling stomach-ache and diarrhœa—" *koo*-năm-bĭ mă-ré-*ĕl*-yĭ lă-rō-*oòng*-kă *mă*-pă-dĭ," where the root *koo-na* (*i.e.*, fæces) is the only syllable intelligible to me. It must not be forgotten that chants and dirges may, on the other hand, be utilised for producing sickness, &c.

283. **Smearing of Blood, of Perspiration; Drinking of Blood, of Seminal Fluid ; Wet-cupping.**—Human blood is used for smearing all over the body, trunk, limbs, and face, in various obscure affections, and internal pains of one sort and another. In the Boulia District this smearing of blood is known as *gim-ba-lo-woon-di-a* (*gim-ba, kim-ba* = blood, *-lo* = prepositional suffix by, with, [sect. 24], *w* = euphonic, *oon-da-* = to grease or smear). The blood itself is removed from any other apparently healthy individual, but never a woman, in one or other of the two following methods :—With a string or other ligature tied tightly round and above the main prominence of the biceps muscle, the elbow is either strongly flexed (Fig. 402ᴀ), or while made to press upon something behind (Fig. 402 ʙ) equally strongly extended ı in the former case, the incision with the stone knife, &c., into the posterior ulnar vein (the blood-vessel ordinarily employed) can be made by the individual himself, in the latter by some other person. The blood is collected into a koolamon, and the wound, dressed with fat, bound round with a leaf or two. By means of a bundle of emu feathers the blood so obtained is dabbed all over the patient from head to heels, while his gin or some male friend, more usually the former, rubs it in with the flat of the hands, the massage, such as it is, lasting often well over a quarter of an hour : in addition to the external application of the remedy, the patient may drink some or even all of it, in the latter case postponing the " rubbing" portion of the treatment for a subsequent occasion. This blood-smearing cure is in vogue throughout North-West-Central Queensland. The Kalkadoon, in addition, apply a method, without rubbing, wherein the whole body, head included, is covered with red ochre. Sweat removed from under the armpits, and smeared in a similar manner as the blood, is also believed to have wonderful curative powers, especially *in extremis*, throughout all these districts. The drinking of seminal fluid in cases of sickness will be referred to in the ethno-pornographical chapter (sect. 305). Wet-cupping, by means of superficial incisions made by stone-knives, &c., is not infrequently practised over an inflamed and painful knee or shoulder-joint.

284. **Smearing of Fat.**—Iguana-, snake-, or any other kind of fat or grease, mixed more or less with mud and dirt, is used as a dressing for cuts and wounds of all description, the latter never been allowed to heal by " first intention": this custom of greasing an incision is very common everywhere. A clean-cut incised wound is called in the Pitta-Pitta language *koo-re-a*, while any open or punctured one, due to a boomerang or spear, is named *wil-pa*. Fat may also be employed as a liniment for rubbing over tired or aching limbs, and in such circumstances affords apparently speedy relief. Independently of sickness, the greasing of the bodies of children and infants is referred to in sect. 328.

285. **Poultices.**—The only application of a poultice that has come under observation is the practice prevailing among the Mitakoodi for the cure of a bad headache : some box-tree bark, subsequently to having been hammered and pounded, is soaked in hot water, and the mass so produced held with a piece of bark, cloth, &c., by the hand—not tied—to the particular part affected. On other occasions, in the same tribe, a bundle of heated fresh leaves may be tied on to the forehead for a similar purpose.

286. Amulets and Charms.—The *min-ma, min-ta-ra,* or *mul-ta-ra* consists of a bundle of emu feathers, either tied up loosely with opossum-string or enclosed in a curved spindle-shaped net (Fig. 403) tied on anywhere where pain may be; for instance, over the forehead for headache (Pitta-Pitta, *ka-ti-pul-ka-le-a*—*see* Vocabulary, sect. 44), over the belly for stomach-ache (Pitta-Pitta, *um-ba put-ya put-ya mul-le-a, tool-chi koon-di koon-di,* &c.—*see* Vocabulary, sect. 44). This charm is met with in the Boulia and Leichhardt-Selwyn Districts.

A rather rare amulet, the *mun-da-koo-e-a,* is of a flattened-spindle form, about 5 or 6 inches long, made of emu feathers, which, after been placed lengthways and bundlewise are wound round and round with opossum-string, and then coated all over with red-ochre grease: a slender piece of bone of some sort is occasionally enclosed in its centre. Originally, in the olden days, this was used as a sign of good faith to be forwarded to some other friendly tribe whose assistance was required in fighting a common enemy: in those times there was but one of them in each camp, and the privileged individual used to wear it on his chest, on which it would hang by means of a string passing round the neck. Subsequently this *mundakooea* came to have remedial properties attributed to it, and, worn in the similar position, has been gradually imitated and supplanted by the more common *wor-a-ka.* [Compare notes on death and burial (sect. 291) for the use of the *mundakooea* among the Mitakoodi.] The *woraka* (Fig. 404) is a similar implement to the preceding, but usually more rounded, and so may be described almost as cigar-shaped: it may also be painted as before, entirely red, or in transverse bands of alternately red and yellow colours. Worn over the chest it is used to relieve obscure pains, a troubling cough, &c., and, as a survival, may still be utilised for collecting aid in case of warfare. The *woraka,* its Boulia District name, is known as *u-la-ri* by the Kalkadoon, who also manufacture it; indeed, it is believed to have been introduced originally to the latter by their northern neighbours, the Workia.

287. Medicinal Plants.—The gum (Pitta-Pitta, *ko-ka*) of the blood-wood tree (Pitta-Pitta, *re-chin-di*) is used both as a local and internal application for venereal sores: in the former case it is used as powder and dusted on, in the latter it is boiled with water. This remedy is used on the Upper Georgina, and in the Cloncurry, Leichhardt-Selwyn, and Boulia Districts.

A species of "penny-royal" (Pitta-Pitta, *po-kan-gud-ye*) is drunk in the form of a decoction, like tea, with apparently very beneficial results, in coughs or colds (Pitta-Pitta, *ka-rin-ga-ri*): a very common remedy in the Boulia and Leichhardt-Selwyn Districts.

In the country of the Mitakoodi, the *u-ka-ta,* a species of rosella growing on the mountains, is also made a decoction of for the same purpose.

Similarly strongly-scented plants are used everywhere for "sniffing at" in cases of headache.

The belief is pretty common that any sort of grass or shrub growing near the water's edge will relieve difficult or painful micturition: various species of Euphorbia are the plants very frequently used for this purpose.

288. Clay-pills.—The aboriginal pharmacopæia for the District ends now with the huge clay or mud pills, one or two of which at a time are prescribed for diarrhœa: these pellets are certainly at least twice the size of those to be seen at any pharmaceutist's. Strange to say that in this respect the therapeutic value of the omnipresent Eucalyptus is unknown in the neighbourhood of Boulia: the Mitakoodi, on the other hand, for similar gastric disturbances, employ both gidyea and eucalyptus gum as well as clay pellets similar to those in use in the Boulia District.

289. Burial: (A) In the Boulia District.—In the Boulia District, when a blackfellow (male or female) dies, some bushes are heaped over a net spread out upon the ground, and on these the extended body is laid, the arms lying at the sides or down the front. Generally, by means of a spear, the net is fixed lengthways above, so as to enclose the corpse in a sort of net-sheet. Two or three men, side to side, carry the body, resting crossways usually on their heads to the burial-place, accompanied by the whole of the camp. The actual spot being now deter-mined upon, some set about digging a grave, while others assist in cutting logs and sticks from 3 to 6 feet long. The depth of the grave appears to vary with the nature of the soil, but about 4 feet is a fair average, though this is often greater. When all is ready, the body is laid in horizontally, face up, with the head pointing in the direction of the north: this is considered to be the orthodox " good-fellow" direction in which the body ought to lie, but too many die nowadays, and the survivors appear too lazy to trouble themselves concerning such details. Some of the longer logs cover the body in, then a layer or two of shorter ones are placed transversely, and next comes the filling up with earth : on top of all this are placed logs and bushes, perhaps some heavy stones, all closely interlaced, and reaching to a height of from 3 to 4 feet above the adjacent surface, which is cleared and cleaned to a distance of a few feet all the way round (Fig. 405). The reason given for the fixing of the logs, &c., is to prevent the corpse from being dug up and tampered with by the dingoes, while the expla-nation of the cleaned space is the prevention of the timber igniting in case of a bush-fire. The various goods belonging to the deceased—boomerangs, spears, &c.—are either buried with him, destroyed by fire, or sometimes, though rarely, distributed among his "brothers," but never his children. Furthermore, his personal individual name (autonym) dies with him, never to be again mentioned, a custom especially marked in the case of near relatives, who do not care to be reminded of the event : it was mainly owing to this circumstance that attempts at forming reliable con-clusions as to possible connections between personal individual names proved to be fruitless (sect. 67). Burial follows almost immediately upon death taking place, though if the closing scene occurs at night it is not carried out until early dawn. The corpse itself is in no ways decorated or painted.

At the grave, and while it is being dug, in the midst of the wailing and the weeping, the women will cut themselves with stone or glass down the outer and anterior aspects of the thighs, in numerous more or less parallel superficial incisions. In the neighbourhood of Glenormiston the women, previous to the cutting, have been known to wash their thighs with their own urine collected in the hands. These signs of grief with the females have their counterpart among the males at Carlo, Glenormiston, Herbert Downs, and Roxburgh, but apparently not at Boulia, who make a single large and much deeper crucial incision on the corresponding portion of the thigh : in the old days, before the advent of the whites, deaths were of infinitely less frequent occurrence than now, with the result that the old practice of a " cross" for each adult male deceased would now be impossible. Occasionally among the elder men one or two of these crucial incisions are still to be observed.

The actual burial being completed, they all return home with many a sob and tear, and plaster their heads with blobs of *pa-ta* or " kopi," a sort of gypsum, these lumps at a distance making the whole hair appear one mass of white. In any camp uncontaminated and away from the settlements, this plastering is adopted by all, no matter whether the deceased be man, woman, or child, though, as might have been expected, it is worn longer by some than by others, even up to six months sometimes in the case of gins mourning their husbands. Owing to this fixing up of the hair a mourner is spoken of as *pata-maro* —*i.e.*, plaster-possessor. In addition, the nearer relatives, and they only, colour-grease themselves down as far as to the waist, after the patterns for male and female respectively in Figs 407A.B. These nearer relatives, in the case of an adult male, are considered to be the wife, and his brothers and sisters by the same mother—not his father or mother : with an adult woman, only the brothers and sisters by the same mother, her husband contenting himself with the plastering. In the case of a young child, no painting would be adopted by anyone. So far as the pattern is concerned, the yellow grease is first of all smeared over by itself, the design being worked by a scraping off with the three or four clawed finger-tips like the teeth of a comb (*cf.* sect. 185) : the red is put on subsequently, and the design on both back and front is similar. An opossum-string armlet is tied on pretty tightly. Exclusive of the nearer relatives, in addition to the "kopi," or more usually when its supply runs short, greased ashes, or mud by itself, may be smeared over the whole body as external emblems of grief.

Crying and weeping, but no singing, is repeated nightly for a week or so, up to a fortnight perhaps, especially by the nearer relatives, who may repair to the grave for the purpose, the sisters continuing when the brothers cease : they generally go in parties to the burial-place, being afraid to go singly on account of seeing the deceased's *Moma* (sect. 260) possibly. Tobacco, matches, food, pituri, a pipe, &c., may be left each night at the grave-side, and the individual departed openly informed to that effect.

When an adult male dies in the Pitta-Pitta country, all his brothers and sisters are called *mun-na moor-ra*, a term literally signifying "no-good sticks," applied probably in reference to the logs lying upon the deceased's grave : his wife, a widow, is henceforth known as *ka-ri-ou-o*, and she remains one for a twelvemonth or more, until such time as another husband can be found for her.

290. (b) Of a Murderer.—When an individual has been killed by the whole tribe collectively—that is to say, in punishment for some serious crime—he is usually made to dig his own grave, which is subsequently closed in similar manner, except that boomerangs are substituted for the long logs immediately covering the corpse. Where, as in cases of murder, the assassin has been caught red-handed, the slayer and slain are buried together in the same grave, previously dug by the survivor after the customary method. In times of open hostilities, those who are killed are left on the field by their enemies, with broken spear or boomerang close beside to show the passing wayfarer how the individuals in question met their death. In the Pitta-Pitta language a grave is called *moorra-kumbo* (= stick-stone), a corpse *koon-ta*, and the act of dying, to die (also = to lie down), *e-che-*.

291. (c) In the Cloncurry District.—In the Cloncurry District, among the Mitakoodi, the corpse, *pa-ra-go* (the same name applied to a white man) is buried usually in a crouching position with head down, enclosed in a net perhaps, then covered with some ti-tree bark, and the earth thrown on top : no logs or sticks are piled up above, but the ground is smoothed to the level of the surrounding surface and a more or less circular area cleaned up. When night falls, a fire is lighted at a few yards' distance from the grave, and some meat, &c., hung up on a neighbouring tree : this may be repeated for three or four nights following, and occasionally now and again during the next few months, until it is believed in fact that the deceased "has got too old, has gone away somewhere else." In the olden days the women used to wear the gypsum as a sign of mourning, but nowadays both sexes only besmear themselves with mud, or else paint themselves red as far down as the waist : incisions used also to be made along the fronts of the thighs, several small superficial ones on the women, and two or three deep ones on the men. Where no visible or otherwise intelligible cause of death presents itself, one of the doctors will find out whether this is due to *Mulkari* or his counterpart who, in the Mitakoodi country, is believed to kill blacks, or to some human enemy with the *munguni* : in the latter case he would make-believe that he had picked up the particular incriminating gew-gaw in the neighbourhood of the grave, and accuse some individual of having committed the crime. In other cases, the near relatives of the deceased may learn something for themselves, by sticking upright a small forked stick on the grave itself, and on it placing a *mundakooea* (sect. 286) : this is done at night, and if on the following morning the *mundakooea* is found on the ground, it is proof positive that the late lamented met his death at the hands of an enemy "from a long way country."

292. (d) In the Upper Georgina District, along the river, from Carandotta upwards, tree-burial is practised. A sort of horizontal platform of logs is built in the tree about 10 or 12 feet from the ground, and upon this, wrapped in its net, &c., the corpse is laid : various sticks and bushes are placed on top, and in and among them the deceased's possessions may be enclosed. Fig. 406 represents a tree-grave which I found a little beyond Roxburgh : the body, that of an old Headingly or Carandotta boy, was lying with head to north-east and feet to south-west.   Among the Yaroinga I am informed by members of the tribe that, in special cases of important personages, when all the flesh has rotted off, the bones are subsequently removed and buried in the ground, with nothing on the surface to indicate their presence beneath. Gypsum is also used as a sign of mourning : the same custom prevails also in the Leichhardt-Selwyn District, though the Kalkadoons use red and yellow paint in addition.

293. Cannibalism.—Though the *primâ facie* evidence of the practice of cannibalism is very meagre, and any information concerning particulars is but charily given by the aboriginals, there is no doubt but that this custom, though gradually becoming more and more obsolete, certainly does take place within certain limitations throughout North-West-Central Queensland.   Thus in the Boulia district, especially with children who die suddenly from no lingering illness, portions of the corpse may be eaten by the parents and by their blood brothers and sisters only : the reason assigned is that " putting them along hole" would make them think too much about their beloved little ones, though unfortunately this is apparently contradicted by the fact that if the child has been ailing a long time previously and become emaciated, &c., it will be buried.   Proofs also are to hand that within the last ten years, since 1885, true-blooded aboriginal children have been killed, with the object of being eaten, at Noranside, Roxburgh, and Carandotta.   In the more northern areas half-caste infants are not uncommonly murdered at the present time, either at the instigation of their white fathers or their assumed black-blooded ones : but to what extent, in the latter case, for the main purpose of providing food, it is impossible to speak with certainty.   My friend Mr. Edwards, late of Roxburgh, is the only European who to my knowledge has been an eye-witness of such an orgie : this was in 1888, between Roxburgh and Carandotta, when he saw an infant being roasted in one of the native ovens, and subsequently watched the blacks opening the body and making for the fat, but he became too sick and faint to observe anything further.   With regard to people of maturer years, those who have died suddenly and who are in good condition at the time of death—not the old or the emaciated—may similarly be eaten : this rarely takes place in the Boulia or Cloncurry Districts nowadays, though many of the older men of these parts will relate numerous instances of its occurrence in the " early " times.   In the Leichhardt-Selwyn District, the Kalkadoon at the present time (1896) will eat any corpse, friend or foe, old or young, even in cases where the flesh is visibly rotten with venereal : *there is no doubt of this.*   Elsewhere individuals who have been killed in intertribal warfare are left exposed where they fall.   At Glen-ormiston, in 1892, on the occasion of a black having been killed by the tribe collectively for murder, a great debate was held as to whether the body should be eaten or not: it was only due to the presence upon the scene of the station-manager (Mr. J. Coghlan, from whom I received the report) that decided the question in the negative.   On the other hand, it is only fair to state that, so far as I have been able to gather information, I know of no case in North-West-Central Queensland where any adult male or female has been killed for the sole purpose of providing a repast.

CHAPTER XII.

RAIN-MAKING, THUNDER AND LIGHTNING-MAKING.

CONTENTS.—Sect. 294. Rain-making in the Boulia District. 295. At Roxburgh. 296. At Headingly, Lake Nash, &c. 297. In the Leichhardt-Selwyn District. 298. Thunder and Lightning-making.

294. Rain-making: (A) In the Boulia District.—With the exception of perhaps a few of the Yunda tribe, there are no individuals in the Boulia District who know how to make rain. When rain is wanted here at Boulia, word is sent down to the Miorli men at Springvale or the Diamantina Gates to come up and make some. This special performance, carried out with a rain-stick (Fig. 408A.), a song, and a dance, takes place somewhat as follows:—The rain-stick, *koo-roo-mun-do*, is formed of a thin piece of a species of "white" wood, about 20 inches long, on to the top of which is fixed a mass of the ordinary cementing-substance: into this the three "rain-stones," pieces of white quartz-crystal, are stuck. Hair cut from the beard is next laid lengthwise on to the cement, and fixed an inch or so below it: over this again are laid leafy branches of "white" wood which is all tied round with string, somewhat after the manner of a straw broom. Three or four of such sticks may be used in the ceremony. At about mid-day, the men proceed to a secluded waterhole, one or more of their number having been previously deputed to dive into the water and fix a hollowed log, about the length and thickness of a man's arm, vertically down into the mud. They now all get into the water, and, surrounding the central individual, who holds the rain-stick, in more or less of a circle, commence proceedings with a stamping movement of the feet, each performer keeping the same relative position to the others: considering that the water may be sometimes 4 or more feet in depth, the "dancing" is maintained with no inconsiderable difficulty. During this part of the performance the water is splashed with their hands, from all sides, onto the *koo-roo-mun-do* held vertically on high by the central figure: there is a singing accompaniment to this, but the Pitta-Pitta men are evidently ignorant of its exact literal purport. The singing over, the central figure dives out of sight, and attaches the rain-stick into the hollow log already fixed there: coming to the surface again he quickly climbs on to the bank, and spits out on dry land the water which while diving he had obtained from below. Should more than one of these rain-sticks have been prepared, the performance is repeated with each in turn. As they return to camp they now and again with a small twig, of any description, just scratch the tops of their heads and the inner aspects of their shins, singing "*pŭn*-jō-pâ-rĭ *pŭn*-jō-pâ-rĭ" (*cf.* Miorli *pun-ja*, the hair of the head, sect. 52) in the former case, and "*wŏn*-kă-pâ-rĭ" in the latter (*cf.* Kalkadoon *wung-ka*, the shin or leg, sect. 52): it is believed that if the scratching were to be done with the fingers direct, it would spoil the whole ceremony. On the arrival of the party back at camp, the men who have been taking part in it paint themselves with gypsum in thick bands: from the top of the head down the middle of the face and neck as far as the umbilicus, a second transverse one over the face across the bridge of the nose, and a third and fourth drawn from the extremities of the last-mentioned down the side of the neck over the shoulder along the front and outer aspects of the arm and forearm to the wrist. During the rest of the day, the scratching process, accompanied by the singing, is repeated at intervals, and the performance comes to a close. No woman is allowed to set eyes on the rain-stick or the ceremony of its submergence; the wife of the "boss" rain-maker may, however, join in the subsequent twig-scratching. There would appear to be no special individual among the Miorli who alone can make the rain: any of the tribe can learn the process, and when once in possession of one of these pieces of white quartz will be successful. When the rain does eventually fall, the *kvoroomundo* is removed from out of the water. At Boulia, during the heavy floods and rains of January and February, 1895, I was assured on native authority that all the rain and water had as usual been produced by the Miorli men: when I begged of them to immediately stay proceedings, the reply came that as the flood had come up too quickly to allow of the removal of the rain-stick from out of its submerged position, the rain would have to run its course! Instead of coming up to Boulia, the Miorli rain-makers may visit Marion Downs: from the former locality they may proceed for similar purposes to Warenda, Noranside, Chatsworth, &c.

295. (B) **At Roxburgh** the following variation of the ceremony may be noted:— A piece of white stone, a kind of white quartz-crystal, the rain-stone obtained from somewhere out in the ranges, is crushed and hammered to powder. Some very straight-stemmed tree is chosen—generally a blood-wood tree with the butt for a long way up free from branches—and saplings from 15 to 20 feet in length are ranged all round it in the form of a bell tent, forming a sort of shed. Outside, in front of this erection, a small space of ground is cleared, a portion scooped out, and some water placed in it. The men, having been previously collected within the shed, now come out, and, dancing and singing all around the artificial waterhole, break out with the sounds and imitate the antics of various aquatic birds and animals, such as ducks, frogs, &c. All this time the women are encamped at from about 20 to 25 yards away. The men next form themselves into a long string, Indian file, one behind the other, and gradually encircle the gins, over whom they throw the crushed and pulverised stone. The women simultaneously hold koolamons, shields, pieces of bark, &c., over their heads, and " gammon " that they are protecting themselves from a heavy downpour of rain.

296. (c) **At Headingly, Lake Nash, &c..,** among the Yaroinga, the rain-making corrobboree always take place at night, commencing with sun-down and finishing with sun-rise. Furthermore, the men, who alone take part in it, are decorated with red and white feathers stuck on with blood in the usual manner (sect. 185), according to the design represented in Fig. 408B. A basis of white over the face, neck, arms, chest, and trunk down to the waist, with two parallel vertical bands of red passing down the centre. On the head is worn a thick roll of emu-feathers, a sort of minma (sect. 286), with one wild-turkey feather stuck on top, to the shaft of which are attached five or six long opossum-string streamers falling down the back. To the usual hair belt are fixed an eagle-hawk feather bundle (sect. 183) at either side, and one of white-cockatoo feathers in front. This rain-corrobboree was " found " in these districts a very long time ago, and hence my informants could render me no interpretation of the song accompanying the performance.

297. (D) **In the Leichhardt-Selwyn District** some of the Kalkadoon can also make rain. The feather-down of the emu is stuck with blood over the whole face, neck, and chest, back and front, down to the waist, including the arms as far as the wrists. The performance, in which two or three old men, never young men or women, take part, is carried out at mid-day, when the sun is high up. They were taught the proper song from the Workia at Carandotta, and so are ignorant of its meaning. At Devoncourt, a sort of soap-stone rubbed with fat is believed to be brought into requisition.

It is true, when all is said and done, that as a rule rain generally follows upon these performances, but then it must be remembered that the rain corrobboree is only held at certain seasons of the year, when to the elders, i.e., the more experienced, the clearer-witted, the various atmospheric phenomena afford a likely indication of its advent.

298. **Thunder and Lightning-making.**—Many Mitakoodi, and several Kalkadoon, are firmly persuaded that other blacks, both of their own and other tribes, can make thunder and lightning: when pressed for the objects and aims of such occurrences, I was assured that they were to drive out the white settlers. In this connection it is interesting to note that the Kalkadoon speak of any European as *yun-yi*, a word synonymous with " bogie "-man, ghost, &c., while the Mitakoodi speak of him as *pa-ra-go*, a corpse (sect. 291); considering how the aboriginals in these parts have up to recent times been treated, these terms are not to be wondered at.

AUTHOR'S NOTE.—*The following chapter is not suitable for perusal by the general lay reader.*

CHAPTER XIII.

ETHNO-PORNOGRAPHY.

299. Degrees of Social Rank.—When the individual reaches the full development of puberty, he or she undergoes a ceremony which entitles him or her on its successful completion to a certain social rank or status in the community. As life progresses, other and higher ranks or degrees are progressively attainable for each sex, until the highest and most honourable grade, that enjoyed by an old man, or an old woman, is reached. Special terms—"climanyms"—are applied for each grade or degree (sect. 68), such names varying with each ethnographical district.

There are four social stages for each individual, male or female, to be initiated into, and it may be many years before all these ceremonials and corresponding grades are reached and passed. It is true that the details of procedure taking place at the initiations into the third and fourth degrees are meagre as compared with the first and second, but the aboriginals were always very chary of imparting information concerning these higher grades even to me who had become intimately connected with them through a knowledge of their written and sign languages and other causes. Further difficulties to be reckoned with were the facts that:—with the gradual depletion of the aboriginal population, the initiation ceremonies of the higher ranks are gradually becoming obsolete, those for the females especially being already very marked; that individuals belonging to the higher grades and consequently older people are not too commonly met with; and that no one is allowed to be present or to assist in the initiation of any degree higher than that of which he is himself a member. As far as my personal knowledge goes, in North-West-Central Queensland the procedures of the first and second degrees only are permitted to be viewed by Europeans.

Before any individual can reach the next higher social stage than that of which he is a member, he must himself pass through all the duties of assisting in the initiating of others into the same rank as himself, until, by reason of his age, he comes to be the leader, chief director, or master of the ceremonies appertaining to his own degree: this coveted distinction having been once attained, he may be admitted into the next rank or degree at the first opportunity which presents itself. Sometimes there will be as many as three or four men accepted into the accorded rank all at the same time. It may be many years, even up to old age, before all the social stages are reached.

There are no pass-words or signs, beyond the presence of certain objects of decoration or attire, by which the members of the different ranks are to be recognised, such information becoming public by word of mouth: every means of

cross-examination has been used to satisfy me on this point.   Furthermore, let it
be borne in mind, that in this portion of Queensland at all events, the knocking
out of the two upper incisor teeth (sect. 177) as well as the cutting of the
" flash"-marks or " brands" (sect. 186) on the shoulders and breast, are
independent of the various ceremonials which give an individual his social status
in the community.

   300. The First Ceremonial (male) (A) in the Boulia District. In the Pitta-Pitta
tribe, as soon as a boy begins to shew signs of puberty in the growth of the pubic
hair, &c., he is known as *koo-e-ri :* at the full development of this physiological
epoch, the commencing moustache, beard, &c., he is called *yup-pi-e-ri,* and the
first ceremonial publicly celebrates this to him important event.   For the first
time in his life, a grass-necklace is put round the novitiate's neck, below this an
opossum-string fringed-necklace hanging over the upper portion of his chest, a
human-hair belt is wound round his waist, a bunch of white-cockatoo feathers is
stuck into his hair, while some white-feather down is fixed on with blood in the
form of a band reaching from shoulder to shoulder (Fig 409).   He must not leave
the camp or his people now, although he may accompany them to fetch up
some friendly neighbouring tribe to join in the ceremony.   In the meantime,
at some distance from the main-camp an *er-rul-li* is built : this is a sort
of bush fence or palisading, in the form of an arc, about 3½ to 4 feet high
and about 30 or more feet long.   Within this enclosure the elder men of the tribe
are sitting, the women either straggling round outside, or else joining (Fig. 410 F)
in bringing up the visitors.   During the latter end of the afternoon, as the
" friendlies" come up, the novitiate is hoisted on to one of the men's shoulders, with
calves dangling over his carrier's chest (same position as in Fig. 419) and leads
the procession ; the other men all follow in Indian-file, and, stamping the feet
as they come up, circle round the *errulli* (Fig. 410 c, D) in front of which they
perform an evolution.   During this procession the singing is done by the men
within the enclosure: it runs as follows :—"nâ-lĭ-lĭ-*lĭn*-jă nâ-lĭ-lĭ-*lĭn*-jă tĭl-pă-*rou*-ĭ
tĭl-pă-*rou*-ĭ," but unfortunately, like all the songs in these initiation ceremonies,
its meaning is unintelligible even to the singers themselves.   As sundown comes
on, the gins' corrobboree commences, the men all sitting down by themselves close
up in the *errulli* around a fire (Fig. 410 E) while the novitiate shifts his position to
some yards further back (Fig 410 A to B) where he sits by himself: the women
now emerge from behind either side of the enclosure, all dressed and painted as
in the Boulia District corrobboree-costume proper (sect. 193, Fig. 287). and dance
to the accompaniment of the men's voices singing " jĭn-ĭn-gŏ-*á*-ra jĭn-ĭn-gŏ-*á*-ra
lâm-*pā*-ră," &c.   This concluded, the evening meal is partaken of, and all together,
both men and women, go to sleep within the palisading; the novitiate alone sleeps
by himself close up to, but not within, the fence.   About the middle of the night,
the proceedings re-commence, the women dancing as they did at sundown, but
instead of coming from behind the "wings," they advance from the front, and
dance in the fire-light to the men singing the same song as on the previous
afternoon.   The singing and dancing continue till daylight, when the gins,
after returning to the main-camp and collecting all the spears, boomerangs,
shields, and other weapons, remove to a distance remote from both camp
and enclosure, in order to decorate themselves after the manner of warriors
about to fight, *i.e.,* with white bands of gypsum upon the thighs, chest, face
(sect. 238).   These would-be amazons next pretend that they are black-fellows
going to engage in combat, and shout " Hoo! hoo! hoo!" as they advance up to
the enclosure, also making pretence of fighting one with the other and using their
weapons.   At last they get closer and closer, and, after circling round the *errulli*
in Indian-file just as they did in the procession of the previous day, squat down
for some little time behind the novitiate : when sufficiently rested they depart once
more to the main-camp.   The novitiate next lies on his back on the ground, and
one by one the elder men, *i.e.,* those that have been " whistled" (sect. 317, &c.),
pass over him from foot to head—the lad is really between their legs—and as they
pass (Fig. 411), each keeps on jagging the cicatrix of his introcised penis more
or less transversely with a piece of flint, &c., thus covering him almost completely
with the sprinkled blood : there may be as many as a score of men engaged in

this performance. The young man is now taken away to where the women are located, and though he stays with them alone all day until sundown, he is on no account allowed to take any liberties with them. If any "introcision" is to be done on any other members of the tribe, it is performed now within the enclosure while the women are absent. During the remainder of the day, the men "paint" themselves in readiness for sundown. Their costume consists of a head ornament of white-cockatoo feathers, a grass necklace, human-hair waist-belt, and large phallocrypt; the face, back and front of chest, and mid-thigh are covered with white feather-down stuck on by means of blood, varied with a cross-band of charcoal on the two former situations, and with three transverse bands on the latter (Fig. 412). At sundown, thus decorated, they go and fetch the novitiate, and the whole company, both men and women sit down once more within the precincts of the palisading. Both sexes in the same locality now join in dancing to the song of " koo-*lŭp*-pō-*lŭp*-pō wâ-*pool*-kâ mâ-rĕn-*jŭn*-nă" while the novitiate sitting on the open thighs of a fellow-aboriginal (Fig. 413), in company with four or five other men, is located at some little distance in front. On the completion of this dance, two of these men walking side-by-side carry the young man in their arms close up to the fence, swinging him laterally to-and-fro as they advance (Fig. 414) to the accompaniment of themselves and others singing " wŭl-pâ-*kĕr*-rŭm *bĭl*-lĭ jŭn-*châ*-lă." The men all dance now until supper-time for which meal they repair to camp, the women (finished now completely with the present ceremony) having slipped away some time previously to get it ready. After supper all the men return to the enclosure with the novitiate, and keep up the dancing and singing—"*lŭm*-mŭng-tă *noor*-pă ră-*lĭn*-yă," &c., without interruption until daylight. Should the women by any chance put in an appearance too early in the morning, some of the men would swing the "whirlers" (sect. 215), the sound of which they know is a signal for them to retire. At the first streak of daylight a fighting-pole (sect. 255) is brought forward on the scene, and fixed firmly and deeply into the ground : from five to six men circle round, and, clasping this protruding stick with their hands, bend their heads forwards and downwards towards each other, so that their backs form a sort of living table—very much after the manner of a football "scrimmage." (Diagram Fig. 415.) Upon this human table the novitiate is laid face up, and the operator sitting astride his chest performs circumcision by removing the fore-skin, held on the stretch with one hand, by a sweep of the stone-knife held in the other. The hæmorrhage being arrested with hot dry mud, the blood-father now gives the fully-fledged *yuppieri* his autonym, or individual personal name (sect. 67) which he maintains for the rest of his life. The *errulli* is next set on fire and, enveloped in flames, soon becomes razed to the ground. During the whole of this, the first of the male initiation ceremonies (the only one of the four which is compulsory on all males when arrived at the suitable physiological stage), the novitiate is only allowed to converse orally with his blood-father, -mother, -sisters, and -brothers. The newly-made *yuppieri* leaves camp until his wounds are completely healed. Henceforth, as the privileges of his rank or social standing in the community, he may wear certain ornaments, *e.g.*, the grass-necklace, human-hair waist-belt, opossum-string phallocrypt, and other opossum-twine articles ; he may furthermore reside in camp and he may marry provided he gets introcised (see *moon-do, nul-la ma-ro, me-ko ma-ro*, in Pitta-Pitta vocabulary).

301. (B) **In the Upper Georgina District.** The following relates only to that portion of the rite which deals with the circumcision as it is carried out at **Roxburgh** and surrounding neighbourhood. About half-an-hour before sunrise any young lad is taken out of the camp and placed standing with his face towards the east to watch for the rising of the sun. At the same time one of the oldest men brings out three stone-knives, which are handed round to be passed sideways through the lips ("kissed," as it were) of all the elder males present. The same old man now produces the fighting-pole, plants it into the ground close to where the watcher stands, and directs the lad how to hold it : returning to the main body of the males he brings up from five to seven boys separately, showing each in turn how to hold the stick, and arranging that all their shoulders should be quite level. These preliminaries are all carried out in strict

silence. The boys chosen to hold the stick are amongst the youngest available:
that is, though they themselves have all been circumcised, they have not yet
arrived at suitable age to permit of their viewing what is about to take place. In
the meantime, the young fellow about to be circumcised has been lying on the
ground at some distance away, but as soon as the sun . begins to peep up
he is carried forward to the required spot by three of the elders walking abreast,
one supporting the head and shoulders, the middle one the loins and buttocks,
and the third one the legs. He is next lifted on to this human table with his face
to the skies. One of these old men now sits astride the chest, and with both
hands pulls the novitiate's fore-skin on the stretch upwards to its greatest limit,
while another elder, standing on the ground, plunges a stone-knife through its
centre, thus, with one sweep, removing the whole of the portion necessary. The
boy initiated does not see the actual operator. Owing to the extreme tension to
which the part is subjected, coupled with the laceration due to the flint-edge,
there is but little hæmorrhage, such as there is being controlled with feather-down,
opossum-hair, &c. When the operation is completed, the newly-fledged *ur-goo-ta*
walks to a remote corner of the camp and two whirlers (Figs. 318, 319) are
sounded as a signal to the women that the ceremony is now over.

302. Among the Yaroinga tribe at **Headingly** and surrounding district, the
complete ceremony may be described shortly as follows. As soon as a few hairs
are visible upon the upper lip, the time is considered ripe for the lad to be
initiated. · He is decorated from the human-hair waist-belt up with a ground-
work of white feather-down interspersed by bands of red-dyed feather-down
arranged in particular pattern (Fig. 416) together with a head-decoration of a
small bundle of white feathers in front, and a large single one stuck in on top
further back. When the women first gaze upon the lad thus ornamented they all
begin to cry, and so do his immediate relatives, his father and mother's brothers,
who further smear themselves over with grease and ashes to express their grief.
He is next packed off for two or three days, not for a moment dreaming of what is
in store for him, and told to gather a lot more of the tribesmen and other visitors
who, understanding the interpretation of the ornamentation, return with him.
That same night, the hair-belt is taken off, and he is again shown to the women
encamped at their fires previously to sleeping apart by himself. All next day he
remains in the company of six women, who allow no liberties of course, and who
at sundown lead him up to the bush-palisading that has in the meantime been
erected, and place him in position. Dancing and singing are now engaged in,
the corrobboree continuing until day-light, when the women all depart, and
the actual circumcision takes place. The method of procedure varies slightly
now from that in vogue in the Boulia District. Three pairs of men stand
close to one another, faces almost touching, each grasping tightly the fighting
pole fixed firmly into the ground: their shoulders and necks are all slightly
bent so that the six heads may form a sort of table upon which a large shield
is placed face upwards. Upon this implement the lad is now placed lengthways, with the result that his head and arms are dangling over one extremity
of the shield, while his legs are hanging over the other, each limb, as well
as the head, being in addition held in position by four or five other individuals
standing outside the central six (Diagram Fig. 417). The operator now sits
astride as before, and pinching up a small piece of the novitiate's fore-skin, shaves
it off in such way with a stone knife as to leave a small aperture: into this
aperture the tip of the knife is inserted and the redundant skin removed while on
the stretch. The wound is dressed with charcoal ashes. From being an *o-we-a*,
the individual is now an *ur-goo-ta*, and can wear the certain prescribed ornaments,
e.g., the human-hair waistbelt, the grass-necklace, the opossum-string phallocrypt,
&c. Furthermore, unlike the practices in the Boulia District, the *urgoota* is now
betrothed to his future gin by her mother, and though he is not yet permitted to
cohabit, he supports her in victuals.

303. (c) **In the Cloncurry District.** Among the Mitakoodi, any very
small infant, boy or girl, is a *ka-ta-go*. A boy at the first sign of pubic hair
is called *kung-gi* or *kur-rung-ga*: (*mung-gun* is a girl at the corresponding

period.) *Kun-ta-kul-poo-roo* is the term applied to a boy at the full development of puberty, there being no similarly applicable term, I believe, for the female. This first ceremonial may be described somewhat on the following lines. The *kuntakulpooroo*, after being caught by some older blackfellow, who sticks a single cockatoo feather into the novitiate's hair, is taken away with a number of *kurrungga* to fetch up some other mob of visitors, occupying some days perhaps to complete the journey: from Cloncurry, for instance, they may travel to Grenada, to Devoncourt, and other places equally distant. During this peregrination, the *kuntakulpooroo* wears no decoration or paint of any description, except the cockatoo feather, the *kurrungga* on the other hand being decked with the *che-ka-ra* chest-ornament (sect. 182) and the *moon-do-lo* waist-belt (sect. 183). On the return home, the elders proceed to the original camping-ground, while the particular novitiate, together with his younger companions, is left at some little distance behind, whither, during the next day or two, food is brought out to them. In the meantime the usual bush-fence is built, the whole camp lending a hand in its construction: the palisading is known among this tribe as the *il-la-ri* (Fig. 418), and differs from that previously described (sect. 300) in being longer, more horseshoe-shaped, and higher at its centre—a height of 12 feet is not uncommon —whence it tapers down towards either extremity. When all is ready, the sun being well below the horizon, the majority of the men get each a piece of bark, set fire to it, and throw it up into the air: this performance being done only outside the enclosure, presents somewhat the appearance of "stars" to the women and other males seated within. After this "star-business" the youngsters are brought up to a spot a little in advance of the *illari* entrance whence each *kurrungga* is carried on some elder fellow-brother's shoulders (Fig. 419), with calves dangling over his bearer's chest, one after the other to where the women are seated within. The *kuntakulpooroo* is brought in last, in similar manner, and made to lie down on his side on the ground with his eyes shut and one hand on his mouth, and allowed neither to speak, move, nor even to scratch himself throughout the night: he is being watched all this time by two of the elders, and should he disobey instructions he would be caught sooner or later with the dreaded "death-bone," and surely die. But while the watching of the novitiate is going on, the remaining elder males sing and the women cry, the singing and wailing continuing all night: the three first verses of the song are " *kĭn-jä-lä wŭng-*gŭn-mŭl-lĭ, *kŭng-gō kou-*â nŭl-lĭl-pă-*wŏl-*lä, *wă-tă nŭn-*ār-gō *kō-rō,*" but the translations offered me were unmistakeably empirical. At the first streak of daylight, a cry of " pĭ-rĭ-pĭrrr......rrou" is made, and immediately after its utterance, all the females return to the main camp. Both *kuntakulpooroo* and *kurrungga* are painted now as in Fig. 420, and each carried on his elder fellow-brother's shoulders as before, round and round the enclosure to which a firebrand is next put and the whole construction burnt. The *kurrungga* are then allowed to run away by themselves to their own camping ground, apart from the women, while the novitiate (supported by two elder blacks holding him under the arm-pits, and accompanied by the main body of the males following close behind) is rushed headlong as hard as he can be made to go in a direction other than that of the main camp or where the *kurrungga* have betaken themselves. All day and night he is here left by himself, unless of course another *kuntakulpooroo* happens to be initiated at the same time, and food brought to him. At daylight next morning the crowd of elder males visits him, and he is dressed now with the single head-feather, the *jum-mul* opossum-hair armlet (sect. 181) tied on as tight as possible (though he must not even wince with the pain) and the grass-necklace, but no belt: human blood is next smeared over him from top to toe. Thus decorated he is carried on his brother's shoulders as before, and brought up to a fire lighted in full view of the women. His carrier then falls on one knee and, bending forwards, "gammons" to put his burden into the fire: after holding him thus for a few seconds, he rushes on a little distance and lets the novitiate down. The newly-made *yup-pi-e-ri* hurries away still further by crawling on his hands and knees, and stays away from the main camp for a week or so, though during this interval he comes up regularly at night. From this time onwards, until he gets a full beard, he may only converse with those who are not *cha-lin,* i.e., fellow-brother (sect. 63, Table 4) to him.

304. (D) In the Leichhardt-Selwyn District. Among the Kalkadoons any little boy is a *koo-e-ri* : at full puberty and after the first initiation ceremony he is called a *yup-pa-ra-ri* (*cf. yup-pi-e-ri*). Within the bush-fence or *pa-li*, from six to ten fighting poles are stuck around in more or less of a circle, only just big enough to allow of one old man to crouch down on his hands and knees within it. At each stick, projecting from 18 inches to 2 feet out of the ground, a young boy fixes his hands, and bends his head well down towards the central individual. The novitiate is then laid upon their respective shoulders, and, supported in addition by the old man directly underneath, is operated on as before. Circumcision is known as *wa-ko*. The *yupparari* can henceforth wear the grass necklace, &c.

305. The First Ceremonial (female) (A) in the Boulia District. Among the Pitta-Pitta and neighbouring tribes there is no special corrobboree for this as in the case of the males. A *mi-ri* (in the Pitta-Pitta language) is a young girl when she first begins to show signs of puberty in the commencing development of the breasts, the presence of pubic hair, &c.: the *ka-na-ri* (Pitta-Pitta) is a young woman at full development of this physiological state. Two or three men manage to get the young woman, when thus ripe enough, all alone by herself away in the bush, and, throwing her down, one of them forcibly enlarges the vaginal orifice by tearing it downwards with the first three fingers wound round and round with opossum-string (*cf.* introcision in the male—sects. 317-322). Other men come forwards from all directions, and the struggling victim has to submit in rotation to promiscuous coition with all the "bucks" present: should any sick individual be in camp, he would drink the bloody semen collected from her subsequently in a koolamon (sect. 289). At this ceremony, any male of any other paedomatronym (sect. 62) than the woman's, except a blood-relative, is permitted to have connection: should, however, a male be present from some distant tribe, and yet belong to the same paedomatronym, he also is allowed to indulge in the common orgie. The celebration of the *kanari* stage, like that of the corresponding male *yuppieri*, is the only one which the tribe insists upon absolutely for all females, the higher ranks not being obligatory. She now has attained the degree in which she is allowed to marry, and can henceforth wear the grass necklace, the human-hair belt, the opossum-string necklet, belt, &c.: she receives no new name, however, like the male (sect. 300). Among the Ulaolinya, as well as those tribes around Glenormiston, any ordinary corrobboree is held during the day-time, and the young woman who has been fixed upon (at full development of puberty, of course) is decoyed by some old woman to come outside the main body of the camp for the purpose of collecting pappa-seed, &c. She is stealthily followed by two or three men who, suddenly pouncing upon her, seize her by the wrists while other bucks, till now in ambush, come rushing upon the scene: she at once realises her position, and, despite all shrieks and intreaties, is thrown on her back on to the ground, the old chaperone clearing away to a distance. Four "bucks" hold one on to each limb, while another presses upon her stomach so as to compel her to draw her legs up: her thighs are now drawn apart and her eyes covered so as to prevent her seeing the individual, probably a very old man, who is beckoned up from some hiding-place to come and operate directly everything is ready. This he does by slitting up a portion of the perineum with a stone-knife, and sweeping his three fingers round inside the vaginal orifice. Before this ceremony the woman was a *wa-pa-ri* : she is now a *ka-na-ri*, her attainment of full puberty having been publicly celebrated. She is next compelled to undergo copulation with all the bucks present; again the same night, and a third time, on the following morning. In the first interval she is ornamented as in Fig. 421, the pattern being worked in bands of charcoal and feather-down of red and white, the latter being stuck on with the blood, &c., obtained from her lacerated vagina. Subsequently to the multi-copulation, the semen is collected into a koolamon, mixed with water, and drunk as medicine: should there be no sick fellows in camp, it is preserved in the vessel until required. The *kanari* receives no new name in this tribe, like the boy does when he is correspondingly initiated (sect. 300): she is, however, entitled to wear the various opossum-string ornaments, the kangaroo teeth on her forehead, the side-bones attached to the hair at the temples, and the grass necklace.

306. (B) In the Upper Georgina District. Among the Yaroinga, three men under the leadership of one of her future husband's brothers catch the young woman, at the period of suitable physical development, and throw her down lengthways, face upwards upon the back of one of them lying face downwards on the ground, where she is held in position (Fig. 422). The actual operator, sitting astride the woman's chest and neck cuts with a stone-knife into the perineum downwards and forwards, turning the implement slightly upwards at the close of the incision. The hæmorrhage is staunched with emu-feathers plugged into the wound. She is next of all feather-decorated according to the design in Fig. 423, in red, white, and bluish-green colours—the last mentioned pigment being obtained from some form of copper ore. On the completion of this ornamentation she is temporarily on loan to her future husband's friends and others in camp, but there would appear to be no subsequent collection of the semen, as in the other districts. The woman, previously an *ul-la-ok-a*, is now an *umb-ba*, and entitled to wear the white fore-head band, &c.

307. (c) In the Leichhardt-Selwyn District. With the Kalkadoon tribe there is no special corrobboree, &c., but the young woman, the *wom-pa* (? or *un-do*) is just seized upon and cut, and publicly proclaimed an *e-ra-ji*.

308. (D) At Birdsville, &c., a wooden stick of very hard wood about two feet long, with a representation of the extremity of a life-sized penis rudely carved at the top, and thinned all the way down to the handle (Fig. 424), is used for the purpose of tearing down the hymen and posterior vaginal wall.

309. Remarks on the Vaginal Laceration. The commonest reason assigned by the aboriginals themselves for this locally-universal practice of lacerating the vaginal orifice, *i.e.*, female introcision (sect. 316), is to make him "big-fellow" not only for the convenience of the escaping progeny, as the men will allege, but also for the progenitor, as the women will say. Among the Ulaolinya it would appear that the women are not operated on when old, when they have already undergone sufficient sexual connection, *i.e.*, in those cases where they have returned to their old camping-grounds after having left them with Europeans and others when of tender age; on the other hand, a report reaches me from Mr. Craigie, at Roxburgh (1894), of a case where a gin upwards of forty years of age, belonging originally to a coastal tribe, was unexpectedly seized upon one night, soon after the death of her husband, and, despite all struggles and protestations, operated on in the usual manner. Whatever the original signification should prove to be, there is no doubt, especially with the use of the stone-knife, that the perineum itself is actually lacerated and cut, *i.e.*, more or less ruptured. I have had dozens of opportunities for making suitable examination in cases of venereal disease and verifying the fact, but as to how far the occasional large extent of the rupture was intentional or accidental on the part of the original operator it is of course useless to express an opinion.

310. The Second Ceremonial (male and female) (A) in the Boulia District: Pitta-Pitta tribe. At about tea-time, having chosen the particular *yuppieri* and *kanari* —there may be several of both—whom they are about to initiate into the next higher grade, the elders stick some broken and torn emu-feathers all over the novitiates' heads. In some locality remote from where the *erruli* (sect. 300) originally stood a *kel-pi* has been already built—this is a horse-shoe shaped enclosure constructed of bushes, &c., reaching to a height of about 7 or 8 feet (*cf.* the *illari* sect. 303), and a fire is lighted close to the entrance. The elder males having feather-painted themselves, now hold a corrobboree in front of the palisading, one portion of the dance consisting of their going down on their knees and thus progressing forwards with simultaneous raised and outstretched arms: their attire is shown in Fig. 425, with a head-decoration in the form of a forehead net (sect. 169), a human-hair belt, and large opossum-string phallocrypt (sect. 184), the portion of the body not feathered being smeared over with red-ochre grease as far as the wrists and ankles. From the fact that all during this ceremony there is some special form of head-dress not only for the performers but also for the novitiate he or she is spoken of now and henceforth, *i.e.*, until attaining the third grade, as the *ka-ti-ka-ti ma-ro* (Pitta Pitta language *ka-ti* = "head"; and *ma-ro*=sign of possession). The dancing being completed they all return to the main camp to sleep, leaving only the newly-made *ka-ti-ka-ti ma-ro* youth, the woman not being troubled about, to sleep all by himself within the *kelpi*. Here he remains by himself alone until early the next afternoon, when he is joined inside the enclosure by the women. The remaining males, who in the meantime have been re-ornamenting themselves, now come up in pairs, dancing but not singing, to behind the palisading, and then separate, each individual advancing round either side and meeting his mate at the entrance. The appearance of one of these fellows is shown in Fig. 426: he is feathered, &c., as in the local Boulia style (sect. 193, Fig. 283), but down to the waist only, the remainder of the body being red-ochre greased, while for decorations he wears the head-net (sect. 168), into which some shag's tail feathers are stuck, the human-hair belt, and the opossum-string phallocrypt: there are no bushes, &c., at the wrists or ankles. When these two meet at the *kelpi* entrance in full view of the women and novitiate or novitiates inside, one throws a spear which the other catches on his shield : they then retire to make room for the next pair who advance from behind in the same manner, and so on. But while this performance is going on, each woman can exercise her right of punishing any man who may have ill-treated, abused, or "hammered" her, and for whom she may have waited months or perhaps years to chastise : for, as each pair appear round the corner at the entrance exposed to her view, the woman and any of her female friends may take a fighting-pole and belabour the particular culprit to their hearts' content, the delinquent not being allowed to retaliate in any way whatsoever—the only occasions in the whole of her life when the woman can take the law into her own hands without fear or favour. By the time that the last pair have completed their part, three men advance from the front towards the *kelpi* entrance, and having enacted their particular dance retire. These three individuals are decorated with charcoal, interspersed with white feather-down bands (Fig. 427), the body below the waist and below the elbows being greased with red-ochre, and bearing a hair-belt and phallocrypt: the leader of the trio alone sports a curious head-ornament, the *ta-ka-le* (sect. 173), in the form of two more or less horizontally-inclined sticks fixed cross-wise, &c., with intermediate strings somewhat after the fashion of a spider-web. The women in company with the novitiate then betake themselves to the main camp, all the men removing to the enclosure now rendered vacant, where, hidden from view, they again re-decorate themselves after a new pattern (Fig. 428). This consists of a wedge-shaped charcoal mark, both back and front, from neck down, the rest of the body being red-greased, while twigs and leaves are tied round the waist and arms, and a small bunch of grass tucked behind the forehead net: the leader of the ceremony alone bears a *ta-ka-le*, though a much smaller one than on the previous occasion. The dressing over, the men turn out of the *kelpi* and retire to make room for the women and novitiate, who now enter it again. Shortly after, the leader with another elder advance once more up to the enclosure-entrance, one throws the spear, the other's shield intercepts it, and then they fall back : another pair advance, go through the same performance, and so on throughout their number, the women coming out to chastise any individual they have "a down on," in the same manner as they did a few hours before. When the last pair have fallen back, the women retire to the camp for good and all, leaving the *kati-kati maro* in the enclosure to be soon joined by the males who tell him to go to sleep—*i.e.*, to close his eyes and hide his face—so as not to see the performance which follows, this belonging to a degree higher than that to which he has as yet attained—viz., the third, or fourth. On the conclusion of certain songs and dances, the fully-fledged *kati-kati maro* being ordered to depart and shelter under some nook, &c., they proceed to pull the *kelpi* down, the bushes composing it are next collected into an immense heap just in front of its former situation, and a fire-brand applied : while the conflagration is taking place, a corrobboree goes on round and round it, the whole ceremony in celebration of this second stage, &c., being completed a little after dark. So long as an individual remains *kati-kati maro* he or she is not allowed to wear the ornaments which were granted at the *yuppieri* and *kanari* stage: the woman lives in the camp as usual, but the man must stay away altogether unless he be married, under which circumstances he can only come home in the dead of night to visit his wife.

311. (B) **In the Leichhardt-Selwyn District.** No special bush-fence is constructed, but only a corrobboree held. From the time that the man is publicly acknowledged as a *wo-brun-ji*, a member of the second degree, until he undergoes introcision at the third stage, a period of one or two months perhaps, he is not allowed to speak by mouth, but employs a sign-language. The woman of corresponding rank is known as a *wol-loo-ma-ra*.

312. (c) **In the Cloncurry and Upper Flinders Districts**, the Mitakoodi and Woonamurra speak of the males belonging to this second stage as *o-brun-ji* and of the females as *wol-la-ma-ra* or *bun-ya*, the last mentioned term signifying in addition any full-grown adult woman in general.

313. **The Third and Fourth Ceremonials (male and female) (A) in the Boulia District.** Particulars of these are not so easily procurable as those of the preceding, and the following comprises the information which can be depended upon. Both initiation rites would appear to take place on the same occasions as when a novitiate is made a *kati-kati maro*, at the interval of his being ordered to hide his head and cover his eyes in the *kelpi* (sect. 310). The third ceremony is signalised among other things, by a particular pattern of yellow design, whence the name of this degree, *koo-koo-ri ma-ro, i.e.,* yellow (ochre) possessor, for both sexes, is derived: the members with this rank have their special ornaments, which were withheld from them at the second degree, now restored, and no restrictions are placed upon their residence in camp. If now there should happen to be present any *kookoori-maro* fully ready by age preference, &c., to be made *mur-uk-kun-di*, a male or female of the fourth and highest grade, he or she is decorated with the *miri-miri* forehead net, which henceforth is allowed to be worn. During the progress of the *muruk-kundi* rite, the novitiate for this degree is allowed to converse orally only with the members of the same paedomatronym, though he may speak in the sign-language with any others—a rule which is strictly enforced and continued for some few days subsequently.

314. (B) **In the Leichhardt-Selwyn District.** Among the Kalkadoon, with the male, the third grade is constituted apparently by the operation of introcision, or *yel-la*, subsequently to which he is known as a *kun-ta-pe-ung-o* or *u-ro*, a fully-developed adult man. There is no particular corrobboree or bush-enclosure to warn him of coming events; however, when once this rite is over and done with, he is allowed to marry, and for the first time permitted to wear the human-hair belt, the opossum-string phallocrypt, and (among the Southern Kalkadoon only) the fore-head net. The same may be said of the females; as the years roll on the *wolloomara*, or second grade woman (sect. 311), without any particular public celebration of the event becomes a *moon-ta moon-ta, i.e.,* an "old woman," and may wear the opossum-hair necklace, or opossum-belt, and (with the South Kalkadoon only) the *miri-miri*.

315. (c) **In the Cloncurry District** among the Mitakoodi, the men of the third degree, who now only for the first time are allowed to marry, are called *ni-ning-in-ni*, and those of the fourth *muruk-kundi*, as at Boulia, &c.; the women at their third, and, for them, last initiation are also known as *muruk-kundi*.

316. **Introcision,** otherwise known as "Sturt's terrible rite," "whistling," artificial hypospadias, &c., is met with throughout the Boulia, Leichhardt-Selwyn, and Upper Georgina Districts: outside these areas it extends westwards into Northern Territory: southwards it is found on the Middle Diamantina, while northwards the ordeal exists among tribes extending as far as Burketown and the Wellesley group of islands. I have designedly introduced the term "introcision," because of, and so as to include, the corresponding mutilation of the females (sect. 305-309). Circumcision is met with only in those areas where introcision is in vogue. The operation, which always takes place subsequently, at least a few months, to circumcision, aims at the permanent opening up of a more or less considerable extent of the penile portion of the urethra by incision commencing at the external urinary meatus. No females, and no males who have not already been themselves introcised, are on any account allowed to witness the ordeal, the sight of which

N

would probably confirm any determination on their part to exile themselves with a view to escaping it : thus, in the Cloncurry District, I came here and there across an appreciable number of Pitta-Pitta and other Boulia Districts males, who admittedly had left their own tribe on this account. Where the custom is in vogue, the individual is not allowed to marry until he has been subjected to it.

317. (A) In the Boulia District, with the Pitta-Pitta tribes, the operation takes place at an interval during the ceremony of the first stage or degree (sect. 300), No young man has the remotest idea that he may be among the individuals secretly agreed upon for its consummation, and indeed may, through absence from the camping grounds, &c., occasionally have reached second, and even sometimes higher grades in the social ladder before circumstances arise and opportunities occur suitable for his selection. Once caught, however, all postponement is refused him : he is brought inside the bush-palisading, the *errulli*, and operated on as follows :—One of the elders will lie face downwards on the ground, a slight excavation having been made there to receive the protuberance of the stomach, and upon this individual's back the victim is laid, face up, very much after the style of the first female initiation ceremony among the Yaroinga (sect. 306) : his limbs are held in position by various assistants, and his body fixed by another who sits astride. While the man on top holds the penis firm and tense with both hands, the actual operator, seated on the ground in front, makes a superficial incision, through skin only, extending from the external meatus down to near the scrotal pouch in a line with the median raphé : a deeper incision is next made with the same stone-knife along the same line as the first, and starting from the external orifice, opens up the canal as it is pushed onwards. The extent of the wound is apparently inconstant : I have observed it varying from a little over half an inch in some cases, to a gash opening up almost the whole of the penis as low down as half an inch from the scrotum, in others (Fig. 429). No bone or stick of any description is inserted within the urethra along which to guide the knife. During the actual introcision no transverse cut is made at the base of the longitudinal one : what sometimes appears to be such is due either to excoriation or disease, or to the voluntary cuts made for the blood-sprinkling when treading over the novitiate during the *yuppieri* ceremony (sect. 300, Fig. 411). Hæmorrhage is arrested by the patient squatting over some smoking embers and heated charcoal placed in a small excavation in the ground beneath him, the wound being subsequently smeared with greased and powdered charcoal : furthermore, for the next two or three weeks he will always try and arrange matters so as to micturate close to, and over, some smoking ashes. After this operation the individual may be described as a fully-developed adult man, a *ka-na*.

318. (B) In the Upper Georgina District, among the Yaroinga, the time at which the introcision is performed on the *urqoota*, an individual after his first initiation, is about when the beard becomes fairly apparent, i.e., when he is ready to become a full-grown man or *ur-twa*, and fit to live along with his gin. The method of holding the man down during the operation is somewhat different to that in vogue among the Pitta-Pitta aboriginals. Here, independently of any corrobboree, during the early morning or middle day his mother's and his own brother will suddenly stand on either side of the unsuspecting individual and hold his arms and wrists, while some other specially strong fellow catches him from behind under the armpits. He is now rushed along to where the main body of the men happens to be, and signs of rejoicing are on all sides expressed. Of course no women are allowed to be present. Two old men lie down side by side, but not too close, with their bellies resting along the lengths of two large shields placed face upwards on the ground ; across their loins, and thus connecting them, is placed another shield, also face up, so as to form a kind of seat upon which the young man to be operated upon is made to sit (Fig. 430). Here he is held by the swarm of men around, some at his thighs and legs to keep them apart, others at his trunk and arms, and one in particular holding his head well back and plugging his fingers in his ears, so as to prevent him either seeing or hearing what is about to follow. The operation consists of two vertical cuts into the urethra extending from the external orifice with a third independently transverse one below, the resulting flap of skin being allowed to take its own time apparently in

subsequently rotting off down to the transverse cut (Fig. 431). The blood from the wound, which is dressed with iguana fat, is collected into a koolamon, whence at night, remote from the sufferer, a few drops or clots are given to each of the women gathered round, the idea being that by this means the wound will heal all the quicker, and the women will themselves benefit by so doing. (Compare the drinking of seminal fluid in sects. 283, 305.)

319. (c) **Among the Undekerebina** tribes living out along the Toko Ranges, there is, what appears to be, a single vertical and an independently transverse incision (Fig. 432), but whether the latter is intentional or not, my examination of the only four or five members of this tribe with whom I was able to get into personal communication, do not permit of my expressing an opinion. In response to inquiries, no bone or stick is inserted into the urethra for the purpose of guiding the knife. Previous to circumcision, the young lad is an *a-we-a*, and after it, an *ur-ur-goo-ta:* subsequently to introcision he is called a *yel-ka*, a fully-developed man.

320. **The Commonly-alleged Object of Introcision Discussed.** Among Europeans, the ordinarily alleged object of this peculiar mutilation in the males is to lessen the struggle for existence, by putting a check upon population and so limiting the demand for food. To show that this view of the matter is untenable, that introcision is *not* intended to restrict procreation, &c., I beg to submit the following facts, taken in conjunction, to the reader's careful consideration :—

a. The alleged object is already met by the universally strict observance of the unwritten laws regulating the permanent sexual union of individuals belonging to one or other of the four paedomatronymic groups whereby the quantity of food available for the progenitors is in no way immediately affected by the number of the offspring (sect. 71*d*).

b. The system of paedomatronymic groups and their derivatives is common throughout the entire North-West-Central Queensland district (sect. 62), and as we know, from other observers, similar organisations exist elsewhere in Australia (*e.g.*, sect. 70), while the practice of introcision is present in a limited portion only and where it is of course co-existent.

c. There is no tradition whatever, and I have made searching inquiry, to the effect that introcision is any preventive to procreation. When asked for an explanation, or the origin, of the ordeal, the aboriginals invariably plead ignorance, or if pressed will answer somewhat to the effect that " *Mulkari* (sect. 260) make him first time." In this connection it is interesting to note that even the possibility of taking artificial measures to prevent fertilisation, &c. (I am not speaking of abortion), is apparently beyond their comprehension : thus I have reports from station-managers who assure me that only with great difficulty could their " boys" be made to understand, if ever they did, the object of spaying cattle.

d. The peculiar method of copulation in vogue throughout all these tribes does not prevent fertilisation, notwithstanding the mutilation of the male. The female lies on her back on the ground, while the male with open thighs sits on his heels close in front : he now pulls her towards him, and raising her buttocks drags them into the inner aspects of his own thighs, her legs clutching him round the flanks (Fig. 433), while he arranges with his hands the toilette of her perineum and the insertion of his penis. In this position the vaginal orifice, already enlarged by the general laceration at initiation (sects. 305-309), is actually immediately beneath and in close contact with the basal portion of the penis, and it is certainly therefore a matter of impossibility to conceive the semen as being discharged for the most part anywhere but into its proper quarter.

e. It must be borne in mind that the forcible laceration and enlargement of the vaginal orifice, *i.e.*, female-introcision (sects. 305-309), only takes place in those districts where male-introcision is practised.

f. Introcision is invariably an indispensable preliminary to marriage : both the man and the woman must have undergone this ordeal.

g. At the suitable age, *i.e.*, full puberty, or as soon after as the opportunity presents itself, every male, where the practice is in vogue, is introcised : ostracism and exile under the protection of the Europeans, or to a district where the ordeal is not practised, is the only chance of escape. The information which on the one hand I have obtained from those reliable, and on the other which I have collected from the dozens upon dozens of personal examinations of my own, is conclusive concerning this matter of every adult male being so mutilated.

h. Proof is not wanting, on the evidence of Europeans, of cases where, in the continued absence of any adult males not already introcised, the birth of true-blooded children to aboriginal women could not . otherwise be accounted for Thus, the late manager (in 1896) of Roxburgh, Mr. Craigie, one of the earliest pioneers on the Upper Georgina, with a record of sixteen years among the blacks of that district, has had opportunity of collecting proof absolute that children have been born to women by introcised fathers, and by them only.

k. In conclusion, granting even that conception under such circumstances be impossible, and that we have a tribe with all the .adult males introcised, a fact that is indubitable, we should be obliged to imagine a condition of things where all the fathers must be mere lads, which, on the face of it, is ridiculous.

321. (A) An Hypothesis Offered. On the other hand, with the limited knowledge at disposal, no explanation of introcision is absolutely satisfactory. Its connexion with marriage is highly probable considering that it is a necessary preliminary, that its consummation is indicated at that period of life when the male arrives at the physiological epoch of full virility, and that, wherever the practice is in vogue, the female, previously to entering upon permanent sexual union or matrimony, has to undergo a corresponding mutilation (sects. 305-309). It is possible that the cutting of the perineum and general laceration, &c., of the female was originally a matter of convenience for the male, the mutilation in her case subsequently coming to signify her fitness, capability, or experience, in the art of the full enjoyment of copulation, and that, on the principle of a form of mimicry, the analagous sign was inflicted on the male to denote corresponding fitness on his part. With this hypothesis, it is interesting to note that in the Pitta-Pitta and cognate Boulia District dialects the term used to describe an introcised penis denotes etymologically the one with a vulva or "slit" (see *me-ko ma-ro* in the Pitta-Pitta vocabulary, sect. 44).

322. (B) Physical Inconveniences. From my own professional point of view the inconveniences of introcision in the male appear to be a frequency of micturition, and a notable increase in the severity of symptoms, perhaps due to increased area of exposed mucous membrane, in cases of venereal inflammation, *e.g.*, gonorrhœa : when on horseback, the former annoyance may cause a good deal of delay in the necessity for dismounting so frequently, an alleged reason why station-managers, &c., will use every endeavour, but usually fruitless, for preventing the operation taking place.

323. Marriage.—The following arrangements concerning permanent sexual union or matrimony hold good throughout the Boulia District. Each male can at least have two wives—an official one supplied him, as a member of the community, by the camp in general council assembled (sect. 238), and an unofficial one of his own choice, whose love, such as it is, he finds reciprocated : the former woman is known as the *no-po*, the latter as the *pun-di-ra*, though both share equal rights and responsibilities. The contracting parties must belong to suitable paedo-matronymic groups (sect. 62*d*), and must at least be of *yuppieri* and *kanari* rank respectively (sects. 300, 305) : the male must be introcised, the female having already been mutilated when initiated into "*kanari*"-hood. Beyond this social stage or degree, people of any rank can marry, provided, of course, that the other conditions, mentioned above, are fulfilled. If the wife happens to be but of *kanari* or *kati-kati maro* rank at the time of marriage she returns to her own mother's gundi every morning, and neither prepares nor cooks her husband's food : only after the birth of her first child does she remain at her husband's apartment permanently. Marriage is never celebrated by any corrobboree, or other public rejoicing. The choice of a wife is determined upon by one or other of the following circumstances :—

a. Supposing that the camp-council consider a man fit and suitable to have a gin " altogether stop in gundi"—*i.e.*, a wife—he has to take whomsoever is assigned to him thus:—The brothers or mother's brothers of the young woman talk among themselves concerning this particular individual being a bachelor, &c., and convene all the other males available, of *yuppieri* rank and upwards, to a sort of camp-council, where the qualifications of the marriageable man are put under consideration : during the deliberations, in which no women are allowed to take part, the person *sub judice* can be present to listen only, but more usually he will leave camp to go on some fishing or hunting excursion. If all is found to be proper and satisfactory, and the vote of the camp-council must be unanimous, the woman's brothers or mother's brothers present the bridegroom elect some time during the day with a smouldering fire-stick. This stick has nothing whatever distinctive about it: any small piece of wood, about five or six inches long, of any material or shape, is sufficient. The same intermediaries some time after sundown give a similar stick to the bride and direct her to her future husband's hut, whither it is obligatory on her part to go and remain. This ceremony is binding on both sides, and except by mutual agreement, the couple can only be parted by death.

b. A man can exchange his true blood-sister, *i.e.*, by the same mother, for the blood-sister of another individual, two marriages being thus simultaneously effected. This arrangement only holds good, however, provided that the respective paedomatronyms are regular, and that the unanimous vote of the camp-council has sanctioned it. At night, the brothers or mother's brothers lead the brides to their respective future homes.

c. In those circumstances where the man is " in love " with a single woman who reciprocates, but the camp-council, for some reason or another, refuses its sanction, they will probably elope some night, and after living together as man and wife for a month or two return to camp. But when they do come back, both have to run the gauntlet of the outraged community, certain members of which will cripple them with knives by hacking into the buttocks and shoulders, will bruise or hammer them about the limbs and head with sticks and boomerangs, or puncture the fleshy parts of the thighs with spears. The perpetrators of the punishment take very good care that the injuries inflicted should not prove fatal, because, were this contingency to occur, they know full well that the death would be avenged by the victims' brothers, &c. (sect. 238). Having undergone the recognised chastisement for breaking the old-established rule, the couple is now recognised as husband and wife, provided the former still wishes it; otherwise, the latter is restored to her brother, &c., as not being required any longer. Even in these cases of elopement, the amorous pair must be of suitable paedomatronyms: the death of both parties, with the tacit consent of the blood-relatives, would be the sure penalty for any breach in this particular.

d. A man may unfortunately take a fancy to a woman—she must belong to the proper paedomatronym if he values his life—already married, and elope with her as in the previous case. After some weeks' absence the couple will return, the seducer bringing the woman back to her lawful husband, who either takes her unto himself again, in which case she would receive more or less chastisement, or else tells her newly-found lover to keep her, and make him some present in exchange. The particular behaviour of the injured husband will vary according as he is afraid or not to fight: where the two men do come to blows, they make no attempt at actual killing, for fear of retribution—their quarrel is not joined in by any others. If the lawful husband refuses to receive his erring spouse, the camp-council sees that she becomes, and is recognised, as the wife of the man she ran away with.

324. Betrothal.—Though I cannot find any traces of the practice in the Boulia District, a form of betrothal takes place at the first male initiation ceremony in the Upper Georgina—certainly among the Yaroinga (sect. 302), apparently among the Undekerebina—and perhaps, independently of the initiation, in the Leichhardt-Selwyn District, among the Kalkadoon.

325. Love-charms.—Among the Yaroinga certain kinds of "whirlers" (sect. 215) are used as "love-charms." This form of implement is obtained from the Workia (? and Undekerebina) tribe, whence its use in this connection has been learnt. It appears to have no special term applied to distinguish it from the ordinary toy-variety, than which it is larger, although it is recognisable by two types of gravings: one (Fig. 320), the ring of concentric circles (*u-run-goo-doo*), represents the smouldering fire-sticks, coolibar-roots, &c., being swung round and round at the camp fires during the "sing-songs," &c., which often occupy the interval between sunset and sunrise; the other (Fig. 318) is a representation of the female genitals, each half-circle indicating a *labium*. The charm is swung at intervals during the hours of night, at a considerable distance from camp, by males only, in the belief that the woman whom they are bent on marrying will reciprocate their passions with increased fervour. The female referred to, of course sees nothing of the web into which she is becoming entangled, though she may feel its effects: she experiences herself as becoming more and more enamoured, and finds herself repeatedly exclaiming, " 1 like this-fellow-boy." No woman is ever allowed to handle, much less to gaze on, one of these whirler love-charms. Among the European settlers around Camooweal, &c., these love-charm whirlers are known by the cacophonous title of "gin-busters."

326. Consanguinity.—Throughout the whole of North-West-Central Queensland, though marriage with brothers-in-law and sisters-in-law is permissible, that of true blood-relatives is strictly forbidden. A man cannot marry his blood-cousin, or his daughter's daughter, and a woman cannot marry her blood-cousin or her son's son, notwithstanding the fact that these particular relationships are necessarily located in those very same paedomatronymic groups (sect. 62*d*: sect. 65, Table) which otherwise would be allowed to join in permanent sexual partnership. Furthermore, a man cannot marry his mother-in-law: everywhere, except perhaps among the Woonamurra, he never sees, speaks to, or approaches this relative.

327. Venery.—The husband sleeps in the same gundi as his wives, and should they quarrel or fight, it is his business to stop them, but whether he actually does so or not will be a matter for himself to decide. If an aboriginal requires a woman temporarily for venery he either borrows a wife from her husband for a night or two in exchange for boomerangs, a shield, food, &c., or else violates the female when unprotected, when away from camp out in the bush. In the former case, the husband looks upon the matter as a point of honour to oblige his friend, the greatest compliment that can be paid him, provided that permission is previously asked: on the other hand, were he to refuse, he has the fear hanging over him that the petitioner might get a death-bone pointed at him—and so, after all, his apparent courtesy may be only Hobson's choice. In the latter case, if a married woman, and she tells her husband, she gets a "hammering," and should she disclose the delinquent, there will probably be a fight, and hence she usually keeps her mouth shut: if a single woman, and of any paedomatronym other than his own, no one troubles himself about the matter. On the other hand, death by spear or club, is the punishment invariably inflicted by the camp-council collectively for criminally assaulting any blood-relative, group-sister (*i.e.*, a female member of the same paedomatronym), or young woman that has not yet been initiated into the first degree. Under such circumstances the blood-brother of the culprit is responsible for his appearance to receive punishment: should the former make any objection or delay, his own life in addition would probably be forfeited.

328. Pregnancy and Labour.—During the latter months of pregnancy a woman will often rub over her breasts and body some warm powdered ashes with the idea of making the child healthy and strong. Among the Yaroinga the woman, when about to be confined, betakes herself to a secluded spot at some distance from the main camp. She lies on the ground upon her back, with open thighs and drawn-up knees: her two hands are clasped behind her head, while the old gin appointed to attend holds her down by the neck and head to prevent her raising herself. The husband, if he be so minded, can take up his position assigned on his wife's left and front, whence, a few paces off, he can witness the whole of the proceeding. The child, as soon as it makes its appearance, is placed on the mother's right, and the navel-string, subsequently to being cut, is tied with opossum-string: the after-birth is buried deep in the ground. The aged attendant brings the newly-born babe into camp, to be followed in a few hours' time by the mother herself, who in two or three days goes about her business and daily occupations as usual. The navel-string, which is preserved, is carefully wound into a ball or roll and forwarded by messenger, at the instance of the father, to his relatives and friends in the neighbouring camps, whence presents will now come pouring in in the shape of blankets, tomahawks, shirts, knives, &c. Immediately after birth (at Headingly, Roxburgh, Boulia, &c.) the baby is "washed" in ashes, mud, or sand, but usually in the last-mentioned, the head and face being alike cleaned. Among the Kalkadoon tribe (at Quamby) the woman leaves camp with one or two old gins or sometimes goes by herself, and does not return until about eight or ten days after the baby is born. A very old man or two may be present during delivery, but no boys or young men on any account. Having made a pretty shallow hole in the sandy soil, she sits over this on her shins and knees, with the thighs well apart: as labour progresses she either throws her body backwards, or strongly forward, so as to rest on her hands, or if conveniently situated, may grasp some overhanging branch (Figs. 434-435). In the intervals, a thick cord, waist-belt, &c., is tied round her pretty firmly to assist in "pushing the child out," while another old woman will take up mouthfuls of water from a koolamon and spit them out again over the distended abdomen; upon which a sort of massage may also be performed. If the patient becomes faint and collapsed, the treatment consists in smearing the perspiration obtained from under her own arm-pits over her forehead, nose, and face (sect. 283). The genital passages are never touched by anyone, and the child, without any guidance, is allowed to fall into the shallow excavation below. The navel-string, before the mother shifts her position, is next held, close to its attachment to the child, between the flats of both hands of one of the old gins, and briskly rolled backwards and forwards until a very marked twist is visible, when it is cut to a length of about 5 or 6 inches. Similarly, the after-birth is allowed to fall into the cavity where it is either buried, or more generally destroyed by fire. When the child is taken out of the shallow rut into which it was allowed to fall, any sand that may chance to be on its face and mouth is removed with leaves: otherwise, it is neither washed or cleaned. Subsequently, however, the infant is smeared from top to toe with iguana fat, which is renovated continuously during its early years, while, at intervals, some powdered ashes are rubbed on the head over the areas of the fontanels.

329. **Abortion** appears to be a common practice in the later months, among the aboriginals of the Boulia, Upper Georgina, and Leichhardt-Selwyn Districts. It is performed by the fixation of thick twine wound very tightly round and round the abdominal walls, combined with the "punching" by hand or stick upon the more palpable and apparently firmer portions of the unborn child as recognised through the abdominal walls. I can find no traces of any other methods being adopted.

330. **Babyhood.**—Very young infants are carried either in a koolamon or else on a sheet of bark, slung up to the side. In the latter form, as practised among the Kalkadoon, it is made from a piece of ti-tree, the bark having been scorched on its inner surface so as to produce a curling over inwards at the sides: this is slung with twine, &c., over the mother's opposite shoulder, and balanced pretty carefully with the hand to prevent the youngster from falling out at either end (Fig. 436). As the child gets older, it is carried on the shoulders or the flank: in the former case it grasps its mother's forehead and neck with its little hands and legs respectively (Fig. 437), while in the latter it sits upon its parent's hips and is supported in position by the protecting arm (Fig. 438).

A mother sings no song or lullaby to her little one beyond a sort of droning, humming sound to send it to sleep: she may slap it after the approved European fashion, and sometimes frighten it by making grimaces, a favourite one apparently being produced by passing a string through the nasal septum and drawing her nose upwards. So far as I have observed, kissing only takes place between mothers and their infants (and between husbands and wives), never between fathers and their children: whether this custom has been introduced in modern times from the whites it is difficult to say, though the presence of a word giving expression to the act in the Pitta-Pitta language, *ing-ga-mul-le-*, is interesting. Suckling may go on up to three, four, even five years of age, and a mother may often be seen with two children at the breast. As they get older they are gradually weaned on honey, kangaroo and opossum flesh, &c. When the children become too big for the gundi, they are sent to sleep with their father's mother-in-law. It is the husband's business in the main to supply the animal food for the family, and although a particular dietary may be forbidden him, he has no compunction in hunting or killing it for his kith and kin. Half-caste children may be destroyed at the instigation of their true white, or presumed black, fathers by a blow with a stick, or allowed to starve : sometimes they will be eaten (sect. 293). True-blooded children may be treated similarly. Among the Kalkadoon, female infants are said to have the top joint of the little finger amputated.

331. **Menstruation.**—In the Boulia District, a woman during her menstrual periods sleeps out of camp alone by herself at night, and in this condition is known as *kim-ba ma-ro*, i.e., the blood-possessor. Among the Kalkadoon, on the other hand, the woman stays in camp, though, if married, a fire separates her from her husband. The Mitakoodi women at these times keep strictly to themselves out of the camp, and will not even walk along the same tracks as the men.

332. **Micturition,** in both sexes, is performed in the squatting position always. In both micturition and defæcation, a few handfuls of earth are scratched up, and in this excavation so formed the emunctories after being discharged are covered over with earth (sect. 101) : earth or sand is further always used to cleanse their persons with. Mr. Coghlan, the manager of Glenormiston (1895), informs me that when out camping with the blacks in the neighbourhood he has often noticed outside a gundi a small mound of earth the top of which is scooped out and subsequently beaten down, with the resulting appearance of a volcano in miniature : this receptacle, which is capable of holding quite a quart of fluid, is intended for the women (he is not sure about the men) to micturate into.

333. **Foul Language** is very commonly made use of under circumstances of contempt, derision, or anger : the foulness does not, however, consist so much in the actual thoughts conveyed as in the particular words employed, there being both a decent and indecent vocabulary to describe the particular region, the generative organs, which are then usually drawn attention to. Thus in the Mitakoodi language, *me-ne* is the "society" term for vulva and nothing is thought of its utterance before a company of people, while *koon-ja, puk-kil,* or *yel-ma-rung-o*, all names for the same part, are most blackguardly words to use. (Refer also to Kalkadoon term denoting "excrement" in sect. 52.)

I have no evidence as to any practice of masturbation or sodomy anywhere among the North-West-Central Queensland aboriginals.

INDEX AND GLOSSARY.

—⚬—

N.B.—The pronunciation of the Aboriginal words is formed on the basis laid down in Section 2.

Unless otherwise stated, the Reference Numbers denote the Sections.

The following Abbreviations are used—namely, Ph.T. and S.L., to indicate respectively the Philological Tables of Chapter II. and the Sign-Language of Chapter IV.

A.

A, Indefinite Article, 9.
Abdomen, Ph.T., 52.
Aboriginal and European Relationship-Equivalents, 66.
Aboriginal-Anglicised Words, 51.
Aboriginal Geographical Nomenclature, 226.
Aboriginal Pharmacopœia, Ch. XI.
Aboriginals : Of the Boulia District, 45 ; of the Cloncurry District, 47 ; of the Upper Flinders District, 48 ; of the Upper Georgina District, 49 ; of the Leichhardt-Selwyn District, 46.
Aboriginals, Number of Pitta-Pitta, 45.
Abortion, 329.
About, Around : Motion, 22 ; Rest, 23.
About to, Just : Special Forms of the Future, 30.
Above, On Top of : Rest, 23.
Abstract Ideas, Signs relating to, 103, 104.
Abstract Ideas, Words relating to, 57.
Acacia aneura, F. v. M. *See* Mulga.
Acacia excelsa, Benth. *See* Iron-wood.
Acacia farnesiana, Willd. *See* Dead finish Scrub.
Acacia homalophylla, A. Cunn. *See* Gidyea.
Accident, Sickness, Disease, Death, Ch. XI.
Acheron Creek, 230.
Acicular-tip Hand-spear, 247.
Acquaintances and Friends, Greeting of, 12, 228.
Across, Over : Motion, 22.
Action, Definitiveness or Special Purpose of, 33.
Action, Indefiniteness of, 33.
Active, Indicative, 17.
Acts, States, Conditions, S.L. 101, 102.
Adjectives, 20.
Adjectives, Comparison of, 27.
Adjectives used as Adverbs, 20.
Adjectives used as Nouns, 20.
Adult Man : Ph.T., 52 ; S.L., 89, 90.
Adult Woman : Ph.T., 52 ; S.L., 89, 90.
Advantage, Benefit, Use, Purpose, 24.
Adverbs, 21.
Adverbs, Adjectives used as, 20.
Adverbs, Comparison of, 28.
After......Before : Idea of Time, 38.
After : To be after, On look-out for, To hunt, 22.
After : Time, 25.
Ague, 262.
Aigrette : Head-ornament, 164.
Ailments, Chants and Dirges for Exorcising 282.
Albizzia basaltica, Benth. *See* Dead-finish Scrub.
All : Idea of Number, 36.
Alley-way, for hunting emu, &c., 132, 138.
Allow, Let, Permit : Special Forms of Imperative, 31.
Alongside of, Among, Through, Up : Motion, 22, 43.
Alongside of, Among, At, In, Close to : Rest, 23.

Also, And : Conjunctions, 26.
Always : Idea of Time, 38.
Among, Alongside of, At, In, Close to : Rest, 23.
Among, Alongside of, Up, Through : Motion, 22, 43.
Amulets, Charms, 286.
Amusements, Sports, Games, Ch. VIII.
And, Also : Conjunctions, 26.
Anger, &c., Language used in, 333.
Anger, &c., Signs expressing, 103, 104, 238.
Anglicised-Aboriginal Words, 51.
Animal- and Folk-Lore, 200.
Animals and Birds, Playing at, 221.
Animals and Birds, Words relating to, 53.
Ankle, Ph.T., 52.
Anklet, 181.
Ant : Ph.T., 53 ; Used as Food, 119.
Apron, 183, 193.
Arm, Forearm, Ph.T., 52.
Armlet, 181, 289, 303.
Around, Roundabout : Motion, 22.
Around, Roundabout : Rest, 23.
Arrangement of Audience at Corrobboree, 198.
Arrangement of Camping Ground, 228.
Art, Mural Painting, Draughtsmanship, 187.
Arthropoda, expressed by signs, 83, 84.
Article, Indefinite, 9.
Artificial Bending and Straightening of Timber, 151.
Artificial Hypospadias, Introcision, 316.
Artificial Whiskers, 167.
Ashes arresting Hæmorrhage, 317.
Ashes : Sign of Mourning, 289.
Assault, Punishment of criminal, 327.
At, In, Close to, Among, Alongside of : Rest, 23.
At, To : Motion, 22.
Atalantia glauca, Hook. *See* Wild Orange.
Audience, How arranged at Corrobboree, 198.
Aunt : Geneanym, 64.
Austral Downs, 231.
Authority of Old Men, 238.
Authorship and Plot of Corrobboree, 190.
Autonym, 67, 300.
Auxiliary Verbs, 8.
Avulsion of Teeth : How Effected, 177 ; Independent of Ceremonial Rites, 299.
Away from, Far, Far off : Idea of Distance, 39.
ă-wē-ă : A lad previous to circumcision (*cf.* o-we-a), 319.

B.

Babyhood, Infancy, 328-330.
Back, Dorsum, Ph.T., 52.
Bad, Ph.T., 57 ; S.L., 103, 104.
Bag, Dilly-, S.L., 91, 92 : 153.
Bag, Water-, 152.
Baking Oven, 156.
Ball Games, 216.
Band-fillet : Ornament, 170.

Excrement : Ph.T., 52 ; S.L., 101, 102 ; Covered with Earth, 332.
Exogamous Groups, 61.
Exorcising Sickness, &c., Chants and Dirges for, 282.
Expression of Ideas by Signs, Ch. IV.
Eye : Ph.T., 52 ; Blindness, 275 ; "Hunt the Eye" Game, 218 ; Eyebrow, Ph.T., 52.

F.

Fables, Legends, Tales, Folk and Animal Lore, 200.
Face, Ornamentation of the, 174.
Fall from Tree, produced by Death-bone, 270.
Family Relatives, Terms Applied to, 58, 63, 64 ; S.L., 89, 90.
Fan or Duster, Phallocrypt used as, 184.
Far Away, How Far? &c. : Ideas of Place, Distance, 39.
Fat. See Grease.
Father : Ph.T., 58 ; 59, 60, 63 ; S.L., 89, 90.
Father, Mother's : Ph.T., 58 ; 64.
Father-in-Law, 64.
Father's : Brother, 64 ; Father and Mother, 58, 64 ; Sister, 58, 59, 63.
Fauna and Flora, Words relating to, 53.
Feathering and Painting of the Body, 185, 296, 297.
Feather-tufts, 164.
Feet, Catching Fish by Treading with, 128.
Female Genitals : Graved on Letter-stick, 236 ; Ph.T., 52. See Foul Language.
Fence, Bush, at Initiation Ceremonies, 300, 303, 304, 310.
Festoons Graved on Boomerangs, 241.
Few : Idea of Number, 36.
Fighting, Methods of, 238.
Fighting-boomerang, 239.
Fighting-pole : Ph.T. 55 ; Bartered, 232, 233 ; How Employed in Fighting, 238 ; Description of Weapon, 255 ; Used at Initiation Rites, 300-2, 304.
Fighting-scars, 186.
Fighting-weapons, S.L., 91, 92.
Figures : Graved on Boomerangs, 213, 214 ; On Letter-sticks, 235, 236 ; Painted on Rocks, &c., 187.
Fillet Head-ornaments, 170.
Finger-posts for Showing the Line of Route, 225.
Fingers, Ph.T., 52.
Fingers, Toes, and Hands : Counting with, 36 ; Mutilation of, 330.
Fire : Ph.T., 54 ; S.L., 101, 102 ; Producing Sickness and Death, 267.
Fire-stick : How Used, 157 ; Sign of Wedlock, 323.
Fish : Ph.T., 53 ; S.L., 79, 80.
Fish, Hunting for : With Dams, 125 ; by Muddying or Puddling the Water, 126 ; with Nets, 124 ; by Poisoning the Waterholes, 126 ; by Spearing, 127 ; by Treading with the Feet, 128.
Fish, Killing and Transport of, 129.
Fish-nets, 124 ; Bartered, 232-3.
Fish and Snake : Lore, 205.
Fishermen, The Two : Lore, 207.
Five : Ideas of Number, 36.
Flake, Flint. See Flint Flake.
Flank, Ph.T., 52.
Flash-cuts, Mutilations, &c., on Body, 186, 299.
Flax, Native (Linum marginale, A. Cunn.): For Nets, 121, 168 ; for Making up the Pituri-roll, 147 ; Bartered, 233 ; how Manufactured into Twine, 153 ; S.L., 85, 86.
Flight of Boomerang, 240.
Flinders District, Upper : Aboriginals and Geographical Limits of, 48.
Flinders River, 48, 241.

Flint-Flake : For Smoothing and Graving, 240, 241 ; used as Chisel, 149 ; as Stone-knife, 257 ; as Spear-tip Sharpener, 253.
Flock-Pigeon : Ph.T., 53 ; S.L., 75-6 ; Hunting for, 137.
Flora and Fauna, Words Relating to, 53.
Flowers and Honey, as Food, 118.
Fluted Boomerang, 242.
Fly : Ph.T., 53 ; S.L., 83, 84.
Folk and Animal Lore, Tales, Legends, 200.
Food, Search for, and Preparation of, Ch. V.
Food : Left at Grave, 289, 291 ; Seed-food, S.L. 85-6, 101-2 ; Food "tabooed," 626.
Foot, Ph.T., 52.
Foot-prints recognised by others, 221, 225.
For : Prepositions of Purpose, Reason, Means 24.
Fore-arm, Arm, Ph.T., 52.
Fore-head, Ph.T., 52.
Fore-head Net : Description of, 169 ; used at Corrobborees, 193 ; Bartered, 233 ; sign of Social Rank, 310, 313.
Forgetfulness, Loss of Memory, S.L., 103-4.
Fort Constantine, 47, 224, 232-3 ; Aboriginal Name of, 226.
Fort William, Aboriginal Name of, 226.
Foul Language, 238, 333.
Four : Idea of Number, 36 ; Ph.T., 56
Fractures : How Treated, 281.
Fresh-water Mussel : As Food, 120 ; S.L., 81-2.
Friends and Acquaintances, Greeting of, 12, 228.
Frog : Ph.T., 53 ; as Food, 121 ; S.L., 77-8.
From : Motion, 22 ; Purpose, Reason, Means, 24 ; Ideas of Direction, Distance, 39.
Fruit : As Food, 117 ; S.L., 85-6.
Fullarton River, Aboriginal Name of, 226.
Fungi, as Food, 116.
Future Existence, Belief in a, 279.
Future Participle, 42.
Future Tense : Active Indicative, 17 ; Special Forms of, 30.

G.

Galah-parrot : An Anglicised-aboriginal Word ?, 51 ; Hunting for, 137, 139 ; S.L., 75-6.
Galah-parrot and Lizard : Lore, 202.
Galah-parrot and Opossum : Lore, 212.
Games, Sports, and Amusements, Ch. VIII.
Gamomatronym, 61.
Gates. See Diamantina Lakes.
Gauntlet, Running the : Punishment, 238, 323.
Gender, 4, 16.
Genealogical Tree, Pitta-Pitta, 65.
Geneanym, 64.
Genitals : Ph.T., 52 ; Mutilation in Fighting, 238 ; in Introcision, 305-8, 316-9 ; Female, Graved on Letter-stick, 236 ; in Foul Language, 333.
Geographical Aboriginal Nomenclature, 226.
Geographical Distribution of Introcision, 316.
Geographical Limits : Of Boulia District, 2 ; of Cloncurry District, 47 ; of Upper Flinders District, 48 ; of Upper Georgina District, 49 ; of Leichhardt-Selwyn District, 46 ; of North-West-Central Queensland, 50.
Georgina District, Upper : Aboriginals and Geographical Limits of, 49 ; Burial in, 292 ; Trade-routes of, 231.
Georgina River, 2, 128, 133, 136-7, 147, 154, 182, 184, 190-1, 207, 213, 216, 230-2, 241-2, 247, 253-4, 257, 320g.
Ghost, 260, 289, 298 ; S.L., 104.
Gidyea (Acacia homalophylla, A. Cunn.), 147, 149, 214-5, 240, 242, 245, 247, 250-1, 253, 255-6, 288.
gĭm-bă : Blood. See kim-ba.
gĭm-bă-lō-woon-dī-ă : Blood-smearing, 283.
Gin (the guttural pronounced soft) : any Adult Aboriginal Woman.
Gin Buster. See Whirler, 325.
gĭn-jă-lă : Leaf, 241.

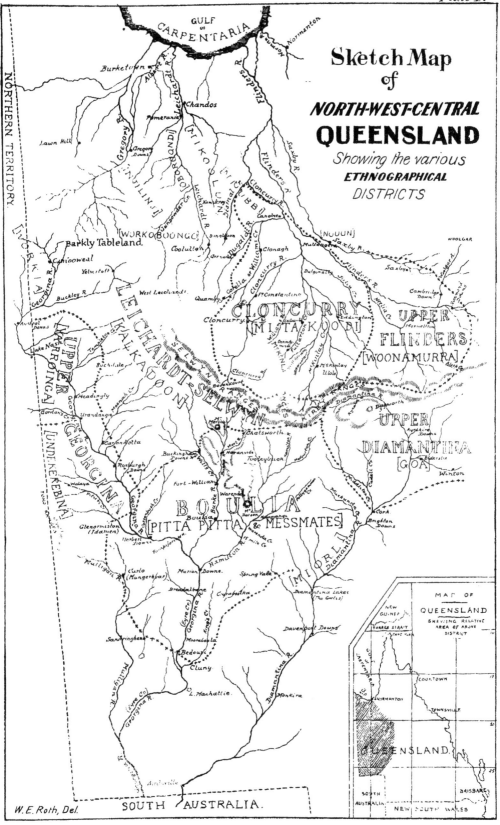

Plate I.

GULF
of
CARPENTARIA

Sketch Map
of
NORTH-WEST-CENTRAL
QUEENSLAND
Showing the various
ETHNOGRAPHICAL
DISTRICTS

NORTHERN TERRITORY

Burketown

Normanton

Chandos

Pomerania

Lawn Hill

Gregory Downs

Barkly Tableland

[WORKOBOONGO]

Camooweal

Yelvertoft

Buckley R.

West Leichhardt

Quamby

Coolullah

Gerrard

Dinnalson

[NOUUN]

WOOLGAR

Clonagh

Muttaburra

Saxby R.

Saxleys

Cloncurry R.

Ft Constantine

Cloncurry

Dalgonally

Cambridge Downs

CLONCURRY
[MITAKOODI]

Cobella or Williams

Oorinda

Eddington

UPPER
FLINDERS
[WOONAMURRA]

Alick

LEICHHARDT-SELWYN

McKinlay

Uiole

Austral Downs

Lake Nash

[UPPER GEORGINA]

[KALKADOON]

Headingly

Manga

Urandangie

[UNDEKEREBINA]

Carandotta

Roxburgh Downs

Buckingham Downs

Tooleybuck

Chatsworth

Noranside

Merino

Fort William

Walaya

Glenormiston
(Idamea)

Herbert
Sionna

Fulchai

BOULIA
[PITTA PITTA & MESSMATES]

Boulia

Warenda

UPPER
DIAMANTINA
[GOA]

Winton

Burke

Mt Ida

Dalton

Cork

Brighton Downs

MIORLI

Mulligan

Curio
(Mungerebar)

Marion Downs

Hamilton

15 mile Cr

Spring Vale

Diamantina R.

Diamantina Lakes
(The Gall's)

Breadalbane

C.Grafootka

Davenport Downs

Sandringham

Moonabula

Bedourie

Cluny

L. Machattie

Monkira

Birdsville

SOUTH AUSTRALIA.

MAP OF
QUEENSLAND
SHEWING RELATIVE
AREA OF ABOVE
DISTRICT

NEW GUINEA

TORRES STRAIT

CAPE YORK

COOKTOWN

TOWNSVILLE

QUEENSLAND

SOUTH AUSTRALIA

BRISBANE

NEW SOUTH WALES

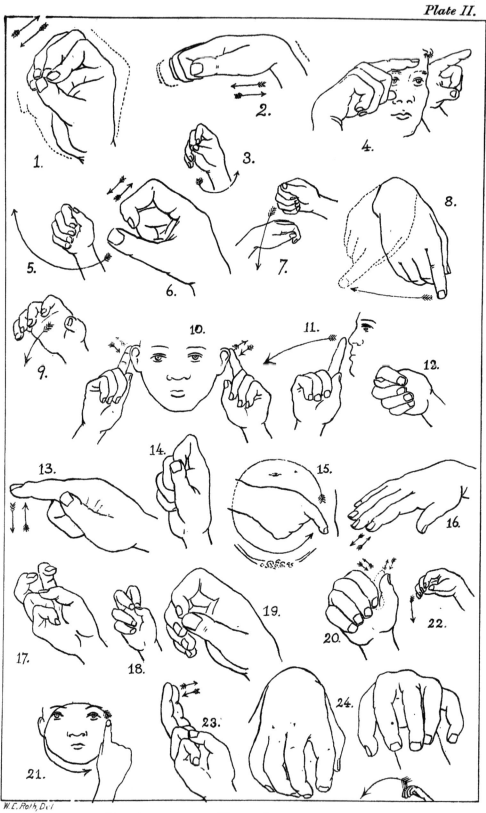

Plate II.

Sign-Language Figs. 1-24, Mammals.

W.C.Roth, Del

Plate III.

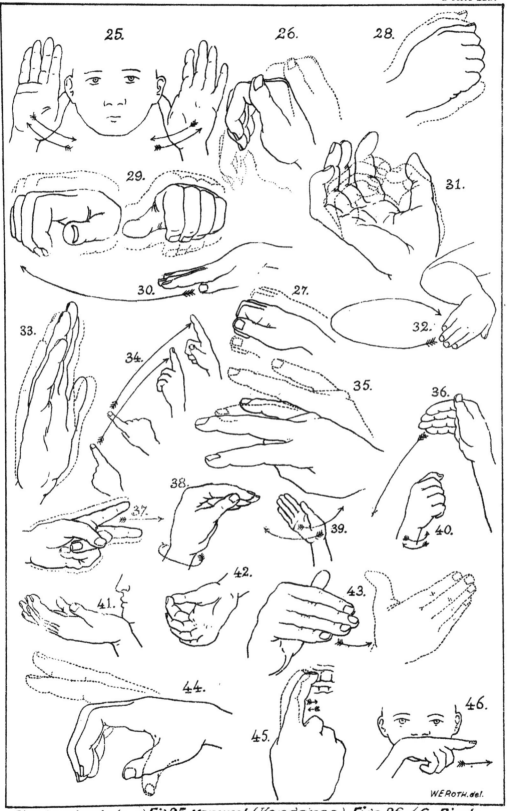

WE ROTH. del.

Sign-Language (Cont.) Fig. 25, Mammal (Kangaroo). Figs 26-46 Birds.

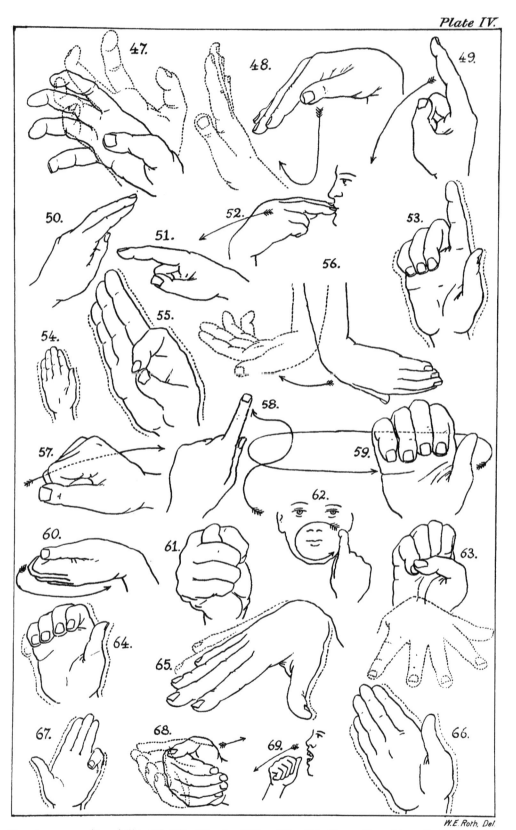

Plate IV.

W.E.Roth, Del.

Sign-Language (Cont⁴) Figs. 47-52, Birds, Figs. 53-63, Reptiles. Figs. 64-69, Fish.

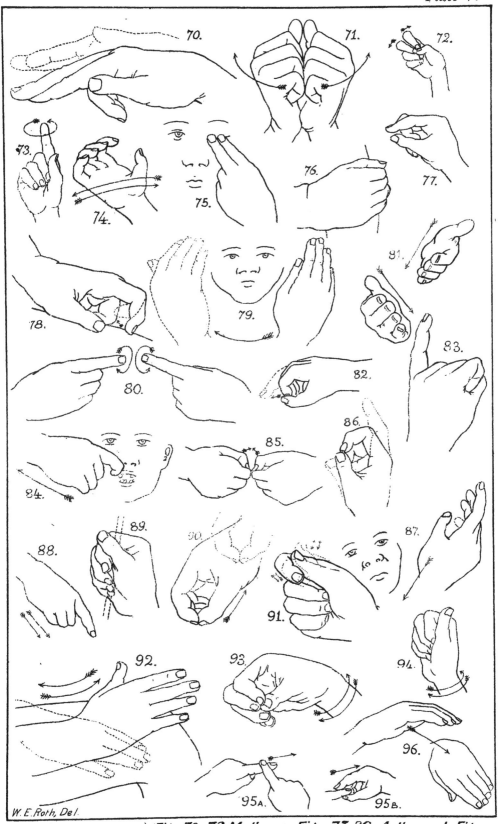

Plate V.

W.E.Roth, Del.

Sign-Language (Contd) Figs. 70-72, Mollusca. Figs. 73-86, Arthropoda. Figs- 87-96, Plants.

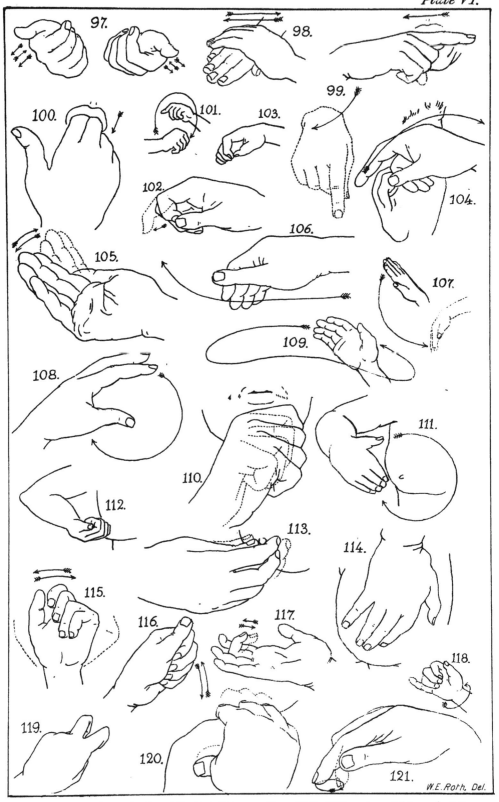

Plate VI.

Sign-Language (Cont^d) Figs. 97-104, Plants. Figs. 105-109, other Objects of Nature.
Figs. 110-121, Individuals, Family Relatives Etc.

W.E.Roth. Del.

Plate VII.

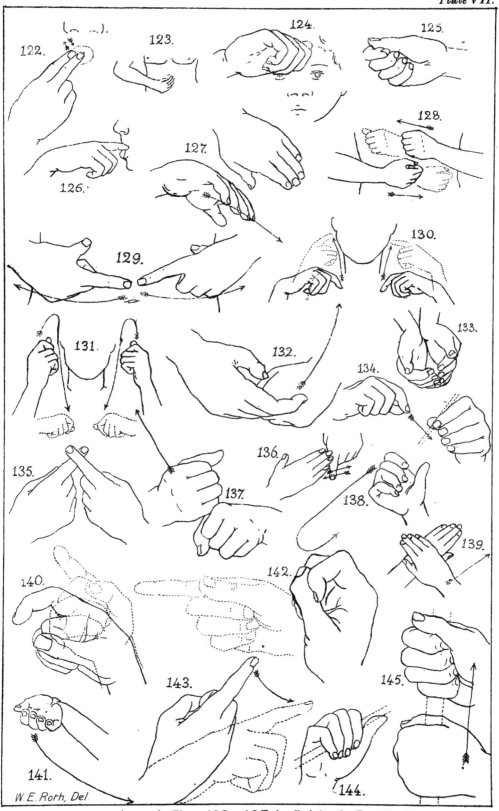

Sign-Language(Cont.d) Figs. 122-127, Individuals, Family Relatives Etc.
Figs.128-145, Articles of Manufacture: Ornaments, Weapons, Implements.

Plate VIII.

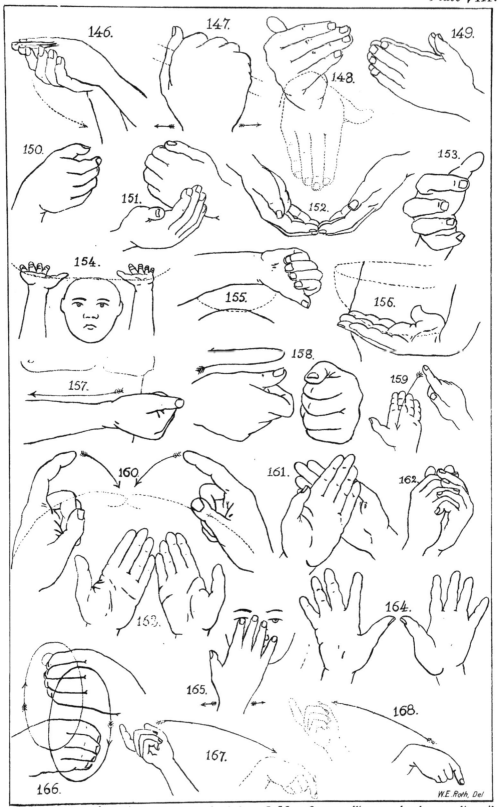

W.E.Roth, Del

Sign-Language (Cont.ᵈ) Figs. 146-162, Articles of Manufacture=Weapons, Implements, Utensils, Huts. Figs. 163-166, Ideas of Number. Figs. 167-168, Ideas of Locality and Direction.

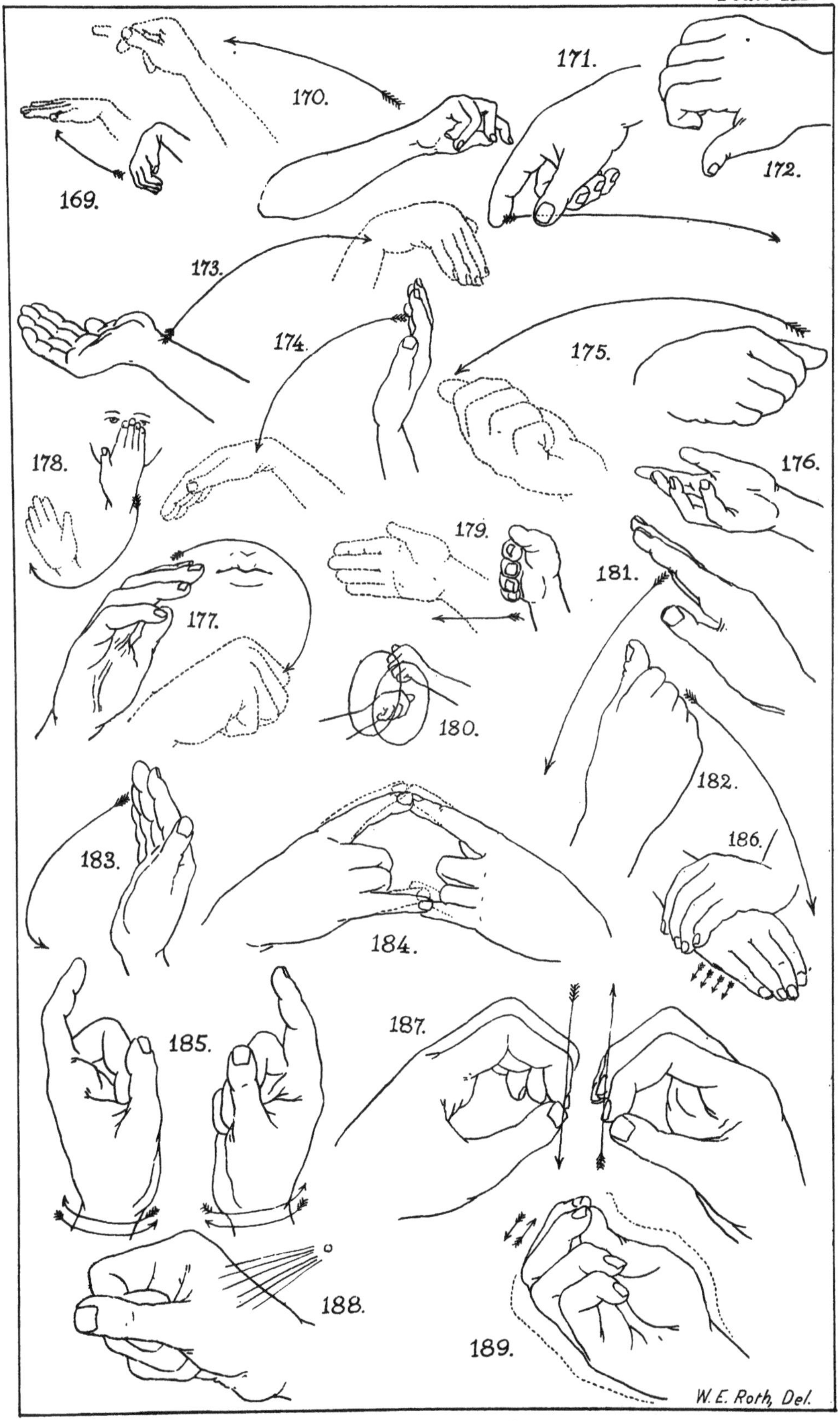

Plate IX.

169. 170. 171. 172. 173. 174. 175. 176. 177. 178. 179. 180. 181. 182. 183. 184. 185. 186. 187. 188. 189.

W. E. Roth, Del.

Sign-Language (Cont'd) *Figs. 169-172, Ideas of Locality and Direction. Figs. 173-174, Ideas of Time. Fig. 175, Interrogation. Figs. 176-189, Simple Acts, States, and Conditions.*

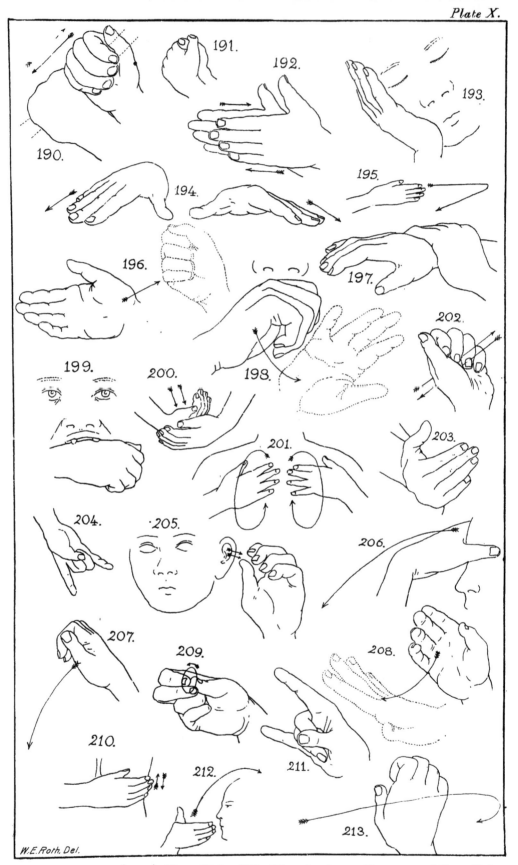

Plate X.

190. 191. 192. 193. 194. 195. 196. 197. 198. 199. 200. 201. 202. 203. 204. 205. 206. 207. 208. 209. 210. 211. 212. 213.

W.E.Roth. Del.

Sign-Language (Cont^d) Figs. 190-198, Simple Acts, States and Conditions.
Figs. 199-213, Complex Conditions, Abstract Ideas Etc.

Plate XI.

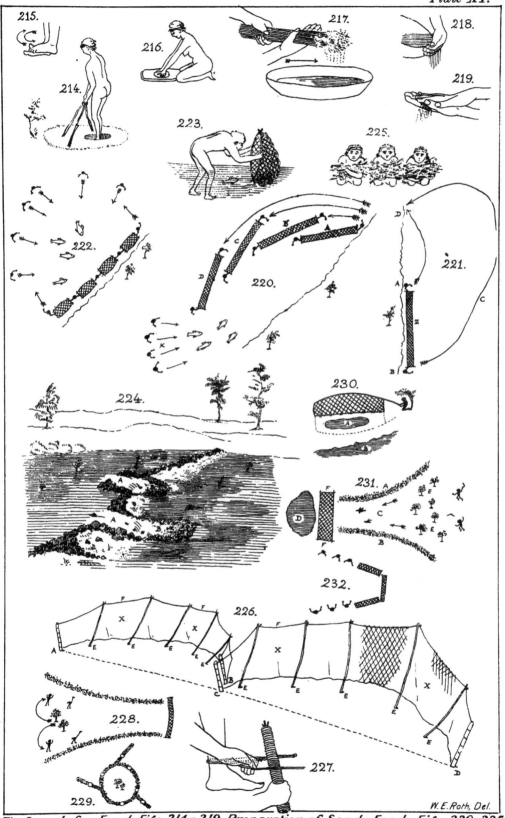

W.E.Roth, Del.

The Search for Food. Figs. 214-219, Preparation of Seed-Food. Figs. 220-225,
Contrivances for Catching Fish. Figs. 226-232, Methods of trapping Emu, kangaroo Etc.

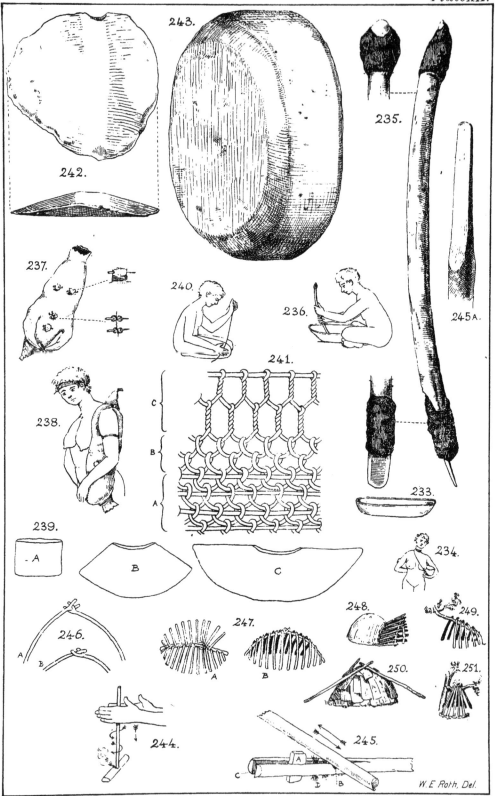

Plate XII.

Figs. 233-251, Domestic Implements and Utensils, Fire-Sticks and Yam-Sticks, Huts and Shelters.

W. E Roth, Del.

Plate XIII.

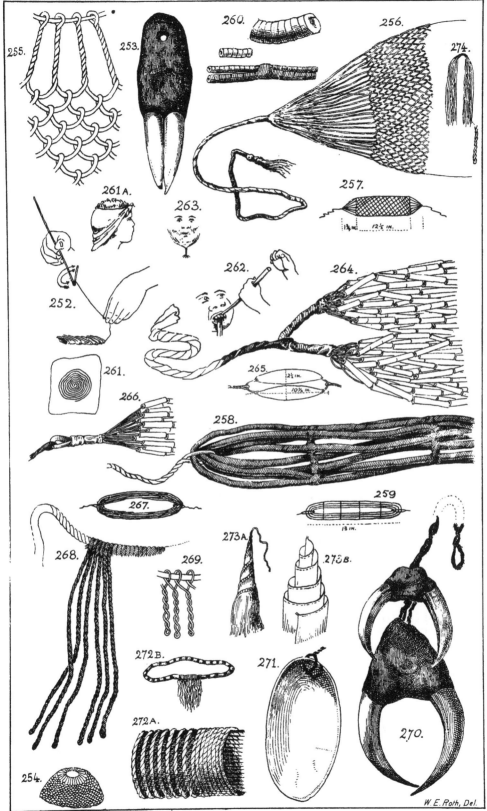

W.E.Roth, Del.

Figs. 252-274, Objects of Personal Ornamentation and Decoration.

Plate XIV.

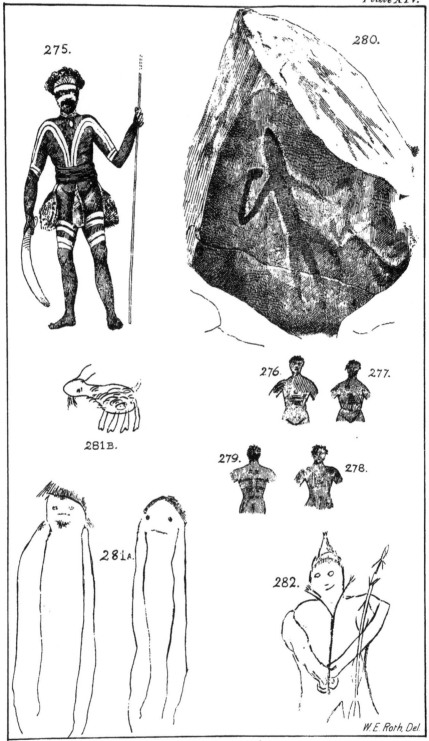

275.

280.

281B.

276. 277.

279. 278.

281A.

282.

W.E. Roth, Del.

Figs. 275-282, Personal Decoration, Mural Painting, Art and Draughtmanship.

Plate XV.

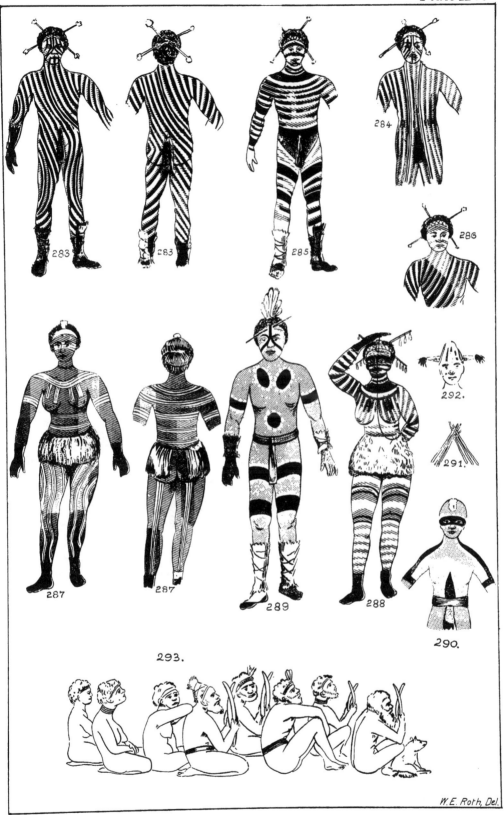

Figs. 283-292, Corrobboree Costumes. Fig. 293, Native Audience.

Plate XVI.

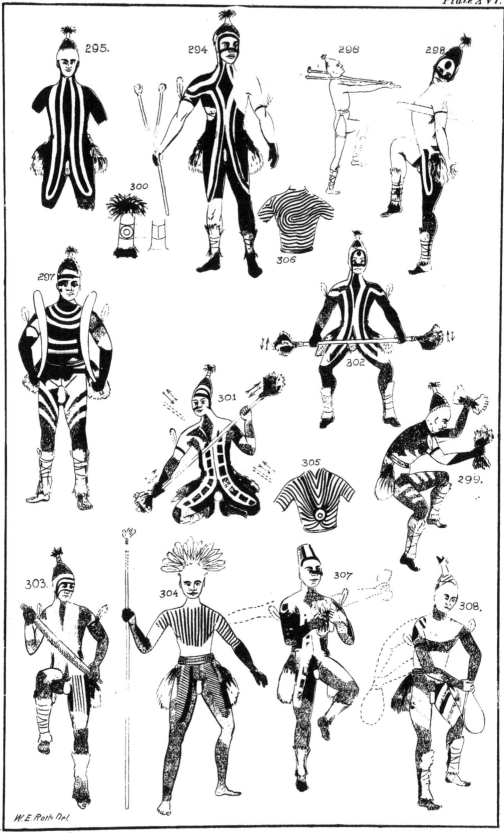

Figs. 294-308, Costumes, Etc. of the Molonga Corrobboree.

W.E. Roth Del.

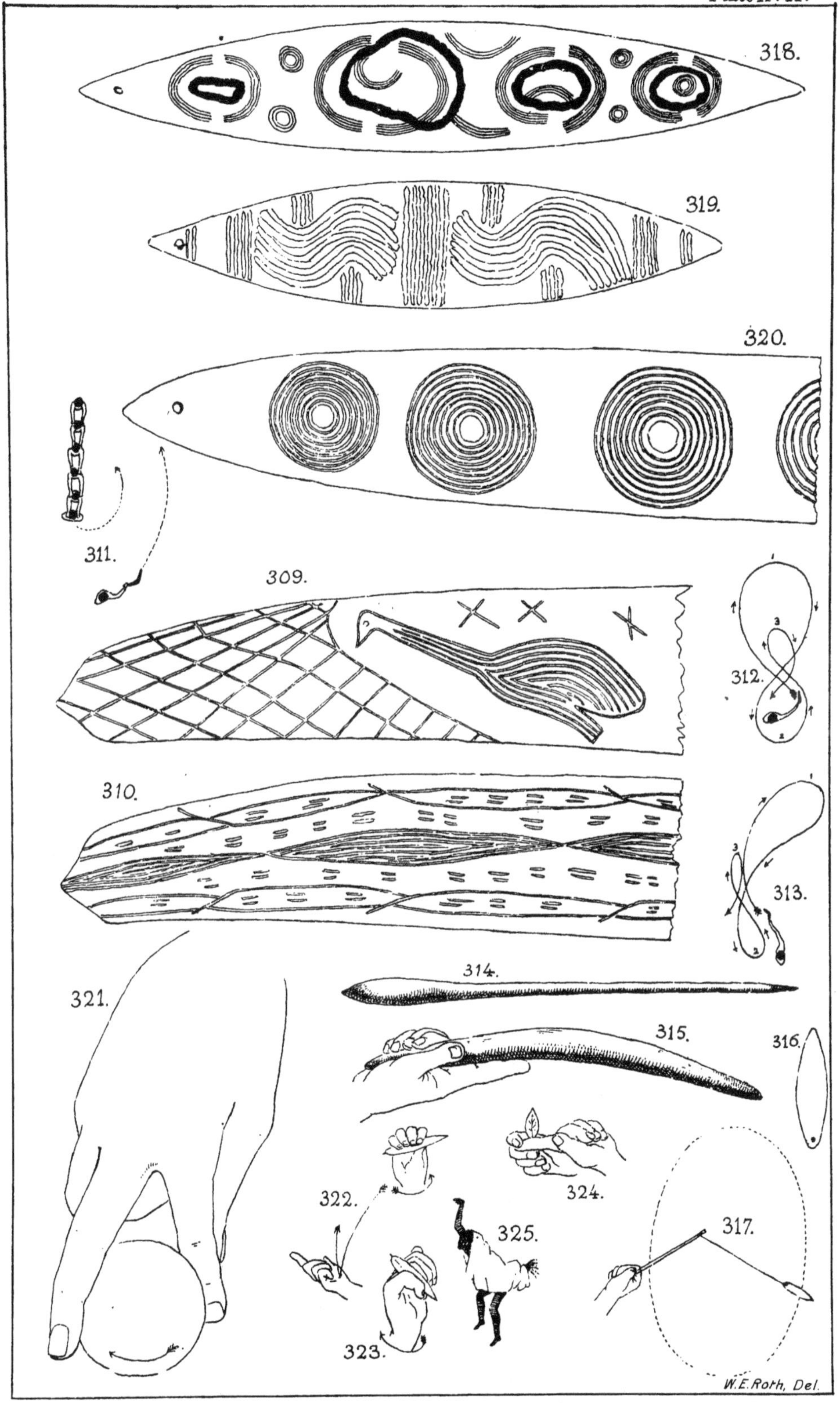

Plate XVII.

Figs. 309-325, Articles Etc. employed in Games and Sports.

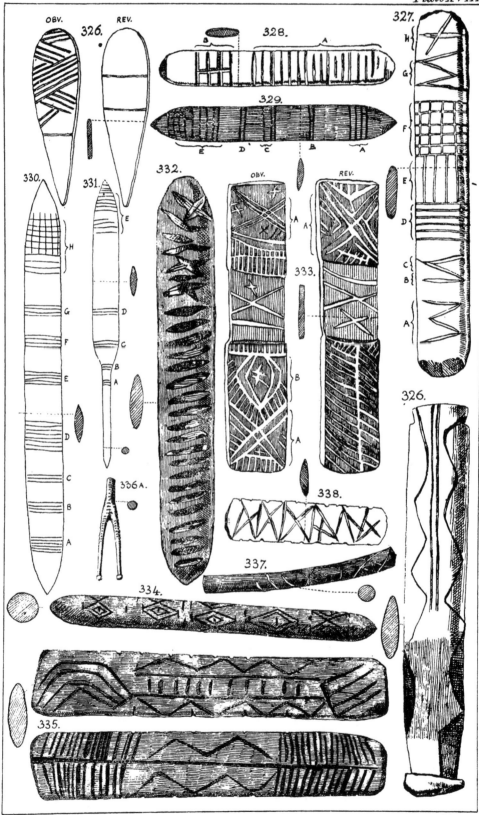

Plate XVIII.

Figs. 326-338, Letter or Message-Sticks.

W.E.ROTH. del.

Plate XIX.

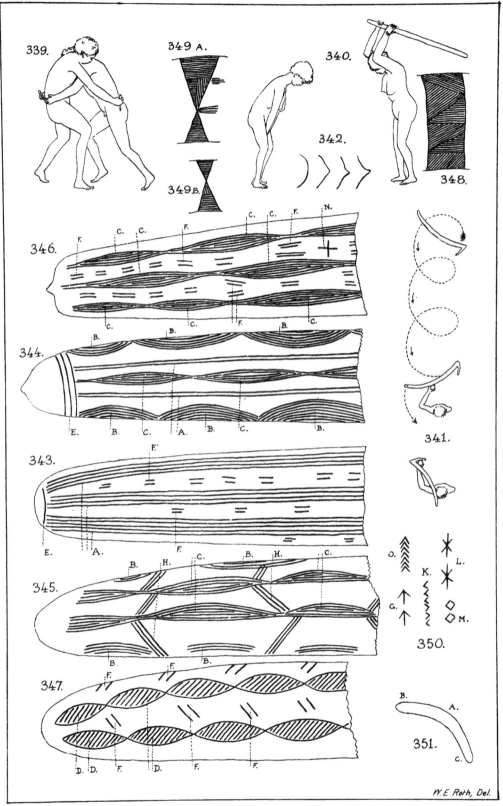

Figs. 339-340, Methods of Fighting. Figs. 341-351, Boomerangs.

Plate XX.

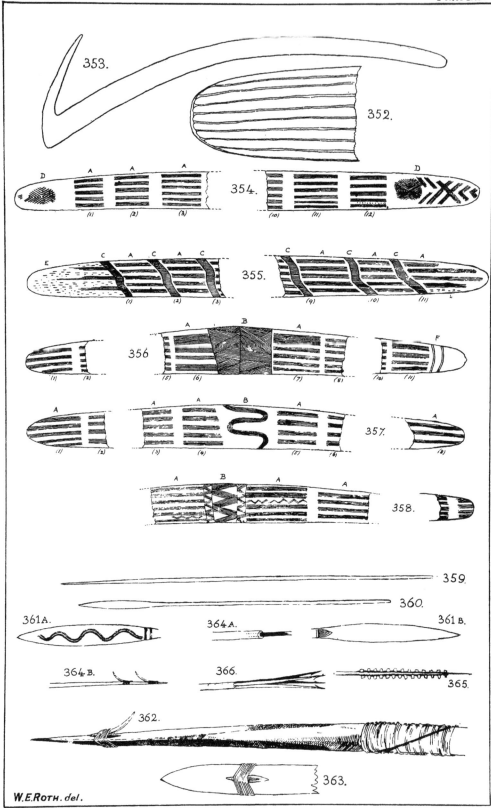

Figs. 352-366; Boomerangs, Two-handed Swords, Spears.

Plate XXI.

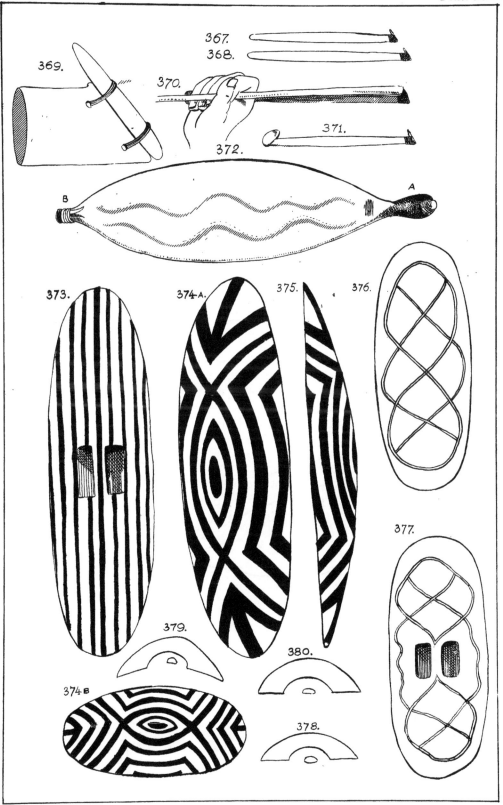

W.E.Roth, Del.

Figs.367-380, Wommeras and Shields.

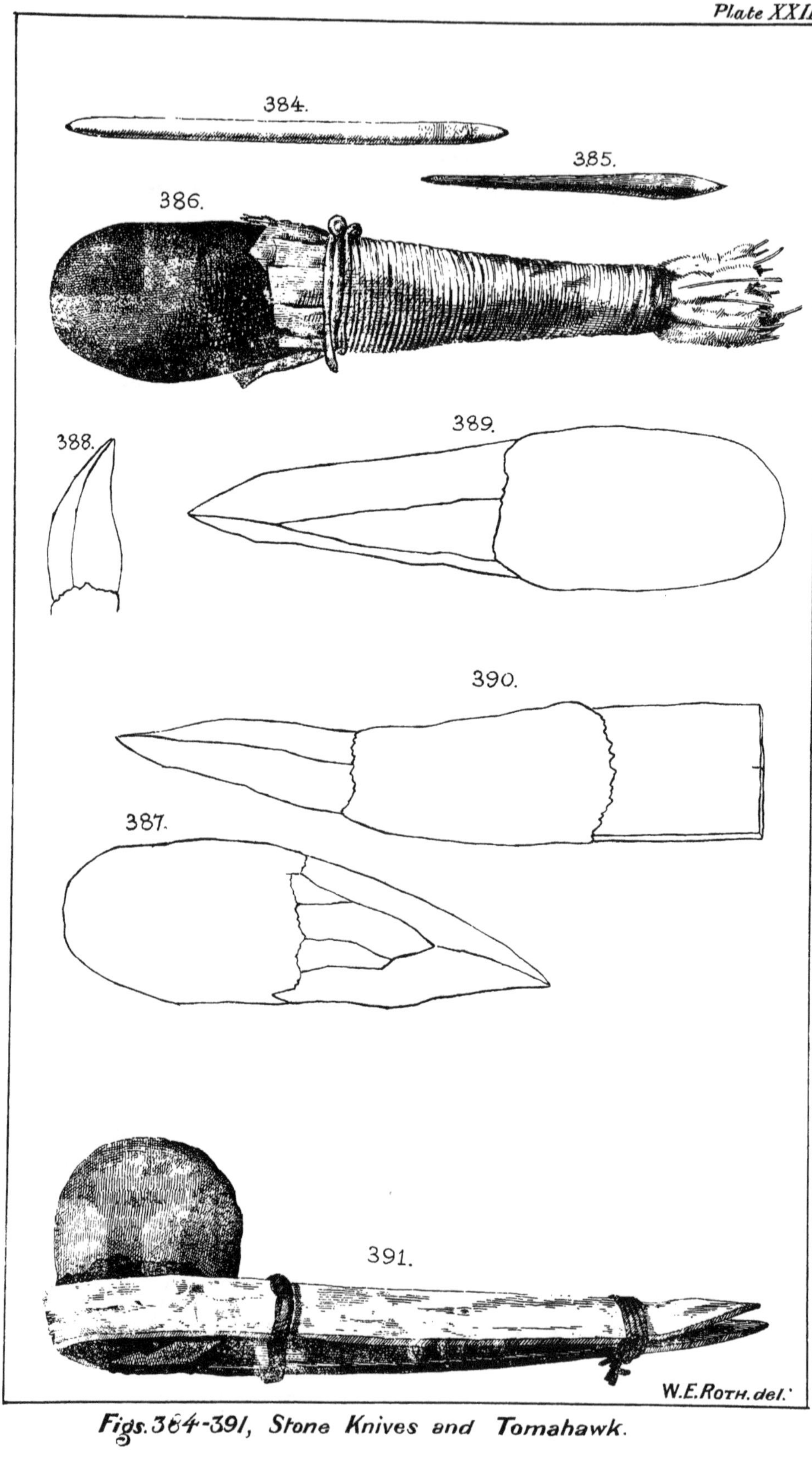

Plate XXII.

384.

385.

386.

388.

389.

390.

387.

391.

W.E.Roth. del.

Figs. 384-391, Stone Knives and Tomahawk.

Plate XXIII.

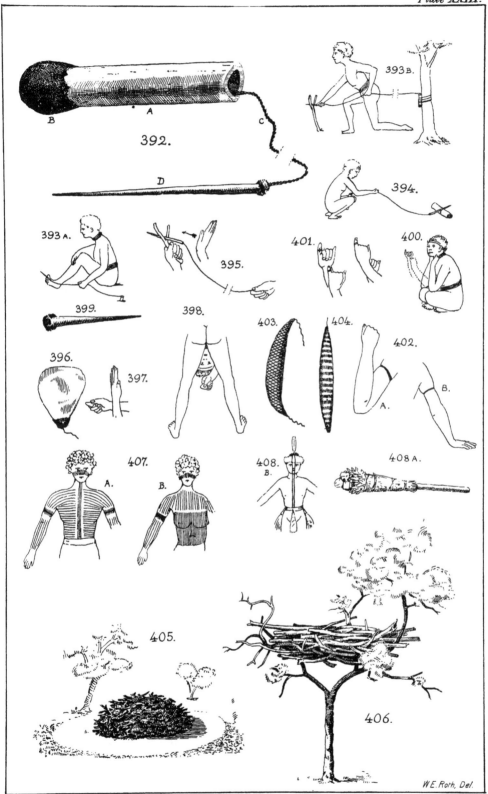

Figs.392-404, Various Devices for Causing or Alleviating Sickness, Disease and Accident. Figs. 405-407, Graves and Mourners. Fig. 408, Rain-maker and Rain-stone-stick.

W.E.Roth, Del.

Plate XXIV.

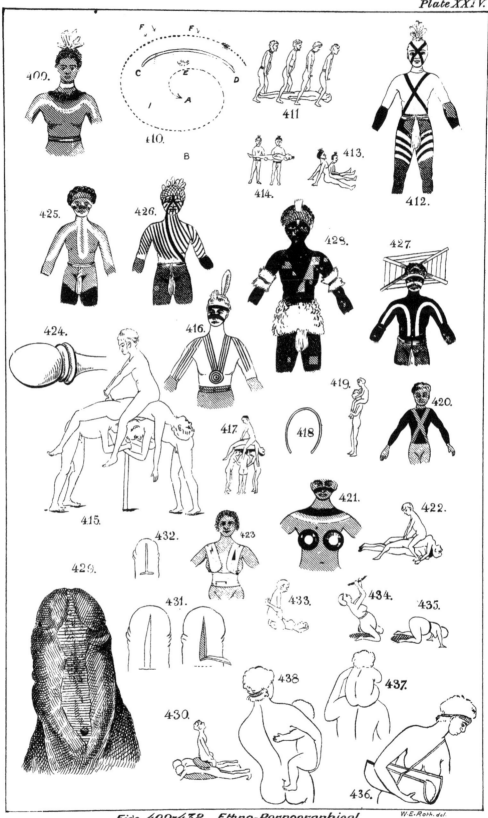

Figs. 409-438, Ethno-Pornographical.

W.E.Roth.del.

For EU product safety concerns, contact us at Calle de José Abascal, 56–1°,
28003 Madrid, Spain or eugpsr@cambridge.org.

www.ingramcontent.com/pod-product-compliance
Ingram Content Group UK Ltd.
Pitfield, Milton Keynes, MK11 3LW, UK
UKHW030901150625
459647UK00021B/2698